FIFTY FAVORITE C

FIFTY FAVORITE CLIMBS
THE ULTIMATE NORTH AMERICAN TICK LIST

MARK KROESE

THE MOUNTAINEERS BOOKS

Published by
The Mountaineers Books
1001 SW Klickitat Way, Suite 201
Seattle, WA 98134

© 2001 by Mark Kroese

All rights reserved

First edition: first printing 2001, second printing 2004

No part of this book may be reproduced in any form, or by any electronic, mechanical, or other means, without permission in writing from the publisher.

Published simultaneously in Great Britain by Cordee, 3a DeMontfort Street, Leicester, England, LE1 7HD

Manufactured in Singapore

Project Editor: Kathleen Cubley
Editor: Kris Fulsaas
Cover and book design: Ani Rucki
Maps, topos, and route overlays: Gray Mouse Graphics

Cover photograph: *Chris Righter belays Randy Leavitt on the fifth pitch (5.12a) of the Needles classic, Romantic Warrior* © Jorge Visser
Frontispiece: *Jack Tackle mixing it up on the crux pitch of A Pair of Jacks, Northwest Face of Mount Kennedy* © Jack Roberts
Pages 18–19: *Steve House enjoying the view down Peak 11,300, Ruth Amphitheater, Alaska* © Michael Powers

Library of Congress Cataloging-in-Publication Data
Kroese, Mark.
 Fifty favorite climbs : the ultimate North American tick list / Mark Kroese.— 1st ed.
  p. cm.
 Includes bibliographical references.
  ISBN 0-89886-728-2 (Hardcover)
  1.Mountaineering—North America. 2. Mountaineers—Biography. I.Title.
 GV199.44.N67 K76 2001
 796.52'2'097—dc21   2001001683

Printed on recycled paper

THE MOUNTAINEERS, founded in 1906, is a nonprofit outdoor activity and conservation club, whose mission is "to explore, study, preserve, and enjoy the natural beauty of the outdoors. . . . " Based in Seattle, Washington, the club is now the third-largest such organization in the United States, with 15,000 members and five branches throughout Washington State.

The Mountaineers sponsors both classes and year-round outdoor activities in the Pacific Northwest, which include hiking, mountain climbing, ski-touring, snowshoeing, bicycling, camping, kayaking and canoeing, nature study, sailing, and adventure travel. The club's conservation division supports environmental causes through educational activities, sponsoring legislation, and presenting informational programs. All club activities are led by skilled, experienced volunteers, who are dedicated to promoting safe and responsible enjoyment and preservation of the outdoors.

If you would like to participate in these organized outdoor activities or the club's programs, consider a membership in The Mountaineers. For information and an application, write or call The Mountaineers, Club Headquarters, 300 Third Avenue West, Seattle, WA 98119; 206-284-6310.

The Mountaineers Books, an active, nonprofit publishing program of the club, produces guidebooks, instructional texts, historical works, natural history guides, and works on environmental conservation. All books produced by The Mountaineers Books fulfill the club's mission.

Send or call for our catalog of more than 500 outdoor titles:

The Mountaineers Books
1001 SW Klickitat Way, Suite 201
Seattle, WA 98134
800-553-4453
mbooks@mountaineersbooks.org
www.mountaineersbooks.org

TO DANIEL AND NICOLE,

PURSUE YOUR PASSIONS, ALWAYS

TOPO KEY

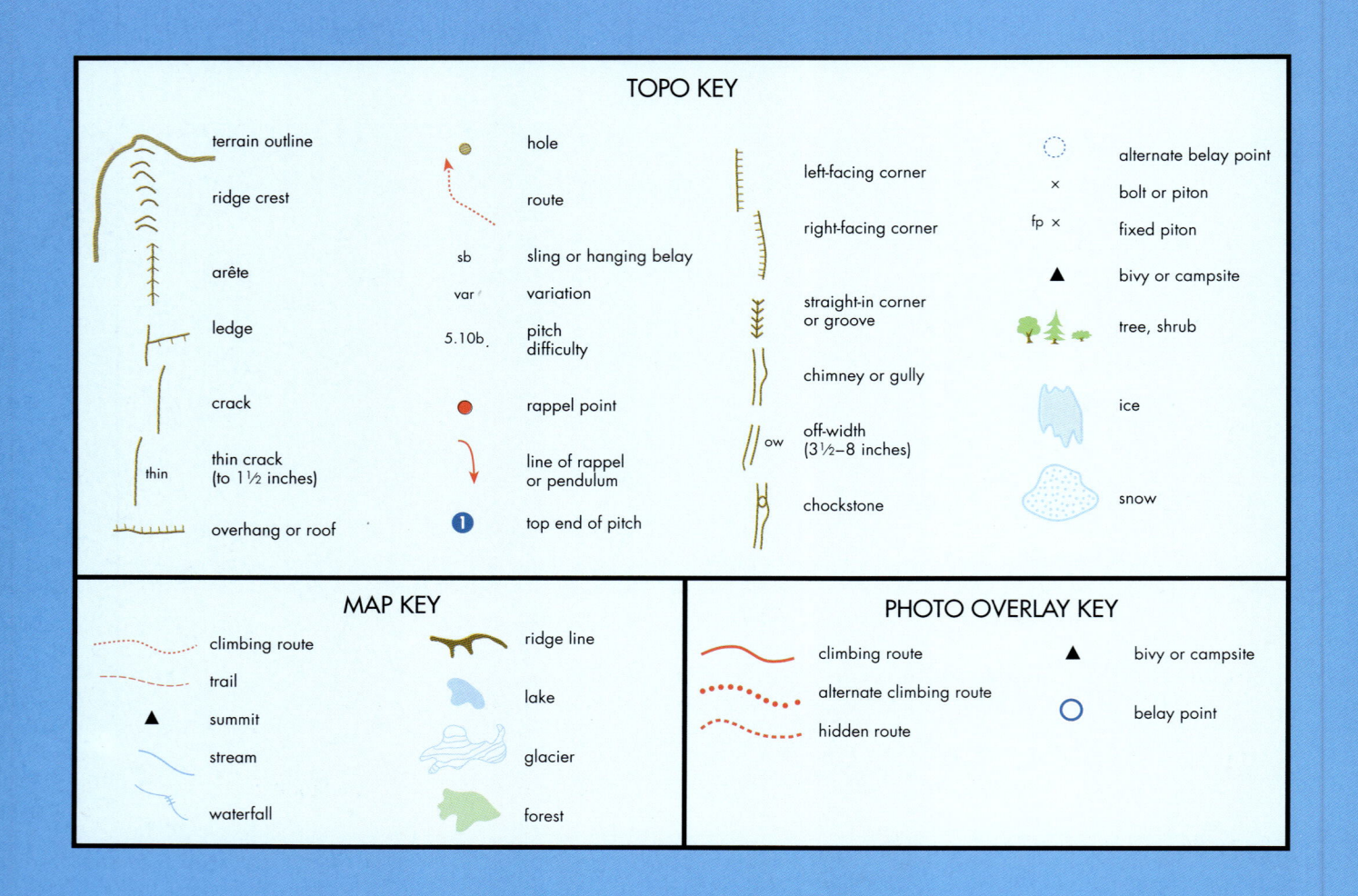

- terrain outline
- ridge crest
- arête
- ledge
- crack
- thin — thin crack (to 1½ inches)
- overhang or roof
- hole
- route
- sb — sling or hanging belay
- var — variation
- 5.10b — pitch difficulty
- rappel point
- line of rappel or pendulum
- ① top end of pitch
- left-facing corner
- right-facing corner
- straight-in corner or groove
- chimney or gully
- ow — off-width (3½–8 inches)
- chockstone
- alternate belay point
- × bolt or piton
- fp × fixed piton
- ▲ bivy or campsite
- tree, shrub
- ice
- snow

MAP KEY

- climbing route
- trail
- ▲ summit
- stream
- waterfall
- ridge line
- lake
- glacier
- forest

PHOTO OVERLAY KEY

- climbing route
- alternate climbing route
- hidden route
- ▲ bivy or campsite
- ○ belay point

CONTENTS

Climb Locator Map 10–11
Acknowledgments 13
Introduction 15

1 CONRAD ANKER 21
STUMP SPIRE, SAM FORD FJORD, BAFFIN ISLAND, NUNAVUT TERRITORY

2 JOHN BACHAR 25
THE NABISCO WALL, THE COOKIE CLIFF, YOSEMITE NATIONAL PARK, CALIFORNIA

3 BOBBI BENSMAN 29
ORIGINAL ROUTE, THE RAINBOW WALL, RED ROCKS NATIONAL CONSERVATION AREA, NEVADA

4 BARRY BLANCHARD 33
NEMESIS, MOUNT STANLEY, KOOTENAY NATIONAL PARK, BRITISH COLUMBIA

5 JIM BRIDWELL 37
PACIFIC OCEAN WALL, EL CAPITAN, YOSEMITE NATIONAL PARK, CALIFORNIA

6 ROXANNA BROCK 41
EPINEPHRINE, RED ROCKS NATIONAL CONSERVATION AREA, NEVADA

7 CARLOS BUHLER 45
EAST FACE OF UNIVERSITY PEAK, WRANGELL–ST. ELIAS NATIONAL PARK, ALASKA

8 TOMMY CALDWELL 49
WUNSCH'S DIHEDRAL, CYNICAL PINNACLE, CATHEDRAL SPIRES AREA, SOUTH PLATTE, COLORADO

9 GREG CHILD 53
BELLIGERENCE, SOUTH BUTTRESS OF MOUNT COMBATANT, WADDINGTON RANGE, BRITISH COLUMBIA

10 RUSS CLUNE 57
THE GRAND WALL, SQUAMISH CHIEF, SQUAMISH, BRITISH COLUMBIA

11 PETER CROFT 61
THE EVOLUTION TRAVERSE, CENTRAL SIERRA NEVADA, CALIFORNIA

12 KIM CSIZMAZIA 65
PRODIGAL SON, ANGEL'S LANDING, ZION NATIONAL PARK, UTAH

13 STEPH DAVIS 69
THE OBELISK, LONGS PEAK DIAMOND, ROCKY MOUNTAIN NATIONAL PARK, COLORADO

14 JIM DONINI 73
THE COBRA PILLAR, MOUNT BARRILLE, ALASKA RANGE, ALASKA

15 NANCY FEAGIN 77
ORIGINAL ROUTE, SOUTHEAST FACE OF MOUNT PROBOSCIS, CIRQUE OF THE UNCLIMBABLES, NORTHWEST TERRITORIES

16 HANS FLORINE 81
BEGGAR'S BUTTRESS, LOWER CATHEDRAL ROCK, YOSEMITE NATIONAL PARK, CALIFORNIA

17 CHARLIE FOWLER 85
SUNLIGHT BUTTRESS, PARIA POINT, KOLOB CANYONS, ZION NATIONAL PARK, UTAH

18 WILL GADD 89
DEEP THROAT, GLENWOOD CANYON, COLORADO

19 KENNAN HARVEY 93
ALL ALONG THE WATCHTOWER, NORTH HOWSER TOWER, BUGABOO GLACIER PROVINCIAL PARK, BRITISH COLUMBIA

20 LYNN HILL 97
LEVITATION 29, RED ROCKS NATIONAL CONSERVATION AREA, NEVADA

21 STEVE HOUSE 101
SOUTHWEST RIDGE OF PEAK 11,300, ALASKA RANGE, ALASKA

22 JOE JOSEPHSON 105
THE WILD THING, EAST FACE OF MOUNT CHEPHREN, BANFF NATIONAL PARK, ALBERTA

23 RON KAUK 109
MIDDLE ROCK TRAVERSE, MIDDLE CATHEDRAL ROCK, YOSEMITE NATIONAL PARK, CALIFORNIA

24 MICHAEL KENNEDY 113
THE INFINITE SPUR, MOUNT FORAKER, ALASKA RANGE, ALASKA

25 GUY LACELLE 117
LA POMME D'OR, HIGH GORGE OF MALBAIE RIVER REGIONAL PARK, QUEBEC

26 RANDY LEAVITT 121
ROMANTIC WARRIOR, WARLOCK NEEDLE, THE NEEDLES, CALIFORNIA

27 ALEX LOWE 125
THE GRAND TRAVERSE, GRAND TETON NATIONAL PARK, WYOMING

28 GEORGE LOWE 129
BLACK ICE COULOIR–WEST FACE LINKUP, THE GRAND TETON, GRAND TETON NATIONAL PARK, WYOMING

29 JEFF LOWE 133
GORILLAS IN THE MIST, POKOMOONSHINE, ADIRONDACK MOUNTAIN PARK, NEW YORK

30 SUE MCDEVITT 137
ASTROMAN, WASHINGTON COLUMN, YOSEMITE NATIONAL PARK, CALIFORNIA

31 JOHN MIDDENDORF 141
TRICKS OF THE TRADE, ISAAC, ZION NATIONAL PARK, UTAH

32 JIM NELSON 145
THE TORMENT-FORBIDDEN TRAVERSE, NORTH CASCADES NATIONAL PARK, WASHINGTON

33 JARED OGDEN 149
BIRDBRAIN BOULEVARD, OURAY, COLORADO

34 ALISON OSIUS 153
PRIMROSE DIHEDRALS, MOSES, CANYONLANDS NATIONAL PARK, UTAH

35 STEVE SCHNEIDER 157
LURKING FEAR, EL CAPITAN, YOSEMITE NATIONAL PARK, CALIFORNIA

36 DON SERL 161
THE WADDINGTON TRAVERSE, COAST RANGE, BRITISH COLUMBIA

37 CHRIS SHARMA 165
NORTH FACE OF THE ROSTRUM, YOSEMITE NATIONAL PARK, CALIFORNIA

38 SETH SHAW 169
HONKY TONQUIN, NORTH FACE OF MOUNT GEIKIE, CANADIAN ROCKIES, BRITISH COLUMBIA

39 TODD SKINNER 173
THE GREAT CANADIAN KNIFE, SOUTHWEST FACE OF MOUNT PROBOSCIS, CIRQUE OF THE UNCLIMBABLES, NORTHWEST TERRITORIES

40 JAY SMITH 177
THE PHANTOM WALL, MOUNT HUNTINGTON, ALASKA RANGE, ALASKA

41 KURT SMITH 181
TIME FOR LIVIN', THE OUTRAGE WALL, EL POTRERO CHICO, NUEVO LEON (MEXICO)

42 STEVE SWENSON 185
NORTH FACE OF MOUNT ALBERTA, JASPER NATIONAL PARK, ALBERTA

43 MARK SYNNOTT 189
VMC DIRECT DIRECT, CANNON CLIFF, WHITE MOUNTAINS, NEW HAMPSHIRE

44 JACK TACKLE 193
A PAIR OF JACKS, NORTHWEST FACE OF MOUNT KENNEDY, KLUANE NATIONAL PARK, YUKON TERRITORY

45 JOE TERRAVECCHIA 197
LEVIATHAN, BLOW-ME-DOWN CLIFF, DEVIL BAY, NEWFOUNDLAND

46 KEVIN THAW 201
THE VAMPIRE, TAHQUITZ ROCK, SAN JACINTO MOUNTAINS, CALIFORNIA

47 MARK TWIGHT 205
EAST FACE OF MOUNT BABEL, BANFF NATIONAL PARK, ALBERTA

48 MARK WILFORD 209
THE PUGILIST AT REST AND WILFORD COULOIR, "POINT BLANCHARD," KLUANE NATIONAL PARK, YUKON TERRITORY

49 JONNY WOODWARD 213
HALL OF MIRRORS, GLACIER POINT APRON, YOSEMITE NATIONAL PARK, CALIFORNIA

50 TONY YANIRO 217
SCIROCCO, EAST FACE OF THE SORCERER, THE NEEDLES, CALIFORNIA

Glossary 221
Selected References 223

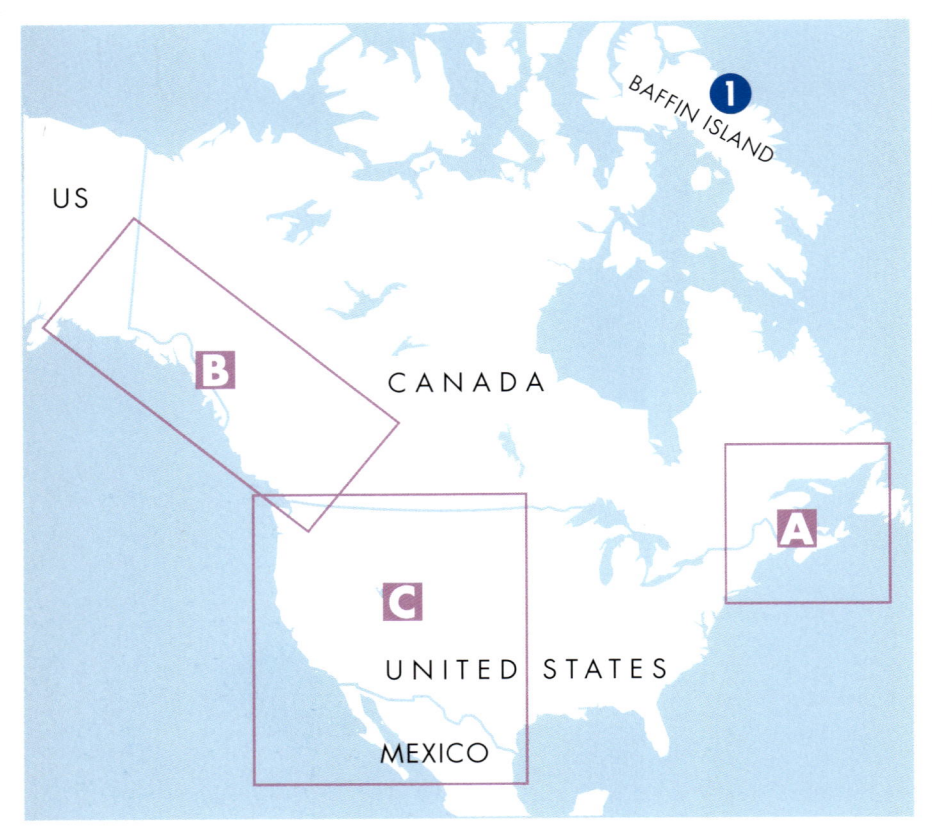

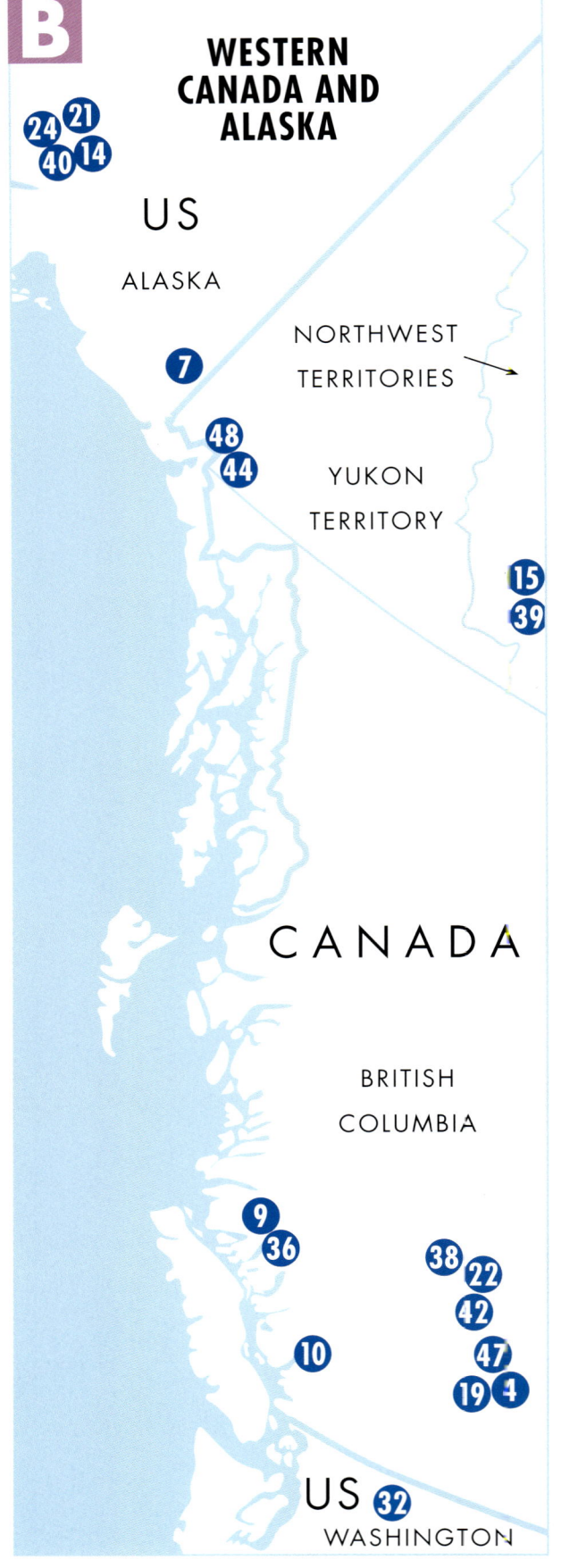

B
WESTERN CANADA AND ALASKA

US
ALASKA

NORTHWEST TERRITORIES

YUKON TERRITORY

CANADA

BRITISH COLUMBIA

US
WASHINGTON

A

CANADA

NEWFOUNDLAND

QUEBEC

US

NEW YORK

NH

EASTERN CANADA AND UNITED STATES

BAFFIN ISLAND

US

CANADA

UNITED STATES

MEXICO

C

WESTERN UNITED STATES AND MEXICO

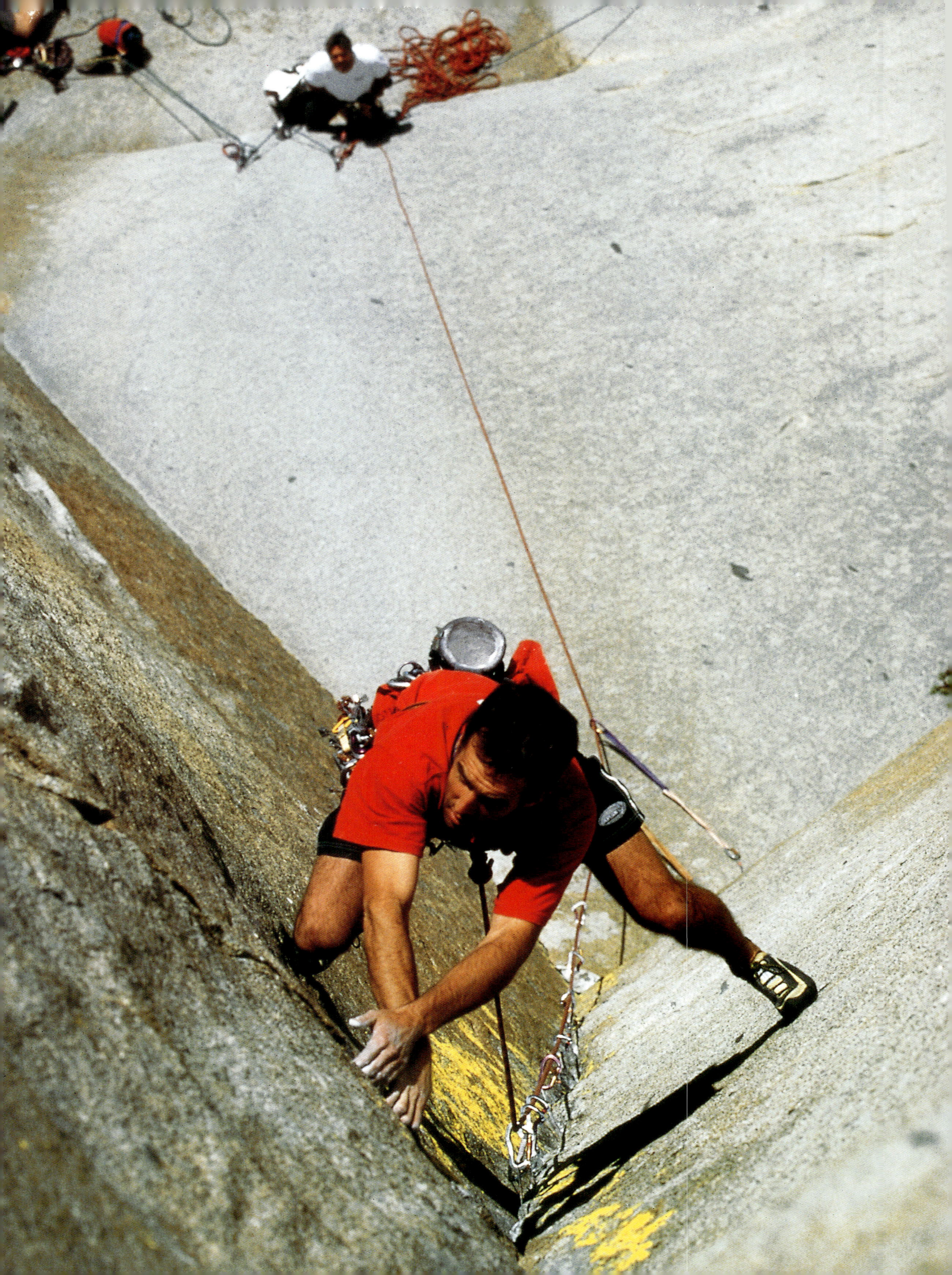

ACKNOWLEDGMENTS

There are many people to thank for their help with this book. The obvious place to start is with the fifty participating climbers; their willingness to share the experience of their favorite climbs is what made this book possible. Most of them also donated the use of their photos. I am also grateful to their climbing partners, most of whom took the time to answer phone calls, respond to email, share trip reports, submit slides, and draw topo maps. Particularly helpful were Kevin Barone, Mike Caldwell, Greg Collum, Greg Crouch, Topher Donahue, Sean Dougherty, Greg Foweraker, Rolando Garibotti, Ed Palen, Paul Piana, Jack Roberts, Charlie Sassara, Grant Statham, Paul Teare, and Jonathan Turk.

I thank the staff at The Mountaineers Books for their skilled and thorough work on this book, particularly Helen Cherullo, Kathleen Cubley, Margaret Foster, Kris Fulsaas, and Ani Rucki.

Thanks to the wonders of email, the following people gave me large doses of insight and encouragement while reviewing numerous chapters: Jane Bromet, Sean Courage, John Fine, Gretchen Huizinga, Bill Jones, Bob Kroese, Kristen Laine, Chris McNamara, Sean Savauge, Kelly Sjolander, Lowell Skoog, and Steve Stroming. I am also indebted to Jim Copacino for teaching me more about writing than he ever realized.

I worked with numerous photographers throughout the process. I greatly appreciate their submissions and inspiring work: Jacqueline Adams, Jeff Achey, Brian Bailey, Barry Blanchard, Tim Bonnet, Jane Bromet, Cameron Burns, Doug Chabot, Mark Chapman, Greg Collum, Sean Courage, Topher and Patience Donahue, Jim Elzinga, Greg Epperson, Joe Josephson, Bob Gaines, Ned Harris, Kennan Harvey, Bill Hatcher, John Heisel, Steve House, Michael Kennedy, Ace Kvale, Randy Leavitt, Charlie Mace, Fly'n Brian McCray, Dan McQuade, Jared Ogden, Kevin Powell, Michael Powers, Corey Rich, Galen Rowell, Grant Statham, Tyler Stableford, Jim Thornburg, Jorge Urioste, Jeb Vetters, Jorge Visser, Beth Wald, Bradford Washburn, Ed Webster, Richard Wheater, Jeff Widen, Mark Wilford, and Gordon Wiltsie.

Thanks to the following people, who provided reference material for the topos in this book: Cameron Burns, Charlie Fowler, Chris McNamara/SuperTopo, Dan McQuade, Greg Collum, Jack Roberts, Jack Tackle, Jeff Lowe, Joe Josephson, Joe Terravecchia, John Middendorf, Jonny Woodward, Kevin Thaw, Kurt Smith, Mark Synnott, Mark Wilford, Paul Piana, Peter Croft, Randy Leavitt, Reynold Jackson, Seth Shaw, Steph Davis, Topher Donahue, Will Gadd.

Finally, I thank my wife, Lisa, and our children, Daniel and Nicole, for their encouragement, patience, and understanding throughout the writing process, and my parents for raising two sons with a sense of decency.

Randy Leavitt on Romantic Warrior's crux pitch (5.12b) © Jorge Visser

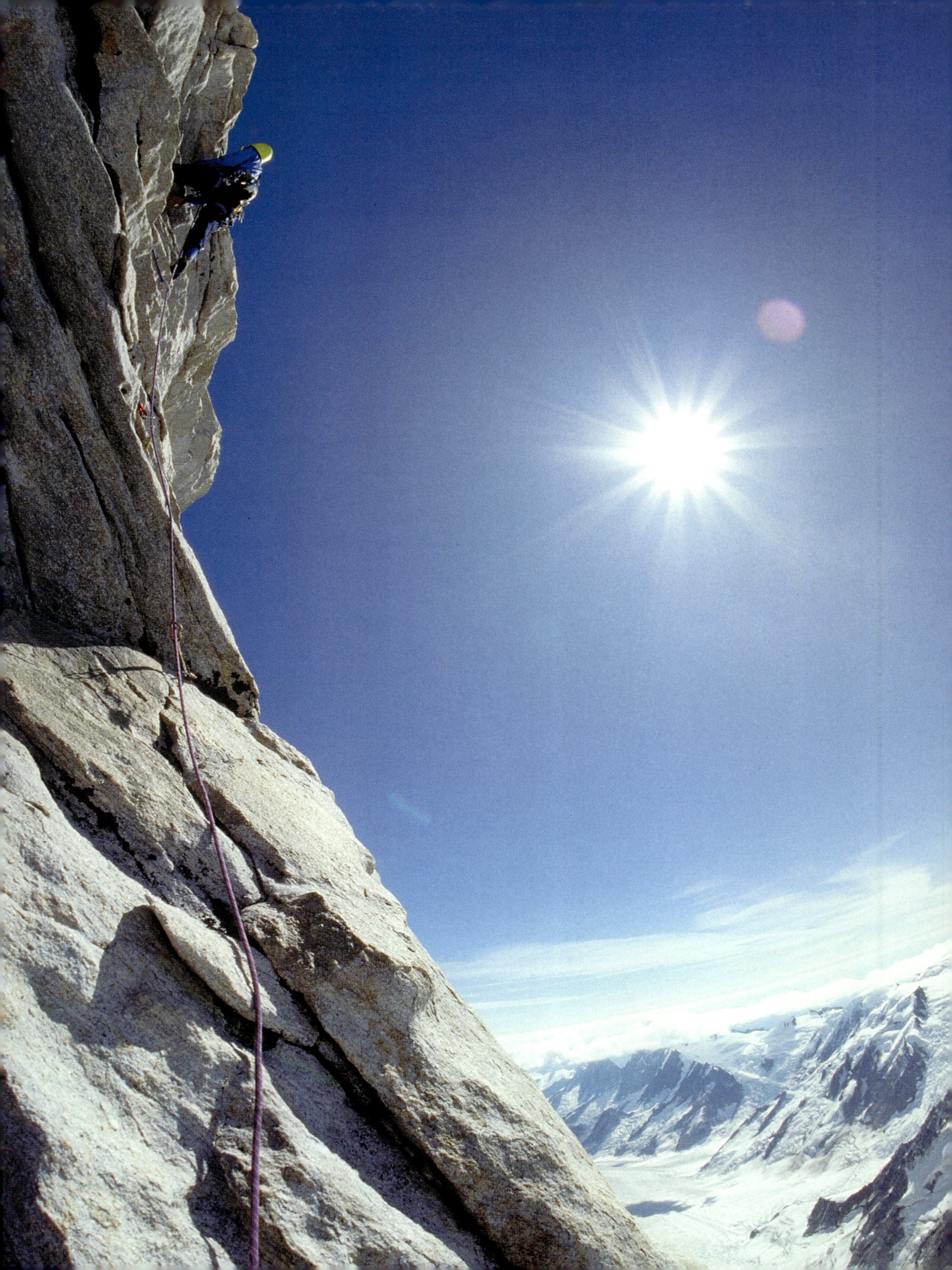

INTRODUCTION

INSPIRATION

In June 1980, when my nineteen-year-old life was ruled by the need to climb, I got my hands on a copy of *Fifty Classic Climbs of North America*. Written by longtime climbers Steve Roper and Allen Steck, the just-published book introduced me to a selection of North America's most classic climbs. I spent the rest of that summer traveling from Canada to Yosemite, sampling routes such as the Northeast Buttress of Bugaboo Spire, the West Ridge of Forbidden Peak, and the Nose of El Capitan. Thanks to the quality of the book's recommendations, it was one of the best summers of my life.

More than twenty years later, after I've climbed many of the so-called "Fifty Classics," a dog-eared copy of *Fifty Classic Climbs of North America* still sits on my shelf, reminding me of routes yet to be done and ranges waiting to be visited. In the spring of 1998, while I was flipping through its pages in search of a cause, I thought about how much climbing has changed since the book was originally published: advances in equipment—sticky rubber, TCUs, high-tech ice tools, and lightweight everything, to name a few—have raised free- and aid-climbing standards to once unimaginable levels. New attitudes and training techniques have given modern-day climbers the confidence to try routes considered impossible by previous generations. Sport climbing and indoor gyms have elevated rock climbing into the mainstream consciousness. And the Internet has enabled instantaneous and global information sharing. The result has been an explosion of new routes and climbing areas.

Aware of the proliferation of new climbs, I began to wonder when the second edition of *Fifty Classic Climbs of North America* was going to be published. I asked around the outdoor industry, talked to some fellow writers, and queried a few outdoor publishers. Everyone I talked to agreed that such a book was long overdue but, surprisingly, no one could identify an author who was working on it. It was then that I decided to take on the project myself.

As I contemplated the selection of fifty routes, I realized that my limited view of North American climbing—the bulk of my experience is in California, Washington, and Canada—would make it difficult for me to choose a representative selection of classic climbs. In search of a broader perspective, I began soliciting input from some of the more accomplished climbers I know. Each had a list of climbs that, in his or her view, deserved more recognition. Climbs each considered to be ultraclassic. Climbs they would recommend to their closest friends. Climbs they would repeat just for the fun of it. The adjective most often used to describe these climbs was "favorite." After I'd gotten a similar response from a dozen or so climbers, Margaret Foster, then the editor-in-chief of The Mountaineers Books, suggested that we take the idea to the next level: Rather than just gathering input from the most accomplished climbers in North America, why not ask fifty of them to each pick a favorite climb? The envisioned book would not only feature fifty classic climbs, it would also profile fifty world-class climbers. And that was it. The concept for *Fifty Favorite Climbs* was born.

THE SELECTION PROCESS

Instead of choosing fifty classic climbs, I was faced with the task of selecting fifty highly accomplished climbers. Twenty years ago, this would have been a relatively simple task. But these days—when climbing is so popular that you're lucky to be the second person in your neighborhood to scale the Seven Summits—it's much more complex. There are thousands of exceptional climbers in North America. I know of at least fifty "big-name" climbers in the state of Colorado alone. Heck, there are probably that many within the city limits of Boulder.

To simplify the selection process, I defined "highly accomplished" in very specific terms. Candidate climbers had to meet most, but not all, of the following criteria. First, they had to be climbing at a modern technical standard. This is not a book about the legendary pioneers of yesteryear such as Yvon Chouinard or Royal Robbins—this is a book about *today's* leading climbers and their favorite climbs. Second, I looked for climbers who have done a significant number of first ascents, because they tend to know about the best new routes. (There are a few "private climbs," such as Joe Terravecchia's Leviathan in Newfoundland, that debut in this book.) Third, I chose climbers who have made important, seminal ascents, such as Lynn Hill's all-free, 1-day ascent of the Nose of El Capitan, and the 1977 ascent of Mount Foraker's Infinite Spur by Michael Kennedy and George Lowe. Fourth, I strove for geographic diversity among the climbers and the climbs. This objective was complicated by the fact that climbers tend to move

Greg Collum on the first ascent of the South Buttress of Mount Combatant (VI, 5.11, A3+) © Greg Child

around, and their favorite climbs are not always in their home state. As you can see by the climb locator map on pages 8–9, most of the climbs are situated in the mountainous West, although there are several gems in the East. All climbers in the book had to be living in North America, although three—Jonny Woodward, Kevin Thaw, and Greg Child—were born and raised abroad.

During the selection process, several very young and extremely talented climbers were suggested for inclusion, but only a few were chosen. When faced with the trade-off between future potential and a concrete list of accomplishments, I placed more importance on the latter. Chris Sharma and Tommy Caldwell are the youngest climbers in the book; despite their youth, both are highly accomplished. I also gave consideration to gender diversity, but did not establish an explicit male/female quota—again, my primary focus was on the climber's accomplishments. Eight women are included in this book.

Anticipating some rejection, I selected ten extra climbers, but didn't get too far down the list; only two declined participation—pretty remarkable, considering I offered no financial incentive and asked each climber for about ten hours of his or her time. Finally, in an effort to give the book as much variety as possible, I tried to avoid "pairs"—married couples and longtime partners with redundant talents, viewpoints, and experiences.

I applied as much rigor and discipline as possible to the selection process, but it was still somewhat subjective. For reasons ranging from practical to visceral, I made many painful "cuts" along the way, silently apologizing to the climbers from afar, wondering if they would even care, if they knew, wishing my choices could be defended with quantitative data. I would like to claim that the climbers in this book are *the* best in North America, but it's more accurate to say they are *among* the best. There are hundreds of climbers who deserve to be in this book. It's not possible to list them, but they know who they are. I thank them for understanding.

CHOOSING A FAVORITE CLIMB

In the context of this book, the term "favorite" is synonymous with the term "classic." By asking each climber to pick a favorite climb, I was really asking them to pick their favorite *classic* climb. A classic climb is one that follows a striking line, offers excellent climbing with minimal loose sections, and has a stunning position, great views, wild exposure, or a spectacular summit. Classic climbs are "the ones to do."

This important distinction was intended to steer the climbers—some of whom have a rather perverse definition of "fun"—away from choosing climbs that are excessively dangerous, scary, or otherwise unpleasant. Because of today's large population of excellent climbers, I did not set limits on technical difficulty, but did encourage the book participants to choose routes that a significant number of climbers can enjoy. For example, Steve Schneider chose Lurking Fear on El Capitan, a route that he climbed at 5.13a, A0. While very few climbers will repeat it as a free climb, it's still a delightful classic when climbed at 5.8, A2. Most of the routes in this book can be done by competent climbers with contemporary skills, but, despite my urgings of the profiled climbers, there are a few climbs that fall into the "aspirational" category and will only be attempted by elite climbers.

Since most of the participating climbers had a long list of favorite climbs, I established the following criteria to help them narrow their selection. First, all climbs had to be in North America. Second, since this is not intended to be a "cragging" guide, each climb had to be 500 feet or longer. (One exception was granted to a very persuasive Ron Kauk.) Third, each route had to offer some technical climbing—"walk-ups" were not allowed. Fourth, no routes could be repeated from *Fifty Classic Climbs of North America*, because the routes in that excellent book are popular enough. Finally, I stressed the importance of choosing a route that could be recommended in good conscience to others who can climb at the technical grade.

INTERVIEWS AND OBSERVATIONS

As I predicted, the highlight of the project was the interview process. I came close to achieving my original goal of *personally* meeting with each climber—forty-four of the interviews were conducted in person. Toward the end of the interview phase, as deadlines loomed and idealism yielded to pragmatism, I conducted six interviews by phone. The rest took place in living rooms, hotel lobbies, restaurants, bars, trade show booths, and, best of all, while climbing.

The interviews were fascinating, thought provoking, inspiring, and most of the time downright fun. In addition to providing the essential information about their favorite climb, the climbers shared their views on everything from ethics to style to training techniques. Each interview gave me volumes of material to work with, although some of the best stuff was either off the subject or off the record.

The interviews yielded countless interesting observations about elite climbers. Sharing them all would fill hundreds of pages, but there are two that deserve inclusion here. The first is the continued importance of Yosemite Valley, specifically El Capitan. While hundreds of crags have been discovered and developed in the past decade, Yosemite still reigns supreme. This book is filled with Yosemite-specific jargon, such as "the Nose," referring to the thirty-four-pitch route up the center of El Capitan, or "The Big Stone" and "El Cap," two nicknames for El Capitan. While Yosemite is as important as ever, its role has evolved. Twenty years ago, scaling El Capitan by any route at any speed was a significant accomplishment. Today, elite climbers use El Capitan as a training ground for the great ranges, routinely making 1-day speed ascents. Virtually every climber in this book has climbed the Nose at least once—most of them in a day. Hans Florine has climbed it more than thirty times, and is one of five climbers who would choose it as their favorite climb had it not been included in *Fifty Classic Climbs of North America*. If I've learned anything while writing this book, it's that the Nose is still the world's ultimate rock climb, and Yosemite is still the ultimate rock-climbing destination. Eight of the climbs in this book are in Yosemite.

The second observation is about style. These days, when gear-intensive siege tactics can virtually guarantee success, elite climbers feel that the style of an ascent is more important than ever. Many of the climbs in this book are considered favorites because of the way in which they were done. Debates about the merits of various climbing styles—from alpine-style vs. capsule-style to aid vs. free to on-sight vs. redpoint—continue to rage, but everyone agrees on one thing: When reporting on the style of an ascent, tell the whole truth—say what you did. Without question, the most respected way to climb in the mountains is alpine style. The phrase "light and fast," which goes hand-in-hand with alpine-style climbing, appears throughout the text. An understanding of the differences between these various styles of climbing is necessary to fully appreciate many of the stories in this book. Please refer to the appendix for further discussion of these terms and concepts.

PASSINGS

During the eighteen-month course of this project, two of the fifty climbers were tragically killed in climbing accidents. Alex Lowe was swept away in an avalanche on the slopes of Tibet's Shisha Pangma on October 5, 1999, and Seth Shaw was crushed by a falling serac in Alaska's Ruth Gorge on May 25, 2000. Both men had chosen a climb for this book and taken the time to be interviewed before the accidents occurred. Since most of the work had been done, the Lowe and Shaw families agreed that the best way to honor Alex and Seth would be to publish the chapters as originally planned. I feel lucky to have known both climbers, and hope this book helps us remember the lasting contribution they made to the climbing community.

CONSERVATION AND CROWDING

Selected climbing guides such as this one are a mixed blessing. On one hand, they reduce crowding on the most popular routes by shifting traffic to newer climbs. On the other hand, they create crowds where they previously didn't exist. While there is no simple solution to this problem, I am donating 25 percent of the proceeds from this book to the Access Fund, a national, nonprofit organization that works to keep climbing areas open, and advocates responsible use of public lands. I encourage all "users" of this book to join the Access Fund *(www.accessfund.org)*, and practice low-impact climbing.

HOW TO USE THIS BOOK

Since this book is about *climbers* as well as *climbs,* it is organized alphabetically, by climbers' last name. Several other organizational schemes were considered, including by climb location, by type of climb (rock, alpine, mixed, etc.), and by type of climber (alpinist, rock climber, etc.). But, since the two most commonly asked questions were "Who's in your book?" and "What climb did they pick?" (in that order), organizing the book by climber names made the most sense. The climb names themselves give the route name, the mountain or feature on which it's located (except for ice climbs and traverses), the area in which it's located—including parks and other protected areas—and the state or province.

Each chapter includes three sections: a profile of the climber, a story about his or her chosen climb, and a route description. The profile is intended to give the reader a feeling for the climber and the type(s) of climbing he or she does. The story—which is the bulk of each chapter—recounts the history of the climb and reveals *why* it's that climber's favorite. The route description, of course, provides the necessary information to do the climb. In most cases, I assume that the route descriptions in this book will be used in conjunction with area-specific guidebooks. If no commercial guidebook is available, as is the case with all of the Alaskan climbs, the route descriptions are more comprehensive.

The route descriptions include an information summary, followed by descriptions of the approach, the route itself, and the descent. All of the info summaries include standard guidebook information: first-ascent party, ratings, time required, recommended equipment, best season, special considerations, and references. If the references listed in the route descriptions are included in the Selected References at the back of this book, just the title and author are listed; otherwise, the references include the facts of publication. I've also included base and summit elevations for high-elevation rock and alpine climbs, and map listings where available.

All difficulty ratings use standard rating conventions, including an overall grade (I–VII), the Yosemite Decimal System for rock (5.0–5.14), aid-climbing ratings (A1–A5, or C for clean, hammerless aid), and ice ratings, which use prefixes such as WI for water ice, AI for alpine ice or névé, and M for "mixed." Most climbs also include a detailed "topo" map; see the accompanying topo key in this section.

Although the *Fifty Favorite Climbs* is, technically, a guidebook, it's also a snapshot of contemporary climbing history and a window into the lives of those who have shaped that history. The climber profiles, the narrative, and stunning color photography are intended to serve as a source of ideas and inspiration for everyone from the armchair mountaineer to the expert climber. Whether you experience the climbs through this book or firsthand, I sincerely hope you enjoy them.

Meeting the climbers and writing this book certainly fueled my desire to climb: More than ever, I want to explore new places, practice the latest techniques, and curb the forces of aging through rigorous training. There is no reason, I now realize, that I can't relive the summer of '80 for at least another twenty years.

—*Mark Kroese, February 2001*

A NOTE ABOUT SAFETY

Safety is an important concern in all outdoor activities. No guidebook can alert you to every hazard or anticipate the limitations of every reader. Therefore, the descriptions of roads, trails, routes, and natural features in this book are not representations that a particular place or excursion will be safe for your party. When you follow any of the routes described in this book, you assume responsibility for your own safety. Under normal conditions, such excursions require the usual attention to traffic, road, and trail conditions, weather, terrain, the capabilities of your party, and other factors. Keeping informed on current conditions and exercising common sense are the keys to a safe, enjoyable outing. The Mountaineers Books recommends that you always carry The Ten Essentials. These include extra clothing, extra food, sunglasses, a knife, a firestarter, a first-aid kit, matches in a waterproof container, a flashlight, a map, and a compass.

—*The Mountaineers Books*

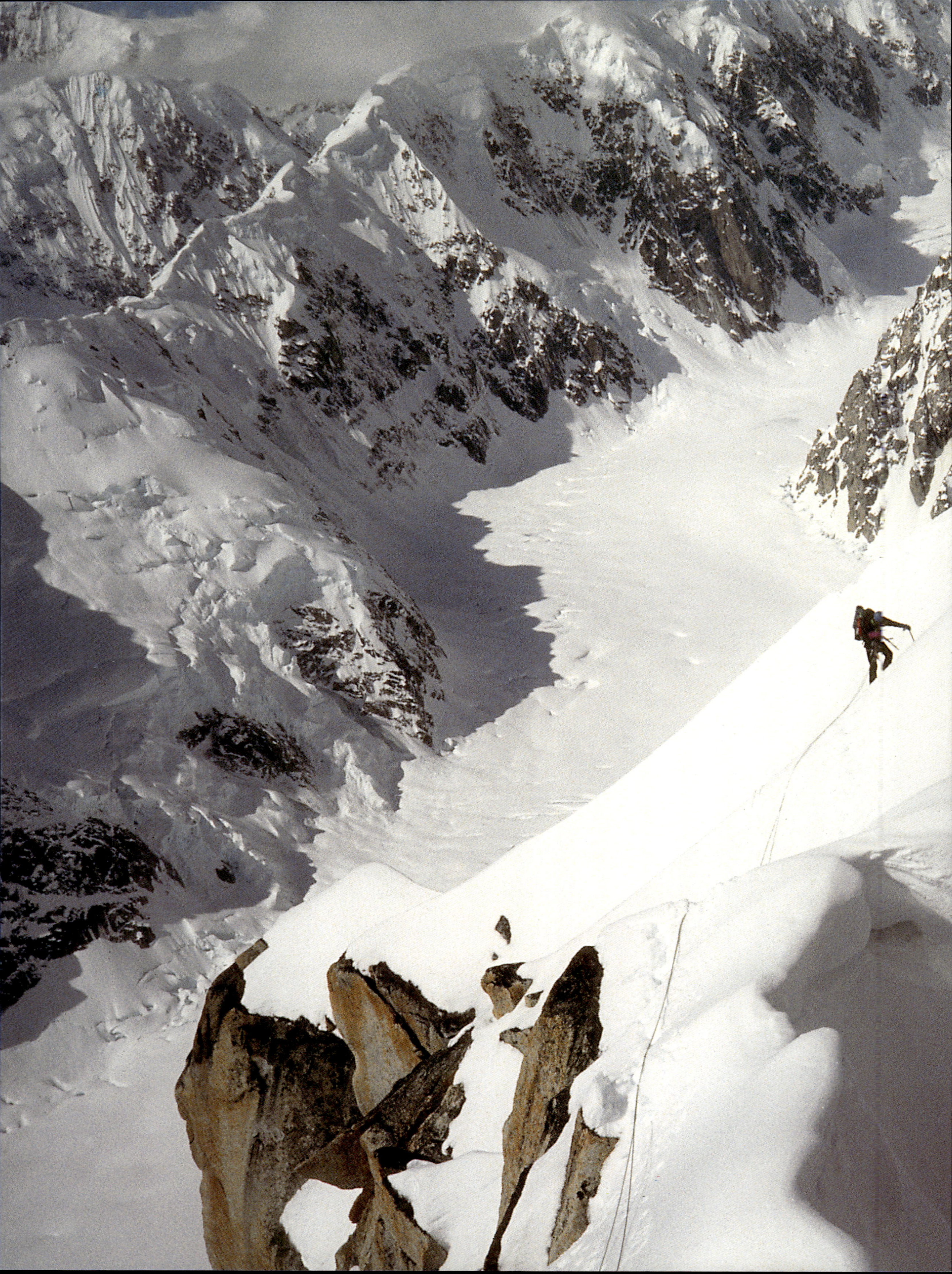

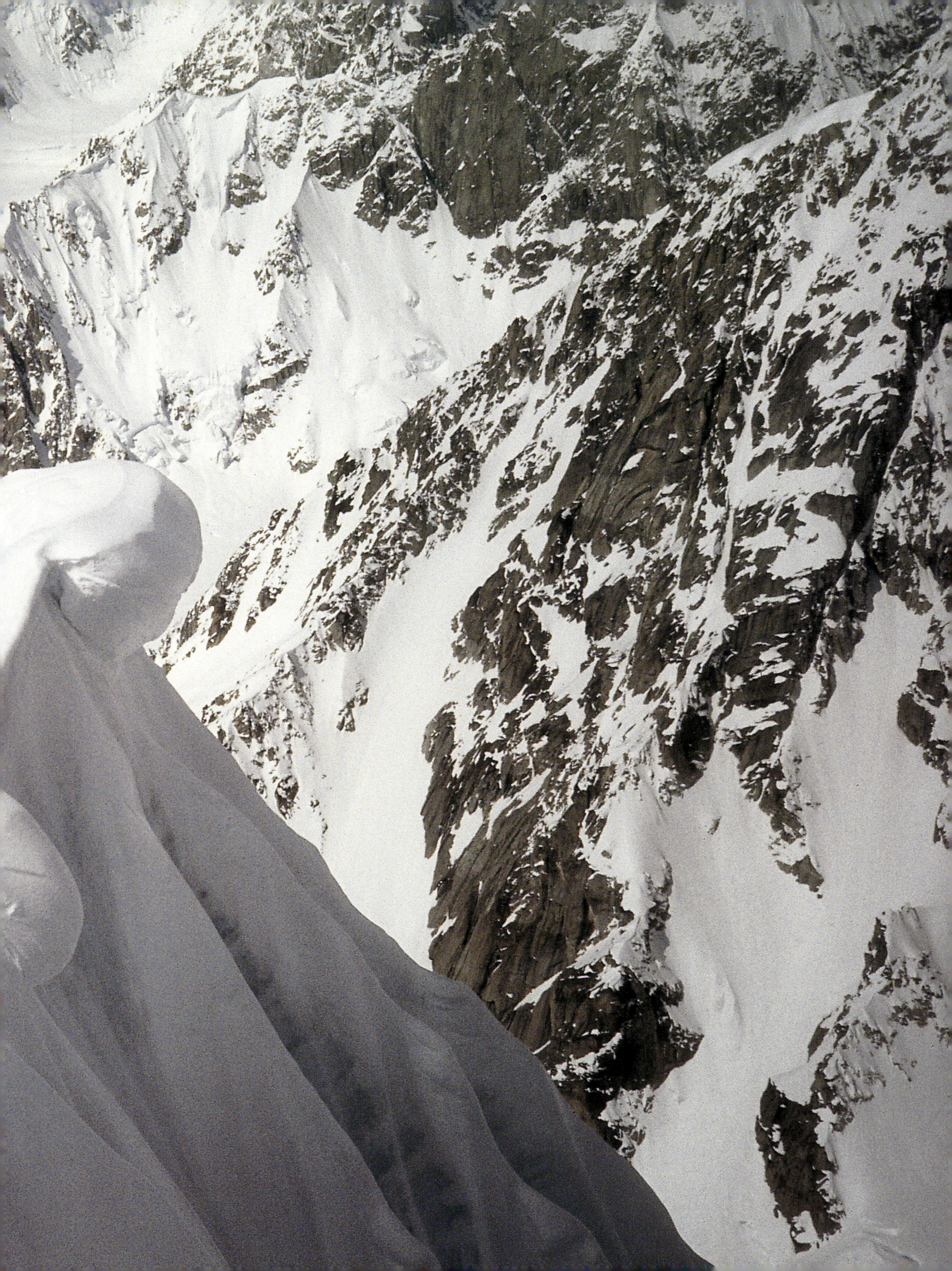

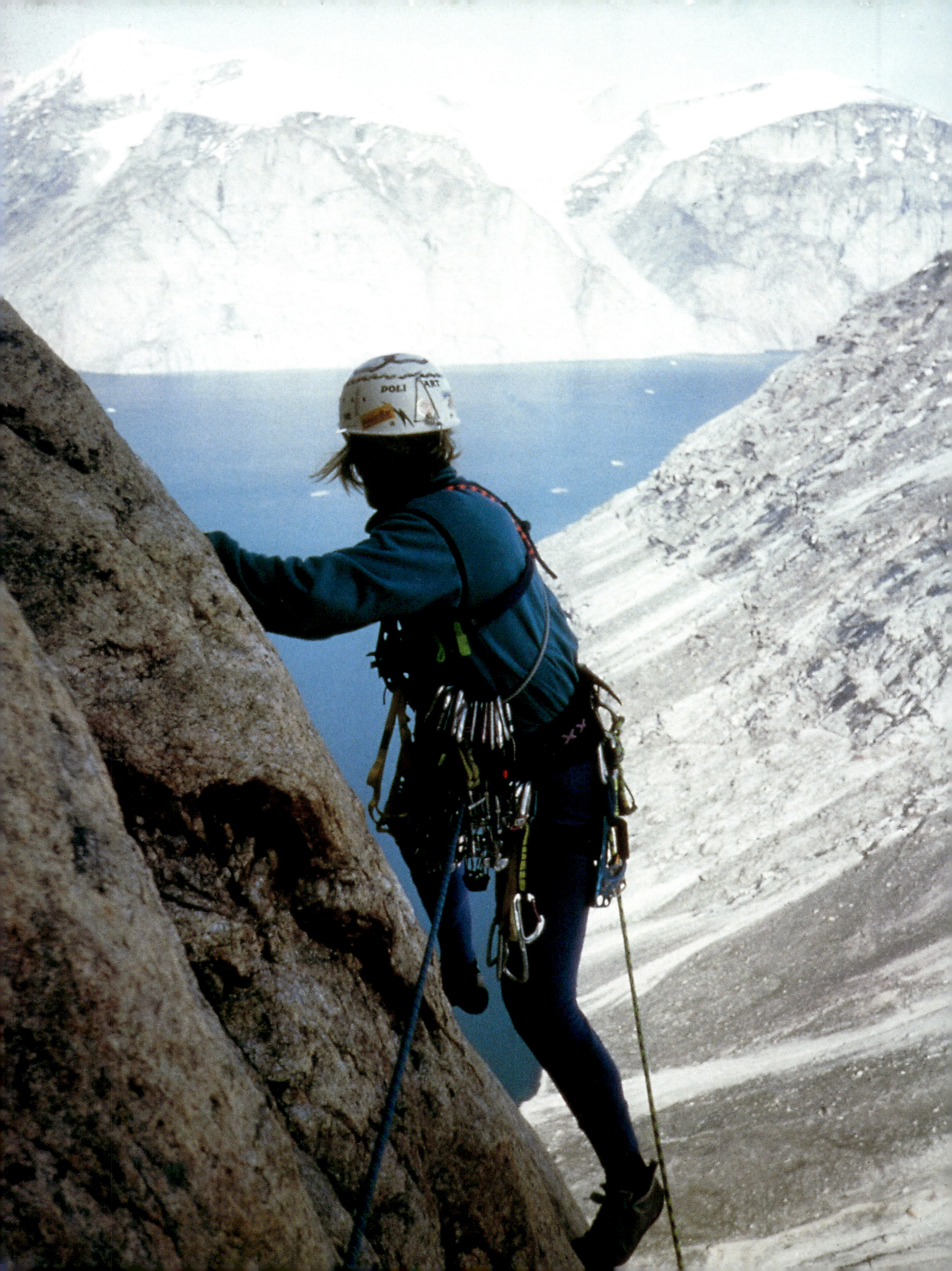
DOLI ART

CONRAD ANKER

STUMP SPIRE, SAM FORD FJORD, BAFFIN ISLAND, NUNAVUT TERRITORIES

CONRAD ANKER—
WILDERNESS WALL EXPLORER

Many people think of Conrad Anker as the guy who found George Mallory on Mount Everest. But to really know him is to understand his accomplishments on big, unexplored alpine walls.

Anker, a native Californian, subscribes to the theory that Yosemite's El Capitan is the ultimate training ground. He has made some thirty ascents of the granite monolith, half of them as sub-24-hour pushes. "For alpine climbing, it's one of the best things you can do," says the big-wall veteran. "You learn to work with your systems, you learn efficiency, and you don't get freaked out by exposure."

Anker has used his Yosemite-honed wall-climbing skills to establish some of the most demanding routes in the world. In 1995, on one of his five trips to Patagonia, Anker put up Badlands (VI, 5.10, A3, WI 4+) on the 3,200-foot southeast face of Torre Egger. After also ticking Cerro Torre and Cerro Standhardt, he became the fifth climber to complete the Patagonia trifecta. In Pakistan, he climbed the enormous, 7,500-foot West Face of Latok II (23,342 feet), often described as "El Cap on top of Denali." And in five trips to Antarctica, he's pioneered numerous routes in the isolated Ellsworth Mountains, including a solo ascent of a 7,000-foot line on the Peak of Kindness.

Anker, now in his late thirties, is the consummate climbing professional. He is well read, insightful, and articulate—an exceptional spokesperson for the outdoor industry. Despite the loss of several close friends, he has no regrets about his chosen lifestyle, and thanks his parents for encouraging him to pursue his passion. Says Anker, "If you can find what you are meant to do in this life, it's really a blessing."

STUMP SPIRE

Jonathan Turk and Mugs Stump were buddies for almost twenty years. Their friendship started in the '70s—when they hung out, skied, and climbed in Telluride, Colorado—and continued until May 1992, when Stump was tragically killed while guiding on Mount McKinley. During that period, both men achieved distinction for their outdoor accomplishments: Stump was regarded as one of America's premier alpinists, and Turk was renowned for his sea-kayaking marathons, such as paddling from Baffin Island to Greenland, or around the tip of South America.

Just before Stump's departure for McKinley, he and Turk organized a trip to the east coast of Baffin Island that would draw on their combined climbing and paddling skills. They planned to use kayaks to explore a remote region known as Sam Ford Fjord, then scale one of the El Capitan–size walls that guard its shores. According to published accounts from six previous expeditions, no technical climbing had been done near the fjord. Their plan was ambitious, and earned them a Shipton-Tilman grant from W. L. Gore & Associates.

Like everyone who knew Mugs, Turk was rocked by the news of his death. His initial reaction was to cancel the trip, but after discussing it with Conrad Anker—Stump's roommate and protégé—they decided to make it into a Mugs Stump memorial. Anker was the perfect partner; he shared Turk's grief, and the desire to find a fitting tribute for their friend. They decided to begin their adventure in mid-July, after the annual breakup of the pack ice.

Transportation in the Arctic is ruled by ice. From October to May, the waterways are frozen solid, making it easy to get around by snow machine. And in July and August, after breakup, travel by water is simple. But in between these seasons, during breakup and freezeup, the ocean is an impassable maze of floating ice that is too thin to walk on and too thick to float through. Anker and Turk figured that by waiting until mid-July, they could make the 100-mile journey into Sam Ford Fjord by speedboat. They envisioned a luxurious base camp from which they could travel to their chosen climb by kayak.

On July 15, they flew to the Inuit village of Kangiqtugaapik, better known as Clyde River, or "The Gateway to the Great Fjords." They were greeted by the disheartening news that, after the harshest winter in several decades, the fjord was in no shape for a speedboat. The first 60 miles were still sealed with ice, and therefore passable by snow machine, but the last 40 miles would have to be navigated by kayak. There was no easy way to get to

Conrad Anker leading into the unknown on 4,500-foot Stump Spire. Walker Arm of Sam Ford Fjord is in the background. © Jonathan Turk, portrait © Michael Kennedy

slabs

© Jonathan Turk

Sam Ford Fjord. Since their arsenal of big-wall gear—haul bags, water jugs, a portaledge—didn't fit into their kayaks, they left most of it behind. They brought only two ropes and a small rack. "We decided to just go free climbing instead," recalls Anker.

Anker and Turk spent the next day in Clyde River, getting organized and acquainting themselves with the Inuit culture. They observed a traditional seal feast, or *alupajaq,* and played simple Inuit games such as the hand-pull, or *aqsaaraq.* As they loaded their high-tech, polyethylene kayaks with supplies, they were reminded that the *qajaq* is an Inuit invention. And because it was their chosen mode of transportation, they were readily accepted by the Inuit people. "That we showed up with kayaks bridged the cultural gap amazingly well," explains Anker. "We were able to sidestep some of the unjust things that the Caucasians who settled North America have done—which is pretty vast—just by being in kayaks."

Anker said that at first, the Inuits didn't understand the point of climbing. "They thought, 'Why would you spend hard-earned money, dress up in colorful clothing, and go out and climb a mountain when life is hard enough as it is?' But then they saw that to us, climbing filled the same psychological need as, say, hunting, where you go out and vanquish this enemy."

After Anker and Turk were shuttled 60 miles by snow machine, the open-water leads became too large to jump, forcing the pair into their kayaks. The adventurous duo bid farewell to their Inuit

Forty miles of late-season pack ice made for a long, tedious approach.
© Jonathan Turk

friends and began the 40-mile journey to Sam Ford Fjord. They alternated between paddling across the leads and dragging their kayaks over the ice. When it looked dangerously thin, they would straddle their kayaks, hover their rear ends over the cockpit, then shuffle across the ice. If the ice broke, they would simply drop onto the kayak's opening as if it were a toilet seat. Four tiring days later, they finally reached their base camp in Swiss Bay.

Their first climb ascended a prominent buttress across from Kigut Peak, which they dubbed Kigut Buttress. They completed the fifteen-pitch route—mostly 5.8 to 5.10 crack climbing—in a continuous 20-hour push. Much of it was clean, but a few wet, ugly chimney pitches detracted from its appeal. It was a decent climb, but not worthy of Mugs's name.

A few days later, the ice melted in a narrow neck of the fjord known as Walker Arm. As they paddled through the pristine passage, they discovered an unnamed, 4,500-foot-high, free-standing pinnacle. "It was a beautiful spire, aesthetic from all angles," recalls Anker, who instantly wanted to climb it. Turk felt the same way. They agreed to take advantage of the good weather and start climbing in the morning.

Their chosen route was what Anker calls "a classic first-ascent line, following the path of least resistance." After scrambling up a few thousand feet of low-angled slabs, the climbers roped up for some moderate, fifth-class terrain. Three relatively easy pitches led to a near-vertical prow of clean, orange granite. At last, they had found what they were looking for. Anker cinched his shoelaces and led a brilliant, 5.10 finger crack to an airy stance. The next four pitches were steep and sustained, rewarding them with Yosemite-quality climbing in an incomparable setting. The last 500 feet were more moderate, winding over steps and ledges, and eventually leading to the top of the spire.

As they sat on the summit, neither Anker or Turk felt like celebrating. Despite their magnificent new route, they suddenly felt melancholy. They were thinking about Mugs: about how much he would have enjoyed this trip, about how much he'd taught them, and about how much they already missed him.

Back at base camp, they used a small piton to scratch Mugs's name into the flat side of a large rock. They placed it at the base of the spire, which now had a name: Stump Spire.

© Jonathan Turk

ROUTE DESCRIPTION

Area: East coast of Baffin Island
First ascent: Conrad Anker and Jonathan Turk, July 31, 1992
Base elevation: Sea level
Summit elevation: Approximately 4,500 feet
Difficulty: V, 5.10+
Time required: 1 full day from base camp
Equipment: Standard rack to 3 inches, including small and medium TCUs and wired nuts, small selection of pitons; 2 ropes
Season: July or August in normal year
Special considerations: Condition of ice dictates timing of trip; this free climb is best done "post-breakup"; many first ascents in this area await the ambitious
Reference: *American Alpine Journal*, (1993, pp 58–65)

Approach: Fly to Clyde River, Northwest Territories; go north past Eglington Fjord into Sam Ford Fjord. Walker Arm is the northerly arm of this fjord.

Route: Eight pitches of fifth-class climbing. From a saddle, scramble up a scree gully and climb three pitches of relatively easy broken rock on the east side of the spire. Climb a steep, 5.10 finger crack, then four more steep pitches to a broken ledge system. Three moderate pitches lead to the summit.

Descent: Rappel the route (the first ascent party left two pitons).

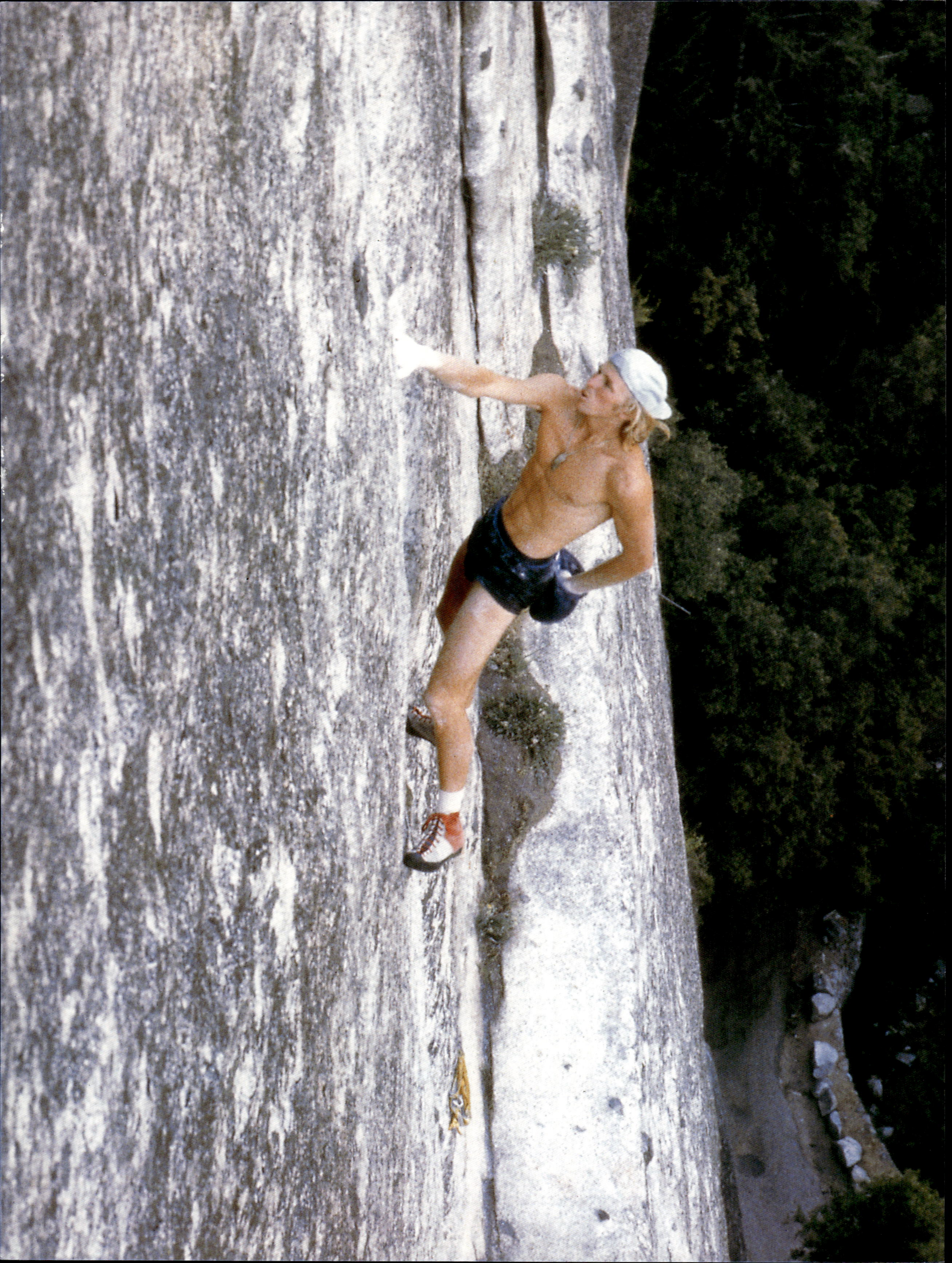

JOHN BACHAR

THE NABISCO WALL, THE COOKIE CLIFF, YOSEMITE NATIONAL PARK, CALIFORNIA

JOHN BACHAR—PARTY OF ONE

People who don't climb—a great majority of the populace, that is—think John Bachar is crazy. When they see pictures of him climbing steep rock faces without a rope, with the strength of his chalk-dusted hands as his only measure of security, they quickly realize the obvious: If he falls, he dies. Yet, after more than twenty years of solo climbing, John Bachar has never fallen. He is very much alive.

His success has very little to do with luck and almost everything to do with his systematic approach. Before Bachar came along, unroped solo climbing was something climbers got away with a few times, then promised never to do again. It was a phase, usually inspired by hubris, a surge of testosterone, or maybe a failed relationship. Bachar saw it differently. Soloing wasn't about being a daredevil or a stuntman. It was about fluid, precise movement—ballet on rock. Says Bachar, "I thought if I did it all the time, I might be able to bring it to an art form where I was in complete control." And he did.

Bachar stunned the climbing world in the mid-'70s when he soloed New Dimensions, the first 5.11 route in Yosemite. That he did it was one thing. That he considered it rational was another. And that was just the beginning.

For more than two decades, Bachar has been showing us a different way, making our palms sweat, teaching by example. Those paying close attention have learned plenty, like the importance of being brutally honest with themselves. One season in Tuolumne Meadows, the supremely confident Bachar decided he wouldn't tie in to a rope for an entire summer. Then he posted a note offering $10,000 to anyone who could follow him for a day.

He never parted with the money. Or his life.

THE NABISCO WALL

On its way south through Yosemite Valley, the Merced River flows past some of the finest free-climbing crags in North America. Although not as big as El Capitan or, say, the Cathedral Rocks, these cliffs are endowed with cracks that are so perfectly formed, so parallel, it looks like they were cut with a laser. By the early '70s, the hard men of Yosemite's post–Golden Age—Jim Bridwell, Henry Barber, John Long—had recognized the canyon's free-climbing potential. New routes were being discovered weekly, and as pitons gave way to "clean" alternatives such as Hexcentric nuts, lines that were once thought impossible were being reconsidered.

Some of the most tantalizing potential routes were on the Cookie Cliff. In those days there was a road right to its base. With a short approach and an abundance of unclimbed "splitter" cracks, the Cookie became the epicenter for advanced free climbing. The first major breakthrough came in 1971. Without the help of modern camming devices and so-called "sticky rubber," Jim Bridwell free-climbed a spectacular crack system on the Nabisco Wall. The route is defined by three aptly named pitches: Waverly Wafer (5.10c), Wheat Thin (5.10c), and Butterfingers (5.11a). It quickly earned a reputation as *the* Yosemite test piece, and saw only four successful ascents during the next two years—all by Bridwell understudies.

The sixth ascent of the Nabisco Wall came in 1973. On a warm spring afternoon at the Cookie, Bridwell and the boys were hanging out at its base, climbing and bouldering. The close-knit clan of Valley denizens knew almost every climber in Yosemite, especially those attempting the hardest routes. They were surprised when, out of the blue, two unknown teenagers from L.A. showed up and started racking up for Waverly Wafer. It was John Bachar and Tobin Sorenson. They were young, earnest, and unaware of the scrutiny they would soon be under.

With skeptical smirks being cast behind his back, Sorenson tied into the rope and started leading Waverly Wafer, a burning 1¼-inch lieback crack. He was a bold climber, bordering on reckless; when he was leading, his belayers were usually more nervous than he was. (Sorenson died in 1980 while trying to solo the North Face of Mount Alberta; see Climb 42). "Tobin's way of thinking was, 'If you're pumped, just start climbing faster and go for it—forget the gear,'" explains Bachar. "So whenever Tobin fell, it was spectacular." Sure enough, Sorenson took a 35-foot fall on the crux section of the Wafer—luckily, wounding only his pride. Adhering to the so-called "yo-yo" style of the day, he lowered to the start of

Fit and focused: John Bachar locked in on Butterballs (5.11c) during his historic solo ascent of the three-pitch Nabisco Wall.
© Mark Chapman, portrait © Greg Epperson

the pitch and led it without falling on his second try.

Next came Wheat Thin. It was more technical, but less pumpy. This time Bachar led, waltzing up the echoing flake without incident. His lead put the youngsters at the base of Butterfingers, the hardest pitch. The crack starts thin, like a sidewalk joint, then widens to what Bachar calls "a hero's hand crack." After a short fall at the crux, Sorenson unlocked the tricky sequence and began blasting up the final hand crack. As Bachar belayed, he noticed about twenty people gathered at the bottom of the wall.

Within an hour the lads had finished the climb and returned to its base. They received a heroes' welcome. "Everyone was there," remembers Bachar, "Bridwell, Chapman, Graham—all the Valley heavies. First they congratulated us, then they were like, 'Fuck, who are *you* guys?'" John Bachar and Tobin Sorenson were strangers no more.

Not long after their ascent of the Nabisco Wall, an alternative to the second pitch was added by Henry Barber, then one of America's leading free climbers. Barber's stunning new route, dubbed Butterballs (5.11c), bisected a blank section of granite 20 feet left of Wheat Thin. At the time, it was the most sustained finger crack of its grade. Butterballs became the ultimate test piece. During the next few years, several elite crack climbers managed to do the route, but it had yet to be "flashed," or done on the first try with no falls. Just as the 4-minute mile was once considered impossible, many didn't think Butterballs would ever be flashed.

Enter Ron Kauk (see Climb 23). Like his friend Bachar, Kauk was young and motivated. He wanted to be the first to flash Butterballs, and after months of rigorous training, he did it. "People were *blown* away," remembers Bachar. Inspired by Kauk's historic feat, and not wanting to be outdone, Bachar repeated the performance a week later. Kauk and Bachar became inseparable —always climbing, always training. One day, while lamenting the lack of good training cracks, they decided to use Butterballs as a workout climb—a radical concept in those days. With the security of a top rope, they did "laps" on the route until they had it wired. "Each time I did it," Bachar explains, "my goal was to use one calorie less."

By the next season Bachar was climbing brilliantly. He was super fit, and had elevated

© Mark Kroese

solo climbing to an art form. Even though he was continually repeating the same climbs, he said he never tired of it. "As soon as you are 10 feet off the ground, you're not bored anymore. It's fresh. You're soloing. You *can't* blow it."

Having climbed the Nabisco Wall with a rope more than thirty times, Bachar felt he was ready to solo it. It was an audacious idea—maybe even crazy—but he *knew* he could do it. "I knew it would blow everyone's buzz," said Bachar, "so one day I woke up and told Mark Chapman that I was probably going to do it that afternoon. I asked him if he would take pictures, and told him not to tell anyone."

As the afternoon shade cooled the Cookie, Chapman rigged a rope for taking photos while Bachar prepared for the climb. "I got there and meditated for 10 minutes and just tried to zone out," remembers Bachar. "Then I threw my shirt off and just fuckin' went for it." For the next half hour, John Bachar played chess with gravity, making deliberate, controlled movements. He was in the zone; only the rock in front of him mattered.

Bachar remembers each pitch vividly. "You get a little bit of everything on the Wafer: stemming, hands, fist, lieback," says Bachar. "Then on Butterballs you're in a sea of blank, vertical granite and there is this perfect finger crack. It's like you're on the side of a building, perfectly vertical and perfectly flat. And then you've got your hero finish on Butterfingers. You're cruising on perfect hand jams on this absolutely bitchin' wall and you're feeling like king of the world."

ROUTE DESCRIPTION

Area: Lower Merced Canyon, Yosemite Valley
First ascent: Jim Bridwell and various partners, October 1970–August 1971
Difficulty: II, 5.11a or 5.11c (depending on second pitch)
Time required: A few hours to a half day
Equipment: Cams and nuts, 3/16 inch to 2½ inch, extra TCUs, ¾ inch to 1¼ inch
Season: Spring and fall
Special considerations: If you want to climb in the shade, wait until late afternoon
Reference: *Yosemite Climbs, Free Climbs* by Don Reid

Approach: Use the State Highway 140 park entrance into Yosemite Valley. Parking is prohibited, so have somone drop you off at one of the turnouts directly below the cliff. Follow a climbers trail somewhat left of the talus field to meet the old road at the base of the cliff. The Nabisco Wall is in the center of the cliff. Approach the first pitch(es) from third-class ledges on the left.

Route: First pitch: Choose either Bev's Tower (5.10a) or Waverly Wafer (5.10c). Second pitch: Choose either Wheat Thin (5.10c) or Butterballs (5.11c). Third pitch: Climb Butterfingers (5.11a), or climb an alternate start to the right, Ladyfingers (5.11a).

Descent: Rappel the route, or descend to the climbers path to the climber's right.

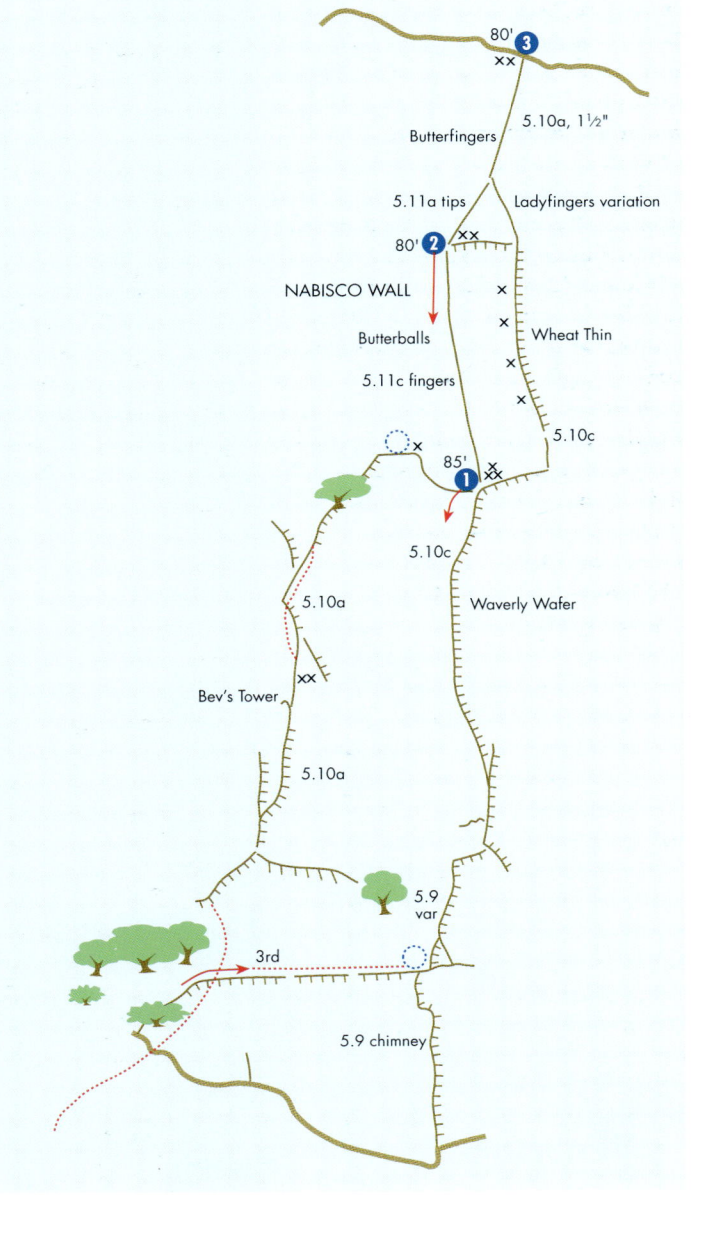

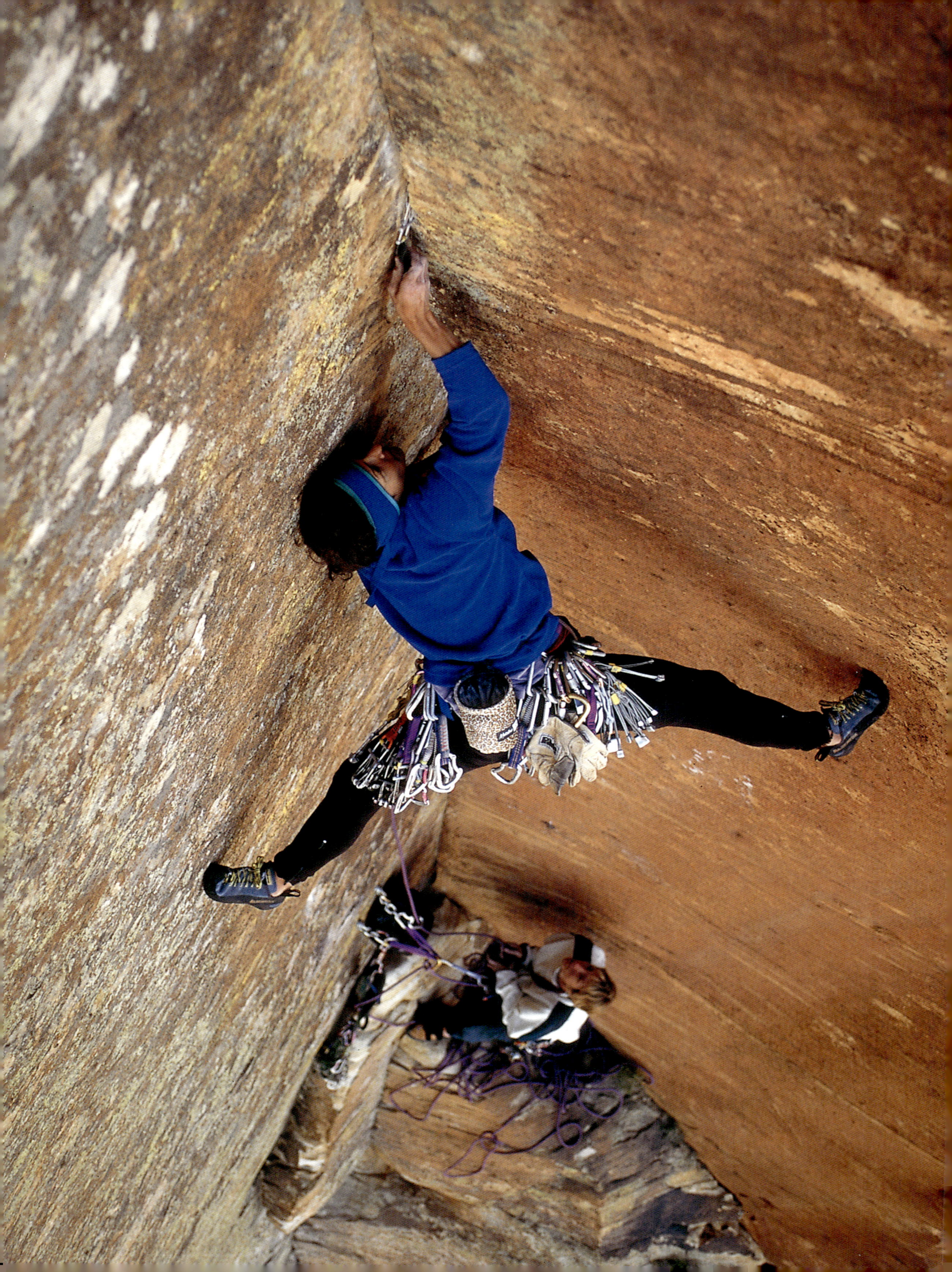

BOBBI BENSMAN
ORIGINAL ROUTE, THE RAINBOW WALL, RED ROCKS NATIONAL CONSERVATION AREA, NEVADA

BOBBI BENSMAN—HARD WORK, HIGH NUMBERS

Watching Bobbi Bensman glide through a 5.13 overhang is an awesome sight: Her svelte body hangs like a feather from her sinewy arms. Her washboard stomach goes drum-tight as she hooks her heel on the lip of the roof and pulls through the crux in a single flowing motion. Minutes later, she flosses the anchors and lowers to the ground with a smile. "The route is totally cool," she enthuses. "But the moves are a little *gnar-gnar*."

Such hip expressions are a tip-off that Bobbi has spent the last twenty years hanging on and around the best crags in the world. Her two-decade career has been an intense blend of traditional, sport, and competitive climbing—from Yosemite to Australia to the south of France.

Bobbi spent her first eight years jamming up classic crack climbs, including early ascents of Half Dome and El Capitan. She discovered her amazing power in 1987, when Yosemite veteran Dale Bard encouraged her to step up her training program. "Dale got me focused on the gymnastic approach," says Bobbi. The following year, when sport and competitive climbing swept the nation, she was ready for the challenge.

Her intensely passionate nature and legendary training regime vaulted her to the top of the game, where she has remained for more than a decade: Bobbi has made redpoint ascents of more than 130 5.13 sport climbs, won the Phoenix bouldering contest 13 times, and, on plastic, earned more than 20 national championships.

By the late 1990s, after almost a decade of clipping bolts, Bobbi rekindled her love for traditional climbing. Since then, she's made numerous trips to her favorite haunts, including Red Rocks, Utah's Indian Creek, and Yosemite. "I'll always love sport climbing," she explains, "but it's the hard traditional routes that I remember the most."

ORIGINAL ROUTE OF THE RAINBOW WALL

In September 1997, Bobbi Bensman steered her fully loaded pick-up into the Red Rocks overlook, a peaceful vista just 20 miles from the neon chaos of the Las Vegas strip. She'd driven almost nonstop from her hometown of Rifle, Colorado, and was sitting before a 7-mile stretch of meandering canyons and striped sandstone towers—her playground for the coming months.

Bobbi had lived in Rifle—a place known as much for limestone sport climbing as its embrace of gun culture—long enough to do most of the area's 500 or so bolted routes. She had become totally immersed in sport climbing and, despite her roots as a "trad" climber, had hardly placed a piece of gear in eight years. When she got the urge to do some long, traditional routes, she packed her truck and headed for Red Rocks.

Bobbi's wish list included many classic routes, the hardest being the Rainbow Wall—a 1,300-foot multicolored arc of sandstone. She first saw the wall in 1980, but didn't consider climbing it until 1997, when her friend Dan McQuade made an all-free ascent. "When Dan did it free, I was super psyched," recalls Bobbi. "I promised myself I wouldn't leave Red Rocks until I'd climbed it."

By the spring of 1998, the Rainbow Wall had seen a handful of free ascents—all of them by men. As Bobbi considered her options for a free attempt, she concluded that the most memorable way to do the climb would be with another woman. She approached longtime friend Roxanna Brock (see Climb 6) with the idea. At first, Roxanna had her doubts but, fortunately, her reservations didn't last long. A month later, after doing the route with her husband, she had a change of heart. "When I was up there with Brian," explains Roxanna, "I kept thinking, 'Bobbi and I can do this.'"

Roxanna signed on, and the pair formulated an ambitious plan: They would spend the first day hiking toward the base of the Rainbow Wall with full packs, stopping along the way to "warm up" on Cloud Tower. (Cloud Tower, also know as the "Astroman of Red Rocks," is a nine-pitch crack climb with two 5.12 pitches and plenty of 5.11.) After polishing off Cloud Tower, they planned to hike to the bivouac site near the base of the Rainbow Wall. The next day, they assumed, they'd simply waltz up the thirteen-pitch classic.

"We bit off way more than we could chew," laughs Bobbi. "We both fell on our respective 5.12 pitches on Cloud Tower, and our

---

Bobbi Bensman stretching for a cam placement high on the Rainbow Wall. She led the eleventh pitch (5.12a) without falling on her first try.
© Dan McQuade, portrait © Dan McQuade

© Mark Kroese

ropes got stuck on the descent. It was pitch-black by the time we got back to our packs." Although they were thrashed from Cloud Tower, the strong-willed Sagittarians donned their packs and marched toward the base of the Rainbow Wall by headlamp.

Early the next morning, they stashed their overnight gear and racked up for the climb. Roxanna cruised up the easy first pitch, putting them just below the 5.12b crux. Bobbi started up the second, but was stopped by a gymnastic sequence involving a controlled lunge to a 1-inch edge. "The move is really, really reachy. It's heinous," remembers Bobbi. After several failed attempts, she lowered off and traded places with her partner. But being an inch shorter than Bobbi, Roxanna's valiant efforts were also in vain. They were forced to retreat. "We were totally demoralized," she remembers.

The failure hung over them like a dark cloud. Unwilling to accept it, they decided to try again in 3 days. Their new plan, however, allowed for a longer rest between the two climbs: After Cloud Tower, they would give themselves an entire day to hike to the base of the Rainbow Wall.

The plan worked like a charm. "Roxanna led her 5.12 pitch perfectly. Then I cruised my 5.12 pitch," enthused Bobbi. "We went up and *walked* Cloud Tower." Without so much as getting a rope stuck on rappel, they made the round trip with daylight to spare.

The following evening found Bobbi and Roxanna camped at the base of the Rainbow Wall, rested and ready for their second attempt. They discussed the possibility of switching leads, but decided to stick with their original plan: Roxanna would lead the odd-numbered pitches, and Bobbi would take the even leads. This meant that Bobbi, who is taller than Roxanna, would lead the height-dependent second pitch.

The eager climbers got an early start, regaining their previous high point by 7:00 A.M. Bobbi started up the second pitch, placing a cam as high as possible before dynoing for the elusive edge. She stretched like a basketball player going for a rebound, but still missed the hold and skidded 20 feet down the wall. Adhering to redpoint-style ethics, she lowered to the belay and tried again. And again. "I tried five time and couldn't do it," laments Bobbi. "Eventually I told Roxanna that I was sorry, but today wasn't the day. That's when she convinced me to give it one last try. Somehow, I went up there and just fired it."

It was now 9:00 A.M. They had spent 2 hours on the first crux, and still had eleven long pitches in front of them. With renewed momentum, Roxanna took the lead and put it in high gear. The next nine pitches, which are mostly 5.11, were pure joy. "It was like dancing," remembers Bobbi. "There were lots of thin cracks, fingertip edges, really technical climbing." Racing against the clock, they swung leads all the way to the eleventh pitch, the second crux. Although slightly easier (5.12a) than the first crux, it was a more daring lead. Since Roxanna had already done the moves (following her husband), she took the sharp end, succeeding on her first try. This put Bobbi in position to lead the twelfth pitch—the third and final crux. "It was a full-on, delicate stemming corner," she remembers. "I was super psyched to lead it on-sight."

The victorious duo topped out at 5:00 P.M. After taking in the view, they simul-rappelled the entire route, a time-saving technique used by only the most trusted partners. As they slid down the ropes side by side, they marveled at the route's breathtaking position. "That's what I love about traditional climbing," muses Bobbi. "It puts you in places that sport climbing never will."

ROUTE DESCRIPTION

Area: Juniper Canyon, Red Rocks
First ascent: Joe Herbst and Larry Hamilton, April 1973; first free ascent: Leo Henson, April 1994; first free ascent, Rainbow Country variation: Dan McQuade and partners, December 18, 1996
Difficulty: V, 5.9, A2, or 5.12b (5.12d via Rainbow Country variation)
Time required: 1–2 days
Equipment: 2 60-m ropes; double set of Camalots to no. 3, 1 no. 4 Camalot; set of wired nuts; set of RPs or equivalent; 1–2 sets of TCUs; many slings
Season: Year-round; spring and fall are best
Special considerations: Rainbow Country variation, pitches six through nine, give an even more sustained experience
Reference: *Rock Climbing, Red Rocks* by Todd Swain

Approach: Allow 3–4 hours. Start hiking at either the Pine Creek or Oak Creek parking areas on the loop road, which is accessed from Road 159, or the old Oak Creek campground. Hike to the mouth of Juniper Canyon. Follow the Juniper Creek drainage upstream to a big, white lump of rock that divides the drainage. Climb slabs left (south) for 600 yards to the base of the wall. The Original Route starts at an obvious dihedral system about 100 feet left of the prominent red arches on the right side of the wall.

Route: Thirteen pitches of classic crack climbing up a multi-colored corner system. See topo for details.

Descent: Rappel the route.

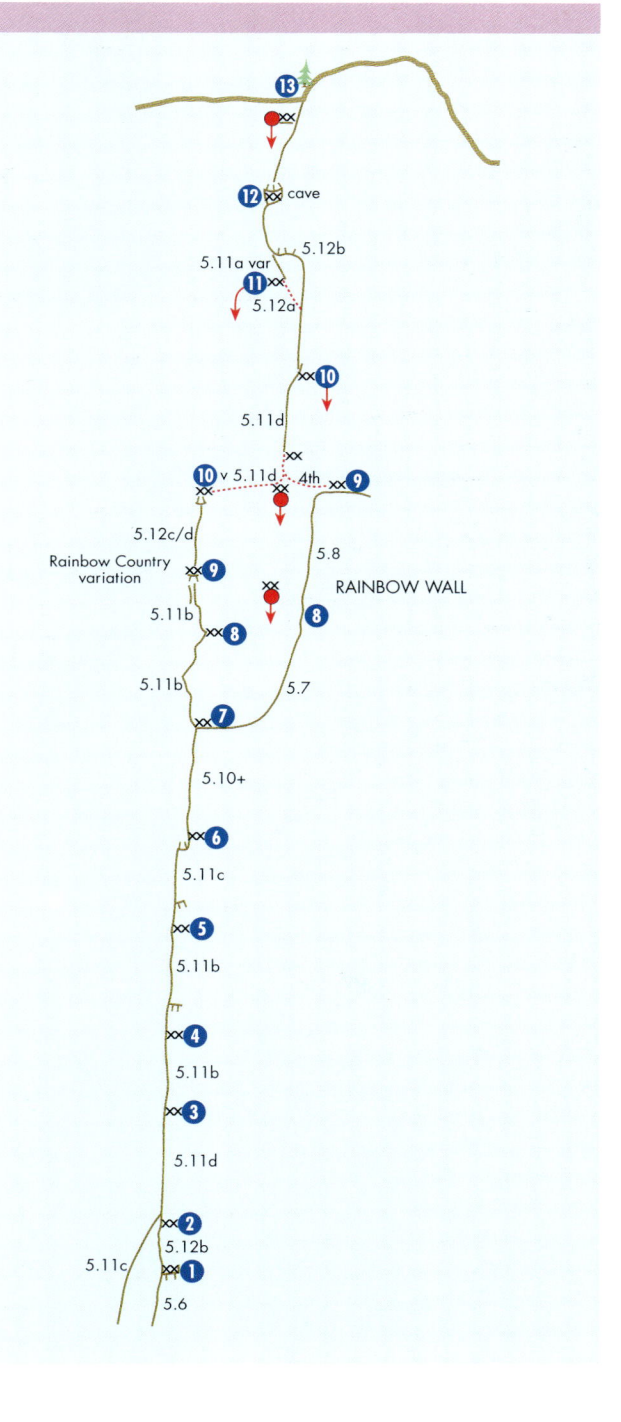

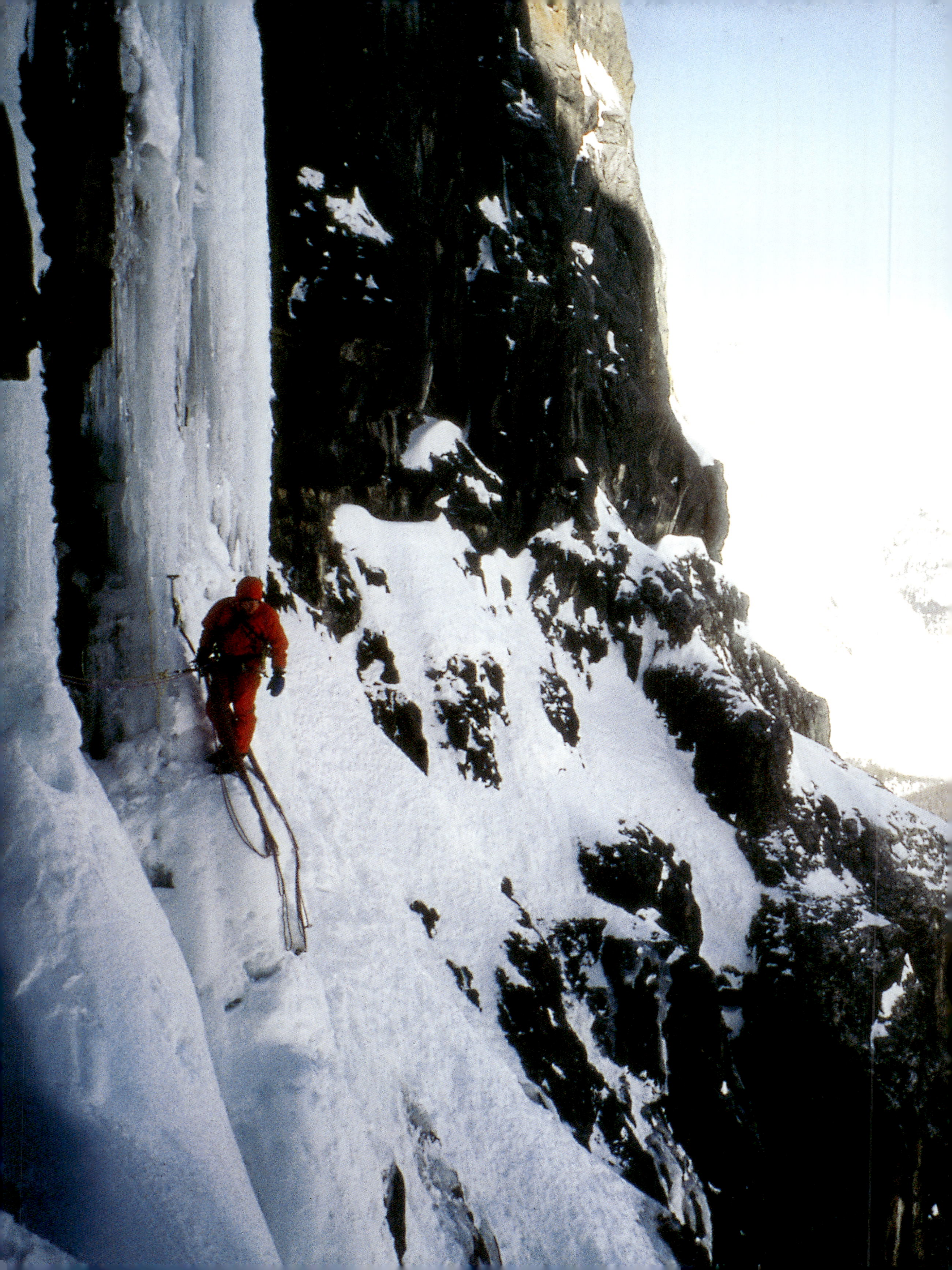

BARRY BLANCHARD

NEMESIS, MOUNT STANLEY, KOOTENAY NATIONAL PARK, BRITISH COLUMBIA

BARRY BLANCHARD—TOTALLY COMMITTED

Barry Blanchard's life is defined by climbing. If he's not guiding a climb, working on a film about climbing, being interviewed by *Climbing* magazine, or writing about his most recent climb, then he's probably out climbing.

Blanchard has been one of North America's most prolific alpinists for more than twenty years. His career highlights alone span four single-spaced pages, and read like a wish-list for the modern hard man. A quick perusal through a guidebook to the Canadian Rockies reveals about half of his notable ascents, including the east face of Mount Fay, the north pillar of North Twin, and the northeast face of Mount Chephren (see Climb 22). The rest of his big routes are scattered throughout the great ranges of the planet—from Alaska to Argentina, Nepal to New Zealand, Pakistan to Peru.

Born and raised in Calgary, Alberta, Blanchard is a seventh-generation Metis—French Canadian and American Indian—a cultural legacy that has shaped his love for the wilderness. He started climbing while in high school, "as an alternative to juvenile delinquency," then moved to Canmore, near Banff, where he still lives.

Despite losing several close friends to climbing accidents, Blanchard has remained totally committed to climbing. In fact, in June 2000, the journeyman alpinist made the third ascent of one of Alaska's most committing routes, Mount Foraker's 9,000-foot Infinite Spur (see Climb 24).

NEMESIS

During the first few years of their obsession, when the need to climb completely overwhelms the desire to work, many climbers quit their jobs in favor of an extended climbing trip. For Barry Blanchard, the itch came in the spring of 1980. Inspired by Europe's great alpinists—legendary figures like Walter Bonatti, Reinhold Messner, and Lionel Terray—he packed his rucksack and headed for Chamonix, France.

Blanchard and his partner, Kevin Doyle, another gung-ho Canadian, spent the summer cutting their teeth on the most classic routes in the Alps. It was a pivotal season for Blanchard: as he describes it, ". . . back before my knowledge and equipment had caught up with my enthusiasm." Fueled by desire and raw talent, he and Doyle climbed with religious fervor. By the end of the summer, they'd pulled off some of the most challenging routes in the region, including the Bonatti pillar on the Petit Dru and the north face of Les Droites.

When Blanchard and Doyle returned to the Canadian Rockies in September, they were brimming with confidence. Climbing in the Alps had been a powerful growth experience. "We were quite psyched," recalls Blanchard of the realization that expert-level routes were now within their reach. "The first thing we did was make a list of the ice climbs we wanted to do in the coming winter." At the time, there were only four routes in the Canadian Rockies rated WI 6—then the most difficult ice rating. And they were all on their hit list.

Their top priority was an early-forming wall of ice on the north side of Mount Stanley called Nemesis. The route was named by ice pioneer Bugs McKeith, who made numerous attempts to climb the 500-foot curtain before finally succeeding in 1974. McKeith's ascent was a significant achievement, but garnered mixed reviews since it was done as an aid climb. Rather than free-climbing the ice with a tool in each hand and a crampon on each foot, McKeith hung all of his weight on his ice tools while his feet stood in nylon stirrups. Each stirrup was connected to the head of its respective tool, forcing him to move each hand-foot combination in lockstep—an awkward if not precarious system that relied on no more than two points of contact.

Nemesis didn't earn its reputation as a testing ground for advanced ice climbers until March 1980, when it was climbed free by John Lauchlan, with partners Albi Sole and James Blench. The ascent was considered a major breakthrough for the sport, and confirmed Lauchlan's reputation as Canada's leading alpinist. Not only was Lauchlan a talented climber, he was a friend and mentor to Blanchard and Doyle. Lauchlan was the one who convinced them they could do the north face of Les Droites, and when they returned from Europe, it was Lauchlan who encouraged them to try Nemesis. (Lauchlan died in 1982 attempting the first solo ascent of Polar Circus, one of Canada's longest ice climbs.)

By February 1981, Nemesis was in perfect shape—as were Blanchard and Doyle. They had been ice climbing regularly for

Joe Josephson contemplating the crux pitch of the Canadian Rockies classic, Nemesis (WI 6) © Barry Blanchard, portrait © Steve House

rappel

three months and were ready for the challenge. A predawn start put them at the base of the first pitch just as it was getting light. After cinching his Salewa strap-on crampons tightly onto his leather boots, Blanchard took the lead. Although the upper half of Nemesis was "fat," the ice on the lower half of the curtain was characteristically thin. The climbing was delicate. Sometimes, in lieu of whacking his tools into the ice for a solid placement, Blanchard would construct a hold by carefully tapping a hole in the ice curtain and hooking his pick on the opening.

Doyle practiced the same technique while leading the second pitch, which brought the enthusiastic teammates to a comfortable stance halfway up the route. The ice above them was much thicker, but went from steep to very steep. As Blanchard led the crux third pitch—a 60-foot dead-vertical pillar—he tried to convince himself that the primitive Salewa ice screws he was placing would hold if he fell. Fortunately, he didn't fall. With daylight to spare, Doyle started up the last pitch, comforted by the thunk of solid tool placements. "It's a sheet of deep blue Canadian ice," explains Blanchard. "And it's *meters* thick—really classic stuff." Even though it was technically the easiest pitch of the climb (WI 5), an untimely freak of nature caused it to be the most memorable.

Nemesis is one of those waterfalls that forms an ice dam near its top. As the season progresses and the dam gains strength, a reservoir of water accumulates between the rock and the back of the ice curtain. During the course of a normal winter, random acts of hydrology will cause the dam to break and indiscriminately spray a few thousand gallons of water onto whatever is in its path. That year, unfortunately, it was Kevin Doyle and Barry Blanchard.

Doyle was halfway up the pitch when it happened. As if he was standing below a helicopter dropping its payload onto a forest fire, he was suddenly hit by a falling wave of water. "There was literally a ton of water falling on us," recalls Blanchard. "It went from being a dry, pleasant ice climb to this insane thing." Apart from the obvious discomfort of being soaked to the skin, the dousing created serious problems for the climbers. The subzero temperatures caused the water to instantly freeze to whatever it touched. Their rope became an inflexible, 30-pound cable that tugged on Doyle's harness and threatened to pull him off the wall. And their Gore-Tex suits were coated by an unbending armor of ice. After a few minutes of chaos, the flow reduced to a tolerable spray, enabling Doyle to struggle to the top of the frozen waterfall. Since the rope wouldn't bend through his belay device, he used a waist-belay to bring Blanchard up.

Standing safely at the top of Nemesis, they were forced by ice-clad knots to cut the rope from their harnesses. The rope was useless, and rappelling was out of the question. Their only choice was to hike and downclimb to the base of the route—a long, unsavory, and avalanche-prone alternative. Two frigid hours later, they returned to Doyle's car, stripped off their clothes, and cranked up the heat.

Author's note: *Blanchard has returned to climb Nemesis seven times since the winter of 1981—thankfully, without another dam-breaking incident. He has climbed it with his wife, Catherine, with friends, and as a guide.*

ROUTE DESCRIPTION

Area: Banff-Radium Parkway, Canadian Rockies
First ascent: Bugs McKeith and partners, March 1974; first free ascent: James Blench, John Lauchlan, and Albi Sole, March 1980
Difficulty: V, WI 6 or 6+
Time required: 1 long day
Equipment: 10–14 ice screws, various lengths; 4 stoppers; 2 knifeblade pitons, 1 shallow angle, 1 1¾-inch angle (rock gear important on light ice years); double 60-m 9 mm ropes (dry)
Season: Late October–April
Special considerations: Do not attempt this climb if the avalanche danger is greater than moderate; Nemesis is high and north-facing
Reference: *Waterfall Ice, Climbs in the Canadian Rockies* by Joe Josephson
Maps: 82 N/8, Lake Louise; 82 N/1, Mt. Goodsir

Approach: From Trans-Canada Highway 1, take Highway 93 South 8.4 miles (13.5 km) west to the Stanley Glacier trailhead. Allow 2 hours. Follow steep switchbacks to the valley above, toward a large cliff band on the right. Nemesis is the sixth climb on your right as you head up the valley.

Route: This continuously steep route is usually climbed in four pitches, but can be climbed in three. The first two pitches lead to a small ledge, and can be thin. The third pitch is the crux.

Descent: Rappel the route on the climber's right.

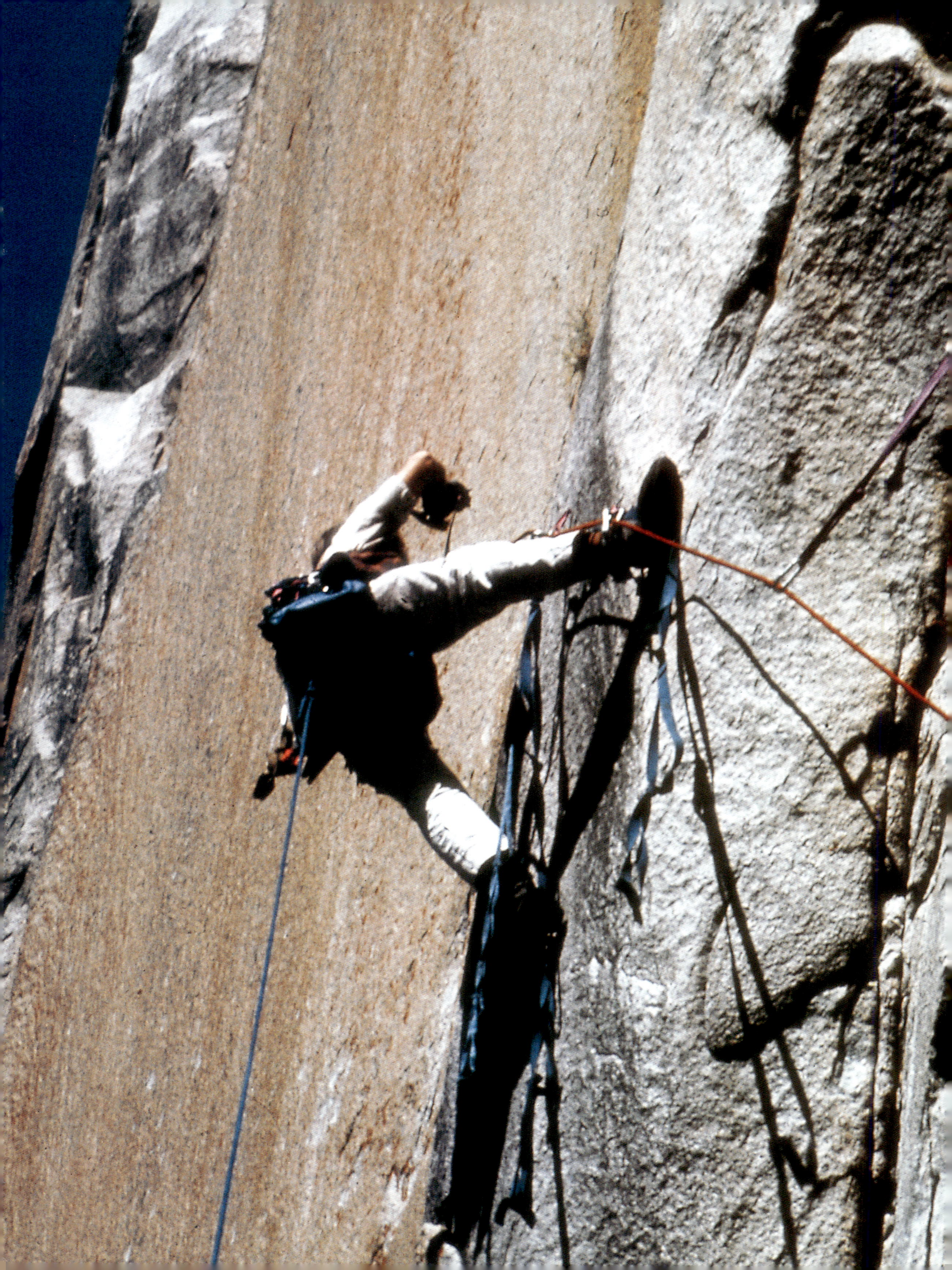

JIM BRIDWELL

PACIFIC OCEAN WALL, EL CAPITAN, YOSEMITE NATIONAL PARK, CALIFORNIA

JIM BRIDWELL—THE BIRD

For almost forty years, Jim Bridwell has been pushing the standards of big-wall climbing—from Yosemite to Alaska to Patagonia. In Yosemite, where Bridwell earned his nickname, he is a totemic figure. His legacy includes countless first ascents and always-entertaining "Bridwell stories." The visionary but flinty wall veteran is notorious for pushing himself—and his partners—to do the impossible. It would take an entire book to chronicle the accomplishments of this granite astronaut, but the highlights alone are inspiring—see the list of selected climbs below.

The Bridwell File (first ascents unless otherwise noted)

1968: Second ascent, Direct Northwest Face of Half Dome
1968: First 2-day ascent of the Nose on El Capitan, first free ascent of stoveleg cracks
1969: First two-bivouac ascent of the Salathé Wall, El Capitan
1971: First free ascent of the Nabisco Wall (5.11), Cookie Cliff, Yosemite
1974: "Geek Towers" (5.11+), Yosemite Falls
1975: First 1-day ascent of the Nose (15 hours), El Capitan; Pacific Ocean Wall (VI, 5.10, A5), El Capitan
1976: Mirage (VI, 5.9, A4), El Capitan; two grade V routes in Patagonia
1977: Bushido (VI, 5.10, A4), Half Dome
1978: Sea of Dreams (VI, 5.10, A5), El Capitan
1979: Southeast Ridge of Cerro Torre (5.10, A3), Patagonia
1981: East Face of the Moose's Tooth, Alaska (in winter); Zenyatta Mondatta (VI, 5.10, A5), El Capitan
1982: South Face of Pumori (23,448 feet), Himalayas; Kangsi III (22,723 feet), Himalayas
1987: The Big Chill (VI, 5.10, A5), Half Dome
1988: Cerro Stanhardt (WI 6, 5.10), Patagonia
1989: Shadows (VI, 5.9, A4), El Capitan
1992: Successful ascent of North Face of the Eiger, Switzerland
1997: Newfoundland ice routes; repeat ascent of Wyoming Sheep Ranch (VI, 5.10, A5), El Capitan
1999: The Bear's Tooth, Alaska (VI, 5.10, AI 5)

PACIFIC OCEAN WALL

June 1975 was arguably the most groundbreaking single month in the seven-decade history of Yosemite climbing. During the last two weeks of that month, the first 1-day ascent of the Nose was made, the east face of Washington Column was freed and renamed Astroman, and the hardest big-wall route of its day—the Pacific Ocean Wall—was established on El Capitan. Two of these feats were accomplished under the tutelage of Jim Bridwell.

Today, more than eighty routes crisscross virtually every aspect of mile-wide El Capitan, but in 1975 there were only about twenty routes. The big-wall pioneers of the sixties and early seventies had left a conspicuous gap between Mescalito and the North American Wall. The Pacific Ocean, or "P.O.," Wall was an obvious but intimidating line. It had been noticed by many, but it remained nothing more than a gauzy fantasy until the fall of 1974.

By then Bridwell had done two first ascents on the Big Stone—the Triple Direct and the Aquarian Wall—but nothing on its steeper right side. Convinced that the P.O. Wall could be climbed, Bridwell recruited two of "his boys"—Werner Braun and Dale Bard—for the effort. In two separate attempts during the fall of '74, the threesome reached the Continental Shelf, a large, sloping ledge ten pitches up the wall. With only a third of the route completed, they had already advanced the standard of aid climbing by establishing two A5 pitches. "It was the first serious use of copperheads," explains Bridwell, who used a blunt chisel to secure dozens of "bodyweight" placements. Bridwell was energized by their progress, but with winter fast approaching, realized that the rest of the P.O. Wall would have to wait. As a statement of his commitment to the project, he left most of his gear stashed on the Continental Shelf.

Bridwell returned to the P.O. Wall the following June, just 4 days after securing his place in history by doing the Nose in a day. With his confidence soaring, Bridwell decided that he wanted to climb the P.O. Wall in one continuous push from the ground. To do this, he would need the gear that was stowed on the Continental Shelf. Somehow, he persuaded Bard and Braun to retrieve the gear by climbing the first third of the neighboring North

Installing a rivet ladder on the twelfth pitch of the Pacific Ocean Wall. Bridwell and three others spent nine days making the route's first ascent in July 1975. © Jim Bridwell Collection, portrait © Brian McCray

then helicoptered to the Bay Area. Emergency brain surgery saved his life, but Rieder never fully recovered. "After that he was epileptic," laments Bridwell. "He never climbed again."

After heroically saving his partner, Graham told Bridwell and Westbay that he didn't want to continue with the climb. Bridwell understood Graham's decision, but remained unflinchingly focused on the P.O. Wall. The next morning the unfazed wall maverick marched into the local cafeteria and found the guys who would go the distance: Fred East and Jay Fiske.

With everything finally in order, Bridwell and Westbay led the team back to their previous high point, the Continental Shelf. Looming above them were several imposing roofs and puzzling overlaps. Using close-up photographs for navigation, Bridwell and Westbay used cotton-swab-size copperheads and hooks as small as a screwdriver blade to connect a series of incipient seams and shallow corners. In *Yosemite Climber,* Westbay wrote about the nerve-wracking, 4-hour leads. "One copperhead placement follows another, as I inch my way up the wall. Absolute precision and finesse are the key, as any excess motion can bring about a long plummet."

The first long plummet came on the twenty-first pitch. As Westbay led left from the top of the Black Tower, he broke a rivet—a ¼-inch stub of aluminum drilled into a blank section of rock—and took a diagonal 30-foot fall into a corner. Scraped and bruised, but not broken, he called on Bridwell to finish the pitch. Higher up, Westbay broke a second rivet, this time taking a 50-foot screamer. Not until then did they realize why this was only happening to Westbay. Bridwell had stocked the bolt kit with a bunch of Kelty clevis pins, the kind used to secure shoulder straps to a pack frame. Before placing one in the rock, Bridwell would first break off the end with the hole in it. "They were brittle," he explained, "and Billy didn't know he needed to break the ends off. Once we figured that out, he didn't fall again."

The weary foursome reached the top of El Capitan after nine laborious days on the wall. They suffered eight spine-crunching nights without a portaledge, drilled seventy-six bolt holes, established seven A5 pitches, and logged enough air time to qualify for a pilot's license. Despite the magnitude of their achievement, there was no media fanfare. Unlike Warren Harding's 1958 ascent of the Nose, Bridwell and company were greeted only by the level ground in front of them.

Twenty minutes later, while quietly organizing their gear, Bridwell heard something. "Hey, JB, you up here?" called a familiar voice. Out of the bushes came Dale Bard and Dean Fiedelman carrying two ice-cold six-packs of beer. Bridwell's spirits soared. Finally, he could taste success—12 ounces at a time.

© Mark Kroese

American Wall and rappelling down to the Continental Shelf, "saving" the lower pitches on the P.O. in the process.

Bard and Braun climbed to the Shelf with a small parachute in tow. Instead of arduously lowering the piton-filled haul bags to the ground, they would simply let them float to the valley floor in the afternoon breeze. The plan sounded good, remembers Bridwell, "but the updrafts were too strong and the parachute was too big." Much to Bard and Braun's chagrin, the payload drifted due west, hugging the wall as it headed toward the Nose. The wind sucked the bags into the wall, and, in a random act of cruelty, deposited them onto Lay Lady Ledge, a spacious platform seven pitches up the New Dawn Route. So much for saving time and energy.

Two days later, after retrieving the stray cargo, Bard and Braun had completely lost interest in the project. As far as they were concerned, Bridwell was on his own. Still determined to scale the P.O., Bridwell recruited Nose-in-a-day partner Billy Westbay and two other talented Valley climbers, Mike Graham and Rik Rieder. Saving himself for the upper pitches, Bridwell sent Graham and Rieder up to lead the first part of the route.

While leading the tricky fifth pitch, Rieder gingerly lowered off of a small piton and prepared for a short pendulum. When he was 10 feet below the pin, it suddenly popped, pulling a basketball-size block onto his helmetless head. Rieder was immediately knocked unconscious, dangling helplessly in space as blood spurted from his fractured skull. He was quickly lowered to the ground by Graham,

ROUTE DESCRIPTION

Area: Southeast face of El Capitan, Yosemite Valley
First ascent: Jim Bridwell, Bill Westbay, Jay Fiske, and Fred East, July 1975
Base elevation: 4,000 feet
Summit elevation: 7,000 feet
Difficulty: VI, 5.9, A3+
Time required: 6–9 days
Equipment: 2 RURPs; 2 beaks; 5 knifeblades—1 each no. 1–5; 8 lost arrows—2 each no. 1–2, 3 no. 3, 1 no. 4; angles—2 ½-inch, 3 ⅝-inch, 2 ¾-inch sawed, 2 1-inch sawed, 1 2½-inch (optional); 2 sets of nuts (offsets useful); 2 sets of RPs (offsets useful); cams—3–4 each ⅖-inch–1-inch, 3 each ½-inch–2-inch, 2 each 2½-inch–4½-inch; 20 heads including circle heads; 2 hooks; cam hooks; 12 rivet/keyhole hangers; 2-inch angle or no. 5 Tri-Cam for pitch 7
Season: May–October
Special considerations: Heat, water, human waste disposal
Reference: *Yosemite Big Walls: SuperTopos* by Chris McNamara (SuperTopo Publishing, 2000)

Approach: Use the State Highway 140 park entrance into Yosemite Valley. Park 0.1 mile west of El Capitan bridge. Follow the trail that heads directly to the Nose, then right, skirting the base of the cliff.

Route: Twenty-seven pitches of spectacular aid climbing. See topo for details.

Descent: Descend the East Ledges (recommended) or hike the long way down the Yosemite Falls trail.

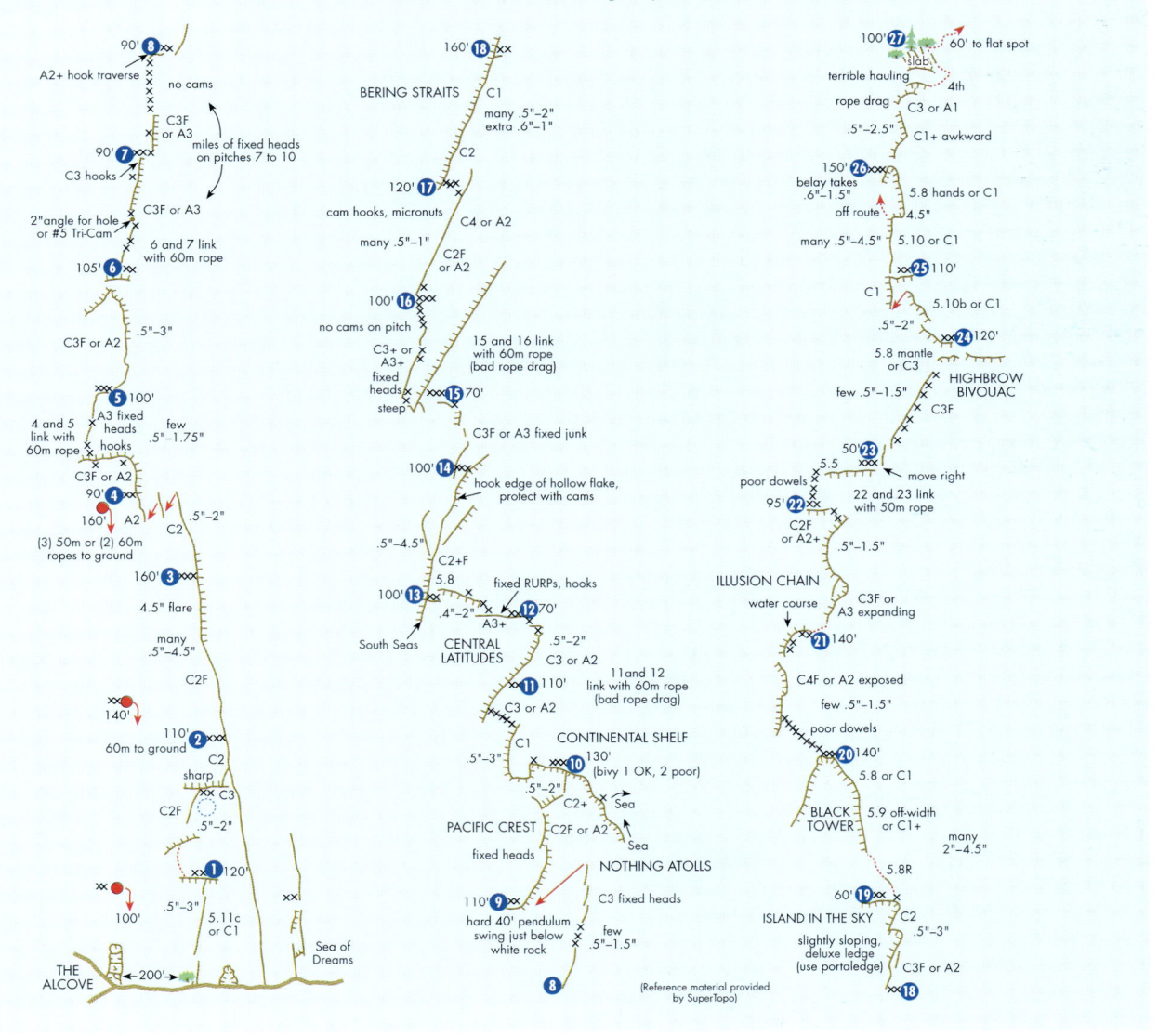

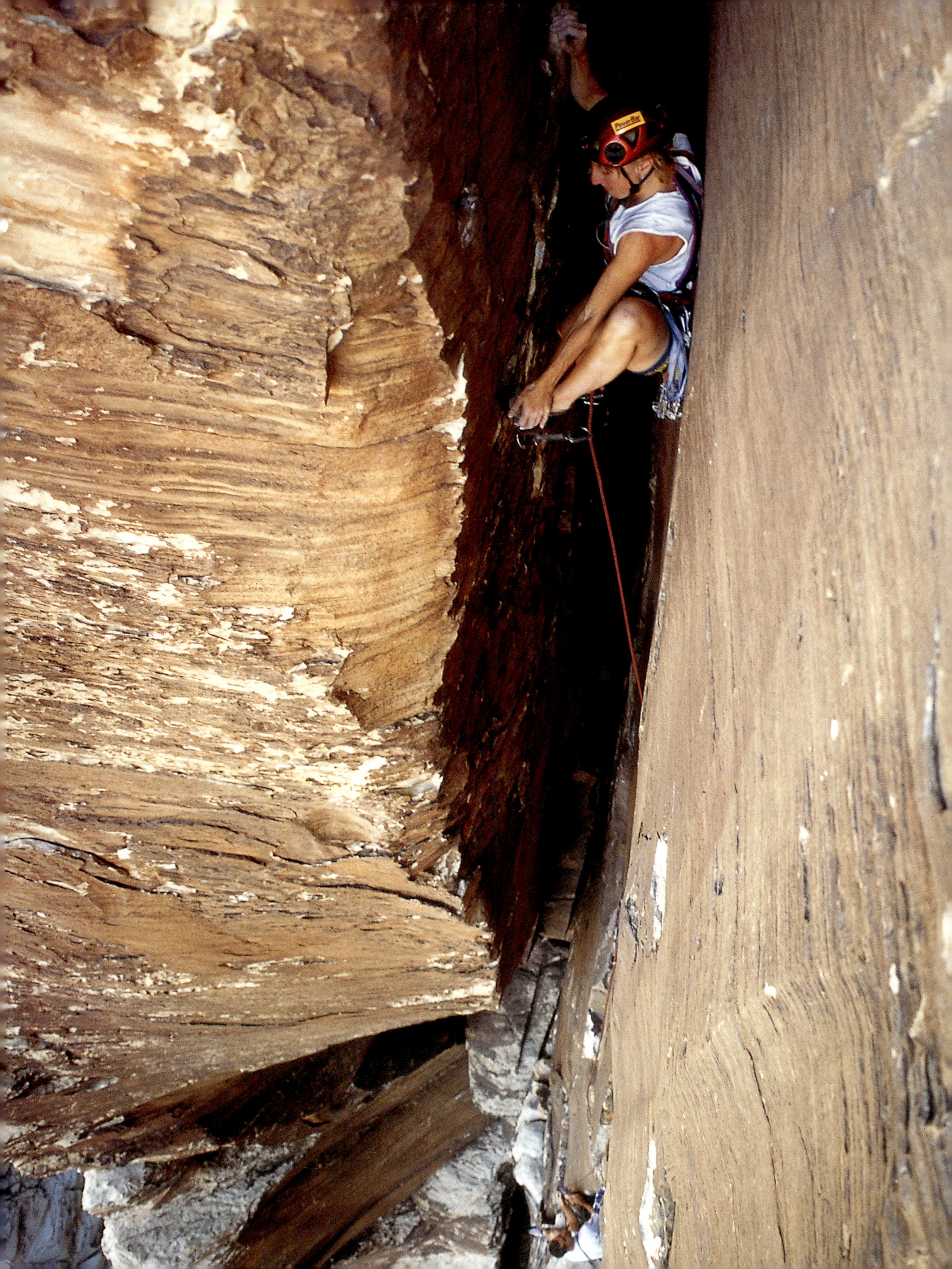

ROXANNA BROCK

EPINEPHRINE, RED ROCKS NATIONAL CONSERVATION AREA, NEVADA

ROXANNA BROCK—PURE AMBITION

Whatever Roxanna Brock does, she does well: She completed high school early, graduated from college with a degree in chemical engineering, then accepted a big job with IBM. Had she not discovered rock climbing at the age of twenty-two, she would have certainly become another corporate overachiever in the new economy.

Brock was overtaken by the desire to climb just as IBM was getting overtaken by competition. In 1993, when Big Blue was looking for volunteers to help them "downsize," she shifted her focus from climbing the corporate ladder to climbing rocks.

Her full-time climbing career started in West Virginia's New River Gorge. She lived there almost full time from 1993 to 1997, funding her modest lifestyle by working as a climbing guide. (She used the continuing education allowance from her IBM severance package to take American Mountain Guides Association guiding certification courses, then founded New River Mountain Guides.) In "the New," she's done at least twenty 5.13 climbs and dozens of first ascents—all of which are listed in the NRG guidebook she co-authored with Fly'n Brian McCray.

During West Virginia's sultry summers, Brock and McCray took extended road trips to the best crags in the West. She learned to love big-wall and crack climbing in Yosemite, where she ticked off classics such as Astroman—leading every pitch (see Climb 30)—and El Capitan's Pacific Ocean Wall (see Climb 5). In 1999, she exported her big-wall skills to Kyrgyzstan, making the first ascent of 3,000-foot Stars and Stripes Forever (VI, 5.11, A4). And in 2000, she made the first ascent of 3,600-foot Hainblak Tower in Pakistan via an all-free (5.12a) new route.

Brock now lives in centrally located Las Vegas, where she and her husband make frequent trips to nearby areas such as Mount Charleston, Red Rocks, and Zion National Park. Never one to sit still, she spends her "rest" days tackling a long list of freelance projects. "No matter what I'm doing," says Brock, "I like to go home at the end of the day and be really tired."

EPINEPHRINE

Sometimes Roxanna Brock just likes to cruise. Even though she thrives on the challenge of a 5.13 sport climb, or the tedium of tapping her way up El Capitan, there are times when she'd rather spend the day in constant motion on a long, moderate route.

Brock's urge to cruise usually comes on the heels of an extended international trip. In the fall of 1999, after a successful expedition to Kyrgyzstan, Brock felt like she'd spent more time at airports and base camps than on rock (although she did establish a big route on a remote, wilderness wall). When she returned to Las Vegas, her first priority was to crank out some vertical mileage.

One of the best ways to do so, she realized, was to start with a good dose of Epinephrine—a route she'd done twice before. She knew the eighteen-pitch classic would provide maximum climbing for minimum logistics: 30 minutes of driving, 30 minutes of hiking, and 12 hours of nonstop movement. Says Brock, "It's the kind of all-day affair I love."

Epinephrine is located deep in Black Velvet Canyon, in the northwestern corner of the 195,000-acre Red Rocks National Conservation Area. Getting there from Las Vegas is an experience of contrasts. The 25-mile drive starts in the mad plastic world of glitter and slot machines, passes through a rural strip of double-wide mobile homes and battered pickups with "CHARLTON HESTON IS MY PRESIDENT" bumper stickers, and ends in a high-desert oasis of Joshua trees and warped sandstone canyons. Short of being beamed aboard the Starship *Enterprise,* it's hard to imagine a more abrupt change of scenery.

The Black Velvet Canyon gets its name from the black minerals that cover the rock with a hard, textured varnish. Over the years, this very climbable Wingate sandstone has yielded more than seventy routes on virtually every aspect of the shady canyon. Many of the popular lines, such as Prince of Darkness, are bolted face climbs. But the most obvious route, which was spotted by Jorge and Joanne Urioste in the late '70s, follows a natural corner system: It starts below an ominous-looking chimney, then sneaks up a shallow dihedral on the upper headwall. "Epinephrine was the only natural line we could see that went to the top of the wall," remembers Jorge. "It was the ultimate climb."

As Jorge predicted, Epinephrine quickly earned a reputation as *the* 5.9 classic at Red Rocks. And despite the ever-changing

Roxanna Brock getting a dose of Epinephrine (5.9). Three consecutive chimney pitches highlight the route. © Mark Kroese, portrait © Mark Kroese

tastes of rock climbers, the route has timeless appeal. Brock was no exception. Even though she didn't make her first visit to Red Rocks until 1997, after dozens of easily accessible sport climbs had been added to the area, Epinephrine was still at the top of her ticklist.

Brock first climbed Epinephrine with her good friend and roommate Kevin Barone. It was so much fun that she jumped at the opportunity to guide the route the following year—giving her a chance to do all of the leading. And in 1999, after returning from Kyrgyzstan, she decided she still hadn't had enough. Since Kevin felt the same way, they did the route again.

One of the things Brock loves about Epinephrine is its variety—which rivals the dinner buffet at the MGM Grand. "I like routes with lots of different movement," she says, "and it has everything: wide cracks, hand and finger cracks, slabs, face climbing, and chimneys!"

Although many climbers dread the three-pitch bomb-bay chimney, it's the highlight of the route for Brock. "Once I'm in the chimney, the climbing is simple because of my short legs," she says. "Sometimes I wish I was taller, but on this route, being 5 feet 3 inches is perfect." Chuckling, she adds, "I always feel sorry for Kevin when he gets jammed into the narrow part of the chimney."

Brock also appreciates the consistent nature of the climbing. Although never desperate, it's seldom easy. "I'm never thinking, 'Oh, this is going to be a breeze,'" she notes. "I'm always amazed at how the route continues to be a challenge." For many, the biggest challenge is simply finishing. After completing the eighteenth pitch, weary climbers often lose their momentum when they realize there is still another 700 feet of scrambling. The ramp system that leads to the summit has been the site of many unplanned bivouacs.

The fact that Brock spends her time climbing routes like Epinephrine instead of gambling proves that she's been unaffected by the Las Vegas environment. But when she submitted the following list of reasons to do the route, it became obvious that she *does* watch David Letterman.

Roxanna's Top Ten Reasons to Do Epinephrine

10. Excellent workout—an all-day affair, hiking and climbing
9. Impressive views: majestic sights of Red Rocks and the bustle of Las Vegas, the great "city of sin" (from a distance, of course)
8. Secluded and quiet: no "tourons" here
7. A long route: eighteen pitches plus 700 feet of scrambling, in Vegas—can you believe it?
6. Bomber fixed anchors: two to three pieces of stainless at every belay!
5. Killer belay stances: ledges, baby; we're talkin' deee-luxe
4. Run-outs: an adrenalin junkie's dream on not-so-difficult terrain
3. The chance to use the wide gear stored in your closet
2. Variety: vertical faces, slabs, pockets, edges, smears, squeezes, thin cracks, hand cracks, fist jams, mantels, liebacks—the list goes on

And the number-one reason to do Epinephrine . . .

1. The best chimneys in the world—chimney heaven!

ROUTE DESCRIPTION

Area: Black Velvet Canyon, Red Rocks
First ascent: Jorge Urioste, Joanne Urioste, and Joe Herbst, August 1978
Difficulty: IV, 5.9
Time required: 1 long day
Equipment: Double set of Camalots to no. 3, 1 no. 4, set of TCUs, set of wired nuts; 1 60-m rope (2 recommended for retreat)
Season: Spring and fall
Special considerations: Allow about 90 minutes for final 700 feet of climbing from top of last pitch to "summit"; can be done in 14 pitches with a 60-m rope; ideal, but not essential, to "carry over" and not leave gear at base
Reference: *Rock Climbing, Red Rocks* by Todd Swain.

Approach: From its intersection with Nevada Highway 159, drive west on Nevada Highway 160 for 4.6 miles to a dirt road (no sign). Turn right at the cattle guard and follow the dirt road for 1.9 miles until forced left at the third dirt road on the left. Drive 0.5 mile to a T intersection, then turn right and drive 0.3 mile to the parking area at road's end. Follow the main trail into Black Velvet Canyon (passing popular climbs like Prince of Darkness). Epinephrine is a few hundred yards past Prince of Darkness, 60 yards upcanyon from a waterfall. The route starts on a gray wall with three red bolt hangers.

Route: Fourteen to eighteen pitches of classic cracks and chimneys; see topo for details. From the top of the last pitch, angle right up a 700-foot, mostly third- and fourth-class ramp to the right shoulder of the cliff. Cut left, then back toward the summit above.

Descent: Walk off. From the highest summit, follow the ridge to the top of Whiskey Peak, making sure to go in the general direction of the parking area (do not be lured down the gully to the right). Stay on the south (right) side of the ridgeline and continue toward the parking lot, following the descent for Frogland.

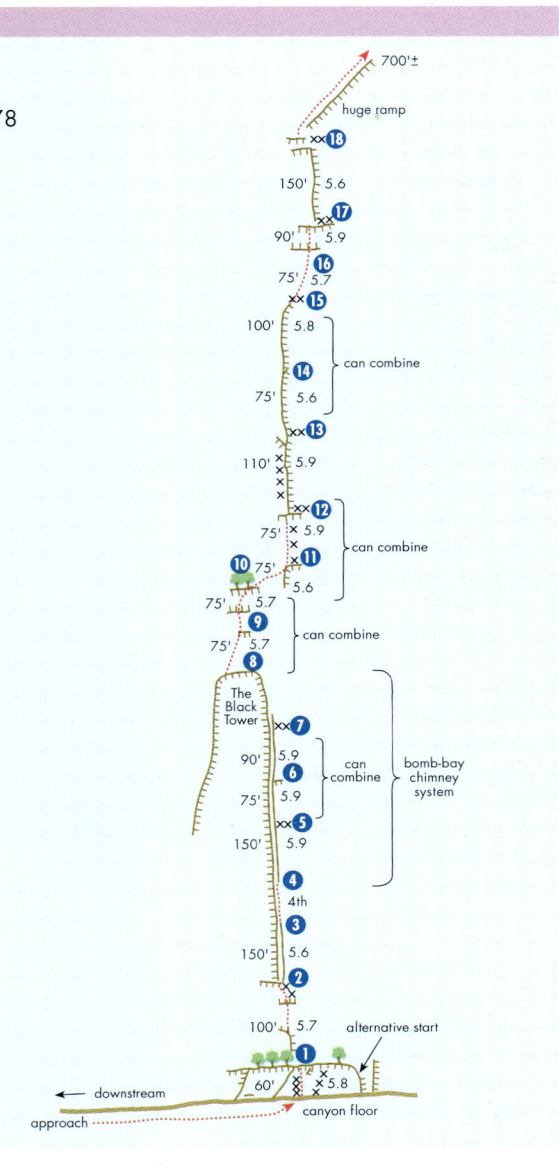

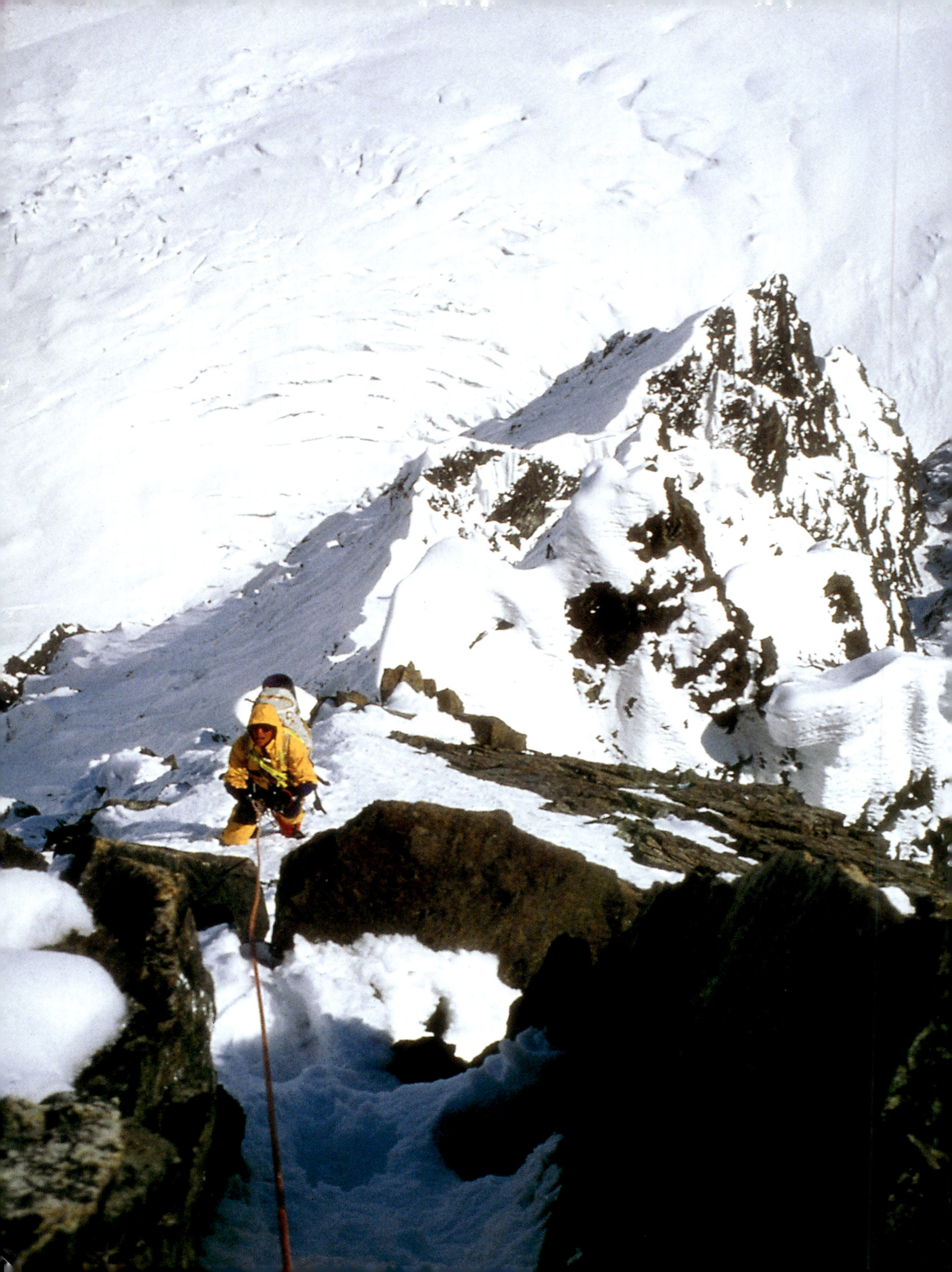

CARLOS BUHLER

EAST FACE OF UNIVERSITY PEAK, WRANGELL–ST. ELIAS NATIONAL PARK, ALASKA

CARLOS BUHLER— A LIFE IN THE GREAT RANGES

Carlos Buhler is North America's most accomplished high-altitude mountaineer. His resumé is a magnificent quilt of slender ridges and steep faces on the world's tallest mountains. Buhler's three-decade climbing career has taken him on more than thirty expeditions to Alaska, Ecuador, Peru, Bolivia, Argentina, Uganda, Kenya, Pakistan, Nepal, China (Xinkiang Province), Kyrgyzstan, Tajikistan, and Tibet.

For Buhler, it's not enough to just climb high. He usually goes for the most technically demanding route with a small, lightweight crew. In 1983, he was part of the American team to make the first ascent of Mount Everest's Kangshung Face—a route that is still unrepeated. His ascents of the north ridges of K2 and Kangchenjunga make him one of a handful of climbers to reach the world's three highest summits by nonstandard routes (the latter two without oxygen).

Not one to limit himself to "big-name" summits, Buhler has made countless first ascents of aesthetically beautiful routes on lesser-known peaks. Exemplary climbs in Asia include the East Ridge of Baruntse, the North Face of Changbang, the Northeast Face of Ama Dablam, and a new line on Kokshaal Tau in Kyrgyzstan. In Peru, his new routes include the west faces of Siula Grande and Extremo Ausangate, and the Anqosh Face of Huascaran-Sur.

Much of Buhler's success can be attributed to his analytical yet intuitive approach. He is acutely aware that statistics aren't kind to thirty-year climbing veterans, and is always willing to back off when things don't feel right. In 1984, he spent sixty-eight days on the West Pillar of 27,766-foot Makalu, only to retreat in a storm within an hour of the top. Says Buhler, "It was extremely disappointing not to reach the summit, but we made it down safely and lived to climb another day."

EAST FACE OF UNIVERSITY PEAK

Each year, dozens of climbers travel to Southeast Alaska to climb Mount St. Elias and Mount Logan, the highest and most popular summits in the area. Along the "flight corridor" to base camp, they fly by one of the most overlooked gems in the region: University Peak. The mountain was first climbed in 1955, via its north ridge, but didn't see a second ascent for forty-two years.

There are two reasons for lack of interest in University Peak. The first is its relatively low elevation. At 14,800 feet, it's not one of the area's "big" peaks, and is therefore below the radar screen of visiting climbers. The second is its technical difficulty. There is no easy way up the mountain; the 4,800-foot north ridge is a complex maze of yawning crevasses, and its south and east faces are enormous, towering 8,500 feet above the surrounding glaciers.

When Alaskan climber Charlie Sassara first saw the peak's East Face in 1989, he immediately wanted to climb it, but knew he'd need just the right partner for such an undertaking. He found that partner in 1995, when Carlos Buhler made his first visit to Southeast Alaska, and laid his eyes on the Himalayan-like face. It was one of the most impressive lines he'd seen in North America.

Buhler and Sassara returned to Southeast Alaska in 1996, but decided to make the first ascent of Mount Miller and leave University Peak for the following year. When they came back in April 1997, the second ascent of the north ridge (and the mountain) had just been made—but the East Face remained unexplored.

Their friend Paul Claus—who, not coincidentally, would be flying them in to the mountain—was part of the team who made the second ascent of University Peak's north ridge. Paul's detailed description of the ridge, which would be their descent route, convinced them that if they could get to the top, they could get back down. Not only were they attempting the first ascent of the East Face, but the first traverse of the mountain.

Paul flew them in to the glacier below University's colossal east flank on April 27. Carrying only a 5-day supply of food and fuel, they skied to the base of the mountain and got to work. They established their first camp 1,500 feet up the face, and awoke the next morning to low clouds and swirling snow. It looked like another Alaskan false start. They decided to retreat, but agreed to wait until the cooler evening hours when the avalanche danger would be lower. They spent the day relaxing in the tent—and eating.

To their surprise, the weather began to clear in the afternoon.

Carlos Buhler moving light and fast on the first ascent of the 8,500-foot east face of University Peak © Charlie Sassara, portrait © Charlie Sassara

© Ruedi Homberger

Indecision set in. The prospect of high pressure was enticing, but they were worried about their food supply. Finishing a climb on meager rations is one thing—starting it that way is another. After much debate, they put the food bag away and decided to stay put until morning.

They awoke to a breathless blue sky. In his account of the climb in the 1998 *American Alpine Journal*, Buhler wrote: "I'm not sure if I was happy or not to see the blue skies in the morning. It meant we would go upward." They snapped on their crampons and began what promised to be a true adventure.

Like ants on a whitewashed wall, they spent the next 4 days inching up the ice-clad face. The route was consistently challenging, but never desperate. The majority of the climbing was 55-degree alpine ice, with some steeper sections and mixed pitches along the way. But more than anything, the mile-and-a-half-high face was committing. As soon as they made the diagonal rappel below the second camp, retreat would have been awkward and unsavory.

The committing nature of the climb did have its rewards. Once they realized that the only way off the mountain was over the top, they were freed from indecision. Says Buhler, "Once you cross the line where you can't go back down, it's very liberating. You just go."

The climbing was rewarding too. On the second day, as they crossed the rock rib in the middle of the face, Buhler was treated to a spectacular mixed pitch that led to an airy stance on the spine of the ridge. The next pitch, according to Sassara, was even more thrilling. "Imagine stemming a broken corner at the apex of a 70-degree arête, in bright sunshine, with 4,000 feet beneath your toes," he enthused. "It was electric." It seemed too good to be true. And, as if the mountain wanted them to succeed, a perfect bivouac spot appeared just when they needed it.

Clouds engulfed the mountain later that afternoon. At first, they worried that a front might be moving in. But when they heard the distinctive whir of Paul's Super Cub, they realized that it was just local cloud buildup. It was music to their ears. Paul checked on them every day, usually with clients from the nearby Ultima Thule Lodge. Buhler and Sassara became the week's favorite sightseeing tour. One couple from Atlanta, who had never seen big mountains, didn't believe the climbers were alive until they saw them move. Then cameras flashed in what looked like an exchange of gunfire.

The next day was an odyssey through a sea of rolling white foam and blue ice, ending below a 300-foot overhanging serac that guarded the summit ice field. They awoke early the next morning and climbed stealthily through the final crux. The brittle, boiler-plate ice tested their nerves—and their ice tools. Buhler broke a pick just below the serac, but completed the lead with one of his partner's tools. Sassara led the last hard pitch to the gentler slopes above and, eventually, the summit.

Feeling as isolated as two people can feel, and out of food, they began to contemplate the descent. Suddenly their thoughts were interrupted by the sound of a prop plane rising above the vaporous mist. It was Paul. Before they knew it, he and their friend Ruedi Homberger were swooping just 100 feet above them. On Paul's second pass, Ruedi leaned out the window and tossed out a red stuff sack. Unfortunately, his timing was off, and the goody bag went sliding into the void. His next toss was better. It was a bottle of white gas, but they were using a butane stove and had plenty of fuel. And his third drop was perfect: Three freeze-dried dinners landed right at their feet.

The descent wasn't going to be so bad after all.

ROUTE DESCRIPTION

Area: Wrangell–St. Elias Range
First ascent: Carlos Buhler and Charlie Sassara, April 29–May 5, 1997
Base elevation: 6,300 feet
Summit elevation: 14,800 to 15,000 feet, depending on various maps
Difficulty: VI, AI 4+, WI 4+
Time required: (First-ascent party) 5 nights on ascent, 1 on descent
Equipment: (First-ascent party) 1 60-m 8.8 mm lead rope, 50-m section of 5 mm Kevlar cord for rappels, 1 Jumar, 6 ice screws with quickdraws on shafts, 6 titanium pitons, 6 stoppers, 30 slings, 16 carabiners, several V thread wires
Season: April–May
Special considerations: Route's moderate technical difficulty belies its seriousness; long, committing climb in remote area, involves traverse of mountain; ascent and descent both very condition dependent
Reference: American Alpine Journal (1998, pp 78–87)
Map: McCarthy, Alaska, 1:250,000, no. 61141-A1-TF-250

Approach: Fly to Anchorage, then drive State Highways 1 and 10 to Chitina. From there, pilot Paul Claus will fly you to the Ultima Thule Lodge, about 40 miles west of the Canadian border.

Descent: Descend the crevasse-ridden north ridge to a small pocket glacier at about 10,000 feet. Arrange air pickup there. It is mostly 40- to 50-degree downclimbing, with a few rappels.

Route: Mostly 55- to 65-degree ice; about fifty roped pitches; some mixed climbing and rock to 5.8 (Alaskan "grade 6-" rating); subsequent parties may consider bringing more gear than the first-ascent party. The route starts up the obvious snow gully that splits the northeast (right) side of the lower rock rib. From there, continue up snow flutings on 50- to 60-degree ice to the ridge proper. Climb to the base of the rock rib in the middle of the face, then do a diagonal rappel/traverse left (first crux) and follow the left side of the rock rib. Look for a passage back to the right side of the rock rib (second crux) after about 700 feet. Once on the spine of the ridge, follow it straight up for about 2,500 feet, to the summit serac. Climb steep (80-degree-plus) alpine ice (third crux) right, then back left, to easier ground above.

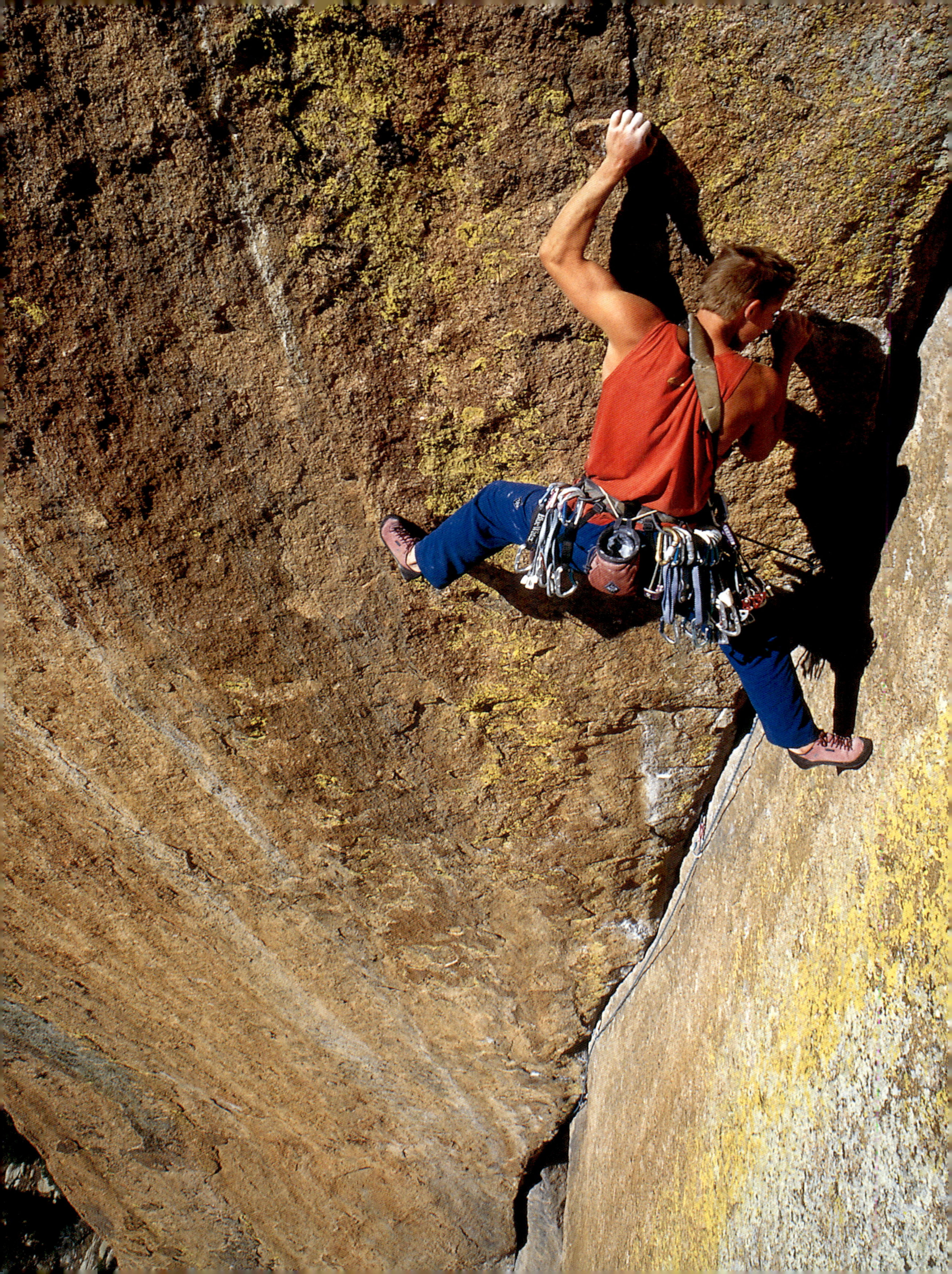

8

TOMMY CALDWELL
WUNSCH'S DIHEDRAL, CYNICAL PINNACLE, CATHEDRAL SPIRES AREA, SOUTH PLATTE, COLORADO

TOMMY CALDWELL— THE NEXT GENERATION

Tommy Caldwell is widely regarded as America's best all-around rock climber. A product of an enthusiastic father, an early start, natural talent, and raw desire, Caldwell embodies the potential of a new generation of climbers. Before reaching the age of twenty-one, he became the first American to lead every pitch of Yosemite's Salathé Wall (5.13b, only one fall) and established the country's hardest sport climb (Colorado's Kryptonite, 5.14d)—pretty amazing for a guy who is too young to know the lyrics to *Stairway to Heaven* and doesn't think about *Jaws* when he swims in the ocean.

Mike Caldwell, Tommy's father and a longtime climber himself, taught his son to climb when he was three years old. Having cut his teeth on El Capitan in the late sixties—using a Goldline rope and a canvas haul bag—Mike saw the importance of exposing Tommy to a wide variety of climbing disciplines. The result is a well-rounded athlete who is as comfortable clipping bolts on overhanging limestone as he is slithering up a flaring Yosemite chimney.

In addition to his physical prowess, Tommy is as well known for his modest, unassuming nature. Despite his emerging celebrity, he remains totally unaffected—he's probably the nicest 5.14 climber you'll ever meet. He is exceedingly gracious, and feels lucky that he can make a living as a sponsored climber, a profession his father never dreamed of. Says Tommy, "I pretty much get to pick where I want to go and climb full-time. It's awesome. I can't imagine a better life."

WUNSCH'S DIHEDRAL

Name a destination rock-climbing area, and chances are good that Tommy Caldwell has been there. Since graduating from high school in 1996, the globe-trotting wunderkind has tested his skills on some of the finest crags in the world, including those in France, Slovenia, Italy, Switzerland, England, Germany, Spain, South Africa, China, Korea, and Mexico. (Caldwell has even climbed the perfect granite in Kyrgyzstan's Kara-su valley, where in August 2000 he and three partners were taken hostage and held at gunpoint by Islamic rebels. See *Climbing* no.199 for the complete story.) Yet, after sampling the best rock in each of these countries, some of Caldwell's favorite climbs are still in his home state of Colorado. When Caldwell was three, his dad took him up a spire called the Twin Owls at Lumpy Ridge. Since then, Tommy and Mike Caldwell have shared a rope in virtually every corner of the mile-high state, from Rifle's limestone sport routes to the long, granite crack climbs in Rocky Mountain National Park.

Like his father, Tommy kept a list of his favorite climbs. The more he climbed, the longer his list became. It included classics from areas such as Eldorado Canyon, Horsetooth Reservoir, and Fremont Canyon. One day, when reviewing his father's favorite climbs, Tommy noticed one that wasn't on his list: Wunsch's Dihedral. According to the elder Caldwell's notes, he'd climbed the route *five* times—with friends and as a guide. Tommy had heard him rave about the route: the perfect cracks, the pigmented granite, its commanding position. Yet, for some reason, they'd never climbed it together.

Wunsch's Dihedral is located in Colorado's South Platte, a 500-square-mile landscape of rolling hills and boulder-strewn rivers situated amid the foothills of the Front Range. Unlike the closely spaced sandstone climbing areas near Boulder, the granite formations of the South Platte are scattered along hilltops and ridges and in hidden valleys. The Tuolumne-like domes offer two very different types of climbing: delicate face routes on rounded, granite slabs and steep, athletic cracks on sheer faces. "The South Platte is really a place of contrasts," offers Mike, who began exploring the region in the 1960s.

After returning from an overseas trip in the fall of 1999, Tommy decided it was time he finally climbed Cynical Pinnacle. As a solid 5.14 climber, he certainly didn't need his dad to guide him up the route, yet he never really thought about doing it with anyone else. "My dad is my favorite climbing partner," says Tommy. "And I knew he'd be willing to do it again."

Tommy caught his first glimpse of Cynical Pinnacle from the dirt road that leads to its base. It looked impressive—almost improbable. "It's like a Titan booster sitting on a launch pad," he explains. "You just look up there and think, 'Oh my god, we're going to climb *that*.'" Staring at it, he wondered how Steve Wunsch ever considered free-climbing the route in the early '70s. Mike, who

Tommy Caldwell on the exquisite third pitch of Wunsch's Dihedral (5.11b) © Topher Donahue, portrait © Topher Donahue

remembers feeling intimidated when he first saw the ominous-looking spire, notes that "Like a lot of good climbs, it looks impossible, but it turns out to be easier than it looks."

As they humped their way up the steep slope that leads to the base of the spire, Tommy marveled at the perfectly sculpted granite that loomed above. He noticed that the left wall of the dihedral—which looks like a giant exclamation point—leans to the right, as if it were in italics. Tommy couldn't wait to tackle the irresistibly steep corner. He was so inspired that he asked his dad if he could lead the entire climb. Having guided many clients up the route, Mike was happy to follow Tommy's lead.

As he prepared for the first pitch, Tommy realized that climbing Wunsch's Dihedral involves making several choices—fortunately, there are no bad ones. His first choice was between the original line (5.8) and the Breashears finger crack (5.12a), a stout variation named after talented climber and filmmaker David Breashears. Naturally, he chose the latter.

Tommy climbed the next part of the corner, which is sometimes broken into two 65-foot sections, as a single pitch. "It's a perfect splitter crack with nice little face holds and little pockets

Like father, like son. Mike and Tommy savoring the experience.
© Topher Donahue

to stem out on," he exclaims. "The hand and fist jams are really solid, and the rock is amazing." The 130-foot pitch put Tommy and Mike at a stance below the steepest part of the corner: The main face is dead vertical, while the left wall overhangs by 25 degrees. A thin crack is all that separates the two masses of granite.

Tommy savored the moves of the third pitch while his dad relived the experience from the belay. "After you pull through the roof, the exposure is crazy," remembers Mike. "But the gear just drops in. To be in such a wild place with such great protection is just a delight. It's one of the most classic pitches I've ever done." Drawing on three decades of local knowledge, Mike then explained that the pink-hued granite of the South Platte is so exquisite that it was once quarried for use on the government buildings in Washington, D.C.

After 30 minutes of pure pleasure, Tommy finished the third pitch and put his dad on belay. Before long, they were both sitting comfortably on a ledge at the top of the dihedral, staring at the short bolt ladder that leads to the summit.

Using the five closely spaced bolts for protection—not aid—Tommy waltzed up the 5.12c face without hesitation. Mike followed, but opted to climb the bolt ladder (like most people do). By early afternoon, the partners were atop Cynical Pinnacle. As they took in the view and shared a bottle of water, Mike asked his son where Wunsch's Dihedral ranked on his list of favorite climbs. Tommy cracked a satisfied smile and said, "At the top, Dad."

ROUTE DESCRIPTION

Area: Southern Colorado
First ascent: Tom Fender and Bill Roos, 1964; first free ascent of pitches one–three: Steve Wunsch, 1972; first free ascent of final bolt ladder: Jeff Lowe and Paul Sibley, 1977
Base elevation: 6,500 feet
Summit elevation: 7,000 feet
Difficulty: 5.11b, A0 or 5.11c, R, or 5.12c; Breashears finger crack variation, 5.12a
Time required: 4 hours
Equipment: Set of wired nuts; 2 sets of cams to 3½ inches, heavy on 2–3 inches; 2 50-m ropes
Season: September–November is best, summer and winter also OK
Special considerations: Cliff closed for peregrine falcon breeding March 1–July 31; Cynical Pinnacle dangerous in summer lightning storms; pets not recommended at base of route—two deaths are known
Reference: *Rock Climbing Colorado* by Stewart M. Green (Falcon Publishing, 1999)

Approach: From Denver head west on US Highway 285 to Pine Junction. Turn south, down a long, winding hill, past the town of Pine, to Foxton Road (dirt). Turn left, parallel to the South Platte River. Cynical Pinnacle is on your left. From the big pullout on the left, or a smaller pullout farther downriver (recommended), start hiking. Allow 3 hours. Ascend a climbers trail to the southwest base of the pinnacle, then along the base of the west face to the start of the route.

Route: Pitch one follows the blocky main dihedral corner (5.8); the Breashears finger crack (5.12a) variation is on the left wall. Belay on gear. Pitch two can be done as a 130-foot pitch (recommended) or be broken in half. Climb the hand and fist crack on the left (65 feet) to a stance on the right (possible belay), then back left into the main corner (thin) to a hanging belay below a roof. On pitch three, pull the roof (use a 3½-inch piece) and continue up splendid stemming and a finger dihedral to the top of the subpinnacle and base of a bolt ladder. Pitch four climbs the bolt ladder (A0 or 5.12c). Or bust out left halfway up (5.11c, R).

Descent: Old anchors indicate several possible rappels. The best goes 60 feet due south to the top of the Center Route. Two 150-foot rappels lead down the west face.

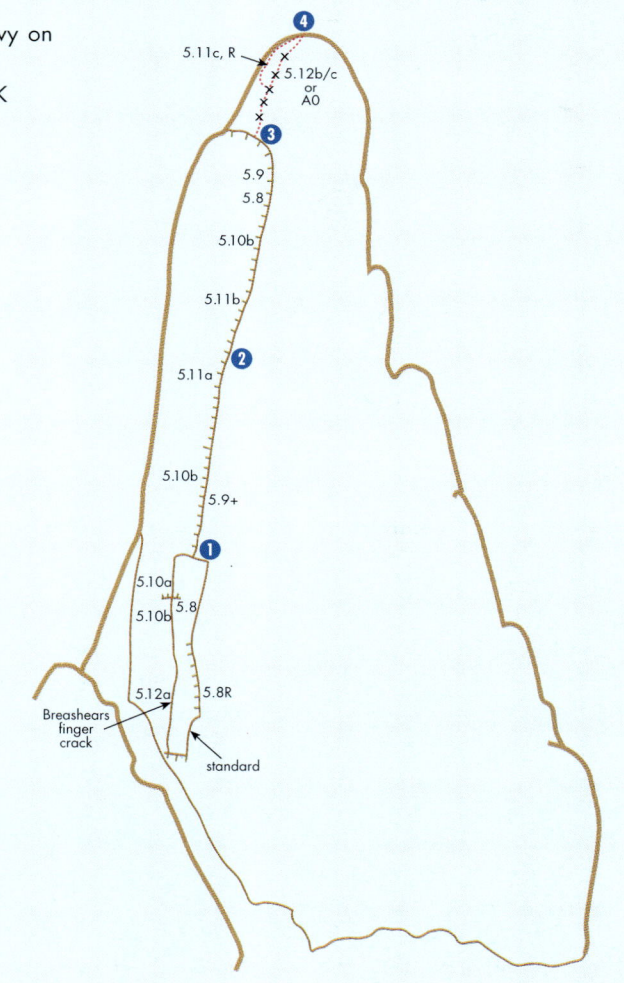

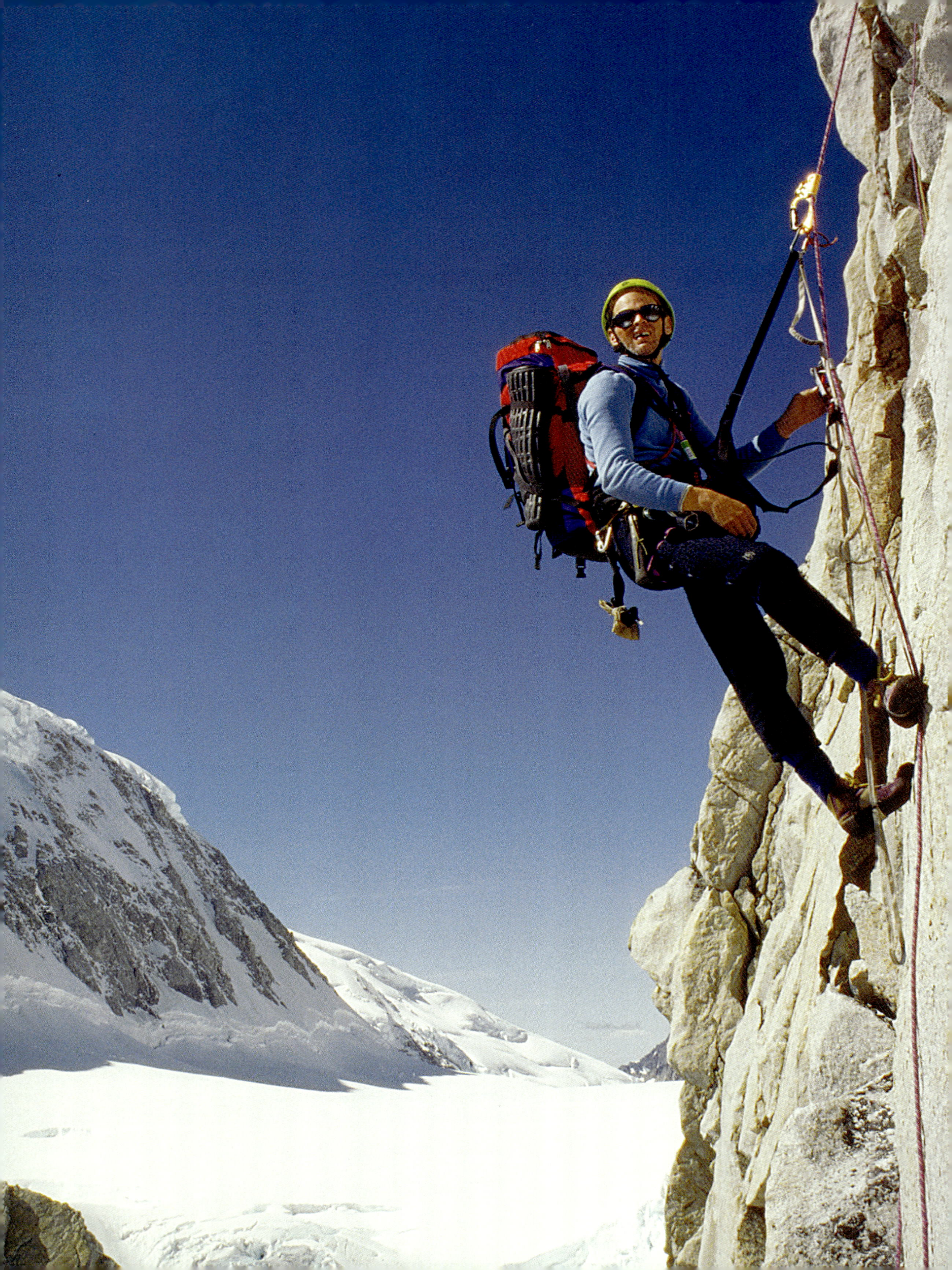

GREG CHILD

BELLIGERENCE, SOUTH BUTTRESS OF MOUNT COMBATANT, WADDINGTON RANGE, BRITISH COLUMBIA

GREG CHILD—THE PROFESSIONAL

After his first eureka moment in the Blue Mountains of Australia, high-school-aged Greg Child vowed to spend the rest of his life exploring the high and wild. Three decades later, with notable ascents in virtually every corner of the globe, it appears that he's kept his promise.

Endowed with a broad array of talents, Child has parlayed his passion for the mountains into a comfortable lifestyle centered around climbing. In lieu of a 9-to-5 job in a fabric-lined cubicle, Child earns his living as a sponsored climber, a mountaineering writer (four books, countless articles, numerous awards), a photographer, and, at times, a videographer for the adventure-loving film industry. Climbing is not only his avocation, but his vocation.

The result is a climbing resumé that touches every corner of the world—and every climbing discipline. Greg Child is a generalist who refuses to be bad at anything. On rock, he's done everything from 5.13 sport climbs to new routes on titanic walls such as Baffin Island's Sail Peak, Pakistan's Trango Tower and Shipton Spire, and, of course, Yosemite's El Capitan. And in the mountains, he's pioneered new routes in Alaska and climbed Everest, K2 (without oxygen), Gasherbrum IV, and many other Himalayan giants.

Child's brilliance is his persistence. Like a diesel engine, he never quits and rarely needs a tune-up. The compact Australian is well known for his ability to push ahead in the face of seemingly insurmountable odds, as well as for his sardonic, cutting wit. As a gifted storyteller with so many tales to tell, Child's biggest challenge is staying on the ground long enough to commit them to paper.

BELLIGERENCE

Having climbed in virtually every time zone of our spinning blue planet, Greg Child was surprised to learn of an unclimbed granite wall of Patagonian stature just 500 miles north of his home in Seattle. He'd seen the 4,500-foot south buttress of Mount Combatant from a distance in 1990. But awash in big projects abroad, he never found time to learn more about it. Four years later, frequent big-wall partner Greg Collum told him that it was still awaiting a first ascent. A glossy photo and the elusive promise of good weather convinced Greg Child and Steve Masceoli to commit to a late-summer trip. In mid-August, the threesome piled into Collum's van and headed for Whitesaddle Air Services in Bluff Lake, British Columbia.

It wasn't until the next day, when Mike King's Jet Ranger helicopter swooped around Combatant's vast southern flank, that Child got a close look at its south buttress. It was way bigger than he expected—soberingly big. "When Greg Collum put the trip together, it sounded relatively low-key," crowed Child. "Then we landed at the base of this rock tower and it's *enormous*. I suddenly realized this is hardly a casual outing."

Combatant's south buttress is actually a series of independent granite towers that weave a circuitous route to its 12,324-foot summit. The first spire, which Collum dubbed the Incisor, is a 2,000-foot symmetrical cone of sparkling granite. The rock is so good that if the Incisor was located in the more accessible Bugaboos, at least a dozen routes would lead to its tiny summit. Behind the Incisor is a long, slender ridge that arcs gradually toward a broad scree ledge, gaining 1,000 vertical feet in a 2,000-foot horizontal span. The team named this complex traverse the Jawbone. Above the scree ledge is the second spire, towering another 1,000 feet and every bit as clean as the Incisor. And beyond it is another ridge traverse, followed by a third, 500-foot tower leading to the summit.

After unloading the helicopter and bidding farewell to Mike, they began humping loads to the base of the Incisor. Anyone who's seen Yosemite climbers prepare for an ascent of El Capitan can appreciate how much technical gear it takes to scale a big wall. To envision the Combatant team's load, start with the El Cap arsenal, then add a stove, mountain boots, crampons, ice tools, and a pile of bulky clothing. Despite their desire to go light, the northern latitude dictated otherwise.

They started up the wall the next day, following an obvious series of flakes and fissures. While the leader enjoyed remarkable climbing, the others witnessed a geologic conversation between

Pakistan or Patagonia? Neither. Greg Collum pauses to take in the view from the enormous South Buttress of Mount Combatant (VI, 5.11, A3+). © Greg Child, portrait © Michael Kennedy

rock, ice, and gravity. Around 10:00 A.M., as the first rays of sun warmed the glacier, seracs would groan, then explode into a jumble of giant ice cubes. In a story about the climb titled "Mortals on Combatant," Child later wrote, "Safe on the wall, we blithely watched from our hanging belays as hour by hour the serac remodeled itself."

The vertical, central section of the Incisor turned out to be the technical crux of the route. The climbers followed a stunning seven-pitch crack system that featured difficult but safe free climbing, and four pitches of challenging aid. Their efforts were rewarded with a spectacular bivy ledge at the top of the twelfth pitch, and the promise of moderate free climbing above.

When they reached the top of the Incisor the next afternoon, they realized that, despite the lower angle of the terrain above, their ascent was far from complete. In front of them was the Jawbone traverse, a sidewalk-narrow obstacle course that guaranteed several days of tricky climbing and arduous hauling. Child described the process in his account of the climb. "We rigged Tyrolean rope traverses to ferry the bags from pinnacle to pinnacle. Our ropes wove through the stony teeth like dental floss." Three pitches into the Jawbone, Masceoli nudged a refrigerator-size boulder into the void. It barely missed Child and Collum, almost chopping their rope on its way to the glacier—a close call. (Four years later, Masceoli was killed on Mount Hunter's Moonflower Buttress when he was struck by a huge block of falling ice.) The cautious trio spent the next 48 hours navigating the Jawbone, treading delicately like paranoid soldiers in a minefield.

On the sixth day the weather took a turn for the worse. As they approached the top of the Jawbone, snow flurries numbed their digits and slowed their progress. Then, just as they pulled onto the spacious platform below the final tower, the sky unloaded. It snowed all night and most of the next day. They rested comfortably inside the tent, relieved to have the tedious and committing Jawbone behind them.

Having completed twenty-seven pitches, they had reached the intersection of the south buttress and the upper tier of the Combatant Glacier—the starting point for their descent route. There was still 1,500 feet of climbing between them and the summit, but much of it was moderate. And best of all, they were now in a position to leave their haul bags and race to the summit with light packs. All they needed was a break in the weather.

The eighth day dawned clear, urging the summit-hungry climbers out of their sleeping bags. They climbed solo until the cliff steepened, then roped up for five extraordinary and increasingly difficult pitches. The final rope length took them to the top of Toothless Tower, named in honor of Greg Collum, who lost his capped front tooth just before the trip began. More ridge traversing was followed by three crack pitches on a bone-white wall, and 200 feet of scrambling to Combatant's summit.

The next day, as they listened for the *thwock-thwock* of Mike King's Jet Ranger, they considered a variety of names for their thirty-six-pitch creation. Collum finally settled on Belligerence, a pun on Combatant's combative name. Reflecting on the eight-day experience, Child countered that it wasn't a belligerent climb at all. "It was a smooth ride, and a bargain to boot—a Trango Tower–scale route for the price of a 12-hour drive from Seattle and a $900 helicopter ride, and all done in less than two weeks."

ROUTE DESCRIPTION

Area: Southwest British Columbia

First ascent: Greg Child, Greg Collum, and Steve Masceoli, August 1994

Base elevation: Approximately 8,000 feet

Summit elevation: 12,324 feet

Difficulty: VI, 5.11, A3+

Time required: (First-ascent party) 8 days

Equipment: 2 60-m ropes and a tag line, lots of webbing; 8 knifeblades, 8 lost arrows, 4 baby angles; 2 sets of brass nuts, stoppers, TCUs, and regular cams to 3½ inches; 1 no. 4 Camalot; 3 ice screws, 3 ice tools per 2 people

Season: August–September

Special considerations: Climbers should be proficient with alpine ice climbing and glacier travel for approach/descent; water can be found on route in normal snow year so bring water bags; good natural ledges obviate need for portaledge, but bring bivy tent; retreat from the Jawbone would be difficult and unsavory

Reference: *The Waddington Guide* by Don Serl (Elaho Publishing, 2000)

Map: 92/N6 Mount Waddington, 1:50,000

Approach: Drive to Williams Lake, British Columbia, then follow Highway 20 west 140 miles (225 km) to Tatla Lake; Bluff Lake is 12.5 miles (20 km) south, located northeast of the Waddington Range, 432 miles (695 km) and 10–12 hours from Vancouver. Fly by helicopter from Bluff Lake. Mike King's Whitesaddle Air Service can be reached at 250-476-1182. (Alternatively, Long Beach Helicopters, 250-286-8863, flies out of Campbell River on Vancouver Island. The flying route is 50 percent longer, and therefore more expensive.)

Route: This is mostly a free climb, with four pitches of aid on the Incisor. The route on sparkling alpine granite in a true wilderness setting has no mandatory 5.11 free climbing, e.g., it goes at 5.10 with more easy aid. See topo for details.

Descent: Rappel the upper third of the route, then descend the glacier to the arranged pickup spot.

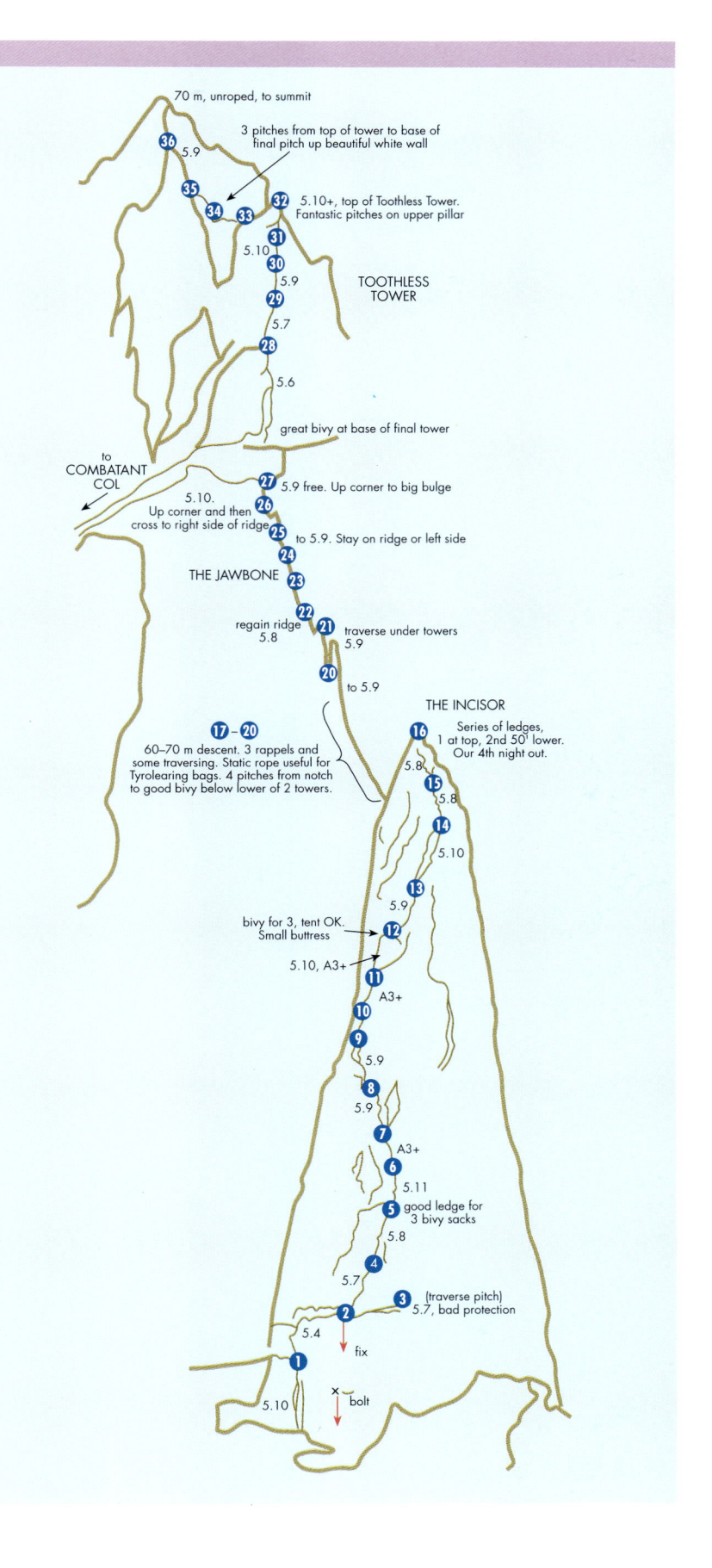

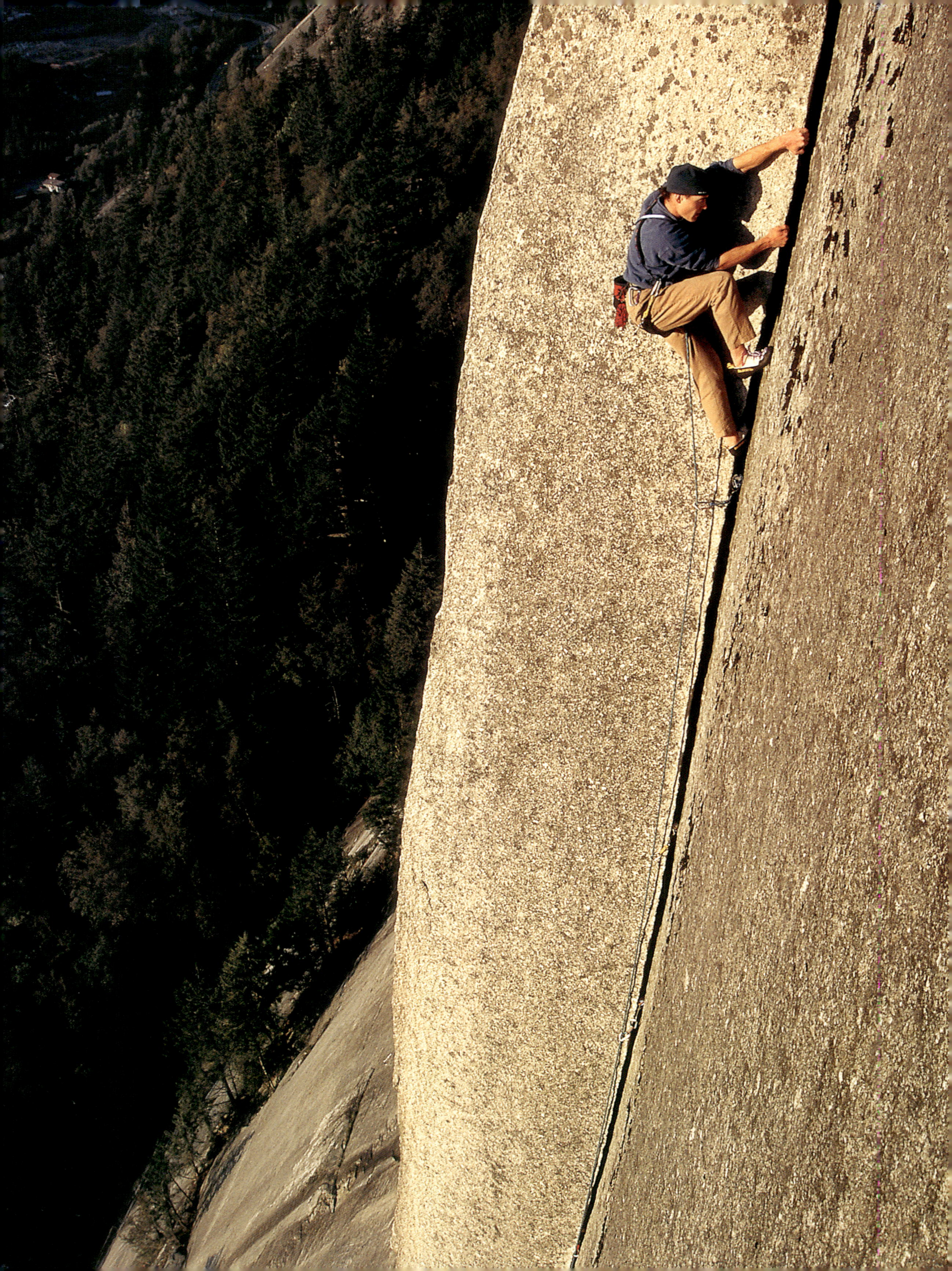

RUSS CLUNE

THE GRAND WALL, SQUAMISH CHIEF, SQUAMISH, BRITISH COLUMBIA

RUSS CLUNE—THE TRAVELER

Russ Clune's most important piece of equipment is probably his passport. Since he started climbing in 1977, he's used it on more than forty overseas trips to twenty-eight countries, logging thousands of climbs at hundreds of different crags. Name a type of rock—gritstone, limestone, sandstone, granite, quartzite, basalt, diorite, volcanic tuff—and he's climbed on it.

Clune cut his teeth at the staunchly traditional Shawangunks in the Northeast. There he met some of the world's leading rock climbers, including Kim Carrigan, an Australian who was visiting in the late '70s. Carrigan told Clune that the best way for him to realize his potential was to climb at as many different crags, in as many different countries, with as many different people as possible. Carrigan's advice, plus Clune's wanderlust, inspired him to head for the gritstone crags of England after graduating from college in 1980. "I saw climbing as a great way to see the world," grins Clune. "It was either that or get a job."

In lieu of full-time employment, Clune spent the next decade on a whirlwind of multimonth trips. After several visits to western Europe, the gregarious American began making forays into the then-Communist countries of East Germany, Czechoslovakia, and Russia. His border-crossing tales are almost as hair-raising as the poorly protected, chalkless routes he's done in Dresden, East Germany.

Clune pushed his limits at home too. In the 'Gunks, where the obvious lines had all been plucked by the early '80s, he added hard, sporting routes such as Drop Zone (5.12, R) and Vandals (5.13). He has more than eighty first ascents in the 'Gunks, more than fifty of them rated 5.12 or harder. In the mid-'80s, during a soloing phase, he made an unroped ascent of the famous Supercrack (5.12c/d). Clune has also climbed extensively in the West, making notable ascents from Yosemite, California, to Squamish, British Columbia.

Now in his early forties, the affable New Yorker is as fit as ever. The location of his home in New Paltz, which is just 8 miles from the 'Gunks, affords him frequent trips to his hometown crag. And when he can't get there, he cranks at his home gym until veins crisscross his Popeye-size forearms like a Los Angeles road map. Why all the training? Who knows?—maybe Clune earns frequent flyer miles when he climbs, too.

THE GRAND WALL

If there was ever a game show that tested people's knowledge of rock-climbing destinations, Russ Clune would be the grand-prize winner. He has spent more than two decades climbing at the finest crags on the planet, taking copious notes on every route he's ever done. The information stored in his head—not to mention his climbing journal—would fill at least a dozen CD-ROM disks.

Want to know the ten best climbs in West Virginia's New River Gorge? Clune can tell you. Planning a trip to Australia? He knows the best crags to visit. Curious about climbing in Korea? Clune's been there, too. And when it comes to his beloved Shawangunks, only Clune can give move-by-move beta for some 500 routes, complete with first-ascent history and hilarious anecdotes.

Clune put his encyclopedic knowledge to use in 1998 while planning a climbing trip to the West Coast with his wife, Diane. She wanted to round out her skills by doing a long, granite crack climb—something classic, but not too difficult. A quick query of his mental database came up with the perfect outing: the Grand Wall at Squamish. He has considered the ten-pitch route a favorite since first doing it in 1987. "I'd rate every pitch on the climb at least two stars," he raves. "And the Split Pillar is one of the best individual pitches I've done, anywhere in the world." In addition to having a great time on the Grand Wall, Clune was impressed by the entire Squamish area. "I remember thinking that the place was a total sleeper," he says of his first trip to Canada's premier crag. "It's a microcosm of Yosemite without the intimidation factor."

For the past two decades, Squamish has existed in the shadow of the sprawling Whistler resort to its north. Skiers, snowboarders, and golfers think of it as the town with a big cliff, a McDonalds, and a gas station that is on the way to the land of endless alpine terrain and twenty-seven-hole golf courses. Climbers think of it the other way around; Squamish is the main attraction.

Like Whistler, Squamish experienced a development boom in the '90s. The once crusty logging town has transformed itself into a climber- and tourist-friendly community. Amenities now include

Approaching the top of the spectacular Split Pillar (5.10b) on the Grand Wall © Rich Wheater, portrait © Michael Kennedy

a Starbucks, a microbrewery, and a decent selection of restaurants. And in 1998, the park service added a beautiful, government-subsidized campground near the base of the Grand Wall. Route development has been brisk, too. There are now more than 1,000 routes in the entire Squamish area, making it the best granite climbing destination north of Yosemite.

Even without Squamish's present-day amenities, Clune's 1987 trip there was a rousing success. Taking full advantage of a spell of good weather, he and his partner ticked off several area classics, including the Grand Wall. Rather than taking the easiest and most popular path up the Grand, which starts with two moderate routes known as Apron Strings (5.10b) and Merci Me (5.8), Clune and his partner opted for the six-pitch edging test, Cruel Shoes (5.10d). "It's the most direct route to the base of the Split Pillar," he says of the variation. "The standard route is less continuous—more like an appetizer before the entrée." Although he doesn't usually seek out slab climbs, Clune remembers the route fondly. "Unlike the nothingness nightmare slabs in Yosemite, Cruel Shoes actually has holds on it—nice, positive edges."

When Clune returned to Squamish to do the Grand Wall with his wife in 1998, his overriding goal was to make sure she had a good time. With that in mind, he suggested starting with Apron Strings/Merci Me, the standard route to the base of the Split Pillar. Even though Diane had never done a ten-pitch granite wall, she wasn't intimidated by the Grand. "The nice thing is that it doesn't feel like a big, scary climb," says Clune. "It's like a bunch of smaller climbs put together. It's friendly in that way."

The bottom half of the route went quickly, and proved to be an excellent warm-up for the Split Pillar—the most spectacular pitch on the climb. Diane had a moment of doubt when she saw the soaring, gradually widening crack, but soon realized it was well within her ability. After liebacking the first 10 feet, she slipped into a comfortable rhythm of secure hand jams. "Diane did really well on the Pillar and the rest of the climb," remembers Clune. "The last five pitches just keep coming at you, and she handled them really well."

The happy couple climbed under sunny skies into the late afternoon, when they reached Bellygood Ledge at the top of the twelfth pitch. Since the venerable Roman Chimneys—an optional, four-pitch continuation rated 5.11d—were still wet, Clune didn't even consider tempting his bride to continue. "Maybe that's why we had such a good time," he laughs. "For once in my life, I quit while I was ahead."

As the Clunes sat on Bellygood Ledge and watched sailboards zip across Howe Sound, Russ thought about the Grand Wall in the context of the best granite free climbs in North America (all of which he's done). "The Grand Wall is where things start to get interesting," he explains. "If you can do the Grand without any problems, you're probably ready for the other Squamish classic, Freeway. If you can do Freeway, you can easily do the Rostrum. After doing that, you should be able to do the West Face of El Cap. And with the fitness you gain from the West Face, you might be able to go up and do the hardest of them all—Astroman. Basically," he continues, "anyone who aspires to do the classic granite free walls in North America should start by doing the Grand Wall."

ROUTE DESCRIPTION

Area: North of Vancouver, British Columbia
First ascent: J. Baldwin and E. Cooper, July 1961; first free ascent: assorted parties free-climbed pitches 2, 3, 4, and 6, pitches 5, 7, 8, and 9 were free-climbed by Peter Croft and Greg Foweraker, March 1981
Difficulty: IV, 5.11a, A0
Time required: 1 day
Equipment: Standard rack of cams to 3½ inches, doubles in hand sizes; set of TCUs and stoppers; 50-m ropes OK
Season: April–October
Special considerations: Rain and car break-ins both common at Squamish, so have foul-weather backup plan and don't leave valuables in your car
Reference: *Rock Climbers' Guide to Squamish* by Kevin McLane

Approach: From Vancouver, British Columbia, follow Highway 99 north for about 37 miles (60 km). Park at the pullout located just below the Grand Wall. Follow the obvious trail for 0.6 mile (1 km) to the base of the wall, about 20 minutes.

Route: Ten to twelve pitches of varied, consistently wonderful granite climbing. Choose from two starts: Apron Strings/Merci Me (easier) or Cruel Shoes (harder but way cooler). See topo for details.

Descent: Exit right (south) on Bellygood Ledge (plan to crawl) after the twelfth pitch, then descend the hiking trail down the right (south) side of Squamish Chief. Hard men and women continue for four more pitches up the Roman Chimneys (5.11d), which are often wet until late July.

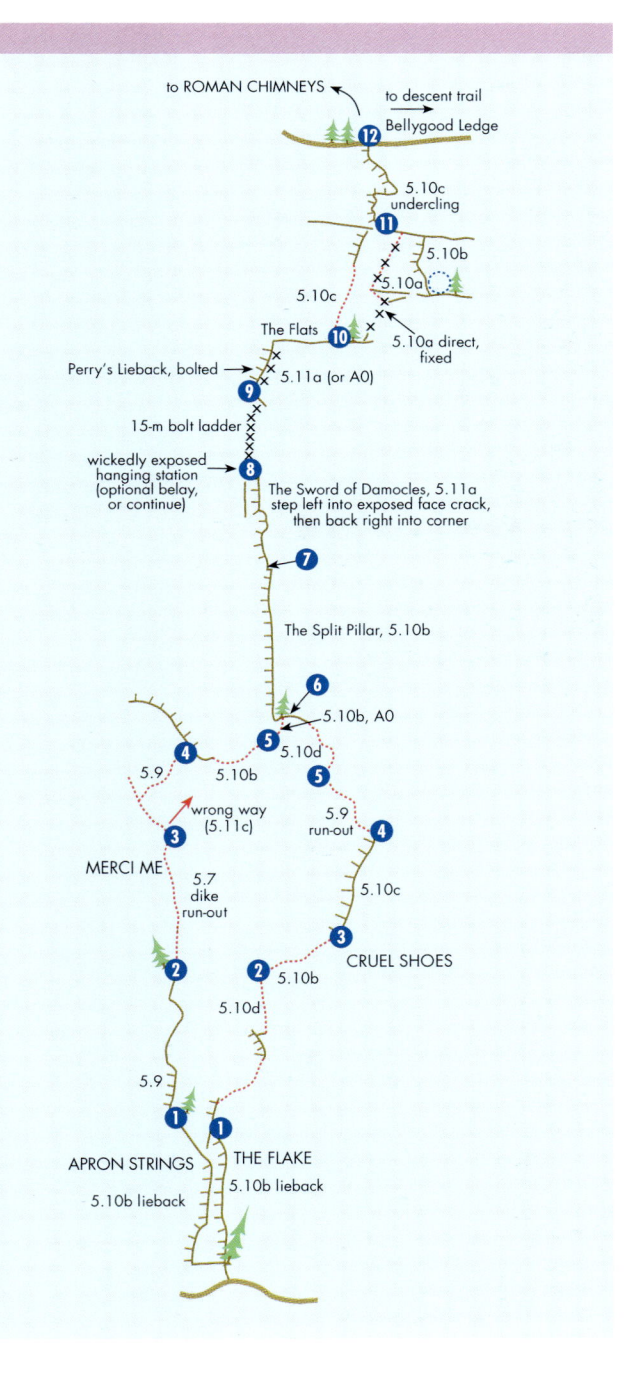

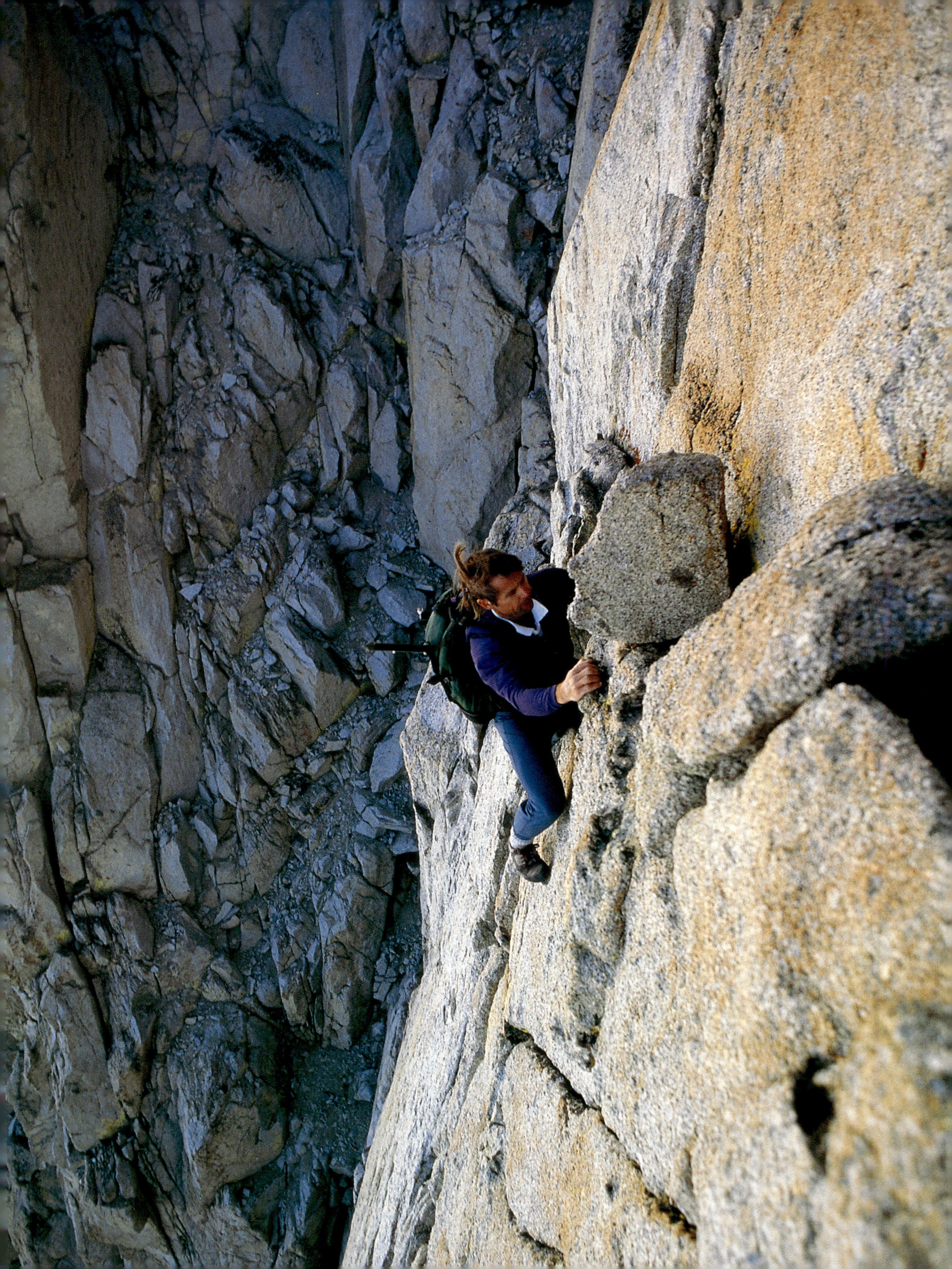

PETER CROFT
THE EVOLUTION TRAVERSE, CENTRAL SIERRA NEVADA, CALIFORNIA

PETER CROFT— THE EVOLUTION OF ENDURANCE

Peter Croft's exploits on rock cause even the most accomplished climbers to shake their heads in disbelief. It takes an especially strong crack climber to get up Yosemite's Astroman (see Climb 30), yet Croft soloed it without a rope. It takes a really fast team to do the Nose of El Capitan in a day; Croft did it in 4 hours, 22 minutes. It takes an even faster crew to make a 1-day ascent of El Cap's Salathé Wall; Croft climbed it *and* the Nose in 18 hours. And it takes still more endurance to solo an 8-mile ridge with 10,000 feet of technical terrain, at altitude, in a day. Croft, of course, has done that too.

Croft was drawn to such endurancefests from the very beginning. Despite the fact that he is a solid 5.13 climber, he always knew that simply "bumping up the grade" wouldn't satisfy him. It was too much like the competitive sports he was trying to get away from. He needed pure adventure. And lots of it.

Croft's definition of adventure evolved with his abilities. First he was happy with long, aesthetic free climbs such as the eleven-pitch University Wall at Squamish Chief, British Columbia. Then he started doing several long routes in the same day, often solo. For example, in 1984 he tagged five summits in Canada's Bugaboo range in a forty-two-pitch, 1-day effort. In Yosemite, Croft became famous for "endurance days"—multiroute marathons that would exhaust several partners. In 1986, Croft and John Bachar upped the ante again by climbing El Capitan and Half Dome in a day. The sixty-eight-pitch sprint was the first 1-day "enchainment" of two grade VI walls. Many more followed.

When running laps on Yosemite's biggest walls wasn't enough, climbing's Energizer Bunny turned his attention to the mountains. Ridge traverses, he realized, had virtually unlimited potential for granite mileage. Croft may have an insatiable appetite for climbing, but he won't be running out of ridges anytime soon.

THE EVOLUTION TRAVERSE

> **No excursion can be made into the Sierra that may not prove an enduring blessing.**
>
> —*John Muir*

On July 6, 1999, the weather was perfect for climbing in the high Sierra, but Peter Croft spent the day doing something he rarely does—resting. He had just returned from the nearby Evolution Range, where he completed his most ambitious project to date: an 8-mile, nine-summit ridge traverse. The 15-hour solo binge involved countless sections of 5.9 free climbing and more than 10,000 feet of elevation gain and loss. Compared to climbing El Capitan in a day, says Croft, it was "way, way harder."

As he described his grand adventure, his enthusiasm for ridge traverses was practically leaking from his pores. "I'm surprised that more people don't do this type of climbing," he beams. "Normally, you do a route, get to the summit—the prettiest place of all—and then you just go back down to the valley. But when you do a ridge traverse, it's like being on a summit all day long."

For Croft, simplicity is a big part of the appeal. "It's about the most basic type of mountaineering you can think of," he explains. "To a nonclimber who is trying to understand what I'm doing, I can say, 'See that ridge of jagged mountains there? That's it. I start at the beginning and go to the end.' It's not like I'm trying to invent some wacky new sport like you find in the X Games."

Croft's passion for linking multiple summits dates back to the '80s. In 1985, he teamed up with Squamish partner Greg Foweraker and Coast Range explorer Don Serl to complete the first traverse of the remote Waddington Range (see Climb 36). And in 1989, he did an entire summer's worth of climbing in a single day when he traversed the six main summits in Washington State's Stuart Range. But it wasn't until 1993, when Croft moved to the east side of the Sierra, that he fully realized the potential for such traverses. Just as Yosemite is the ideal place for big-wall routes, the Sierra Nevada is tailor-made for ridge traverses: The access to the backcountry is abundant, the weather is perfect, and the jagged granite ridges often connect for miles on end.

Over the course of two separate outings with different partners in 1997 and 1998, Croft climbed the entire Evolution Traverse, but never more than two-thirds of it at once. In July 1999, he returned to climb the entire ridge, in a day.

Peter Croft, sans rope, navigates a tricky section of the Evolution Traverse. He climbed the eight-mile, nine-summit ridgeline in fifteen hours.
© Galen Rowell, portrait © Galen Rowell

Ridge traversing, explains Croft, "is like being on a summit all day." © Galen Rowell

Getting to the beginning of the traverse involves about 10 miles of mostly cross-country travel. Croft remembers seeing the first major summit on the ridge, Peak 13,385, as he hiked through Lamarck Col. "It's pretty overpowering to see this thing that would be considered a big alpine rock climb by itself," he says, "and then realize it's only the first of nine peaks."

After acclimating for a day, Croft awoke at 4:00 A.M., revved himself with a pot of Peet's coffee, and bid farewell to his hiking partners. With only a small pack and a chalk bag, he spent the day in constant motion. Like a restless Huck Finn on a granite raft, he traversed roughly the distance from El Capitan to Half Dome, stopping only for an occasional drink of water. The profile of the knife-edge ridge—which goes up and down between 12,500 and 13,835 feet—looks like the readout from an EKG machine.

For Croft, the climbing was never technically difficult, but the routefinding was a constant challenge. "You can have tunnel vision on crack climbs," he explains. "But on these long ridges, you've got to be constantly looking ahead, anticipating, poking your head around corners." He made several wrong turns along the way, but always took them in stride. "The whole idea is not getting depressed when you've made a bad decision," he stresses. "On these big traverses, you can't afford to lose a lot of psychological energy when you do something that's inevitable."

After 15 hours of jamming, stemming, smearing, and scrambling, Croft eventually ran out of ridge to climb. His adventure ended just as Mount Mendel was casting its stegosauruslike shadow into the Darwin Canyon. The ridge stopped as definitively as it started. For the first time that day he had only one choice—to step onto level ground. A 3-mile hike to camp was all that remained.

Croft has enjoyed dozens of Sierra ridge traverses over the years, but insists that the Evolution Traverse is the most classic. "The rock is superhigh-quality alpine granite," he says, "and you're always in a spectacular position, right on the crest of the ridge. No other traverse I've done even comes close."

Croft's enthusiasm for ridge traverses reflects his evolved way of thinking about endurance climbing. "If you view rock climbs only as going up a steep face or buttress," he explains, "you're quickly going to realize that the biggest climbs in the Lower 48 are about 3,000 feet. But if you view a long, knife-edge ridge as a legitimate rock climb, things start to look pretty limitless."

ROUTE DESCRIPTION

Area: Evolution Range, Central Sierra Nevada
First ascent: Mount Mendel to finish, Peter Croft in part with Galen Rowell, July 1997; start to Mount Haeckel, Croft and Dale Mazzeralla, August 1998; entire 8-mile traverse, Peter Croft, June 1999
Base elevation: 11,160 feet
Summit elevations: Peak 13,385, 13,385 feet; Mount Mendel, 13,691 feet; Mount Darwin, 13,830 feet; Peak 13,332, 13,332 feet; Mount Haeckel, 13,435 feet; Mount Wallace, 13,377 feet; Mount Fiske, 13,524 feet; Mount Warlow, approximately 13,300 feet; Mount Huxley, 13,117 feet
Difficulty: VI, 5.9
Time required: 1 day for approach, 1 day to acclimate, 2–5 days on rock, depending on speed and party size
Equipment: Medium-size rack of stoppers and cams to 4 inches; many, many slings and a few cordelettes; single-wall tent or bivy bags; 1 60-m rope for climb, extra rope for hauling
Season: July–mid-September
Special considerations: Obtain overnight camping permits at Bishop Ranger Station (760-873-2500); only water on traverse is from occasional snow patch, so carry plenty and get it when you can
References: *Sierra Classics, 100 Best Climbs in the High Sierra* by John Moynier and Claude Fiddler (Chockstone Press, 1993), p. 148 (map); *The High Sierra: Peaks, Passes, and Trails*, 2nd ed, by R. J. Secor (The Mountaineers Books, 1998)

Approach: From Bishop, take State Highway 168 west 17.8 miles, then right on North Lake Road, continuing 1.2 miles to the parking area, and then another 0.8 mile to the trailhead. Follow Lamarck Lakes Trail to just before Upper Lamarck Lake, then go south on a cross-country trail that improves after 0.25 mile. Follow it to Lamarck Col (12,960 feet), then down to Darwin Canyon. The trail disappears 1 mile west of the col. Camp at the lowest lake (11,160 feet), below the ridge.

Route: Head south-southeast from the small lake to the toe of the buttress. Pretty much follow the ridge crest for the next 8 miles, with only small detours off the ridge. Lots of third- and fourth-class rock, with bits of class 5, lead to Peak 13,385. To Mount Mendel, skirt the first sharp pinnacle on the east side, then some tricky knife-edge and notches lead to the summit. Follow the very crest to Mount Darwin (first crux). Cross the summit plateau to the top pinnacle, then begin the crux traverse to Peak 13,332. Several hundred feet of loose climbing lead to better rock; stay right on the crest—fantastic climbing. From Peak 13,332 to the base of Mount Haeckel, the climbing eases off. Climb Haeckel's classic northwest arête to the summit, then climb Wallace (nontechnical) and around to Fiske, Warlow, and Huxley. The last three summits are tricky on the way up (north), but easy on the way down (south). It is much, much better to go from north to south.

Descent: From the top of Huxley, head north, then drop down to the John Muir Trail. Follow until approximately 1 mile past Evolution Lake, then go up the trail beside the outlet stream back to camp.

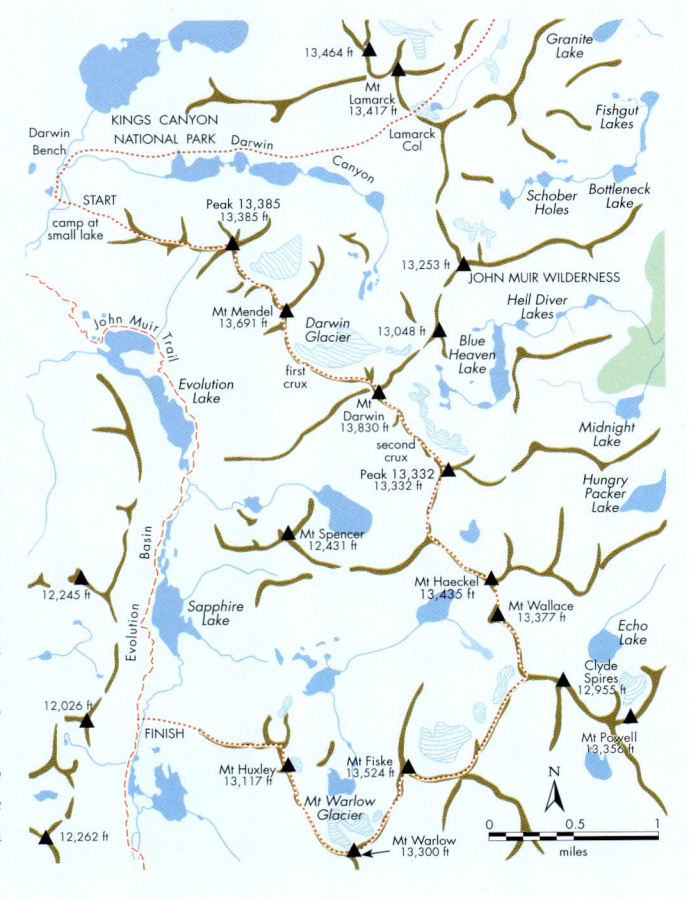

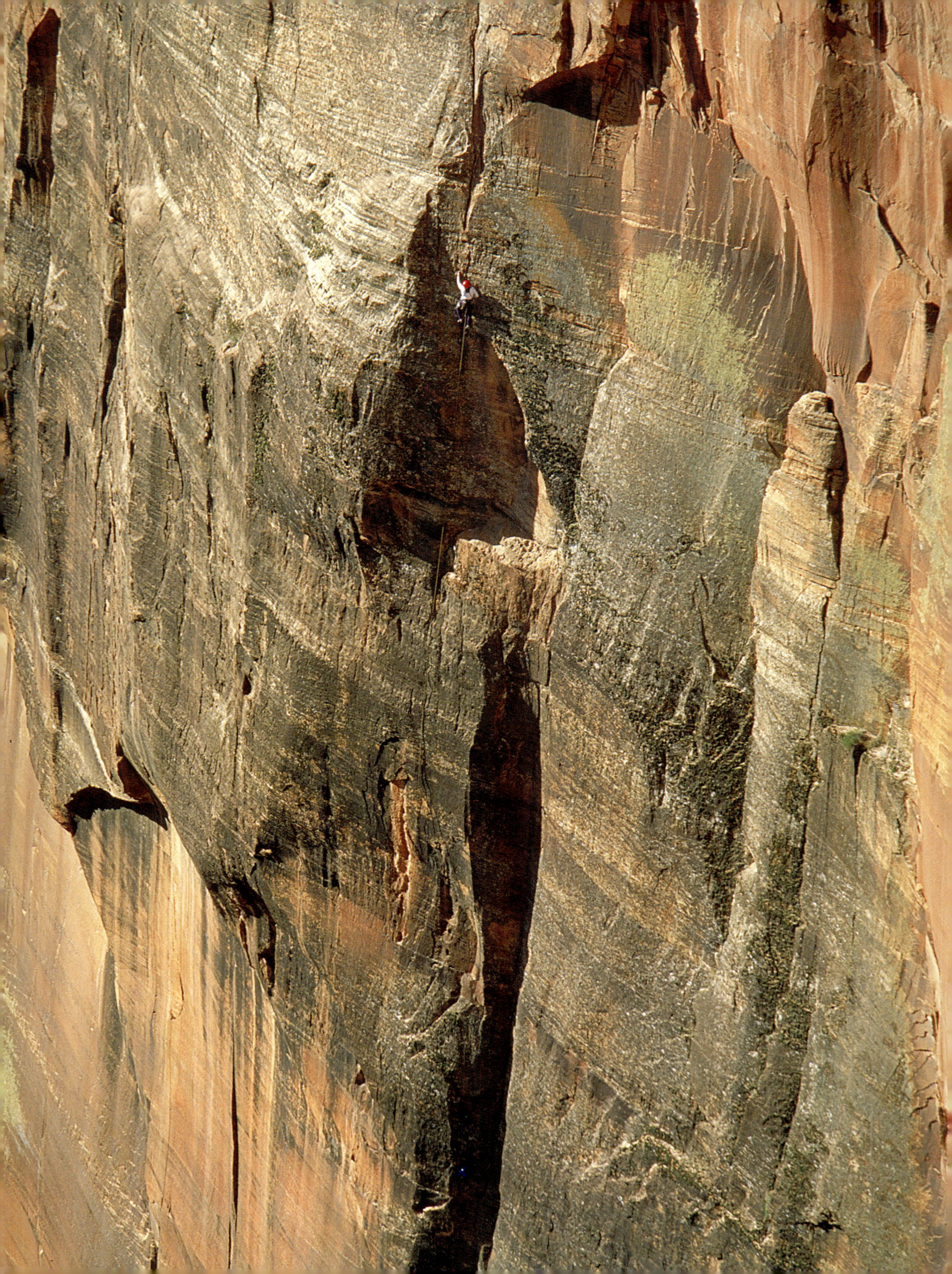

KIM CSIZMAZIA

PRODIGAL SON, ANGEL'S LANDING, ZION NATIONAL PARK, UTAH

KIM CSIZMAZIA—MASTER OF ALL TRADES, JACK OF NONE

When Kim Csizmazia won the ice-climbing competition in the 1998 X Games, her friends and family were delighted but not surprised. At the time, she'd been ice climbing for two years—about the time it takes her to master a sport.

Raised in mountain towns—Whistler, British Columbia, then Sun Valley, Idaho—by mountain-loving parents, Csizmazia (pronounced chiz-ma-ZEE-uh) was introduced to outdoor sports at an early age. Her youth was spent following her parents' ski tracks; she became a nationally ranked Nordic ski racer by age fifteen. Her father, a "training fiend," and her mother, "a natural athlete," set the pace while she and her two brothers followed closely.

In 1985, Csizmazia earned a scholarship to the University of Utah, where she joined its NCAA-leading Nordic ski team. She was introduced to rock climbing during college and loved it, but her rigorous ski-training schedule kept her from pursuing it seriously. After graduation, says Csizmazia, "I got full-bore into it."

By applying her ski-training regimen to climbing, she improved quickly, and was on-sighting 5.12 sport climbs by her second season. Although initially she was uninterested in ice climbing, a 1996 Jeff Lowe slide show changed her mind. Two years later she was the country's top-ranked female ice climber.

Csizmazia's technical prowess has taken her all over the world—from Europe to the Canadian Rockies—and attracted lots of attention. But despite all the hoopla, she hasn't forgotten her roots. "No matter where my technical climbing takes me," she maintains, "I'm always going to tromp around the mountains and bag peaks and go out for ski tours. That's a given."

PRODIGAL SON

After spending three long weeks in the spring of 1998 working on an ice-climbing film in a desolate, wind-swept corner of Iceland, Kim Csizmazia was glad to be heading home. Spring is Csizmazia's favorite time of year in Utah, and April 1998 was especially dear. Between the filming gig in March and a trip to Mount McKinley in May, she had less than a month to get her annual desert fix. In search of stark blue skies, cascading waterfalls, and warped sandstone canyons, she packed her van and headed for Zion National Park.

Csizmazia chose Zion because, in addition to its singular beauty, which the Mormon settlers deemed worthy of its Biblical name, it has an abundance of 1-day, moderate wall climbs. She'd done bigger, harder walls before—such as El Capitan's Zodiac and Salathé Wall—but had never done an aid climb without a partner. Suddenly enamored with the idea of scaling a wall by herself, she saw Zion as the perfect training ground.

Solo aid climbing appealed to Czismazia because, like Nordic ski racing, it involves constant motion for extended periods of time. She knew it also demands considerably more mental and physical endurance than doing a wall with a partner. "When you climb a wall with a partner," notes Csizmazia, "you do lots of sitting around." Climbing solo, on the other hand, sounded much more intense. It was just what she was looking for.

Among the various climbing disciplines, solo aid climbing occupies a peculiar niche. Success as an aid soloist has little to do with one's forearm strength or aerobic fitness. Rather, it depends on technical craftsmanship, mastery of mechanical systems, and ruthless efficiency of movement. Like a dog running ahead of its owner on a trail, the soloist covers three times as much ground as a traditional team of climbers. After leading each pitch, the soloist must remove all of the gear on rappel, then regain the high point by using mechanical ascenders to climb the rope. All told, it's a tedious endeavor.

Most first-time aid soloists start with a modest goal, like a three-pitch aid climb that can easily be done in a day. But not Kim Czismazia. In typical Csizmazian style, she set out to solo five walls in 5 days—never mind that she had never actually done a single pitch of solo aid climbing. "I'd read about solo aid climbing in a book," she laughed, "but I hadn't really done it." Fortunately, she's a quick study.

For her first wall, Csizmazia chose Space Shot, an airy but straightforward classic on the Leaning Wall. After she fumbled through the first few pitches, the process began to make sense, and by the fourth pitch it felt like second nature. She easily finished the seven-pitch climb before dark. The next day she found her way to the

Kim Csizmazia feeling small on her one-day solo ascent of Prodigal Son © Greg Epperson, portrait © Will Gadd

base of the Touchstone Wall. Unfortunately, there were two parties in front of her. After giving them a 3-hour head start, she fixed a few pitches and called it a day. But with an early start the following morning, she finished the eight-pitch classic with daylight to spare.

Although she had fallen behind her wildly ambitious schedule, Csizmazia was still pleased with her progress. She was getting faster and her confidence was soaring. She also found the solitude surprisingly enjoyable. "It was one of those funny trips where you are laughing with yourself the entire time," she remembers.

The next climb on Csizmazia's hit list was Prodigal Son, a stunning line that bisects a broad sweep of sandstone known as Angel's Landing. Although two pitches longer than the Touchstone Wall, it was still within the realm of a 1-day outing for a fast party. Her friend Doug Heinrich, who had done the route and seen her in action, encouraged her to go for it. His only advice was to bring a good selection of small nuts.

Armed with all of the right hardware, Czismazia got an early start and began ticking off the pitches. Although Prodigal Sun was supposedly easier than the Touchstone Wall, she found it consistently more challenging. The cracks were thinner and the climbing was more intricate. But it didn't matter. She was totally dialed in, and fully absorbed in the climb. "I was in my own little bubble world," she remembers.

By midafternoon she was at the base of the eighth pitch, a grand, left-facing arch that leads to easier climbing above. Knowing it was the last full pitch of aid, and anxious to complete the route, she began to get hasty. Emboldened by solid gear placements, she would pay out several arm-lengths of rope at once—a shortcut that saves time but increases the length of a potential fall.

As she hung from a fixed piton near the top of the pitch, Czismazia was confronted by a very thin crack. As she stared at it, she remembered Doug's advice. "I was thinking, 'This must be one of those sections where I need to do small nutting,'" recalls Czismazia. Without searching for an alternative placement, she slid a brass nut the size of a pencil eraser into the crack, paid out some rope, and, without even testing the placement, committed her weight to it. The next thing the overconfident neophyte knew, she was skidding down the near-vertical wall in a jingle of hardware. Thanks to the extra slack she had just given herself, what should have been a 10-foot fall had become a 30-foot, knuckle-scraping whipper. Unhurt but surging with adrenalin, Czismazia immediately grabbed the rope and hoisted herself back to the piton that held her weight. When she regained her high point, a perfectly sized slot for a small camming unit suddenly appeared in front of her. Or had it been there all along? "It was a classic case of tunnel vision. I just didn't see it the first time," laughs Czismazia. "It's one of those things that happens in climbing—you just pull a bozo maneuver and have to laugh at yourself."

Csizmazia placed a bombproof TCU in the now-obvious slot, enabling her to finish the pitch without raising her blood pressure. Another 300 feet of easy free climbing led her to the top of the wall, and the Angel's Landing Trail.

As she ambled her way back to the car, she basked in the tingling afterglow of her most memorable wall climb to date. The quality of the rock was superb, its position was magnificent, and it had been an incredible learning experience. Only one question remained: Which wall would she climb tomorrow?

ROUTE DESCRIPTION

Area: Zion Canyon
First ascent: Ron Olevsky, September 1981
Difficulty: IV+, 5.8, C2
Time required: 1 full day
Equipment: Complete set of camming units; several sets of wired stoppers with many medium stoppers; 2 ropes, 1 10.5/11 mm, 1 8.5/9 mm, 50-m ropes OK; Lowe balls extremely useful
Season: Spring and fall
Special considerations: Some parties do the route in 2 days (overnight permit required); rope drag can be bad on pitch 8; exit gully above eighth pitch is really loose
Reference: *Selected Climbs in the Desert Southwest* by Cameron M. Burns

Approach: From the T intersection of Zion Canyon Road–Mount Carmel Highway, drive on Zion Canyon Road about 5.5 miles; Angel's Landing is on the left. Wade the Virgin River, unless it's too deep. In that case, head downcanyon to the Zion Lodge area, park, and use the Angel's Landing Trail bridge to cross. Once across, hike to the first switchback. A small, very rough trail leads down and right, into the underbrush. Follow this trail along the river's edge for 2.5 miles, to the base of the route.

Route: See topo.

Descent: From the top of the route, hike north to join the Angel's Landing Trail. Follow this paved trail down the southwestern side of Angel's Landing to the Zion Lodge area.

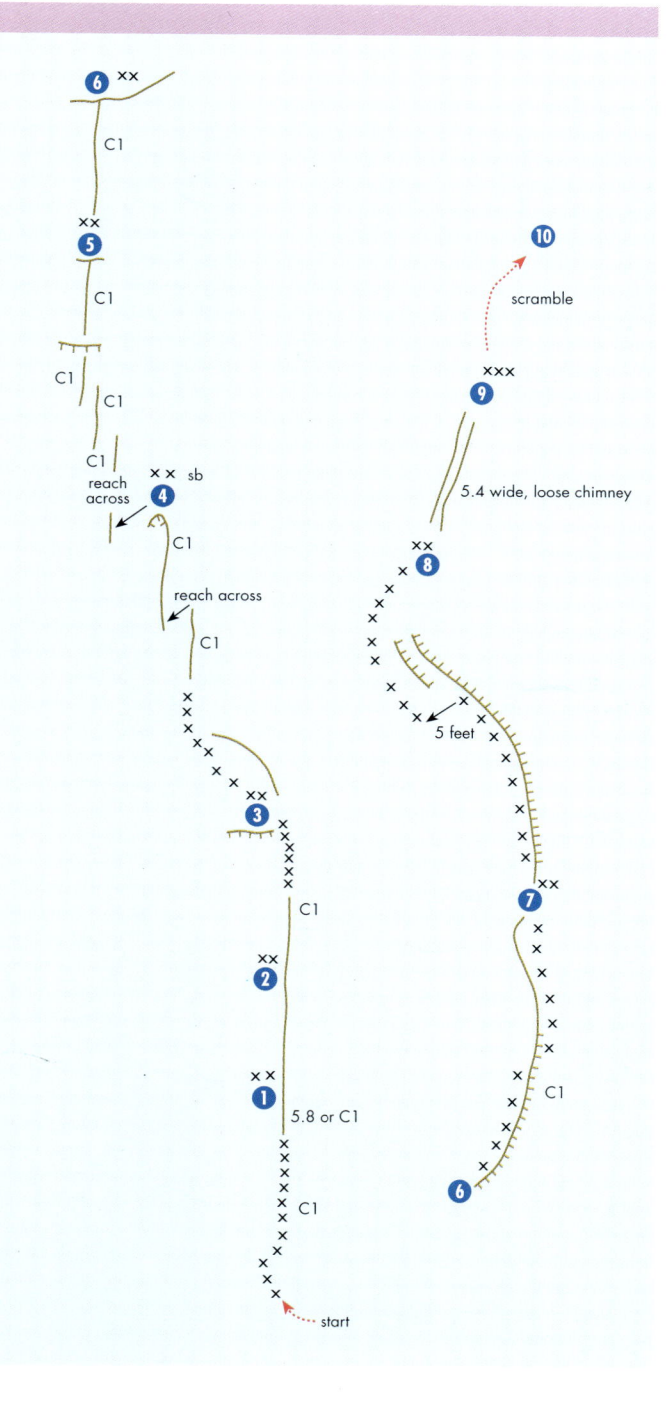

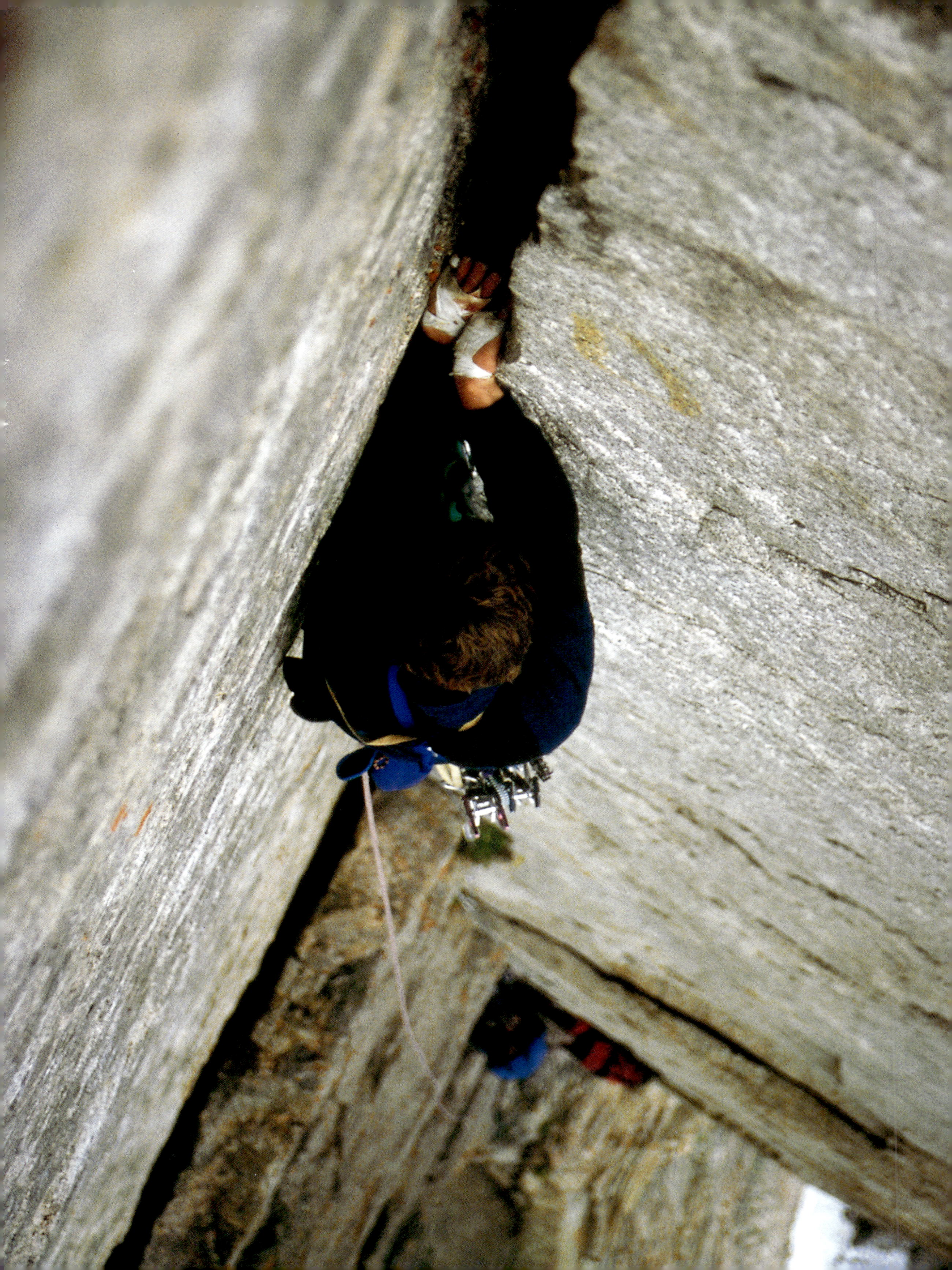

STEPH DAVIS
THE OBELISK, LONGS PEAK DIAMOND, ROCKY MOUNTAIN NATIONAL PARK, COLORADO

STEPH DAVIS—
ADVENTURE ROCK CLIMBER

Steph Davis spent the first eighteen years of her life training hard—to be a musician. Raised in suburban Maryland, Davis began playing the piano when she was three. "And when I wasn't playing the piano, I was reading books," she laughs about her scholarly upbringing. But when she was eighteen, she was introduced to rock climbing at nearby Carderock, and was instantly hooked. "I thought, 'I want to do this all the time,'" remembers Davis. So she did.

Davis backed off of the piano and started climbing constantly. After graduating from college, she moved to Fort Collins, Colorado, to pursue a masters degree in English literature. It was there that her climbing really took off. While honing her skills at the local crags, Davis found herself drawn to longer, more adventurous rock climbs such as those found on the Longs Peak Diamond. "Looking back, discovering the Diamond was a really big thing for me because it was the first time that I was exposed to an environment where there was more going on than just the rock climbing," says happy-go-lucky Davis, momentarily serious. Since those formative years, she has climbed all over North America, from Yosemite to Baffin Island, and internationally, from Patagonia to Pakistan.

In the process, Davis has emerged as one of America's most talented, well-rounded rock climbers. The 5-foot-6 dynamo on-sights 5.12, redpoints 5.13, and is perfectly happy to spend weeks at a time on remote wilderness walls. Yet she hardly looks the part. Her wavy, shoulder-length hair and perfectly tiled teeth suggest that she might be a college professor or perhaps a surgical resident. Instead, she's a full-time, sponsored climber. Despite her professional status, Davis is refreshingly spontaneous, often planning international trips in less than a month. "I never seem to have a master plan," she admits. "You just have to do what's exciting at the time."

THE OBELISK
Ob-e-lisk *n*. **A tall, four-sided shaft of stone, usually tapering into a pyramidal point.**

When Steph Davis decided to pursue a masters degree in English literature, Colorado State University was the obvious choice: The English department was strong, a fellowship made it affordable, and, above all, its hometown of Fort Collins was surrounded by some of the best rock climbing in the West.

Like most graduate students, Davis had stacks of work to do, but enjoyed the flexibility of doing it wherever she pleased. She spent many afternoons at nearby Horsetooth Reservoir, often correcting homework assignments between bouldering problems. "You can read and grade papers just about anywhere," she laughs. On weekends she would climb Fremont Canyon, Lumpy Ridge, or Eldorado Canyon. Her life had a simple, happy rhythm: study, climb, eat, sleep.

When the local crags got crowded, Davis would flee to less-accessible areas such as the Diamond. Situated on the northeast face of 14,256-foot Longs Peak, the Diamond is one of the most spectacular alpine walls in North America. Its 1,000-foot face, which sits entirely above 13,000 feet, is graced with highly featured granite, in-cut handholds, and a network of vertical cracks that seem to invite exploration. Today, more than thirty-five routes crisscross the wall—many of them historic achievements from the '60s and '70s. Although good weather is common during the summer months, the Diamond is notorious for sudden storms and epic retreats. Snow-covered ledges, icy cracks, and howling winds are all standard fare. Climbing the Diamond can be serious business.

Such alpine excursions appealed to Davis's adventurous spirit because they require more than just technical skills; they demand endurance, self-reliance, and toughness. During the course of her masters program, Davis climbed the Diamond more than a dozen times. With each trip, she grew more comfortable on the once-intimidating wall. It became a special place, a peaceful sanctuary where she could escape from the pressures of school and everyday life. In the summer months, Davis made such frequent trips to the Diamond that she would stash her climbing and camping gear at its base, reducing the arduous approach to a leisurely hike.

After several successful ascents of the Diamond, Davis set her sights on one of its most classic lines, the Obelisk. Located on the left, or "friendly," side of the wall, the route follows a splitter crack up the side of a massive, detached pillar. The crack starts thin and gradually widens to a 5-inch off-width. Most climbers learn to

Fist fight on the Obelisk (5.11-). Don't forget the large cams. © Kennan Harvey, portrait © Kennan Harvey

climb—maybe even enjoy—hand and finger cracks, but go to great lengths to avoid the knee-scraping, fist-grinding experience of off-width climbing. But not Davis. The talented generalist actually enjoys climbing wide cracks.

When Davis first climbed the Obelisk in July 1993, her partner, Jeff Ofsanko, led the crux pitch, the 5.11 off-width that finishes on the top of the pillar. Although she didn't fall when she followed it, she didn't feel totally solid. In the end, she wasn't *sure* she could have led it. For two years the uncertainty nagged at Davis—who prides herself on being an equal partner, not a "girlfriend climber"— until she decided do the climb again. This time her plan was to lead the pitches that she had previously followed.

Davis recruited her close friend Elaine Lee for the adventure. The pair departed from the bivy area at first light and scrambled up the 700-foot North Chimney, reaching Broadway Ledge by 6:30 A.M. Although they climbed the familiar terrain without a belay, Davis says most parties use a rope in the chimney. "You don't want to fall off the Diamond, like Charlie did," she chuckles, referring to Charlie Fowler's infamous tumble down the North Chimney in April 1984. (After losing his balance in a small snowslide, he bounced 400 feet down the chimney, eventually landing on the pillow-soft Mills Glacier. Miraculously, he wasn't hurt.)

Davis led the first pitch off Broadway Ledge. As she often does, she decided to test herself by climbing the more difficult right-hand variation (5.11-). Davis warns that the first 15 feet are "pretty burly" and protected by manky aid bolts. After pulling through the bouldery start, she climbed up what she dubbed the Garden of Woe—a beautiful corner crack garnished with foul-smelling Hummock plants. "I had just seen the movie *Conan the Barbarian*," she explains, laughing hysterically, "and I kept thinking that this must be Woe's garden." Davis acknowledges that the left start (5.8) is a better choice for most parties, but recommends the right start for seasoned climbers.

Two more pitches of moderate crack climbing took Davis and Lee to the base of the Obelisk pillar. "The first pitch of the pillar is super, ultraclassic," remembers Davis. "It's a beautiful corner—long, steep, and clean." As Lee muscled her way up the pumpy dihedral, Davis got psyched for her next lead, the off-width.

Her largest camming unit was a number 4 Camalot (at the time, it was the largest size available). If she was climbing an off-width crack at a roadside crag, she would carry two or three of the bulky devices on her gear sling. But on the Diamond, where going "fast and light" is crucial, she brought only one. From previous experience, Davis knew she could protect herself by sliding the number 4 Camalot above her head as she moved up the crack. She also knew that at some point, the yawning crack would become too wide for the number 4 Camalot. What she didn't know was just how far from the top of the pillar this would occur.

As Davis slithered upward, the number 4 Camalot expanded with the crack until, about 20 feet from the top, it became "tipped out." Without saying a word, a very determined, very composed Steph Davis nodded goodbye to her last piece of protection and moved above it. With her left shoulder and knee torqued into the 5-inch slot, Davis clung to the wall like a barnacle while she repositioned her hands. When her stacked fists were securely anchored in the crack, she would hang from them, advance another 6 inches, reset her shoulder and knee, then repeat the process. Five long minutes later, she flopped onto the top of the Obelisk pillar and yelled "off belay."

Another day at the Diamond. Another test. And, as usual, another passing grade.

ROUTE DESCRIPTION

Area: Rocky Mountain National Park
First ascent: George Hurley and P. Fowler, 1974; first free ascent: Chris Reveley and partner, 1979
Base elevation: 13,000 feet
Summit elevation: 14,256 feet
Difficulty: IV, 5.11-
Time required: 1 day from bivy area; fast parties go car-to-car in a long day
Equipment: 1 each no. 0.5, 0.75, 3, 4, 5 Camalots; 2 each no. 1, 2 Camalots; set of stoppers; 1 each pink, red, and brown Tri-Cams; 2 60-m ropes
Season: July–August
Special considerations: Permits required to bivy at Mills Glacier; obtain permits from ranger station in Estes Park, not at trailhead
Reference: *Rock Climbing, Colorado* by Stuart M. Green (Falcon Publishing, 1999)

Approach: Take Colorado Highway 7 south from Estes Park for 7 miles to the Longs Peak Campground. Hike to Chasm Lake (left fork at 3 miles). Scramble around the north end of the lake, toward the 700-foot North Chimney, making sure not to climb the chimney to its left. After exiting the chimney, carefully climb left on loose ground to Broadway Ledge. Scramble left to the base of the "mitten" (2-plus hours from camp to here). Choose from two starting pitches (left is easier).
  Route: See topo.
  Descent: Descend the North Face, along the old Cables Route. Extreme caution is advised.

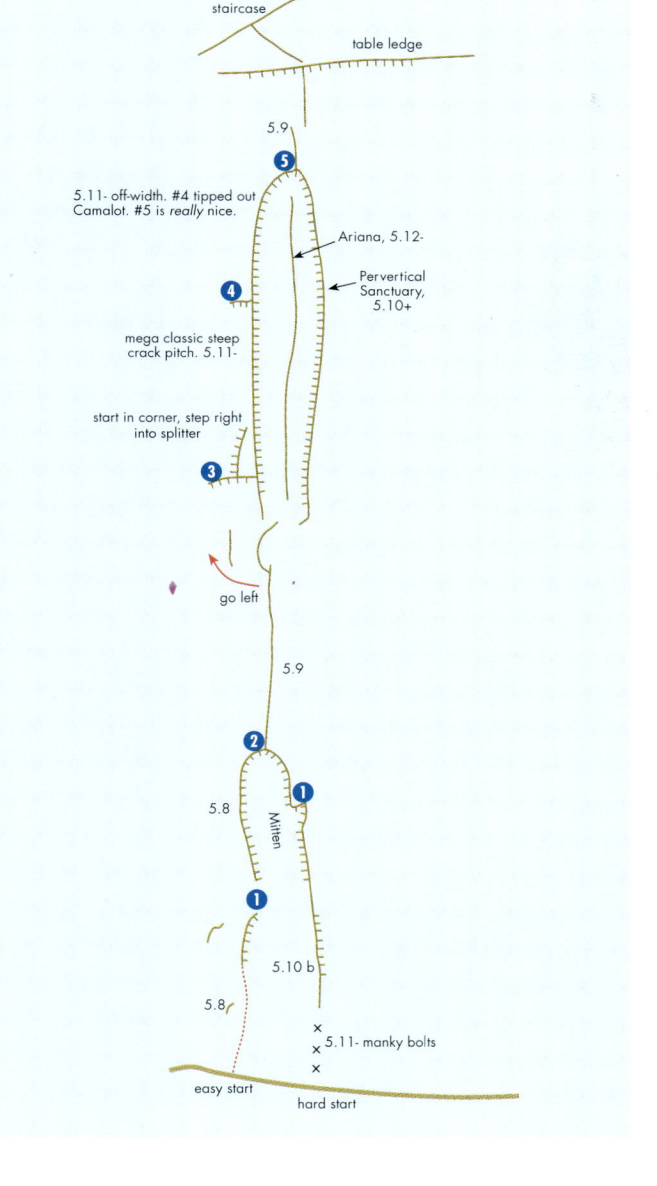

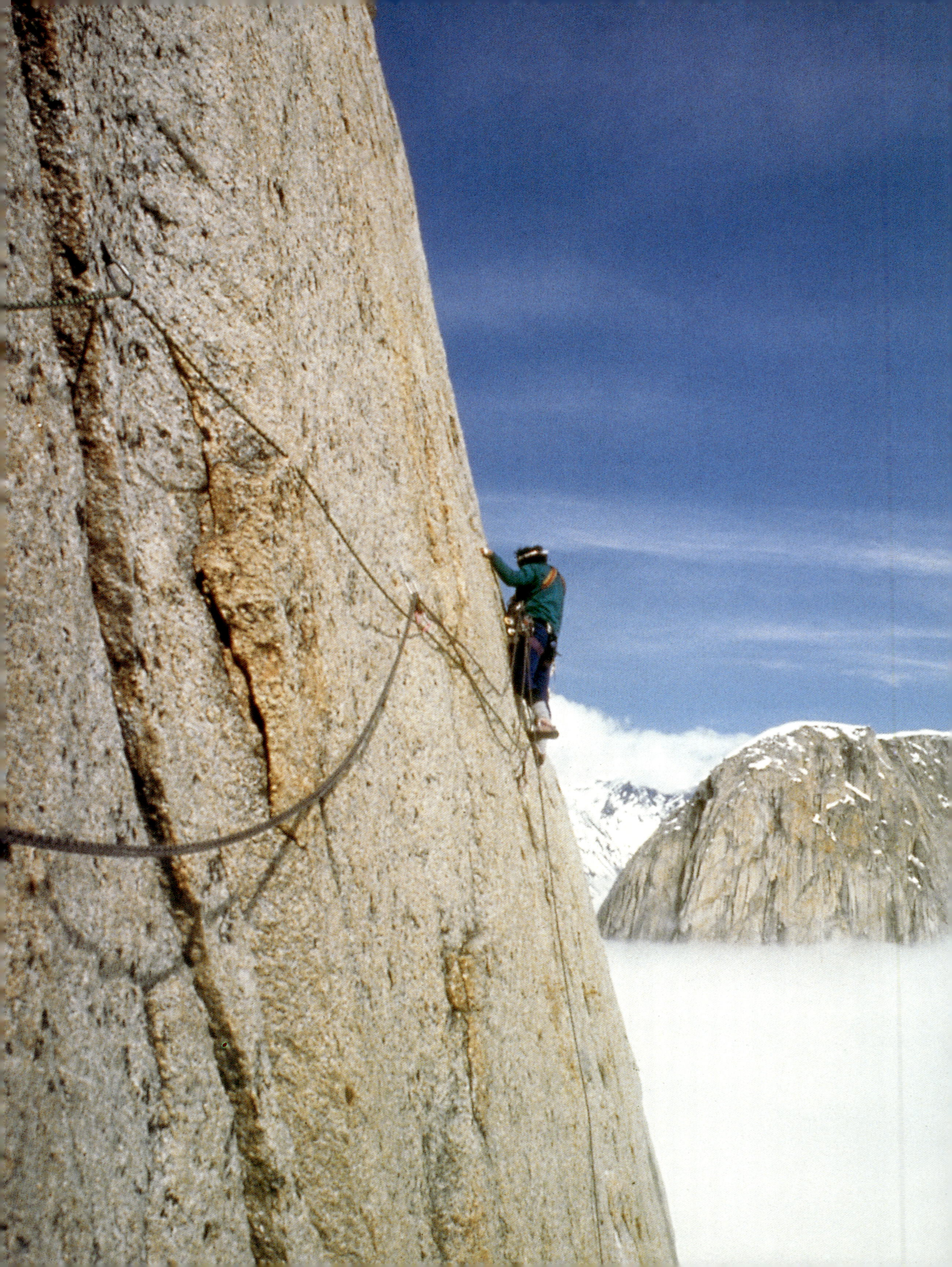

JIM DONINI

THE COBRA PILLAR, MOUNT BARRILLE, ALASKA RANGE, ALASKA

JIM DONINI—STYLE MATTERS

For the past thirty years, Jim Donini has been crisscrossing the globe in search of true adventure. And he's found plenty. With dozens of first ascents to his name—from Alaska to Patagonia to the Himalayas—Donini is a unique blend of traditional ethics and new-age technical skills.

Raised on a steady diet of swashbuckling adventure narratives, he saw climbing as the best way to explore the planet. Donini explains that, for him, the ultimate form of exploration is doing first ascents in the mountains. "Going up on terrain that's never been climbed before, turning a corner that's never been turned, putting my hands on a hold that's never had a hand on it—that's my exploration."

In the spirit of true adventure, Donini climbs fast and light—alpine style—with the smallest possible team. "The best way for me to climb in the mountains is with one partner with whom I have complete and implicit trust. There are fewer moving parts. You move faster. And it's incredibly democratic."

For such a purist, simply getting to the summit isn't enough—it has to be reached by fair means. "For me, climbing is totally about style," says Donini, who tirelessly preaches a doctrine of speed and self-reliance. Disturbed by our creeping dependence on technology, Donini feels that climbing has drifted from its core principals of adventure and risk. "We need to get back to the nitty-gritty," he declares. "That means no fixed ropes in Patagonia, no radios in Alaska, and no oxygen in the Himalayas." The ever-jocular alpinist continues, "If the Army Corps of Engineers built an escalator to the top of Mount Everest, would *that* be climbing?"

Donini's future plans in Patagonia and Alaska elicit nervous laughs from climbers half his age. Greg Crouch, a frequent partner twenty-three years his junior, continues to be amazed by his abilities. "It doesn't do him justice to say that he's a remarkable climber for a guy in his late fifties. He's a remarkable climber for any age." As far as Donini is concerned, he's still a kid. Quoting British author Aleister Crowley, he smiles and says, "My ultimate goal is to extend my adolescence beyond all previous limits."

THE COBRA PILLAR

Jim Donini is a veteran of more than a dozen climbing trips to Alaska, most of them resulting in bold new routes. Although he lives to explore the unknown, Donini is quick to point out that doing first ascents in Alaska can be a scary, miserable affair. He has experienced his share of chopped ropes, frigid bivouacs, and harrowing descents. Knowing this, it was refreshing to learn that Jim's favorite Alaskan climb included none of the above. "I've had epics on almost everything I've done in Alaska," laughs Donini, "but not on the Cobra Pillar."

Donini first set his eyes on the Cobra Pillar in 1987, on his second trip to Alaska. As he and frequent partner Jack Tackle (see Climb 44) flew into the Ruth Gorge, they noticed a beautiful, unclimbed line on the east face of Mount Barrille. They agreed it would be their primary objective, but decided they would first "warm up" on the northeast ridge of nearby Mount Wake. Although the ridge had never been climbed, it looked like a moderate, mostly snow and ice route that could be done in a few days.

As they hoped, Donini and Tackle made good time. By the end of the first day, they were two-thirds of the way up the route—well above the technical crux and only 1,000 feet of moderate climbing from the summit. Unfortunately, they awoke to swirling winds and 18 inches of fresh snow. After setting off a football field–size avalanche that almost killed Tackle, they began what turned out to be an epic retreat. Avoiding the snow-loaded slopes of their line of ascent, they rappelled down the steep, unexplored north face—surrendering both of their ropes on the way down.

After recovering from their epic on Wake, they started up the Cobra Pillar but were weathered off after just seven pitches. "That's when we decided there is no such thing as a warm-up climb in Alaska," says Donini, who returned the following year with a different partner. Plagued by bad weather, he was denied success once again, but remained inspired by the brilliant line. The next year, the ever-persistent Donini was back again, this time with his trusted partner, Jack Tackle.

In June 1989 the weather in the Ruth Gorge—known as the banana belt of the Alaska Range—was exceptionally good. Things

Jack Tackle in search of another crack system on the thirteenth pitch of the Cobra Pillar (V, 5.10+, A2) © Jim Donini, portrait © Jim Donini Collection

Cobra Pillar (1989)   Happy End (1988)

were about as perfect as they get in the Last Frontier; the sun was shining, the south-facing pillar was dry, and days were long. Still smarting from their experience on Mount Wake, the anxious pair decided to forego a warm-up climb and jumped right onto the Cobra Pillar.

As usual, Donini and Tackle climbed alpine style, carrying packs but no haul bag. They moved quickly up the pillar using modern wall-climbing techniques: the leader would free-climb, then the second would Jumar with the heavier pack while the leader hauled the light pack. Unlike Mount Wake, the Cobra Pillar was pure rock climbing; they climbed with bare hands and chalk bags, with oversize rock shoes as their only concession to the northern latitude. Before long they were in that elusive alpine groove, cranking out pitch after pitch of sustained but well-protected climbing on solid granite. "The rock on Barrille is the best I've climbed on in the Ruth Gorge," says Donini. "But just bad enough to keep the Californians away," he adds with a wink.

Well above their previous high point, the seasoned climbers encountered a horrendous-looking 5-inch crack that loomed above them for 40 feet. Their largest piece of gear was a number 3 Camalot—way too small for even the narrowest section of the crack. It was Donini's lead; he mulled over his options. He could place a few bolts, try to find an alternate route, or climb the thing with no protection. Donini, who spent his formative years mastering Yosemite off-widths, chose the last option. Tackle wasn't surprised. "Jim's got the perfect build for wide cracks—huge feet and no ass," he laughs. "He just slides into the crack and heel-toes his way up the thing." After he chicken-winged and arm-barred his way 40 feet up the 5.11a slot, it finally narrowed, enabling Donini to place a good cam and finish the pitch without incident. "That was a scary lead," he allows. "But with 5-inch gear it would be fine."

By the end of the second day, the speedy climbers had reached a comfortable ledge two-thirds of the way up the pillar. They now stood at the intersection of their new route and Andy Orgler's 1988 route, Happy End. Donini and Tackle had completed seventeen new pitches of brilliant free climbing, using only a few points of aid. With the exception of Donini's wrestling match with the 5-inch crack, the climbing had been downright enjoyable; it was consistently challenging but never desperate. About seven pitches of more moderate climbing—the upper third of Happy End—stood between them and Barrille's summit. With any luck, in 24 hours they'd be back at base camp enjoying the company of their good friend Jack Daniels. With the weather still good, the cautiously optimistic climbers cooked a hearty meal and snoozed under the cold, clear skies.

The next day, Donini and Tackle completed their ascent of Mount Barille. On the summit, they basked in the sun and the success of their new route. For once, they didn't have to worry about getting down alive. Barrille has a relatively gentle back side that can be descended in about 2 hours. "It's the easiest descent I've ever done in Alaska," explains Donini. "Put it this way: It's been skied."

Even though the upper third of Barrille's southwest face had been climbed once before, Donini never considered descending from the twenty-one-pitch high point of their new route. Although he would have preferred to climb on virgin rock all the way to the summit, reaching the top still matters to Donini. He scoffs at those who climb partway up an unclimbed mountain face, descend from their high point without reaching the summit, and still call it a new route. "Alpine climbing is about starting at the bottom and getting to the top," insists Donini. "The last meter is the hardest meter because you're pushing the weather window. You're stretching that umbilical cord."

ROUTE DESCRIPTION

Area: Ruth Gorge, Alaska Range
First ascent: Jim Donini and Jack Tackle, June 1989
Base elevation: Approximately 5,000 feet
Summit elevation: 7,754 feet
Difficulty: V, 5.11a, A2; moderate snow and ice
Time required: 2 days
Equipment: 2 ropes, at least 55 m; double set of Camalots to no. 3, 1 each no. 3.5 and 4, TCUs and wired nuts; rock shoes big enough for warm socks; boots capable of taking alpine crampons; 1 short ice tool with hammer head per person; bivouac gear, no portaledge
Season: Early June–mid-July
Special considerations: Route is mostly free with just a few points of aid
Reference: *American Alpine Journal* (1990)

Approach: From Talkeetna, Alaska, fly by ski-plane to the Ruth Gorge. Talkeetna Air Taxi (800-533-2219 or 907-733-2218) and Hudson Air Services (907-733-2321) are the recommended carriers.

Route: Seventeen pitches of mostly free alpine rock climbing in a spectacular setting. See topo for details.

Descent: Downclimb the back side on snow up to 50 degrees.

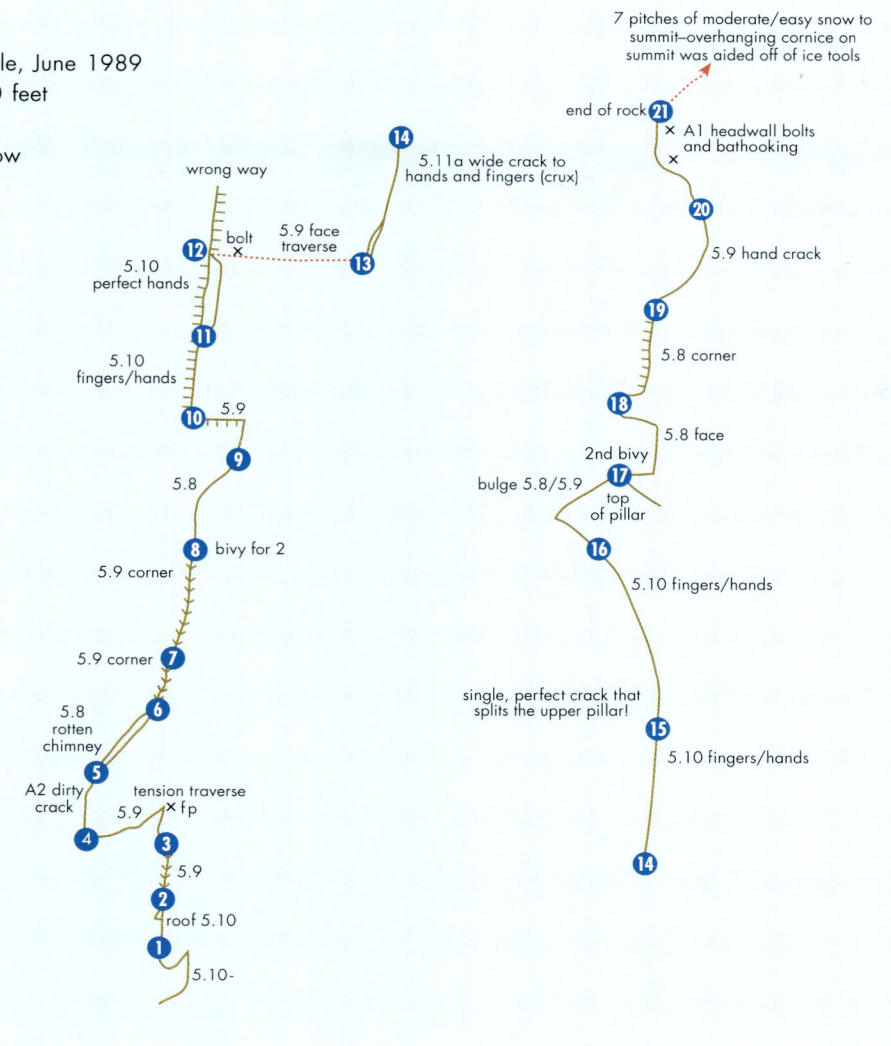

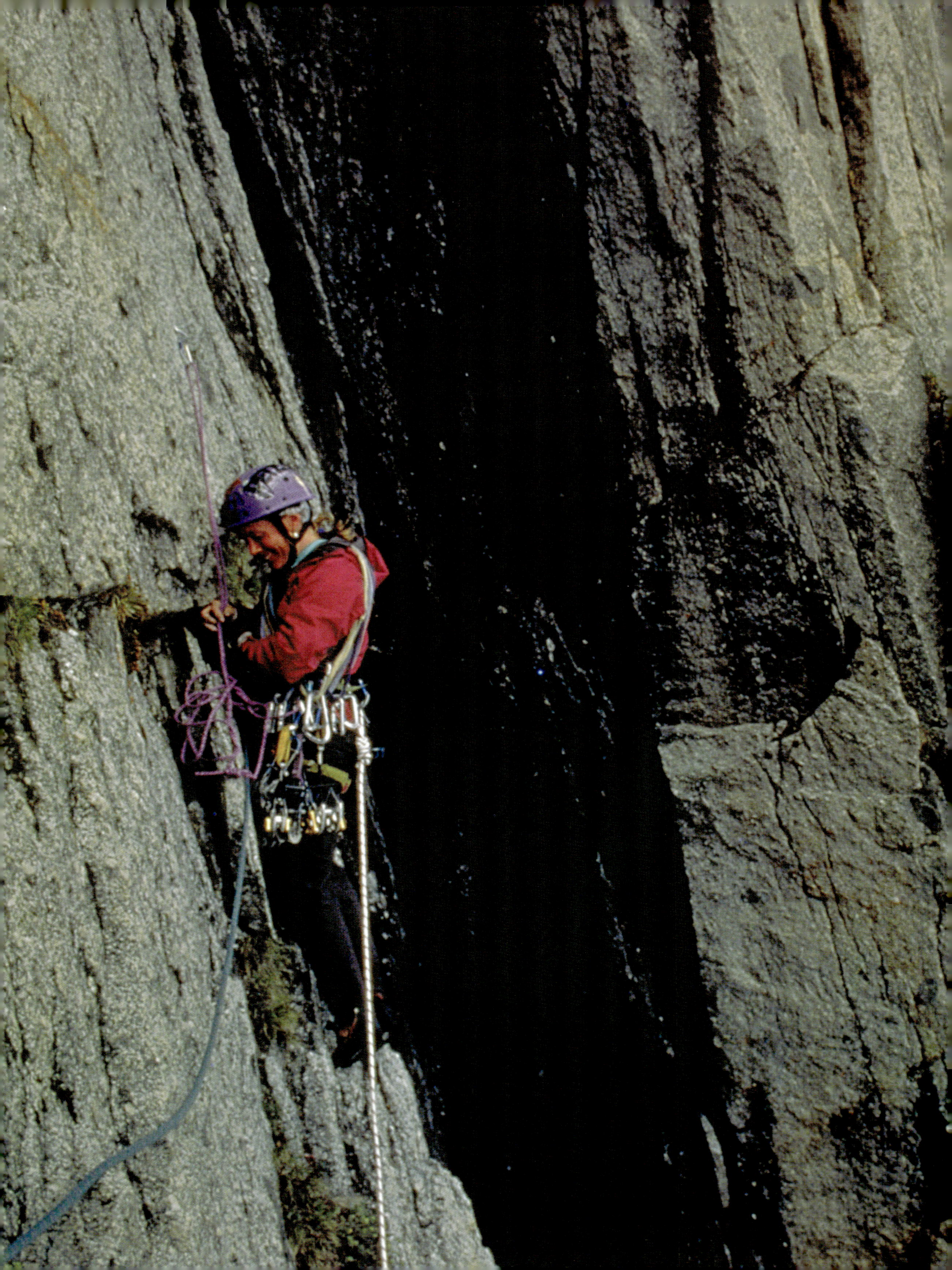

NANCY FEAGIN

ORIGINAL ROUTE, SOUTHEAST FACE OF MOUNT PROBOSCIS, CIRQUE OF THE UNCLIMBABLES, LOGAN MOUNTAINS, NORTHWEST TERRITORIES

NANCY FEAGIN—
ENDURANCE WITH A SMILE

Nancy Feagin was thirteen years old when her outdoor-loving family moved to Jackson Hole, Wyoming. She was introduced to mountaineering that same year when her father—who is a doctor—traded a knee operation for a guided climb of the Grand Teton. Her entire family of five made it to the 13,770-foot summit.

Her successful ascent of the Grand Teton and her love of the outdoors laid the foundation for her lifestyle today. Despite holding two degrees (in computer science and electrical engineering) from Duke University, she chooses to earn her living as a mountain guide and sponsored athlete. "I love my lifestyle," says Feagin. "I get to pick and choose when I want to work."

Although she enjoys all aspects of climbing, the soft-spoken athlete is best known for her endurance on rock. In addition to making 1-day ascents of the Nose and the Salathé Wall on Yosemite's El Capitan, in 1995 she partnered with Hans Florine (see Climb 16) to become the first woman to climb the Nose and Half Dome in less than 24 hours. With the same partner, she also climbed twenty of the so-called "Fifty Classics" (from Roper and Steck's 1979 guidebook of that name) in 20 days, including driving.

Despite her penchant for round-the-clock marathons, Feagin's sunny disposition never seems to wilt—a quality that her partners always appreciate. "Nancy is always a joy to climb with," says Florine. "Just being out there puts a smile on her face."

ORIGINAL ROUTE,
SOUTHEAST FACE OF MOUNT PROBOSCIS

Nancy Feagin knew things were getting desperate when the video camera got zapped by lightning. They'd been racing against the weather all day, and now, she feared, it was going to win. Two hundred feet above, at the top of the sheer, southeast face of Mount Proboscis, was the film crew, hiding under a thin layer of Gore-Tex. And 30 feet below, watching anxiously as hailstones collected in the folds of his parka, was her partner, Barry Blanchard (see Climb 4).

"Just tell them to lower you a rope," pleaded Blanchard, who, under the circumstances, was willing to trade the purity of a self-sufficient ascent for the safety of their hides.

"No way," insisted Feagin as she stuffed a cam into the seeping crack. "That would mean we won't have done the route. I'm not about to give up now." She continued up the delicate, dripping corner.

An hour later, after one of the most harrowing leads of her life, a very determined Nancy Feagin pulled onto a hail-covered ledge and secured the rope for Blanchard. She was soaking wet and chilled to the bone, and just one pitch from a completely free ascent of Proboscis's southeast face. After 8 days of hard work, only 80 feet of scrambling stood between her and the top of the wall.

Barry Blanchard and Nancy Feagin were on a business trip of sorts. They had been invited to climb the southeast face of Mount Proboscis by Richard Else, a British climber and filmmaker producing a series called "The Face: Six Great Climbing Adventures." His concept was to bring unlikely pairs of highly accomplished climbers into the mountains, then let human chemistry and the quest for adventure determine the outcome.

The soaring granite walls of the Cirque of the Unclimbables was the perfect setting for one of the adventures. And to Else's way of thinking, Feagin and Blanchard were the model team. Feagin specializes in long, difficult rock climbs, like those in Yosemite, while Blanchard is an alpinist, renowned for his ice-climbing and mountaineering skills. Putting them together on a 2,000-foot rock face in a remote, alpine environment, he thought, would create some interesting dynamics.

By the time Else's film project got underway in 1997, the southeast face of Mount Proboscis had become a popular destination. Although twenty-nine years passed between the first and second ascents of the Half Dome–like wall, a recent spate of route development had added five new lines to its mile-wide face: the Great Canadian Knife (VI, 5.13b; see Climb 39), a Spanish variation to the original 1963 route, Yukon Tears (VI, 5.12c), Crazy Horse (5.11, A4), and the Grendel (VI, 5.10, A4). Despite the flurry of activity, the original Robbins route—the most historic line on

Nancy Feagin, momentarily dry, getting psyched for the "waterfall pitch" on the southeast face of Mount Proboscis © Barry Blanchard, portrait © Beth Wald

the wall—had yet to see an all-free ascent. Enamored with the purity of the line, Feagin and Blanchard decided to go for it.

Although they would have preferred to climb "light and fast," filming logistics dictated otherwise. Not only would they need to leave fixed ropes for the camera crew, they would have to lead many of the pitches twice to accommodate camera shots from above. It wasn't the way they were used to climbing, but it was a small price to pay for a helicopter-aided, all-expenses-paid trip to a remote, wilderness wall.

The first three pitches went quickly. Swapping leads, Blanchard and Feagin climbed the right-angling ramp in less than 2 hours. At its end, they made a difficult traverse into a chimney that acted as a natural downspout. It took Feagin more than an hour to climb the slick, lichen-covered chimney. As she did, a cold shower of Canadian snowmelt poured down her neck. "When I finally made it to the belay ledge," remembers Feagin, "I was shivering uncontrollably." And then it started to rain.

As Blanchard Jumared through the waterfall, Feagin evaluated the route above. They had a choice to make: either follow the original route to the right, or climb straight up via the Spanish variation. The original route looked clean and dry, but impossibly thin. Feagin knew she couldn't climb it free. The Spanish route, however, looked like it would go after some significant cleaning. They discussed their options when Blanchard reached the belay. Then, in need of some dry clothes, they retreated to camp.

Climbing every pitch free—on-sight or otherwise—was important to Feagin. Blanchard, on the other hand, was more concerned with getting up the wall in a timely manner. He feared that using precious good weather to prepare the lower pitches for a free ascent might foil their chances for reaching the top. Yet Feagin argued persuasively that an all-free ascent would be much more rewarding. And since she was willing to lead the hard pitches, Blanchard agreed.

As they anticipated, cleaning the Spanish variation was time consuming and laborious. Each pitch was led using aid, then scrubbed on rappel. Like window washers on a skyscraper, they spent 3 days preparing the rock for a redpoint attempt. Even the aid climbing was a challenge. On the third pitch, Feagin took a 40-foot fall when she unzipped a series of A3 placements.

The first pitch of the variation went free at a reasonable 5.10d. The next was much harder, but solid protection gave Feagin the confidence to pull through the 5.11d crux after only a few tries. The third pitch was harder still—5.12—and lacked protection at the crux. Unfortunately, in their haste to get on the wall, the climbers left the bolt kit at camp. Unwilling to risk a 50-foot fall in such a remote area, and out of time, Feagin resigned herself to doing it with a top rope. It was a disappointing compromise, but a wonderful pitch nonetheless. "There are these awesome little knobs for your feet," recalls Feagin, "It's one of the most remarkable pitches I've ever done."

With the crux pitches behind them, Feagin and Blanchard awoke in the portaledge with a renewed sense of momentum—and urgency. Although the upper part of the route was much easier than the lower half, there was still 1,000 feet of it. Swapping leads, they raced the weather toward the top of the wall, climbing seven pitches in as many hours.

Then the skies unloaded. The ensuing epic tested their mettle, but it made them stronger as climbers, and as partners. What started as a filming project had turned into much, much more—an outstanding climb, a memorable adventure, and a wonderful friendship.

ROUTE DESCRIPTION

Area: Logan Mountains
First ascent: Layton Kor, Dick McCracken, Jim McCarthy, and Royal Robbins, August 1963; first free ascent: Barry Blanchard and Nancy Feagin, July 1997 (crux pitch top-roped)
Base elevation: Approximately 6,700 feet
Summit elevation: 8,530 feet
Difficulty: VI, 5.9+, A3, or 5.12a
Time required: 2–5 days from lake below Proboscis, depending on conditions and party strength
Equipment: Double set of cams to 3 inches, 1 5-inch piece; double set of TCUs, size 00–3; 2 sets of stoppers; assortment of pitons: 5 lost arrows, 3 knifeblades, a few baby angles; 60-m ropes, extra webbing for slinging rap anchors; portaledge with fly; good rain gear
Season: Late July–August
Special considerations: Beware of bears around Glacier Lake; expect lower pitches of route to be wet through late July
Reference: www.geocities.com/~gibell/cirque/ (George Bell's online guide to Cirque of the Unclimbables)
Map: Mount Sir James MacBrien 95L/4, 1:50,000

Approach: The hike to the base of Mount Proboscis starts at Glacier Lake, goes to Fairy Meadows, then over "What Notch" —a difficult snow and ice col. Most climbers take a helicopter in lieu of the strenuous, 2-day approach. Flying to Glacier Lake, or directly to the Proboscis, is best done from Watson Lake, Yukon Territory, but is equally feasible from Fort Simpson or Fort Liard, Northwest Territories.

Route: Fifteen pitches of crack climbing on highly textured granite. See topo for details.

Descent: Rappel one of the direct routes on the face (such as the Grendel), or downclimb and rappel the South Ridge (5.7, A2) to the climber's left, then down loose, third-class shale to the lake.

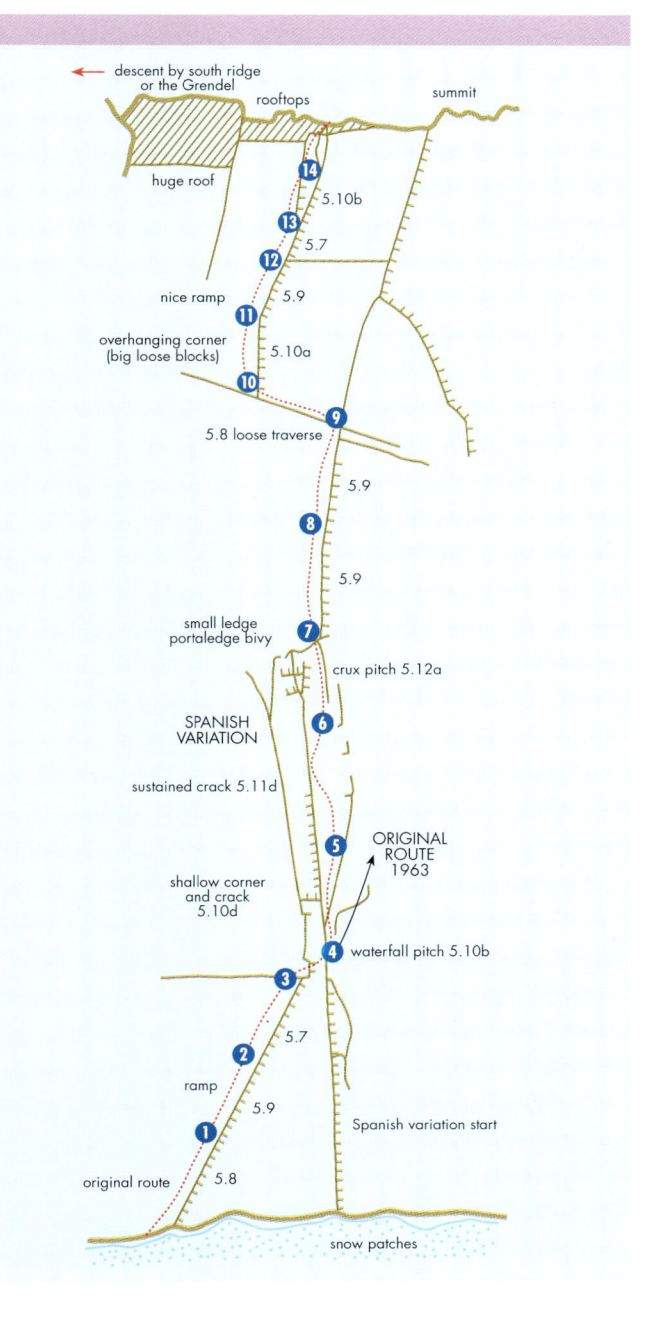

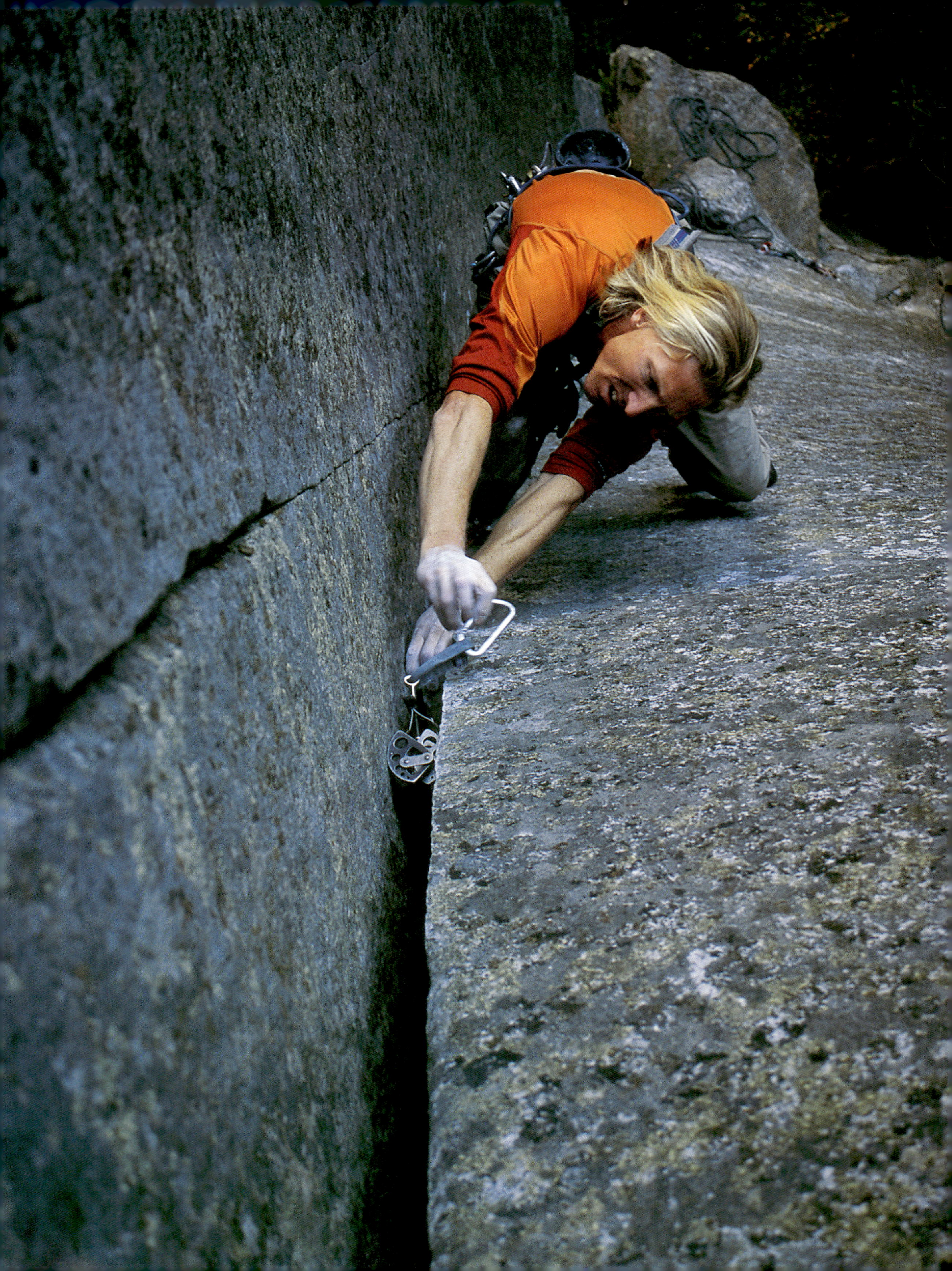

HANS FLORINE

BEGGAR'S BUTTRESS, LOWER CATHEDRAL ROCK, YOSEMITE NATIONAL PARK, CALIFORNIA

HANS FLORINE—
SPEED CLIMBER

My philosophy, in essence, is the concept of man as a heroic being, with his own happiness as the moral purpose of his life, with productive achievement as his noblest activity, and reason as his only absolute.

—Ayn Rand, author of The Fountainhead and Atlas Shrugged, on the philosophy of Objectivism

In Ayn Rand's classic, *Atlas Shrugged,* John Galt is the man without pain or fear or guilt, because he is sure of his convictions. When readers meet him on the pages of this best-seller, they ask, "Could anybody in real life be that sure of his convictions?" When they meet Hans Florine, a self-described Objectivist who has read all of Rand's books, they'll know the answer is yes.

Hans Florine, or "Hollywood Hans," claims to be the world's fastest climber. Is he? That, of course, depends on your definition. If you define it as a less-than-24-hour solo linkup of the Nose of El Capitan and the Regular Northwest Face of Half Dome, then he could be. On July 28, 1999, Florine soloed (with a rope) both Yosemite walls in the same day. His time for the fifty-six pitch effort: a remarkable 20 hours, 43 minutes. With Peter Croft (see Climb 11), Florine also held the Nose speed record for nine years. Their time of 4 hours, 22 minutes was beaten in October 2001, when Florine and Jim Herson climbed the 34-pitch route in a blistering 3 hours, 57 minutes.

It's hard to imagine that it's humanly possible to climb so fast until you see Florine in the flesh. He has the perfect climber's physique: tall, thin, matchstick legs, washboard abs, and sprawling lats that hang from his shoulders like wings. He walks with a self-assured swagger that says he's always been an athlete. Not surprisingly, Florine was a nationally ranked pole-vaulter in college.

In addition to being lean and mean, Florine is intensely competitive. In fact, he candidly admits that competition is his primary inspiration. Telling him he can't do something is like waving a red flag in front of a bull. "Everyone knows that if you want to get me to try something, all you have to say is, 'You can never do that,'" he laughs. Florine typically responds with a brash announcement that he will do the climb in question, fully committing himself in the process—the kind of hubris you'd expect from a professional boxer.

Although Florine is ultracompetitive, he is a model sportsman. He'll share detailed beta with anyone—even if they're attempting to best one of his speed records. Florine is very supportive, always offering words of encouragement to others, including rival speed climbers. He genuinely wants to see others do their best, and then do even better himself.

Florine is also exceedingly generous, constantly sharing his Yosemite home with visiting climbers. While he may not be home when they arrive, you can be sure he'll be back to sleep; his portaledge doesn't get much use. "I'd rather push my body until it drops and then have a really comfortable bed to drop in," quips Florine. "My favorite phrase is 'car to car.'"

BEGGAR'S BUTTRESS

Hans Florine was hiding from the sun when he first climbed Beggar's Buttress. On a warm morning in June, he and fellow hard man Chandlee Harrel were on the first pitch of Hall of Mirrors (see Climb 49), a slick slab of granite at the center of Yosemite's Glacier Point Apron. The first pitch, the notoriously underrated Misty Beethoven, had just come into the sun. As Florine slinked his way up the polished granite slab, his fingertips began to surge with sweat, and his shoes, which normally stick to the microscopic divots in the rock, skated hopelessly for purchase. "I couldn't do it," said Florine. "I backed off."

The day was still young, and Florine and Harrel were keen to climb—but not in the sun. "We were thinking, 'We'll do anything in the shade—just give us shade,'" recalls Florine. It was then that he remembered Beggar's Buttress, which was billed as the perfect outing for a sweltering summer day. The route sounded ideal, but Florine was skeptical; it had been recommended by Greg Murphy, an archetypal Valley traditionalist with a penchant for what Florine calls "epic grovels." Absent a better alternative, they decided to find out for themselves.

Speed climbing ace Hans Florine in motion on Beggar's Buttress © Mark Kroese, portrait © Mark Kroese

Florine, who has lived and climbed in Yosemite for much of the past decade, thinks that one of the hallmarks of a Yosemite classic is a short approach. On this score, Beggar's Buttress did not disappoint; they reached the base of the route in 12 minutes. Murphy told Florine that the route would be out of the sun by 10:00 A.M.—exactly the time they arrived. As promised, the first pitch of the route had just entered the shade.

After climbing a short, left-facing, 5.7 corner, Florine and Harrel were presented with the choice of a 5.8 flare or a striking, 5.11a finger crack. Naturally, they chose the latter. "The 11a is this beautiful, beautiful lieback dihedral finger crack," exclaims Florine with a wry smile, "before it turns into a fist crack." Sensing my distaste for off-widths, he quickly interjects. "It's like two moves, then it's over, so you don't need to be a fist crack master to get through it. But it gives you a flavor for what's coming up," he lets on, raising his eyebrows for effect.

As he describes the top of the first pitch, it sounds a bit like Astroman's famous Harding Slot, a grunty, narrow passage that discriminates against large climbers. Florine scowls at the comparison as if he has just taken a gulp of curdled milk. "Astroman has nothing on this climb," he boasts with an intentionally controversial smile. The first pitch, he explains, is vintage Valley climbing. "It's pretty darn steep, but you don't have to worm your whole body into the crack." Conversely, says Florine, "The Harding Slot is this sicko, impossible thing."

Florine even delights in the less-intense third, fourth, and fifth pitches of the climb. "To get the full Yosemite experience," he insists, "the climb has to have nice, flat ledges with manzanita trees." Florine points to the topo again. "And here, you get the Yosemite classic ledge with trees on it in between beautiful striking cracks." He continues, "And we haven't gotten to the last four pitches, which are even more classic."

On the start of the seventh pitch, Florine and Harrel were presented with delicate face climbing between two crack systems, a situation that Hans thinks a well-rounded Yosemite climber should know how to deal with. "It's supercommon on Yosemite climbs, where the crux is a face climb between two cracks." After what Florine remembers as "a superfocused 10 feet of sport climbing," he entered the long, pumpy 5.11b thin crack. The "better than Astroman" comparisons continue: "Talk about endurance," he says, "the 11b thin crack goes for at least as far as Astroman's Enduro corner, and then you enter the off-width." Despite the effort required, Florine likes the fact that the off-width can be well protected. He adds, "Non-off-width-savvy people should bring two number 4 Camalots, and a number 5 would not go unused."

The variety continued all the way to the ninth pitch—the 5.11c stemming corner that Florine likens to the nearby classic Bircheff-Williams route. The sustained, calf-burning corner demanded his undivided attention to the bitter end. "The beauty is that the hardest move is the *last move* of the route," he raves, "and it has a definitive platform finish. It's like 'Climb, climb, climb. Done.'"

"So there you have it," concludes Florine, as if he were speaking to a jury. "Beggar's Buttress offers the complete Yosemite experience: It's got a superclean 5.11a dihedral; it's got a flaring bomb-bay chimney; it's got classic Yosemite ledges; it's got off-width, but not disastrous off-width; it's got an enduro 11b finger crack; and an awesome stemming finish—all with consistent 5.10 crack climbing in between!"

ROUTE DESCRIPTION

Area: Yosemite Valley
First ascent: Mark Chapman and Kevin Worrall, May 1976
Difficulty: IV, 5.11c
Time required: 1 long day
Equipment: Double set of Camalots up to no. 4, no. 5 optional; selection of wired nuts; 2 50-m ropes or 1 60-m rope
Season: Spring–fall
Special considerations: This north-facing climb goes into shade early
Reference: *Yosemite Climbs, Free Climbs* by Don Reid

Approach: From State Highway 140 eastbound, park at the west end of the turnout that is .3 mile east of the junction with Highway 141. Cross road, then follow horse trail for ¼ mile or so until intersecting talus field with huge white boulder. Head up talus to first major crack system left of toe of buttress.

Route: Nine pitches of classic, varied Yosemite climbing. Choose from the original start (5.7) or the newer, bolted face to its right.

Descent: Head southwest to find chain rappel anchors. Two 30-m rappels (full 60-m rope required) get you to the Overhanging Bypass approach ledges. From there, trend west and descend the wooded buttress used to approach that route (third class).

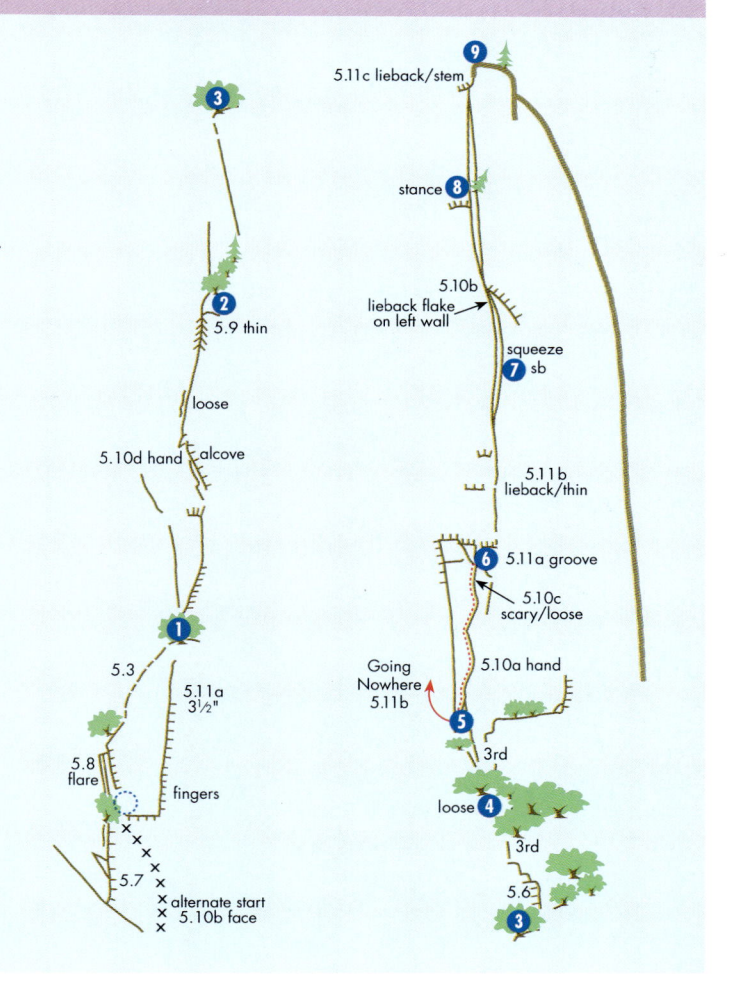

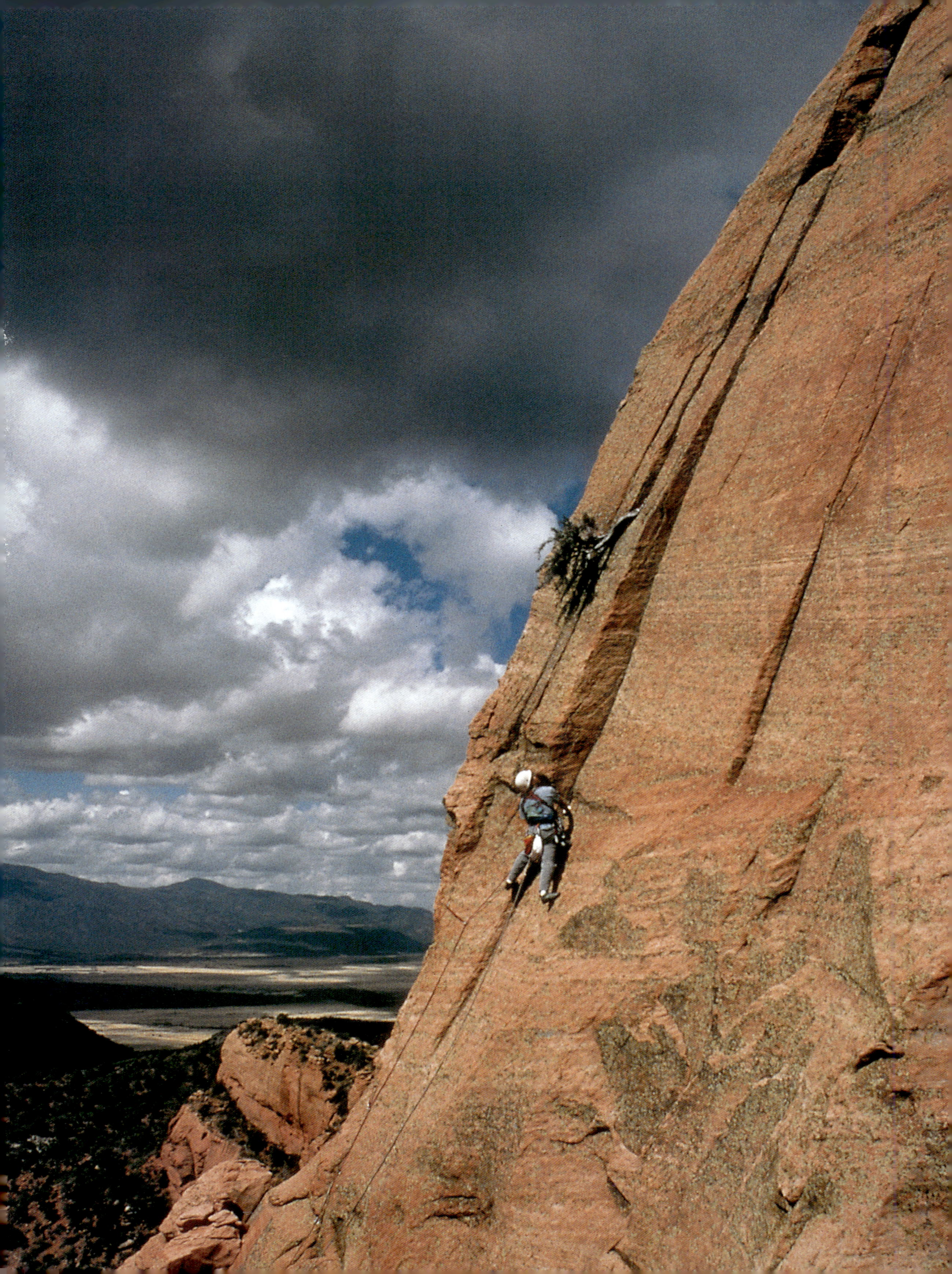

CHARLIE FOWLER

SUNLIGHT BUTTRESS, PARIA POINT, KOLOB CANYONS, ZION NATIONAL PARK, UTAH

CHARLIE FOWLER— UNSWERVING FOCUS

Anyone who believes that all full-time climbers eventually succumb to the security of a regular job and a traditional family life hasn't met Charlie Fowler. Since he started climbing in 1968, the perennially motivated, modern-day Fred Beckey has spent close to 365 days a year fueling his insatiable desire to climb.

Refusing to specialize in a single discipline, Fowler does it all—cracks, sport climbs, big walls, water-ice, high-altitude alpine routes, even nontechnical trekking. And he does it all over the world, all year long. Since his first trip to Patagonia in 1977, he's made dozens of international trips. His wanderlust has taken him to some of the most remote places in the world, including seldom-visited corners of Pakistan, Tibet, Bhutan, Peru, and Bolivia. In 1997 alone, Fowler spent three months in Patagonia and five months in Tibet.

Since Fowler makes his living as a writer and photographer—not a sponsored climber—he doesn't get caught up in industry debates about ratings or the accomplishments of the latest and greatest climbing star. He just climbs. And since he cares more about the experience than the accomplishment, Fowler is happy to climb with partners of all abilities and on routes of all difficulties. He also likes to climb alone. His first of many legendary solo climbs was in 1977, when he climbed the seventeen-pitch Direct North Buttress of Yosemite's Middle Cathedral Rock (V, 5.10) without a rope—on-sight. The daring performance, which he now refers to as "pretty wild," set the tone for the rest of his climbing career.

Now in his late forties, Fowler is in remarkable shape and continues to climb at a high technical standard. When asked about his future plans, he rattles of a list of big objectives in the desert Southwest, Patagonia, and the Himalaya. "Basically," he says with a quiet intensity, "I've got stacks of projects to do."

SUNLIGHT BUTTRESS

Thanks to a flurry of route development in the late '80s and '90s, the breathtaking and compact Zion Canyon has become one of the desert's premier climbing destinations. Where there were once just a few trade routes to fight over, there are now dozens of classic lines for climbers of all abilities to enjoy. Certainly, a zealot with a keen eye can still find new routes to climb, but it's fair to say that most of the obvious lines have been plucked.

Ironically, less than 30 miles from Zion Canyon—and still within the boundaries of Zion National Park—is a relatively overlooked area with unfathomed new route potential. Situated in the northwest corner of the park, the Kolob Canyons are to Zion what Tuolumne Meadows is to Yosemite: a less-crowded but equally spectacular place to extend the climbing season.

In 1992, while driving through Kolob country, Charlie Fowler, Steve Johnson, and Ron Olevsky noticed a striking buttress on a formation called Paria Point. The giant, south-facing hunk of sandstone first made headlines in 1991, when Jeff Lowe and Catherine Destivelle established an eleven-pitch tour de force named Wind, Sand, and Stars (V, 5.12c). The route quickly gained a following among a clan of advanced free climbers but, oddly enough, none of them noticed the line to its right. Even Eric Bjornstad—the Southwest's most prolific first-ascensionist—had missed it. "The funny things is," says Fowler, "it's a pretty darn obvious route. When you drive up the road, you're looking right at it." Realizing that the buttress wouldn't go unnoticed forever, the zealous trio began making plans to climb it.

They made their first visit to the unclimbed buttress later that year, when the crisp autumn days were beginning to smell like winter. They had climbed only two pitches—enough to convince them that the route was every bit as good as it looked—when they were chased off the wall by a sudden storm. Despite the inclement weather, the wall's southern exposure inspired them to name the route Sunlight Buttress. Not only was the appellation descriptive, it made a friendly jab at the ever-popular Moonlight Buttress—another Jeff Lowe creation, and probably the most sought-after climb in Zion National Park. Captivated by what looked like brilliant climbing, they vowed to return as soon as possible.

Fowler spent the next two years on a whirlwind of international trips, missing the prime desert climbing seasons of spring and fall. It wasn't until October 1995 that he, Johnson, and Oleveky found the time to return to their unfinished project. Surprisingly, no one had beat them to it.

Sunlight Buttress follows an obvious, natural line, but was overlooked until 1995. © Charlie Fowler, portrait © Beth Wald

© Charlie Fowler

Sunlight Buttress appealed to Fowler because it promised an interesting variety of climbing, something he has come to appreciate from years of doing first ascents in the desert. "I like sandstone more than any other medium," he explains. "You get everything—cracks, slabs, and faces." The first two pitches of Sunlight Buttress offer an engaging assortment of cracks and face climbing, and from what he remembered, it looked like there was plenty more above that.

Fowler and his partners knew they would have to place numerous bolts on Sunlight Buttress. They figured that most of the belays would need two anchors, and the numerous faces and slabs that connected the discontinuous crack system would require a few dozen more. Because the use of power drills is prohibited in national parks, each ⅜-inch bolt would have to be laboriously hand-drilled—just the thought of it made their hands ache.

Even with three people to share the work, hand drilling is a strenuous, time-consuming endeavor. Anticipating progress of about two pitches per day, the threesome adopted a remarkably civilized approach to the project. Instead of hauling bivy gear and a week's worth of food up the wall, they opted to spend the long autumn nights at Olevsky's house in nearby Toquerville. Each day, after reaching their new high point, they would simply descend a string of fixed ropes to the base of the wall and walk back to the car.

The 90-minute "commute" was a small price to pay for the guarantee of cold beer and a warm bed.

The first two pitches went quickly, leading them to a comfortable stance. Above them, the wall became steeper, reaching an angle Fowler calls "pretty darn vertical." The thin, lightning bolt–shaped crack went free at 5.10+, and was the first of three consecutive pitches of that rating.

Although the technical difficulty was consistent, the nature of the climbing was anything but. The fourth pitch was an entertaining puzzle of technical face moves, requiring six bolts and small wired nuts for protection. Then, as if the climb was pitching change-ups, the next lead followed a thin crack that tested their finger-locking skills.

At the top of the fifth pitch was a commodious ledge that offered a welcome respite from the technical difficulties. The comfortable platform gave them ample time to inspect the sixth pitch, which, in more ways than one, turned out to be the most difficult section of the climb. The steep, delicate face (5.11b) was entirely void of cracks, and required eight bolts for protection. By using sky hooks to climb above each bolt, they avoided the toil of installing a closely spaced bolt ladder.

Above the sixth pitch they could see about 400 feet of mostly 5.9 cracks; it looked like less than a day's worth of climbing. With six demanding pitches and the technical crux behind them, they realized they could complete the route the next day. They spent another comfortable night at Ron's house, but awoke extra early to make the ever-lengthening approach to their high point. A few hours of vigorous Jumaring put them at the top of the sixth pitch.

From there, they climbed the final three pitches—5.9+, 5.9, and 5.10—without incident.

After 5 days and forty-three bolt holes, their new route was completed. "It was a lot of hard work," shrugs Fowler, "but it's definitely my favorite desert climb—so far."

ROUTE DESCRIPTION

Area: Kolob Canyons
First ascent: Charlie Fowler, Steve Johnson, and Ron Olevsky, October 1995
Base elevation: Approximately 6,500 feet
Summit elevation: Approximately 8,000 feet
Difficulty: IV, 5.8, C1 or 5.11b
Time required: 1 long day
Equipment: 1 60-m rope, 2 sets of Camalots to no. 4 (no. 5 optional for pitch 5), 2 sets of wired nuts, set of RPs, extra small cams, 12 quick draws, 1 regular Chouinard hook for aid climbing between bolts on crux sixth pitch
Season: Spring and fall
Special considerations: Be prepared for a desert climate: sun, heat, snakes; spring is better because of longer days; Kolob is about 3,000 feet higher than Zion, allowing for comfortable climbing well into June; there are several good ledges for slower parties; bivouac permits are required
References: *American Alpine Journal* (1996, p. 157); *Desert Rock*, vol. I, by Eric Bjornstad

Approach: Kolob Canyons is in the western part of Zion National Park, about a 3-hour drive from Las Vegas, Nevada. Take Utah Highway 9 west to its junction with Utah Highway 17. Drive north on Highway 17 for about 13 miles to the Kolob Canyons exit. Park at the pullout where the road switchbacks near Paria Point. Follow the trail upcanyon, slightly right of Sunlight Buttress. Ascend a hillside, then third- and fourth-class slabs, to a notch. From the notch, descend left toward the base of the route. Allow an hour.

Route: A nine-pitch desert classic featuring a wide variety of crack and face climbing, with outstanding desert ambience.

Descent: Seven rappels down the route.

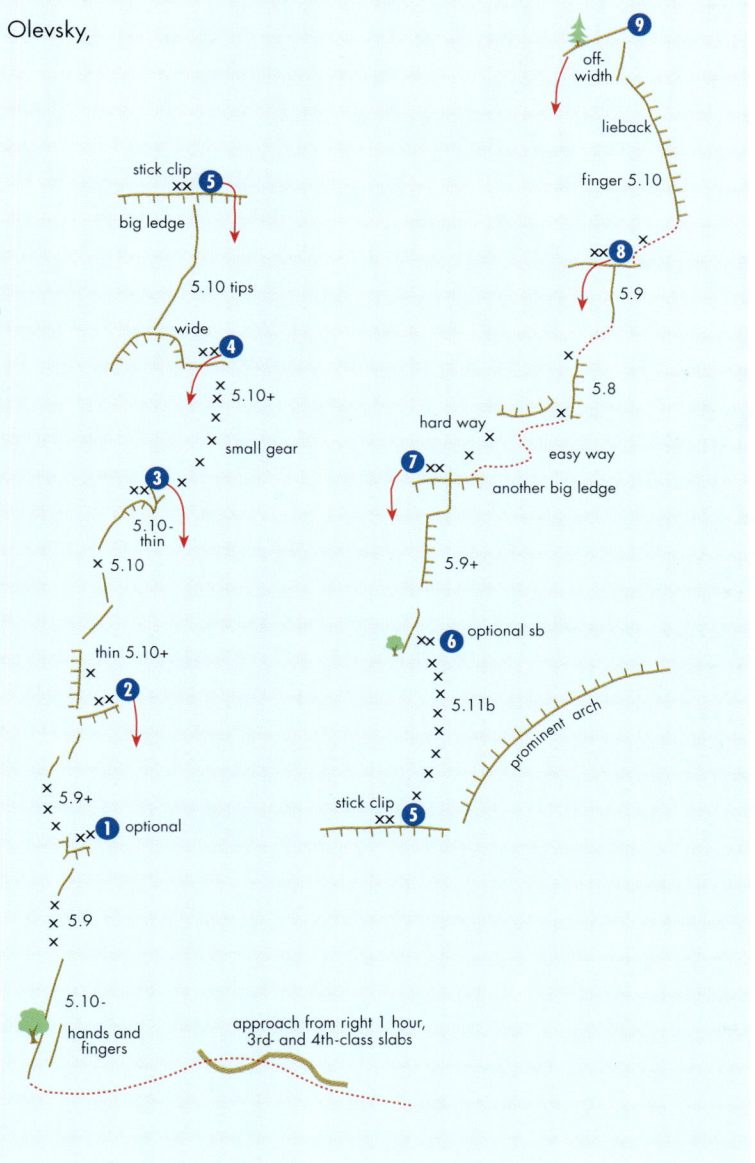

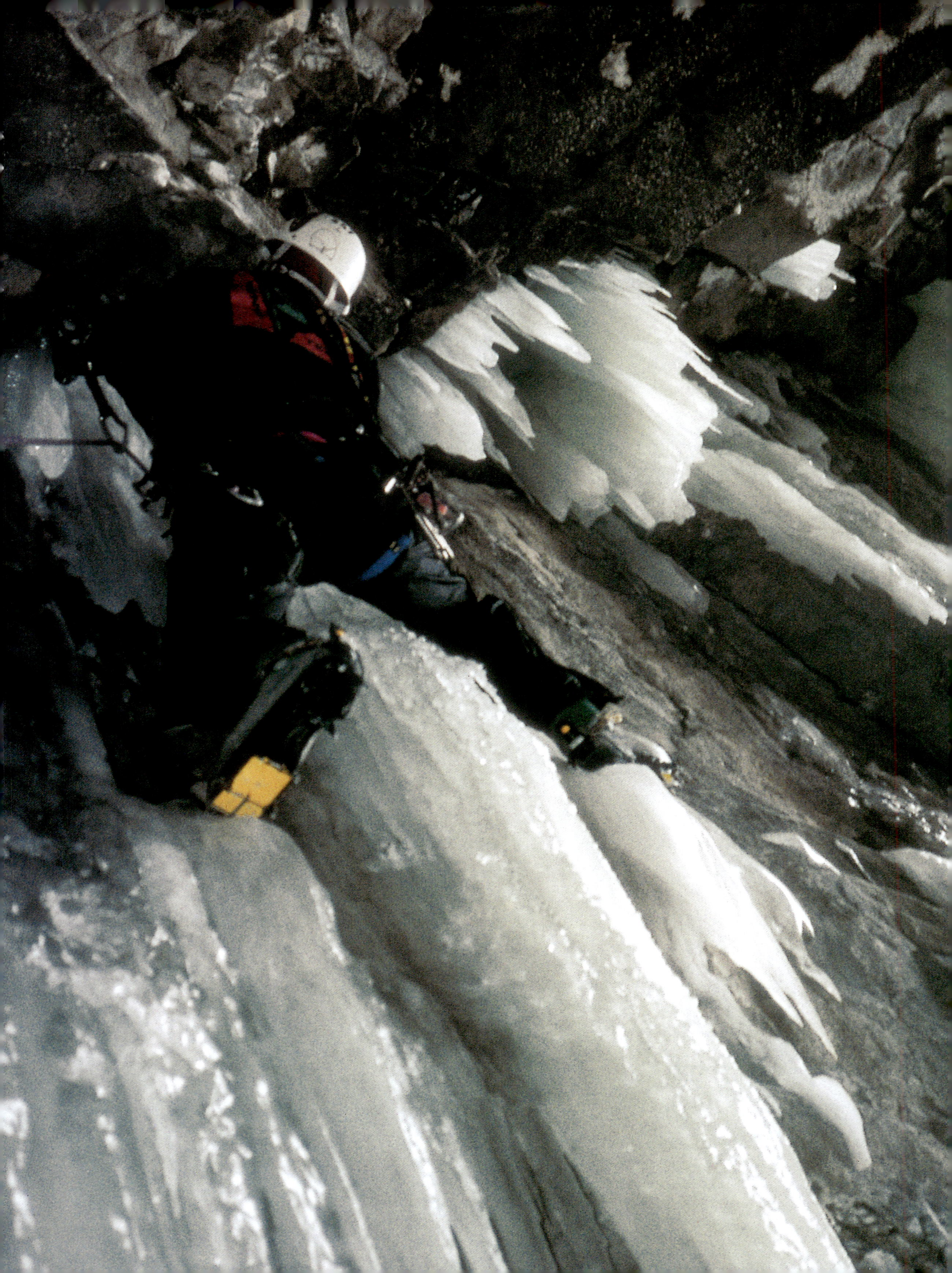

WILL GADD

DEEP THROAT, GLENWOOD CANYON, COLORADO

WILL GADD—THE ULTIMATE GENERALIST

Will Gadd is one of those guys you'd love to hate. He's talented, energetic, smart, articulate, and—wouldn't you know it—modest. He participates at an expert level in at least nine outdoor sports, and dabbles in a half dozen others. Reading his resumé is not only inspiring, but entertaining. Under the heading of "Primary Sports Skills," you'll find pithy statements such as:

Rock Climbing: Up to 5.14, sport and traditional.
Ice Climbing: Climbed first waterfall at age twelve; placed first in every major ice competition in the world in '98 and '99 (ESPN X Games, Courchevel Invitational, France). Won the 2000 World Cup.
Paragliding: Former world distance record holder, 179 miles.
In-Line Skating: Not very good, but can do a weak frontside grind if pressed.
Mountain Biking: Occasional sport-class racer, 16-inch log hop.
Kayaking: Kayaking since age fourteen, solid wilderness and rodeo boater.
Caving: Numerous expeditions in Canada and the United States. Lots of vertical experience.
Other Sports: Scuba certified, hack sailor, lousy but psyched surfer, dynamic snowboarder.
Other: Dual U.S./Canadian citizen. Can get to the airport in almost every major North American and European city. Can hack at Spanish and French, and live on chile peppers and coffee.

In our increasingly specialized world, Gadd is the ultimate generalist. His freakish ability to quickly master new sports has earned him the respect of even the most die-hard specialists. What's his secret? Gadd gives his parents, who are climbers themselves, much of the credit. While living in Jasper, Alberta, they introduced Gadd and his brother to every outdoor activity imaginable. In fact, Gadd's first exposure to rock climbing was in the womb. His mom climbed until she was eight months pregnant, stopping only when she could no longer see her feet. Says Gadd, "I guess I got the intense gene."

DEEP THROAT

Shortly after Will Gadd climbed the Canadian ice classic Polar Circus in 1985, he pronounced the sport of ice climbing dead. Advances in equipment, he felt, had reduced the once-challenging route to a casual outing. When he realized there wasn't a frozen waterfall he couldn't climb, the sport suddenly seemed boring. He sold his ice tools and moved on.

Gadd spent the next twelve years pursing other challenges. He got into sport climbing, paragliding, whitewater kayaking, mountain running, general mountaineering, and more. Not surprisingly, he did them all extremely well. Whenever he got "bored" (achieved expert status), he would simply try something new—just what you'd expect from a fast learner with the outdoor version of attention deficit disorder.

By early 1997, after mastering another half dozen sports, Gadd was getting itchy. While contemplating his next challenge, he came across a copy of Jeff Lowe's (see Climb 29) recently published *Ice World*. The book's cover captured his imagination: On it was a spectacular picture of the author doing an overhanging "mixed" route in Vail named Octopussy. His picks and crampons were being used not only to hang from the ice, but also from small edges and cracks in the rock. Lowe's book explained that this new-age hybrid of rock and ice climbing was called mixed climbing. Gadd was intrigued. "It opened my eyes to a whole new world of possibilities," he remembers. "When I quit ice climbing in the mid-'80s, I thought I was bored. But I just didn't have the vision to see where it could go."

Gadd became interested enough to equip himself with the latest gear and try a few mixed routes with fellow alpinist Mark Twight (see Climb 47). "That got me really fired up," he recalls. "I realized that anything was possible, and that we were in the Golden Age of mixed climbing." And that's all it took. As if he were simply changing channels, Gadd shifted his focus to mixed climbing.

It didn't take long for him to hook up with fellow Coloradian

Jeff Lowe trying not to get spit out of Deep Throat. "It's like being inside the mouth of a crocodile," says Gadd. © Will Gadd, portrait © Beth Wald

© Will Gadd

Jeff Lowe, the sport's most persuasive advocate. Lowe had been focused on mixed climbing since 1992, when a trip to Europe awakened him to its unfathomed potential. Since then, he'd been looking at everything with a different set of eyes. He saw new routes everywhere—even in areas that were considered "climbed out."

One such place is Glenwood Canyon on Colorado's Interstate 70. In January 1997, while driving to the Ouray Ice Festival (an annual event that he organizes), Lowe noticed a prominent corner system on the south side of the freeway. A discontinuous runnel of ice clung to its upper half, but stopped just above a large, shady cave. Below it was several hundred feet of mostly dry limestone. Depending on one's perspective, it was either a few pitches of mediocre rock, an improbable ice route, or the perfect mixed climb. Most climbers wouldn't have given the route a second look, but through the eyes of a mixed climber it looked irresistible. "When I saw that the route was in," says Lowe, "I asked Will to meet me there in 3 days." Gadd jumped at the chance.

The first pitch was what Gadd calls "high-grade Rockies choss"—sparely protected 5.8+ climbing on steep rock. Since it was totally void of ice, they climbed it without crampons. "It was a fun, full-length pitch with a nice belay stance—basically rock climbing in mountain boots," recalls Gadd.

Next was a transition pitch that followed a thin smear of ice up the corner system. "It was a total grin," remembers Gadd. "The gear was adequate—cams, a few stubby ice screws, a few pitons—and the climbing was really beautiful. But the whole time I was looking up at the third pitch. It's this maw, this big cave-thing that hangs out above you. When you reach the belay, it feels like you're inside of the mouth of a crocodile."

On the floor of the cave, Lowe and Gadd stood under a canopy of stalactitelike ice daggers that threatened to reduce them to Sloppy Joe mix. Lowe, who is a veteran of hundreds of mixed climbs, says it's the most unique belay ledge he's ever stood on. "You're staring out at this constellation of icicles, the walls are overhanging in all directions, and you have no idea where to begin."

Because he had spotted the climb, Lowe elected to lead the crux pitch. From the belay stance in the "throat" of the cave, he began a 40-foot diagonal traverse toward its mouth. Every inch of progress was hard fought. Using cracks in the rock for protection, he wove his way through the icy fangs making sure to only hang from the big ones. Clearing icicles out of his way was exhausting and time consuming—it was almost dark when he reached the mouth of the cave. With half the pitch still to climb, he decided to leave the gear in place and come back the next day.

When they returned to Deep Throat the following morning, Lowe offered his partner a chance to lead the third pitch. Gadd accepted without hesitation. Following Lowe's path from the previous day, he made good progress to the lip of the cave. But when he pulled over the roof, he could see that the difficulties were far from over. Above him was a 100-foot series of ice curtains that hung from the overhanging wall like chandeliers. Alternating between the rock and the ice, it took him 4 hours to complete the pitch. "The climbing was really strenuous and the gear was really intricate," remembers Gadd. "I was totally worked—but it's still the best pitch I've ever done."

Prior to climbing Deep Throat, Gadd had hardly climbed in

four years. Since making the ascent, however, he's hardly stopped, and credits mixed climbing with renewing his enthusiasm. "I'll climb anything, even bridge abutments with glue-on holds," quips Gadd. "But mixed climbing is my favorite discipline. It's the most fun because it has the fewest rules—sort of like professional wrestling compared to boxing."

ROUTE DESCRIPTION

Area: Interstate 70, Colorado
First ascent: Will Gadd and Jeff Lowe, January 1997
Difficulty: IV, 5.9, WI 6, M7
Time required: 1 full day
Equipment: 2 60-m ropes; 6–8 ice screws, mostly short; 8–10 pitons, mostly thin; set of TCUs and cams to 2 inches; a few Spectre hooks; ice tools and crampons suitable for dry tooling
Season: December–March, although it does not form every year.
Special considerations: Depending on conditions, third pitch can be very run out, but is steep enough to be safe
Reference: *Colorado Ice* by Jack Roberts (Polar Star Communications, 1998)

Approach: From Denver, drive west on Inerstate 70 to exit 125, and park at the Hidden Lake turnoff. This is a westbound-only exit; eastbound traffic must go to the next exit and loop around. The route is located left of the main Glenwood Icefall (left) route. Approach as for Glenwood Falls but continue past this climb and go uphill for another 20 minutes, following a field of scree and talus until at the base of the main wall. Deep Throat follows the chimney/dihedral system found here.

Route: Three long, involved, intricate pitches; a modern classic for accomplished mixed climbers. Pitch one is mainly rock, M4, 5.8. Pitch two is WI 5+, M5. Pitch three is WI 6, M7.

Descent: Rappel the route. The first-ascent party left fixed anchors at the top of each pitch. In order to rappel from the top of the third pitch, a trail rope must be fixed to the top of the second pitch. This is used to pull the climbers from the lip back into the throat of the cave.

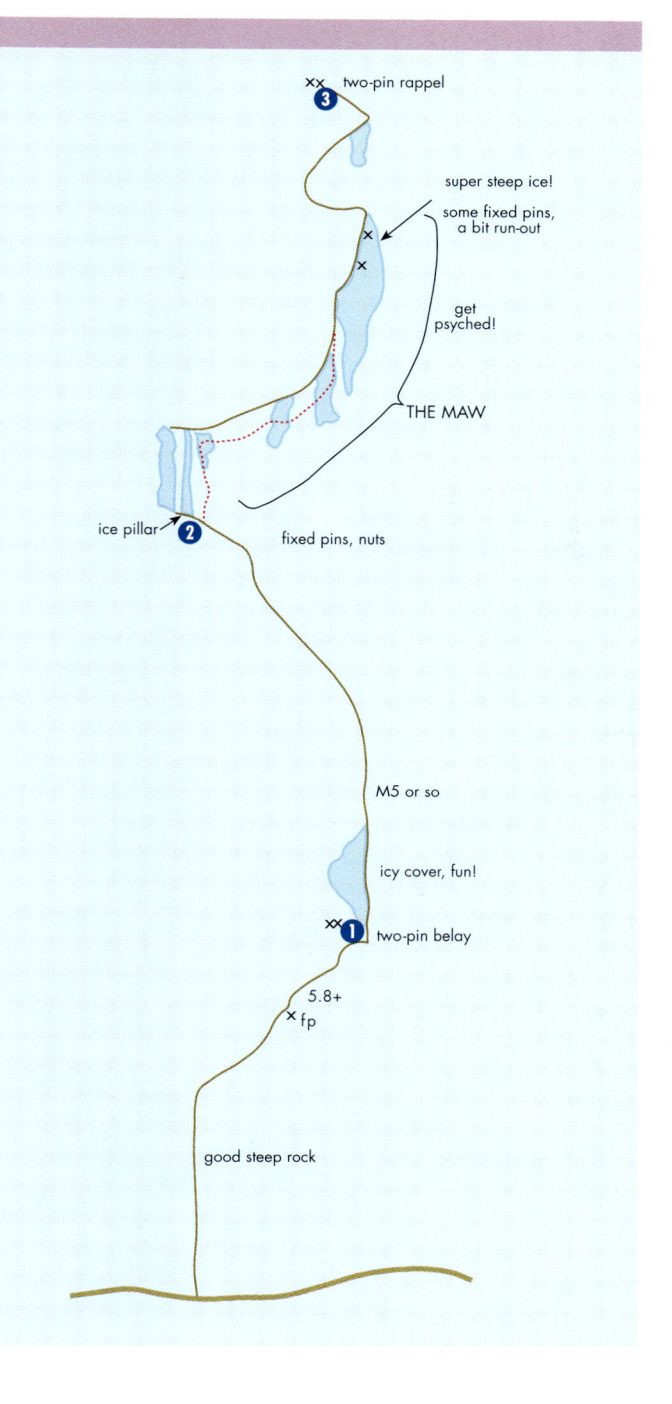

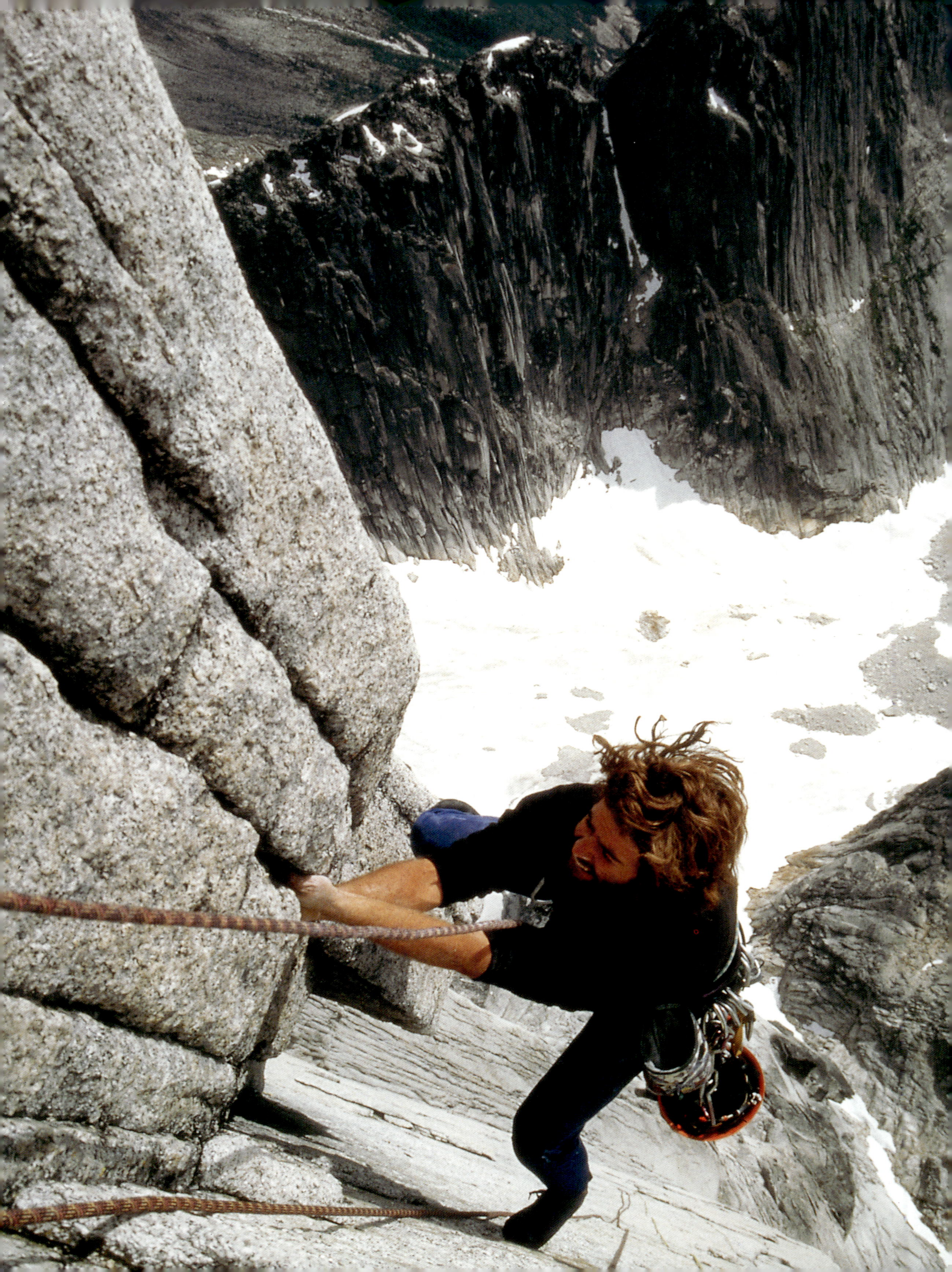

KENNAN HARVEY

ALL ALONG THE WATCHTOWER, NORTH HOWSER TOWER, BUGABOO GLACIER PROVINCIAL PARK, BRITISH COLUMBIA

KENNAN HARVEY—
THE CALL OF THE WILD

Kennan Harvey is a climber and photographer who loves true wilderness. His images capture a vast, untamed world that very few people—climbers included—ever experience, from giant granite towers in the Karakorum to wild, unexplored peaks in Alaska. "I've always been driven to do things that are elegant, beautiful, and wild," says Harvey. "I'm not into culture or crowded cities."

Harvey's quest for raw adventure is backed by well-rounded technical and backcountry skills. Pick a medium—granite off-widths, limestone pockets, sandstone splitters—and Harvey can on-sight 5.12. Water ice and mixed terrain? He's done plenty. And on foot, he has a remarkable tolerance for long approaches and heavy packs. His second-place finish in the 1996 Survival of the Fittest contest says it all: He's a master generalist.

The common thread in Harvey's resume is wilderness adventure. Never one to take the easy route, he climbed Mount Waddington while on a 300-mile ski traverse of British Columbia's Coast Range. In Pakistan, Harvey joined Steph Davis (see Climb 13) and Seth Shaw (see Climb 38) for a 14-day, virtually free ascent of 4,300-foot Shipton Spire via a new route dubbed Inshalla (VII, 5.12, 10 feet of A1). And in Alaska, he and Topher Donahue were the first to explore the 5,000-foot north face of Mount Neacola (they climbed most of the route in a 24-hour push before being shut down by weather).

When Harvey does go to a popular climbing area, he still finds a way to make it interesting. On the Longs Peak Diamond in Colorado, he made a winter ascent of D7 (5.11 in summer conditions), solo, in a record-setting 17-hour car-to-car push. When asked about the adventure, Harvey described it as "pretty wild"—just how he likes it.

ALL ALONG THE WATCHTOWER

When Fred Beckey and Yvon Chouinard made the first ascent of the 2,000-foot West Buttress of South Howser Tower in 1961, they bequeathed the climbing community with a timeless classic: nineteen pitches of moderate climbing on perfect alpine granite in a dramatic glacial setting. Four decades and hundreds of ascents later, the sweeping ridge remains the most sought-after climb in the Bugaboos.

With so much focus on the Beckey/Chouinard route, the even more impressive west face of North Howser Tower wasn't explored for another ten years. Between 1971 and 1981, just four routes were added, All Along the Watchtower among them. There wasn't any new route activity on the west face of North Howser Tower for another thirteen years. Two new lines were added in 1994, but the face still lacked an all-free route. North Howser's serious, Patagonian feel detracted from its popularity. The more accessible and friendly Beckey/Chouinard route continued to be the primary objective on the Howser massif.

In 1995, when Topher Donahue read an account of the first ascent of All Along the Watchtower, he took note of the author's comments on its potential as a free route. Climbing at a reasonable 5.10 standard, the first-ascent party free climbed seventeen of the route's twenty-three pitches, aid climbing only in the flawless, 800-foot dihedral. The article suggested that the soaring corner was ripe for a free ascent. Intrigued, he asked longtime partner Kennan Harvey if he was interested.

Even though some Canadians told him the route was impossible, Harvey was game. The adventure had everything he was looking for: impeccable rock, length, difficulty, a wilderness setting, and the perfect partner. He'd done some of his most memorable climbs with Donahue, including a 50-hour ascent of the 4,500-foot north pillar of Fitzroy in Patagonia.

The weather in the Bugaboos isn't known to be great, but it's better than in Patagonia. The windows of high pressure are longer, and the storms less severe. Knowing this, Donahue and Harvey made a conscious decision to sacrifice the speed of their ascent for the enjoyment of free climbing. Rather than whizzing up the route as fast as possible—where the leader pulls on gear using the so-called "French free" technique and the follower ascends a fixed rope with Jumars—they decided to free-climb the entire route. The leader and follower would both take the time to work out every move.

The first ten pitches of "cruisy 5.9 and 5.10" went quickly, ending at a comfortable ledge. Since they were traveling light—without sleeping bags—hauling the pack was easy too. But getting

Topher Donahue pulling through the 5.12 crux on the first free ascent of All Along the Watchtower © Kennan Harvey, portrait © Jeff Achey

North Howser Tower
Central Howser Tower
South Howser Tower

© Randall Green

a full night's sleep was another story: With only their clothes and a thin Gore-Tex bivy bag between them and the elements, the 10 hours of darkness were reduced to a series of short naps, interrupted by occasional bouts of shivering. The climbers boiled water during the night to fend off the cold. "A hot water bottle on your belly can keep you pretty warm," says Harvey, a notorious minimalist. "It's not luxury, but a stove weighs a lot less than two sleeping bags."

Four more pitches led them to the base of the seemingly endless, 800-foot dihedral. They stared at the perfect corner in awe, and felt lucky to be there. "We were dumbfounded that something so long and beautiful hadn't been freed," says Harvey. "It's the quintessential free-climbing feature."

Swapping leads, the veteran climbers made steady progress up the clean, symmetrical corner. "The rock was perfect," remembers Harvey. "It didn't need a bit of cleaning and the protection was solid." The long and increasingly difficult pitches tested their stemming skills as well as their jamming technique. On the nineteenth pitch, the dihedral jogs left for 20 feet before resuming its upward path. As Harvey approached the traverse, he could tell it was going to be difficult.

Not only was the traverse virtually featureless, it was wet. Determined to climb it free, Harvey started by aiding across the seeping arch, using his tee shirt and chalk ball to dry key footholds. Once the pitch was "prepared," he lowered back to the beginning for a free attempt. He almost got through the crux on his first try, but fell when a small nubbin broke. He succeeded—just barely—on his third try, "grunting and thrutching" the entire way.

After successfully following the crux, Donahue summoned the energy for his last hard lead. He completed the sustained 5.11c pitch without incident, and was relieved to see easier ground above. Although he and Harvey could have raced to the summit and descended in the dark, they decided to savor their success with another night on the tower. It was cold, but sleep came easily.

When they reached the summit the following morning, Harvey and Donahue were greeted by a mysterious rack of hardware, parts of which were frozen under a translucent sheet of ice. They took what they could and left the rest. As they rappelled down the east face of the tower, still more camming devices appeared. "We were giddy about finding all this free gear," explains Harvey. "But we also had this eerie feeling that there had been some sort of epic." They found out what happened soon enough.

As it turns out, the abandoned rack was left by Warren Hollinger and Jerry Gore in 1994. After completing a new route on the west face of North Howser, they were caught on the summit in a violent electrical storm. Hollinger got zapped by lightning and suffered temporary paralysis. Ten hours later, after regaining feeling in his legs, he and Gore fled the scene, sans hardware. They named their new route Young Men on Fire.

Back in the States, Harvey phoned Hollinger and offered to return the gear. Not surprisingly, Hollinger wanted nothing to do with it.

ROUTE DESCRIPTION

Area: West face of North Howser Tower, Bugaboos
First ascent: W. Robinson and J. Walseth, August 1981; first free ascent: Topher Donahue and Kennan Harvey, August 13–15, 1996
Base elevation: 8,350 feet
Summit elevation: 11,150 feet
Difficulty: VI, 5.10, A2 or 5.12
Time required: 4–6 days round trip from Conrad Kain Hut, 2–4 days on route
Equipment: Large free-climbing rack with extra small gear: 3 sets of TCUs to no. 3; 2 sets of cams to 3 inches, 1 no. 3.5 and no. 4 Friend or equivalent; 2 sets of wires with extra RPs (or equivalent brass nuts); 2 knifeblade and 2 lost arrow pitons (optional); 2 60-m ropes, bivy gear, no portaledge; boots, crampons, and an ice tool useful on approach and descent
Season: July–August
Special considerations: Beware of rockfall and thunderstorms
Reference: *Bugaboo Rock, A Climber's Guide* by Randall Green and Joe Bensen

Approach: Bugaboo Provincial Park is located in southeastern British Columbia. Follow Highway 95 north to Radium Hot Springs, then continue 16.7 miles north to Brisco. Follow signs to the Bugaboo Alpine Recreation Area, which takes you left (west) on a good gravel road for 28 miles (beware of logging trucks). From the trailhead, hike 3 miles to the Conrad Kain Hut. From the hut, hike through the Bugaboo/Snowpatch Col, then cross the upper Vowell Glacier. To reach the west side of the North Tower, take the second obvious notch to the north of the main North Howser summit. Allow 4–6 hours from the hut.

Route: A spectacular climb on outstanding granite—worth doing all free or otherwise. Of twenty-three pitches, seventeen are 5.10 or easier. See topo.

Descent: Rappel the east face (the easiest ascent route, 5.4) to the glacier. Crossing the bergschrund usually requires an additional rappel.

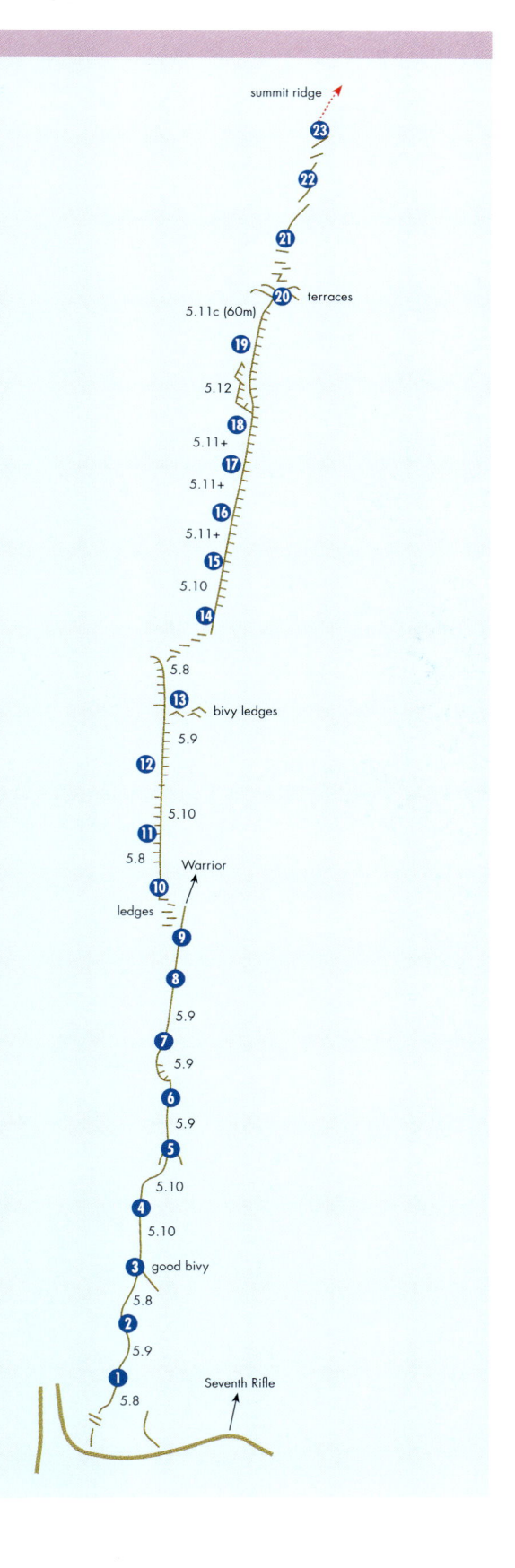

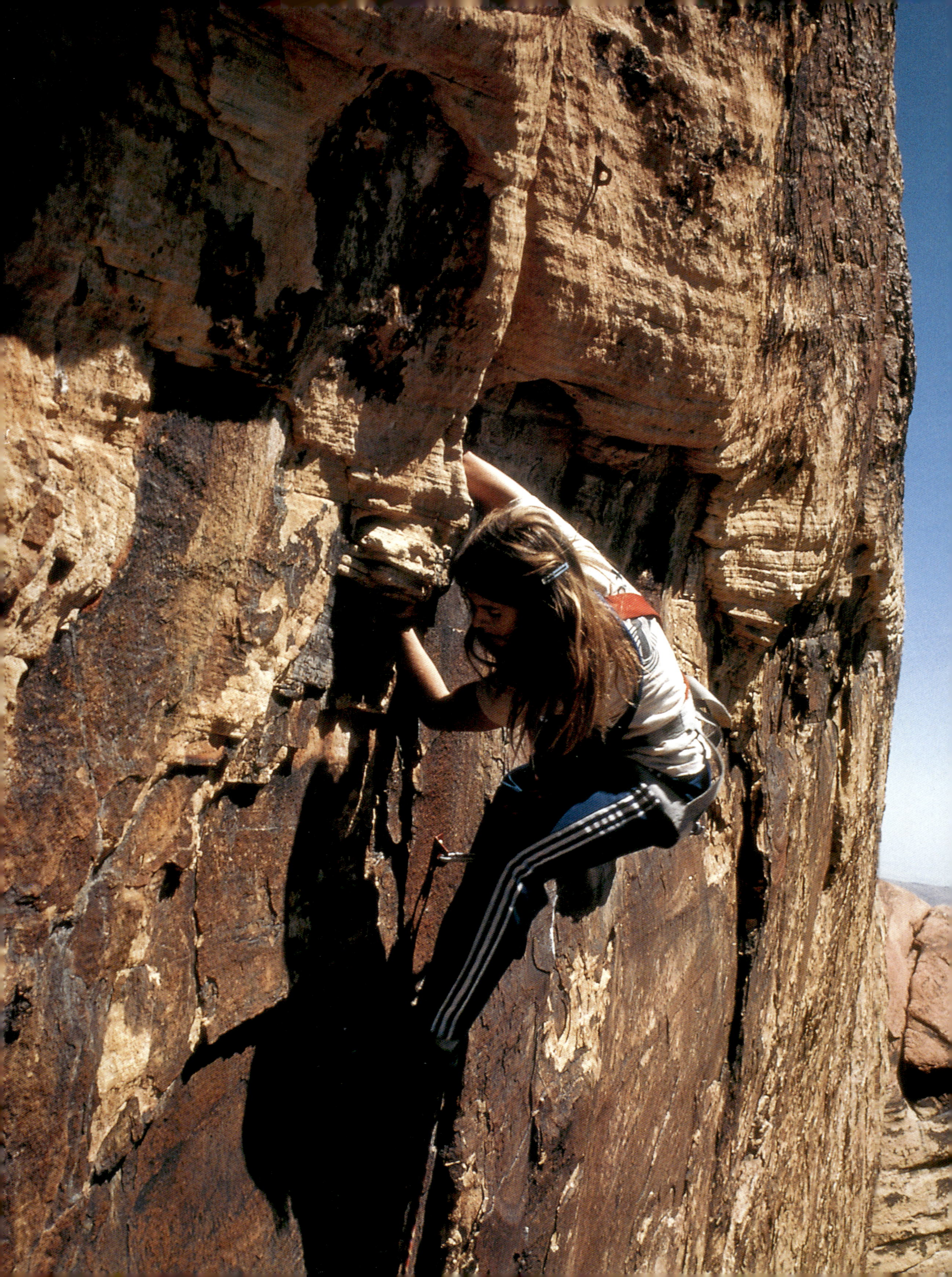

LYNN HILL
LEVITATION 29, RED ROCKS NATIONAL CONSERVATION AREA, NEVADA

LYNN HILL—
DOING THE IMPOSSIBLE

If you haven't met her, then you've probably seen a poster of her in your local mountaineering shop. She's the one clinging to a steep rock face, looking exceedingly calm as her lithe body hangs from an impossible-looking overhang. She's the one climbing in places you've never heard of and doing routes you've only dreamed of. She's Lynn Hill—the world's most accomplished female rock climber.

Hill's climbing career started early. She grew up in the L.A. suburbs, excelled at gymnastics, then found rock climbing at age fourteen. She spent her formative years in traditional areas with old-school ethics: Joshua Tree, Taquitz, and Yosemite. In 1977, at age seventeen, she climbed the Northwest Face of Half Dome, her first big wall. Two years later, Hill and partner Mari Gingery made the first all-female ascent of the Shield on El Capitan, then a serious aid route. She continued climbing through college, supporting her habit with prize money from four consecutive Survival of the Fittest contest victories.

In 1983, Hill went to New York's Shawangunks for a one-week photo shoot—and stayed for eight years. There, she made many bold ascents, including Yellow Crack Direct (5.12c, X; unrepeated) and Vandals, the 'Gunks' first 5.13. Once a die-hard traditionalist, Hill learned to appreciate the merits of sport climbing on a 1986 visit to Europe. That year she entered her first competition in Arco, Italy, and dominated women's competitive climbing until retiring from the World Cup in 1992. (She also climbed harder than most of the male competitors. In the 1990 World Cup in Lyon, France, only Hill and two men completed the finals route.)

In 1993, Hill returned to her roots—adventurous climbs in beautiful settings with close friends. She started with a feat many considered impossible: the first free ascent of the Nose of El Capitan. Then she took her skills abroad, establishing difficult routes in places as exotic and diverse as Kyrgyzstan, Vietnam, Scotland, Morocco, Madagascar, Thailand, and Sardinia. Her globe-trotting lifestyle suits her indomitable spirit. Says Hill, "I love to explore new places and climb things that have never been climbed—especially when someone tells me it's impossible."

LEVITATION 29

In July 1992, about the time she was thinking about retiring from World Cup competition, Lynn Hill spent a few weeks climbing in Yosemite. During her visit she hooked up with speed-climbing ace Hans Florine for a quick romp up the Nose of El Capitan. To ensure a fast ascent, they used a combination of free- and aid-climbing tactics, and often simul-climbed. But on the twenty-third pitch—the famous Great Roof—they took their time. As Hill aid-climbed across the shady overhang, she slid her fingers through the narrow crack and carefully inspected the face for tiny footholds. She was trying to decide if the once-considered "impossible" Great Roof pitch could be climbed free. She concluded it was at least worth a try.

The rest of the story, as they say, is history. Hill retired from competitive climbing and returned to Yosemite in 1993. Over the course a few weeks, she managed to free all thirty-four pitches on the Nose. And if that wasn't enough, in 1994 she did it again—but in a day. Her all-free (5.13c), 1-day ascent is arguably the greatest achievement in the history of rock climbing, by a man or woman. (It was six years before the coveted "first male ascent" was made by Scott Burke after an absurd 261 days on the route.)

Hill's feat solidified her standing as the best all-around female rock climber in the world and, more importantly, represented a turning point in her career. After years of training and competing on artificial walls, she realized how much she'd drifted from the type of climbing that attracted her to the sport in the first place. "I got sucked into the whole trend toward competition and plastic," explains Hill. "But that's not what I started out doing, or what I enjoy doing the most. To me, climbing is about adventure and exploring beautiful places with my friends."

Hill's 1981 ascent of Levitation 29 exemplified the roots she envisioned returning to: It was a long, aesthetic free climb in a beautiful setting. It was a grand adventure shared with a few close friends. And, although she didn't realize it until years later, it was a formative experience that embodied what she loved about climbing.

Young and restless: Lynn Hill making the first free ascent of Levitation 29 in 1981. She led the crux pitch (5.11c), on-sight. © Jorge Urioste, portrait © Greg Epperson

Hill first climbed Levitation 29 just a month after its original ascent. The route was established over a period of two months by a prolific Las Vegas couple, Jorge and Joanne Urioste. According to Jorge, they started "construction" on the route in February 1981, and worked on it every weekend for two months. The middle of the route was steeper than anything they'd ever done; they joked that only a person who could levitate would be able to climb it free. When they finally completed the project on April 5, which was Joanne's twenty-ninth birthday, they named the route Levitation 29.

At the time, Lynn Hill and her then-boyfriend John Long were nearing the end of a nine-month stint in Las Vegas. Hill had already gained a reputation as a fantastic climber, and Long, who was a member of the historic "Nose-in-a-day" team from 1975, was even more well known. The Uriostes were anxious to share their magnum opus with other climbers, especially such a high-caliber team. If anyone could climb Levitation 29 free, they figured, it was Hill and Long. They invited them to give it a try in early May.

Compared to the more popular cliffs near Red Rocks' roadside "pullouts," Levitation 29 is a backcountry experience. The climb is nestled deep in Oak Creek Canyon, miles from the main road. "It's an amazing wilderness for being only 20 miles from the Las Vegas strip," says Hill. "There are bighorn sheep and ring-tailed cats, things you normally don't see." Levitation 29 is also notorious for its confusing approach that—depending on one's route-finding skills—takes from 2 to 4 hours.

Fortunately for Hill and Long, the Uriostes were able to lead them right to the base of the route. When they arrived, they stood below an enormous rainbow of sandstone with an obvious system of cracks just right of center. As Hill's well-trained eye followed the line toward the top of the cliff, she could see that Levitation 29 was blessed with highly varnished Wingate sandstone—the best stuff at Red Rocks. Solid rock means solid protection and, thanks to the Uriostes, the belays were already in place. All they had to do was climb.

Sensing that something historic was going to happen, Jorge decided to spend the day taking pictures instead of climbing. Using the fixed ropes that were still in place from the original ascent, he was able to Jumar ahead of the climbers with his camera. Like a proud father, he documented the entire event.

Lynn Hill starting up the first pitch of Levitation 29 © Jorge Urioste

Unlike many first free ascents, which are remembered for scary leads and heroic falls, Hill and Long's ascent of Levitation 29 was remarkably uneventful. The climbing was challenging—even difficult at times—but every pitch was led free, with no falls, on the first try. The fifth pitch turned out to be the technical and mental crux: Since it was the only pitch that the Uriostes hadn't attempted to free-climb with a top rope on the original ascent, they had no idea how hard it would be.

Hill, who is especially good at on-sight leads, volunteered to lead the fifth pitch. Because there were no chalk marks to follow, she would sometimes hang from crimpy, forearms-draining holds for several minutes while working through a tricky sequence of moves. Jorge, who was dangling just a few feet above her, marveled at her endurance. "One thing that was really impressive was the power of Lynn's arms," he remembers. "On that pitch, you are always on your arms, and Lynn did it beautifully. It was amazing to watch."

The last half of the climb was slightly easier, but still demanded their full attention. With each new pitch came even better views of the surrounding landscape. They could even see the neon glow of the Las Vegas strip when they reached the top of the dome in the late afternoon.

Levitation 29 has been climbed hundreds of times since Hill's free ascent in 1981. Her advocacy has played a big part in the route's popularity. "I recommend it to a lot of people," says Hill. "It's in a beautiful setting. There is lots of aesthetic movement. And the climbing is consistently in the 5.10 range, with only a short bit of 5.11 that can be aided if necessary. It's the perfect all-day route."

ROUTE DESCRIPTION

Area: Oak Creek Canyon, Red Rocks
First ascent: Jorge Urioste, Joanne Urioste, and Bill Bradley, April 1981; first free ascent: Lynn Hill, Joanne Urioste, and John Long, May 1981
Difficulty: IV, 5.11
Time required: 1 long day
Equipment: TCUs and camming devices to 3 inches, assorted wired nuts, 12 quick draws; 2 ropes, 50-m OK
Season: Spring and fall
Special considerations: Approach can be tricky, keen route-finding skills required; spring ideal because of longer days
Reference: *Rock Climbing, Red Rocks* by Todd Swain

Approach: There are two ways to reach Oak Creek Canyon. The first is from the Oak Creek Canyon parking area, just off the scenic loop road, off Nevada Highway 159. This approach is shorter, but requires parties to exit the loop road before dark, or get locked in. Alternatively, reach the canyon mouth via the old Oak Creek Road, which begins at the old Oak Creek Campground, located 1.4 miles south of the exit of the loop road. Either approach takes you to a huge dirt mound at the canyon mouth called the Wilson Pimple. From it, follow a roadbed or trail up the canyon for about an hour, then cut back right (north) when the canyon splits. Continue until a large, slabby ramp leads up and right toward a huge cliffband. From the top of the ramp, descend 400 feet to the start of the route.

Route: Nine outstanding pitches of varied sandstone climbing, with only two pitches of 5.11. See topo for details.

Descent: Either rappel from the top of the seventh pitch, or walk off to the left, making a giant, U-shaped route to the Oak Creek drainage (30 minutes). Follow the drainage east back to the canyon mouth.

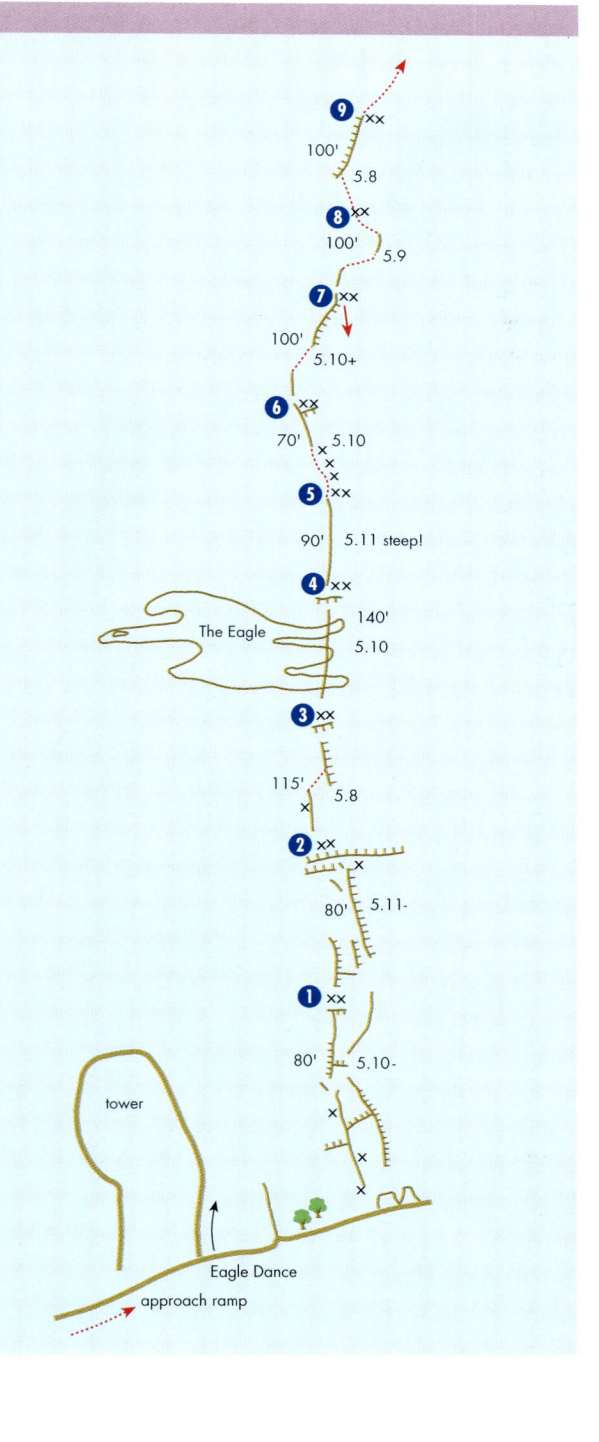

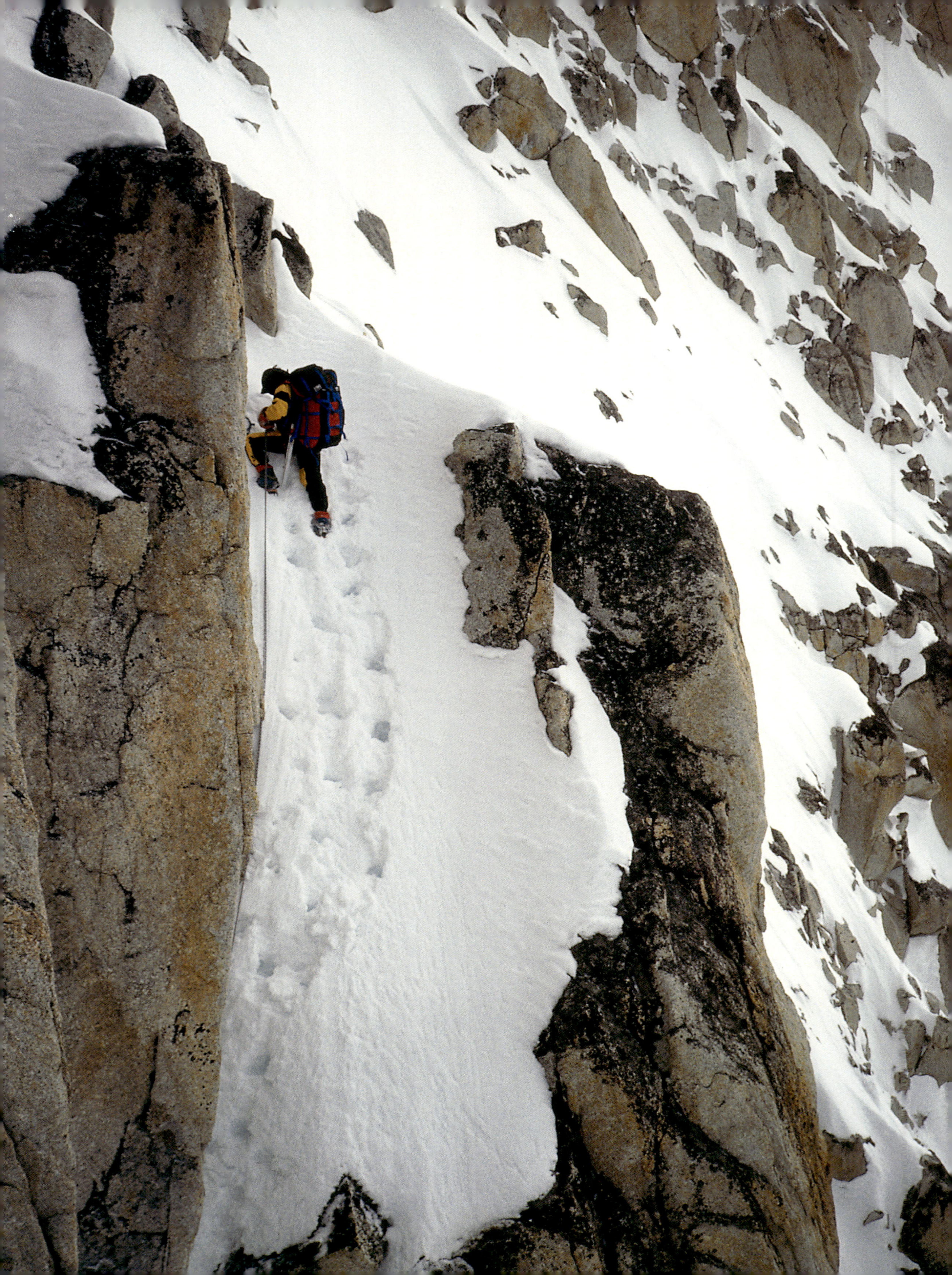

21

STEVE HOUSE

SOUTHWEST RIDGE OF PEAK 11,300, ALASKA RANGE, ALASKA

STEVE HOUSE—LIGHT IS RIGHT

When the history of twenty-first-century alpinism is written, Steve House will go down as the guy who took the credo of "light and fast" to a whole new level. Since the early 1990s, he has been the driving force behind a new era of high-standard, single-push ascents in Alaska and Canada. Because of his impressive record of technically difficult climbs and innovative tactics, many consider him America's most capable alpinist.

House's daring and speedy ascents in the mountains rely on a combination of minimalism, endurance, and technical prowess, all of which support his ideal of alpinism. "To me, it's about climbing the biggest feature on the biggest mountains using as little gear and as much skill as possible," says House.

The scrupulous alpinist is full of little tricks that enable him to do major ascents with as little as 20 pounds of gear. In Alaska, he climbs at night and sleeps during the day: When it's coldest, and conditions are ideal, House is in constant motion. And when the midday sun warms the air, he snoozes comfortably, sometimes without a sleeping bag. His obsession with shaving ounces borders on fanatical. In lieu of a 4-pound tent, he often digs a shelter with a 4-ounce shovel blade. He leads on a skimpy 9.1 mm single rope, and rappels on a 6 mm line. His definition of "safety gear" is a stove with extra fuel—hydration is vital.

House's minimalist mindset is backed by a worldly perspective and impressive technical skills. He spent twelfth grade in Slovenia on a student exchange, climbing almost every day. The formative experience taught him that going light means going fast, and faster is safer. Back in the states, he got his big-wall education in Yosemite, scaling El Capitan eight times by some of its most challenging routes. He completed the curriculum by earning his American Mountain Guides Association certification, which he uses to make a living.

When House turned his attention to the mountains, he began making surgical strikes on unclimbed lines in Canada and Alaska. His new routes in the Canadian Rockies include a 34-hour single push of Call of the Wild on King Peak, the seldom-forming Two Piece Yanks (5.11, WI 7), and the legendary M-16 (VI, A2, WI 7+) on the oft-tried east face of Howse Peak. His Alaskan first ascents include a spontaneous solo on Mount McKinley, Beauty Is a Rare Thing (V, 5.8, WI 4+), and the Gift (VI, WI 7, X, A3) on Mount Bradley.

SOUTHWEST RIDGE OF PEAK 11,300

There are two aspects to Steve House's life in the mountains: climbing with friends, and guiding with clients. When doing the former, House pushes his limits, often resulting in daring new lines or lightning-fast ascents of existing routes. But as a professional guide, he is exceedingly sane, choosing climbs that are well within his clients' abilities.

The challenge for House and other guides of his ilk is to find the perfect climb for a gung-ho client. He looks for something that is aesthetic, accessible, and safe, yet difficult enough to offer a rewarding experience. In May 1994, when he first climbed the Southwest Ridge of Peak 11,300 with three friends, the egalitarian guide knew he'd found such a climb.

Peak 11,300 is situated in the Ruth Gorge, the so-called "banana belt" of the Alaska Range. The Ruth offers a wide variety of choices for the modern climber—everything from long granite free climbs to challenging mixed routes to pure ice. Getting there is relatively simple. From Talkeetna, the most popular departure point, there are seven different air taxis that fly into the Ruth. And once climbers land on the west fork of the glacier, the approach to base camp is done. "You can set up your tent right next to the plane's ski tracks," lauds House. "From there, it's half an hour to the base of the climb."

In addition to the hassle-free approach, House appreciates the route's character. The climbing is reasonable, but never mindless. For example, there are several sections of 5.8 rock climbing, but all of them are short. "The ridge is really steppy," he explains. "None of the rock pitches are more than 80 feet, and the ridge is fairly broad, giving you freedom to find the easiest way around the numerous rock towers." The rest of the route involves straightforward but often exposed ice climbing to 65 degrees.

Another nice feature of the route is the bivy sites. With proper planning, climbers can avoid the toil of hacking out a tiny ledge on an exposed, windswept ridge. The first good site is on a spacious, tent-friendly bench about a third of the way up the ridge.

Steve House cruising on moderate terrain on the southwest ridge of Peak 11,300 © Michael Powers, portrait © Charlie Mace

The Southwest Ridge of Peak 11,300 follows the obvious sun/shade line to the summit. Descend the Southeast Ridge, the right-hand skyline. © Bradford Washburn (neg. 7877)

"It's a cool feeling when you get there," says House. "You climb this 60-foot, 5.7 rock fin, then pull over the top and step down onto this big, flat plateau." Faster parties often make it to the less comfortable, but still adequate, bivy spots near a notch about halfway up the ridge.

On House's third ascent of the route, he and his client decided to spend the night in the notch itself, which is reached with one rappel. Although it offers more protection than some of the flat spots on the ridge, creating a tent platform requires some digging. House advises taking extreme caution in the notch. Although he had been through it twice before, he walked too high on the cornice, causing it to fail and send him on a heart-stopping ride down the north face. Luckily he was still on rappel and had his system backed up with a prusik.

The upper half of the 4,000-foot ridge—which has no good bivy spots—is House's favorite part of the climb. "The route finding is straightforward and the position gets more and more spectacular as you go higher. There is also a feeling of commitment, since you descend a different route. It's not like you can just retreat back to the notch." House always knows he's getting close when he reaches the final ice dome. From its base, a half dozen pitches of solid alpine ice lead to the summit.

The view from the summit is, of course, breathtaking. "Your position at the head of the Ruth Glacier system gives you a fantastic view of the Moose's Tooth, the Great Gorge, and the 6,000-foot north face of Mount Huntington," says House. "And then there is Denali. You can truly appreciate how massive it is from this vantage." As is the case on many Alaskan summits, the view is also elusive; the summit is often shrouded in clouds during the afternoon.

On House's third ascent of the mountain, he and his client reached the summit late in the day. Clear skies and high pressure enticed them to spend the night on top, something he doesn't recommend, but an experience he will never forget. "There was a full moon," remembers House of the late May bivouac. "It was one of life's special memories."

ROUTE DESCRIPTION

Area: Ruth Amphitheater, Alaska Range
First ascent: Heinz Allemann and Niklaus Lötscher, May 1968
Base elevation: 7,200 feet
Summit elevation: 11,300 feet
Difficulty: VI, 5.8, 65-degree ice (Alaska grade 3, Alpine grade D+)
Time required: 3–5 days round trip from camp at 7,200 feet
Equipment: 1–3 pickets or flukes; 3–5 cams up to no. 2 Camalot; 8–10 stoppers; 3–4 ice screws; lots of slings (many natural features), biners; 2 half ropes or lightweight single rope and 7 mm half rope; Bibler I-tent or equivalent and hanging stove, 2 ice tools, crampons, helmets, shovel, clothing for full-on Alaskan conditions
Season: April–June; May ideal
Special considerations: Not possible to pick up weather forecast for Denali from Ruth Glacier on CB channel 19, so best to have lightweight FM radio and find out what time KTNA (Talkeetna Public Radio) broadcasts its "Denali Report," usually 7:00–8:00 A.M.; currently, permits only required for Denali and Foraker (Mountaineering Rangers, Denali National Park, P.O. Box 588, Talkeetna, AK 99676, (907-733-2231), dena_talkeetna_office@nps.gov)
References: Overstuffed binders maintained in Talkeetna by climbing rangers
Map: "Washburn Map" of Denali, 1:50,000

Approach: From Talkeetna, charter a ski plane to the west fork of the Ruth Glacier (to go directly to the route) or the Mountain House (if you plan on climbing/skiing in the area). From the Mountain House, ski west 5–6 miles to reach the toe of the Southwest Ridge of Peak 11,300 (allow 1 day). Expect to pay $200–$300 per person, round trip. For more information, call Talkeetna Shuttle Service (907-733-1725).

Route: The longest section of continuous rock climbing is 80 feet. There are three different topos at the Talkeetna Ranger Station, but the nature of the route makes the topos confusing. Following your nose (and this description) is advised.

To gain the ridge, either go around the north side of the toe (standard approach), ascending a long 40-degree snow slope, or climb a narrow snow gully just to the south of the toe. The latter option has some awkward rock climbing near the top of the gully (exit right) but enables a ski cache that is easily accessible on the descent.

Stay on the ridge crest, passing major obstacles on the right. Some slabby rock and mixed climbing is encountered a few pitches after gaining the ridge. Continue on steep snow with occasional rock steps. Follow easy snow slopes on the right of the crest to an initially awkward, then easier, rock pitch that gains the (obvious) plateau camp (recommended bivy).

From camp, climb increasingly steep snow, then work left into a broad gully (65-degree ice). Ascend the gully to a monolithic block on its top left (possible bivy below rock near ridge crest). Once there, traverse right to a short rock/snow crest, then over it. Continue toward the ridge crest. At the crest, rappel into the notch from a large horn festooned with slings (cramped bivy; clip in for safety).

Move the belay across the notch (80 feet), then climb out the other side, moving up at first, then climbing a ramp on the left (difficult and exposed). Once above the difficulties, follow steep snow on the ridge crest, passing any difficulties on the right side of the ridge. Approximately 2 hours from the notch, encounter an 80-foot rappel down to the right, then climb out of the gully and regain the ridge crest. From here, expect an increasingly spectacular position with no bivy spots until the summit. (A strong team can bivy at the upper notch, then reach the summit and get halfway down the next day.) Ascend the summit ice dome (five to seven pitches of 60-degree ice, decreasing in steepness).

Descent: Descend the Southeast Ridge. From the summit, head east-southeast, keeping to the skier's right (south) of the ridge, which gets more defined as you descend. Farther down, as the ridge gets narrower and steeper, stay below the crest (cornice danger). When forced to rappel, use bollards or v-threads to make four to six rappels, angling toward the ridge crest. Traverse to a bench on the ridge at 9,400 feet (good camp).

Continue down the now-broad ridge crest, making one 150-foot rappel down steep ice to a small bench. Downclimb on the ridge crest, working along the top of a rock band and downclimbing as far as comfortable before rappelling through it. Stay as close to the ridge crest as possible for six to ten rappels (serious, exposed rappels; expect to leave gear). From the base of the rock band, walk easily down a short glacier to the West Fork of the Ruth.

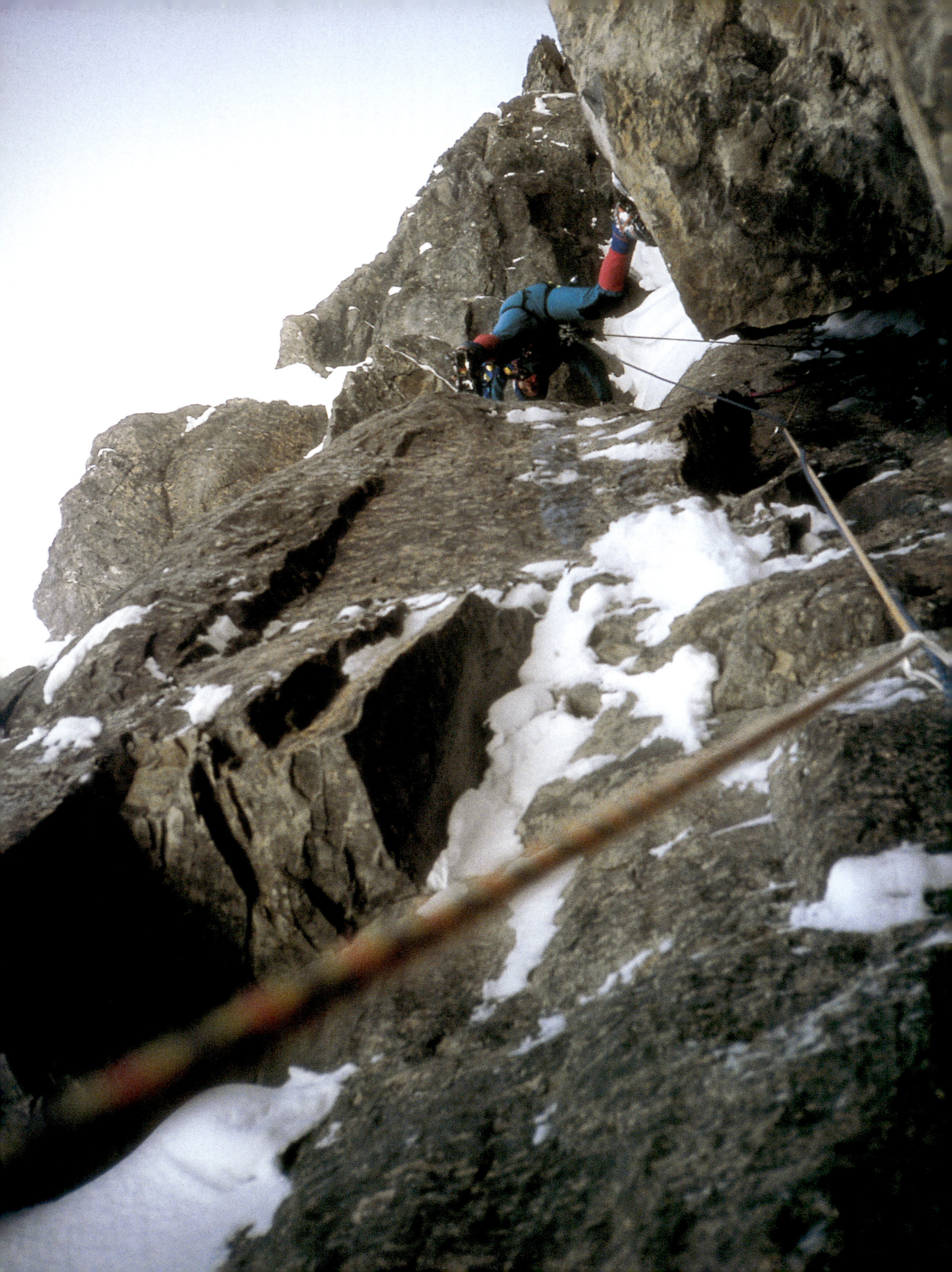

JOE JOSEPHSON
THE WILD THING, EAST FACE OF MOUNT CHEPHREN, BANFF NATIONAL PARK, ALBERTA

JOE JOSEPHSON—TEAM PLAYER
Joe Josephson was fifteen years old when family friend Bruce Anderson taught him how to climb. In addition to the basics, Anderson instilled in Josephson a sense of caution and respect for the mountains. "He told me, 'Never lose your fear,' " remembers Josephson. "That advice has always guided my climbing."

Josephson's first adventures were in the Beartooth Mountains in his home state of Montana. In 1987 he moved to Canmore, Alberta, to attend the University of Calgary. There he fell in with a group of hard-core alpinists from the Canadian Rockies, and his climbing took off. After honing his skills on numerous area classics, Josephson began to establish new climbs of his own. A small sample of his ice routes include the Replicant (WI 6+), Rainbow Serpent (WI 6), Fearful Symmetry (WI 6, X), and Sea of Vapors (WI 7+, R). A more complete list can be found in his comprehensive guidebook *Waterfall Ice Climbs in the Canadian Rockies*.

In addition to pure ice climbs, Josephson likes to challenge himself on large alpine faces that require commitment and a variety of technical skills. With Steve House (see Climb 21), he established Call of the Wild on King Peak in Kluane National Park in a 34-hour single push. The swift, technical ascent exemplifies his ideal of alpinism. Beyond going light and fast, Josephson is not a "numbers-driven" climber—solid partnerships and memorable experiences are what matter the most. "I care more about who I'm with than what I'm climbing," he explains. "I've never finished a route and wished it was harder."

THE WILD THING
As Grant Statham pounded a piton into Mount Chephren's limestone midriff, Joe Josephson fed a bight of rope through his belay device and reflected on the team's progress. It had been a good day. Since leaving Lake Louise more than 18 hours ago, he, Grant, and Sean Dougherty had climbed all the way to the base of the steep rock band more than halfway up Chephren's northeast face. En route, they had endured a frigid stream crossing, wallowed through waist-deep snow, and climbed a 3,000-foot ice gully that poured with spindrift. He was exhausted. But now, knowing that Grant had just finished fixing the first pitch of the rock band and that Sean was below digging a snow cave, Joe realized he'd soon be cocooned in goose down, enjoying a warm brew. Maybe, he hoped, Sean would have dinner ready as well.

It was almost dark by the time Grant rappelled the fixed line and rejoined Joe at the belay—but the day's work was done. A 100-yard snow slope was all that stood between them and the comfort of the snow cave. Five minutes later, when Joe crawled into the cave, he was alarmed by what he saw. The envisioned living room was only slightly bigger than the trunk of his car, and in it, slouched against the back wall, was Sean. Shivering and disoriented inside a frozen armor of burlap-style Gore-Tex, he slurred out a few sentences that confirmed Joe's fear: He was hypothermic. Too little sleep, too few calories, and wet clothing had rendered him helpless.

The severity the situation escalated a few minutes later when Sean started to vomit. "That snapped us both into action," remembers Joe. He and Grant immediately started reviving their friend—the first of several selfless acts of partnership that defined the 4-day experience. Joe stripped off his clothes and zipped him into a sleeping bag while Grant fired up the stove. After a few hours of hot soup and shared body heat, their friend began to recover. To ensure that his core temperature would return to normal, Joe spent the rest of the night inside the double sleeping bag with Sean, laughing heartily at Grant's jokes about "spooning."

Although they never discussed it, Grant and Joe both assumed they would descend in the morning. But Sean awoke feeling strong, and was the first to suggest they continue. Since the weather was still good, they had no reason to go down. The pleasantly surprised trio shouldered their packs and began ascending the fixed rope.

Before long they were standing at the base of the crux pitch—an overhanging slot choked with snow and ice. Despite the pitch's history, and partly because of it, Joe volunteered to the lead it. It had taken Barry Blanchard (see Climb 4) and assorted partners five tries to complete the Wild Thing. During those attempts, Blanchard and Ward Robinson, another revered Canadian alpinist, took 30-foot falls at the roof while leading that pitch. As Joe organized his gear

Joe Josephson leading the crux pitch of the Wild Thing on the route's second ascent © Grant Statham, portrait © Grant Statham

rack, he tried to forget about the pitch's history and focus on the task at hand.

Thirty feet into the lead, he dislodged a TV-size rock that just missed the belay—the first of two close calls. Several aid placements later, he was confronted by a VW bus–size block of snow wedged into the throat of the chimney. He climbed behind it and began to chip at a vein of ice that bonded it to the rock. Figuring it would take a while, he hacked at the ice with reckless abandon. But after just a few swings, the entire mass suddenly dropped into space like an elevator with a broken cable. The Friend at shoulder height held him in place as the giant snow cube headed for the belay. A huge plume of powder filled the air while the snow roared down Chephren's face. "I was thinking, 'This is it,'" recalls Joe. "I thought it was going to rip the belay off the mountain." A few seconds later—it seemed like an eternity—Grant and Sean emerged from the white cloud. They were covered with snow, but miraculously unhurt. And, since the fallen snow had exposed the remainder of the thin crack, Joe was able to continue aid-climbing through the overhang. He completed the pitch a draining 4 hours after starting it.

After another pitch of mixed climbing, they reached the next snow band and dug another snow cave. They were physically and mentally drained, but relieved to have the crux pitch behind them. Sleep came easily.

Their third day on the Wild Thing was spent climbing through alternating bands of rock and ice that look like the layers of a wedding cake from a distance. Although the climbing wasn't desperate, it was consistently challenging and often hard to protect. Thin to sometimes nonexistent ice made for exciting leads and creative belay anchors. After Jumaring one of Sean's leads, Joe arrived at the belay only to find him sitting on the ledge, braced in a corner with locked knees. He then realized that the rope he was hanging on was connected directly to Sean's harness. Unwilling to fully trust the belay, which consisted of two rickety, tied-off pitons, Sean had endured 30 minutes of dead weight on his harness.

The excitement continued until well past midnight. Grant finished leading the last pitch of the Wild Thing at 12:30 A.M. Like Sean on the earlier pitch, he was unable to find a suitable anchor on the summit. Dead tired and chilled to the bone, he laid flat in the talus, clipped the rope to his harness, and instructed his friends to start Jumaring. As the tension from the rope ground his hips into the shattered limestone, he gazed at the starry sky and listened to the wind swirl around him until 2:00 A.M., when Sean and Joe finally reached the summit. The Wild Thing had lived up to its name.

Many years and many summits later, it remains Josephson's favorite climb. "The route's quality, variety, length, and position make it a classic," he explains. "But it's the camaraderie and partnership that I remember the most."

© Barry Blanchard

ROUTE DESCRIPTION

Area: Canadian Rockies

First ascent: Barry Blanchard, Ward Robinson, and Peter Arbic, March 1987

Base elevation: Approximately 5,300 feet

Summit elevation: 10,715 feet

Difficulty: VI, 5.9+, A3, WI 5

Time required: 3–4 days; second ascent required 45 hours of climbing

Equipment: Full-on alpine clothing; Friends, 1 each of no. 0.5–no. 4; set of wired nuts; 2 RPs, 0.5 Tri-Cam; 3 baby angles, 1 shallow angle, 2 lost arrows, 7 knifeblades; 5 ice screws; Jumars or equivalent; 12 slings/carabiners; 3 aid slings; 2 55-m 9 mm ropes

Season: Winter and spring

Special considerations: Banff National Park requires a car pass to enter the park and bivouac permits; climbers should abide by voluntary sign-out system

Reference: *Selected Alpine Climbs in the Canadian Rockies* by Sean Dougherty (Rocky Mountain Books, 1999)

Map: 82 N/15 Mistaya Lake

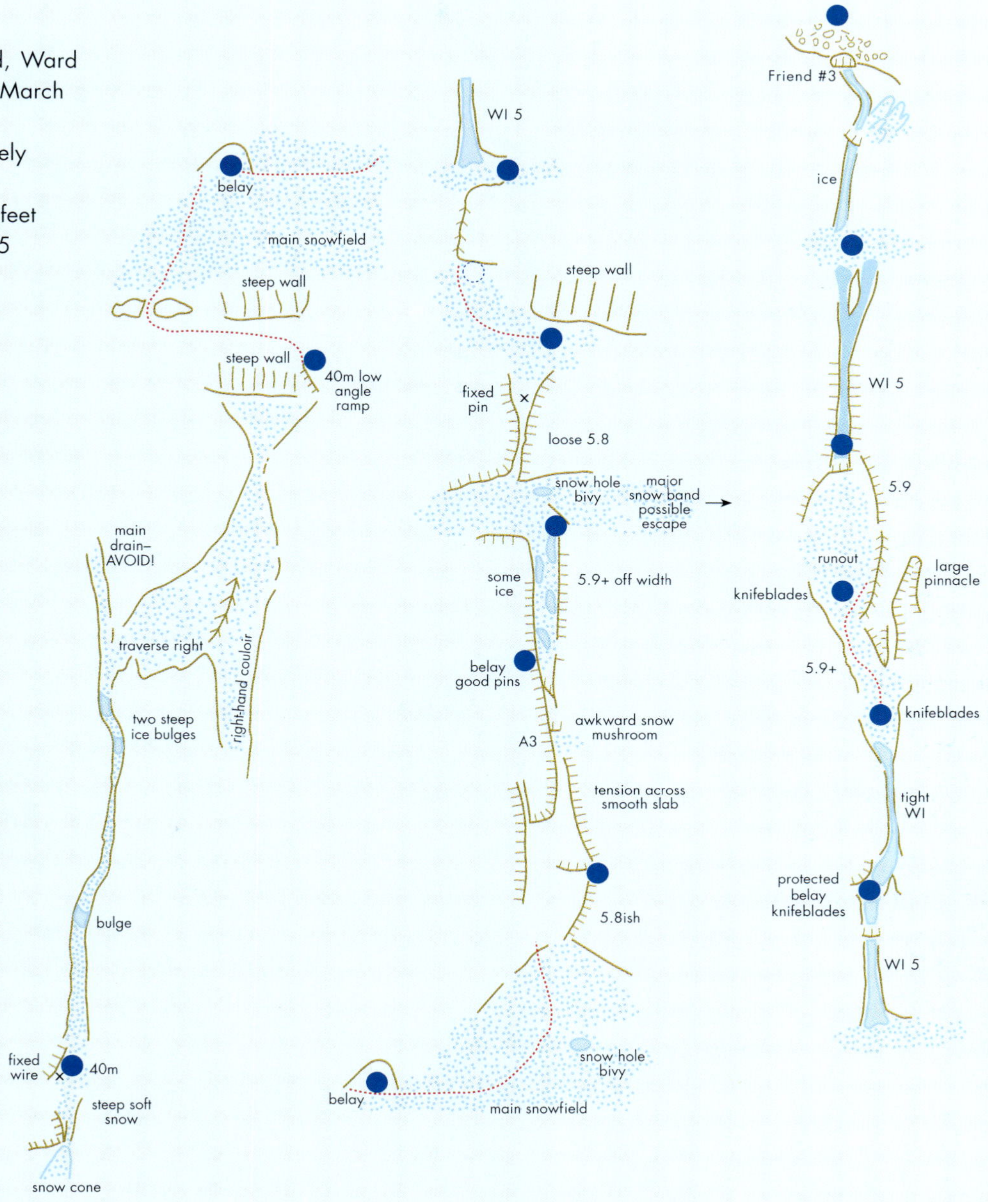

Approach: From the Icefields Parkway (Highway 93, north of Lake Louise), drive to Waterfowl Lake, 10.9 miles (17.5 km) north of Bow Summit or 10.25 miles (16.5 km) south of the Saskatchewan River crossing. Park at the roadside pullout at Waterfowl Lake, about 90 minutes from Banff. The East (right) Face of Mount Chephren is split by numerous gullies that rise into steep headwalls above. The Wild Thing starts up the left-hand gully and traverses right about a third of the way up. Use skis to make the 4-hour approach.

Route: Three thousand feet of mostly snow and ice followed by thirteen technical pitches of outstanding mixed climbing. Slab and spindrift avalanches are the primary hazard, although there is some loose rock. The first two ascents were in March and late April, respectively. Banff Visitor Centre has weather info (403-762-4256); also Lake Louise Visitor Centre (403-522-3822), Lake Louise Warden Office for emergencies (403-522-3866), Avalanche Bulletin (800-667-1105). See topo for details.

Descent: Follow easy snow slopes down to near the col between Mount Chephren and White Pyramid. Continue south (skier's left) above large cliff bands and eventually to the top of a broad avalanche gully. Go down the gully (crevasse danger) and onto the slopes leading to the moraines near Chephren Lake. Beware of seracs off Howse Peak to the right. Cross Chephren Lake and bushwhack back to Mistaya Lake. Allow 6 hours.

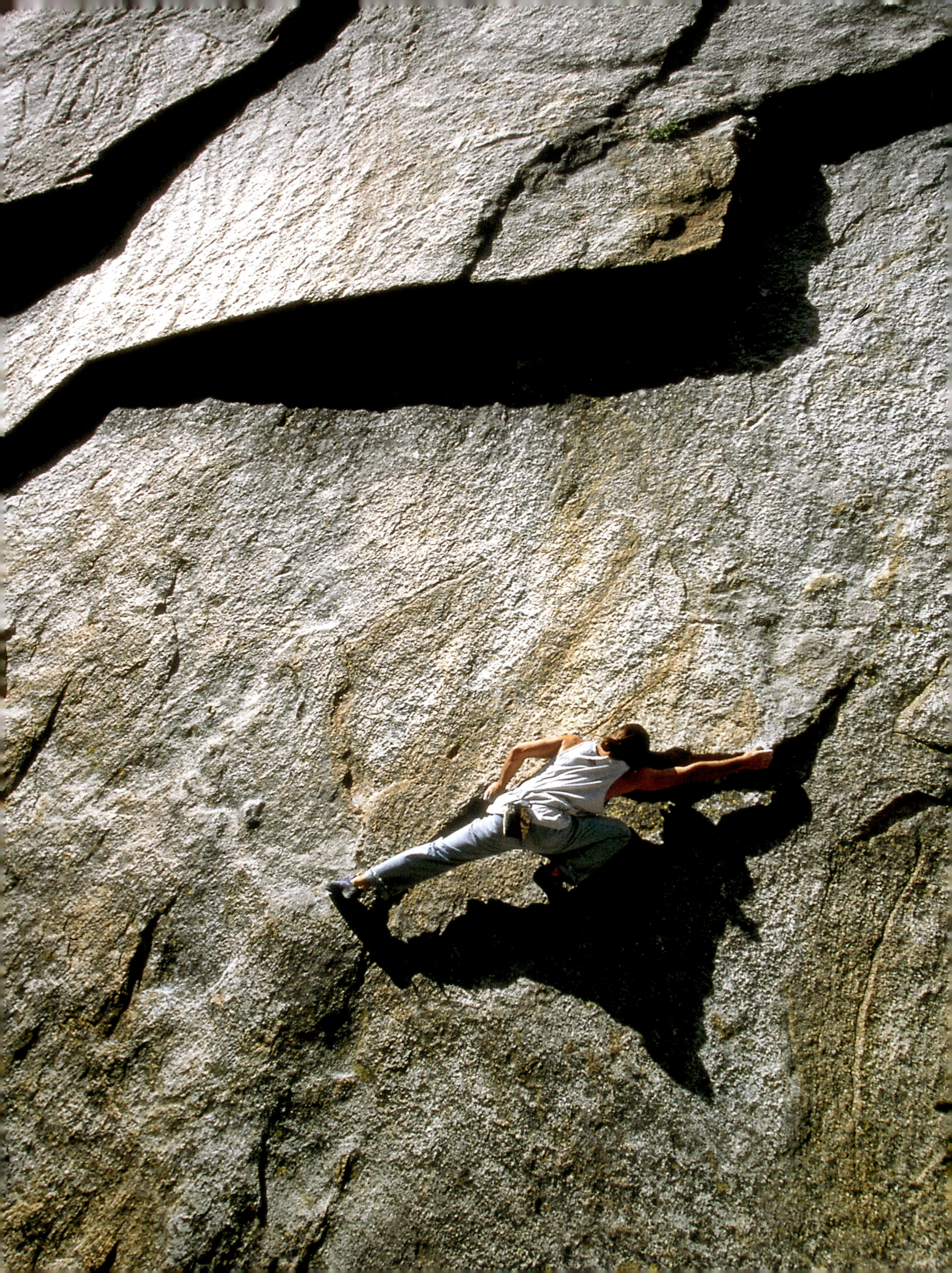

RON KAUK

MIDDLE ROCK TRAVERSE, MIDDLE CATHEDRAL ROCK, YOSEMITE NATIONAL PARK, CALIFORNIA

RON KAUK—LIFE IN YOSEMITE

It seems that no matter where in Yosemite Ron Kauk goes, he is well known: Visiting climbers recognize him when he pulls into Camp 4 on his motorcycle. They know him at the mountain shop. And he's always welcome at the Ahwahnee Hotel. Having lived in Yosemite for at least part of every season since 1974, he is the park's most enduring figure. "I've been able to call Yosemite home," he says proudly, referring to not only his residence, but the free lifestyle that's gone with it.

Kauk was only sixteen when he initially settled into Camp 4. "I was dreaming, eating, and sleeping climbing," he remembers of his first complete season. "It was a landmark summer for me." Climbing and training constantly, he progressed quickly, and was soon challenging the free-climbing standards of the day. In his inaugural year, he did the first ascent of Freestone (5.11c) with Jim Bridwell (see Climb 5) and Dale Bard. And early the following season, he did the first free ascent of the east face of Washington Column with John Bachar (see Climb 2) and John Long, renaming the all-free (5.11c) route Astroman (see Climb 30). Both routes remain revered classics to this day.

Although he excels at all aspects of Yosemite climbing—he's done numerous aid routes on El Capitan, including two first ascents—Kauk is best known for short, hard, and beautiful free climbs such as Tales of Power (5.11d), Separate Reality (5.11d), and Magic Line (5.14a). Kauk was the first to flash Butterballs (5.11c) and, in 1978, was the first to do America's most famous boulder problem: Midnight Lightning (V9). It was nine months before John Bachar pulled off the second ascent, and almost a year until it was repeated for the third time. Kauk's success is not just a function of his vise-grip strength, but of genius and determination. "Kauk is probably the most talented climber I've ever seen," says Bachar, a close friend and frequent partner during the '70s. "When he puts his mind to something, you know he is going to do it." The movie industry has noticed Kauk's talents too. He has appeared as a stunt double in several motion pictures, including *Mission Impossible II*, where he climbed as actor Tom Cruise.

At the heart of Kauk's relationship with Yosemite is a deep love of nature. His life in the Valley has been defined not only by the conquest of natural wonders, but by a Zen-like coexistence with them. "Mother nature has been the best teacher I've ever had," says Kauk. Although he has experienced her teachings all over the world—from Asia to Africa to Europe—he always returns to Yosemite with a renewed appreciation of its beauty. "I have a curious connection to this place," says Kauk. "It has a timeless feel to me."

MIDDLE ROCK TRAVERSE

By 1976, his third season of full-time climbing, Ron Kauk was one of the leading free climbers in Yosemite. Like the other top dogs, Kauk trained hard: He lifted weights, did fingertip pull-ups, and often bouldered until after dark. The harder he worked out, the better he climbed. And the better he climbed, the more he felt like working out. Kauk's world was brimming with possibilities.

At the time, the potential for new routes in Yosemite was staggering. On Middle Cathedral Rock, Kauk spotted an unclimbed line between two existing classics, the Kor-Beck route and the Central Pillar of Frenzy. The devious-looking passage followed a series of flakes and overlaps up a featured, 80-degree face. Kauk teamed up with fellow climber Kevin Worall to tackle the project. Their new route—later named Space Babble (5.11a, R)—turned out to be a six-pitch, mind-blowing face climb. Unlike Kauk's other routes, which demanded forearms of steel and expert crack-climbing skills, Space Babble was about footwork; it was a dance on dime-thin edges.

While working on Space Babble, Kauk realized he would need to train his EB rock shoes to stand on the tiny quartzite crystals and shallow divots that peppered the otherwise blank face. One afternoon, in an effort to improve his footwork, he started bouldering across the slabby, granite belly of Middle Cathedral Rock. First he went 10 feet, then 20, then 50, and before long, he had traversed 150 feet. He found himself just inches off the ground on some sections and 15 feet up the wall on others. The traverse was tricky in places, but never desperate. The friendly holds and rhythmic, continuous movement offered a refreshing change of

Ron Kauk finds his rhythm on Middle Cathedral Rock. He has repeated the bouldering traverse countless times since first discovering it as a teenager. © Corey Rich, portrait © Corey Rich

© Corey Rich

pace from the power-oriented bouldering Kauk was accustomed to. Not only was the traverse good for his footwork, it was fun.

Later that summer, Kauk and Worall finished Space Babble—a brilliant but seldom-repeated opus known for its long run-outs. Even though he wasn't planning any new routes on Middle Cathedral Rock, Kauk found himself returning to its base just to do the traverse. When the pressure to climb increasingly harder routes wore on him, Kauk would find solace in the peaceful setting and the uninterrupted flow of the moves. "It sort of puts you back to your roots," says Kauk. "You're completely free to enjoy the climbing. It's kind of an egoless thing to do in which you are not competing with anyone."

As the years went on, the traverse became an indispensable part of Kauk's routine. If he wanted some solitude or just needed to relax, he would spend a few hours doing laps on the traverse. Kauk described his sessions as cathartic, even spiritual. "It's an incredibly scenic environment, and since you're not in any big risk, you can concentrate on what's inside you and discover yourself in a really peaceful way."

In 1986, as the controversy over sport-climbing ethics divided Yosemite climbers, Kauk spent the season in Europe. There he met some of the best rock technicians in the world: Antoine LeMenestrel, Jerry Moffet, and Patrick Edlinger. The Europeans introduced Kauk to new techniques, new ethics, and new ways of thinking. The open-minded Yosemite veteran was reenergized by the experience. "It was like being born again," remembers Kauk, "like when I first started coming to Yosemite." He spent the next four seasons climbing and competing in Europe.

By Kauk's fourth season abroad, the structured, rule-based nature of competition climbing was starting to wear on his psyche. The discipline had been good for him, but he missed the free-form lifestyle he had in Yosemite. He missed climbing the endless granite cracks the Valley was famous for and, more than anything, he longed for the Middle Rock Traverse. "All I could think about during my last season in Europe was getting back to Yosemite to do the traverse. I know it sounds weird," says Kauk, "but I just wanted to walk up there by myself and boulder, just go back and forth along the rock."

Since returning from Europe, Kauk has gone back to the Middle Rock Traverse countless times. He's been there in all seasons, at all times of day, and appreciates its many moods. But most of all, he sees it as a point of stability in a constantly changing world. "Coming here always regrounds me," says Kauk. "In twenty-five years, it hasn't really changed. It's a constant reflection of history for me."

Unlike many bouldering problems, the Middle Rock Traverse is primarily about footwork. © Corey Rich

ROUTE DESCRIPTION

Area: Yosemite Valley, California
First ascent: Ron Kauk, 1976
Difficulty: 5.12a
Time required: 1 hour, more if you do laps
Equipment: Rock shoes, chalk bag
Season: Early spring–late fall
Reference: *Yosemite Climbs, Free Climbs* by Don Reid

Approach: Park at the turnout 1.3 miles east of the Highway 41/140 junction. Hike west along the horse trail until the path to the Central Pillar of Frenzy can be found. The traverse starts at the base of the Kor-Beck route.

Route: Traverse between Kor-Beck route and Central Pillar of Frenzy. Kauk recommends going high or low, "whatever feels right."

Descent: Not applicable.

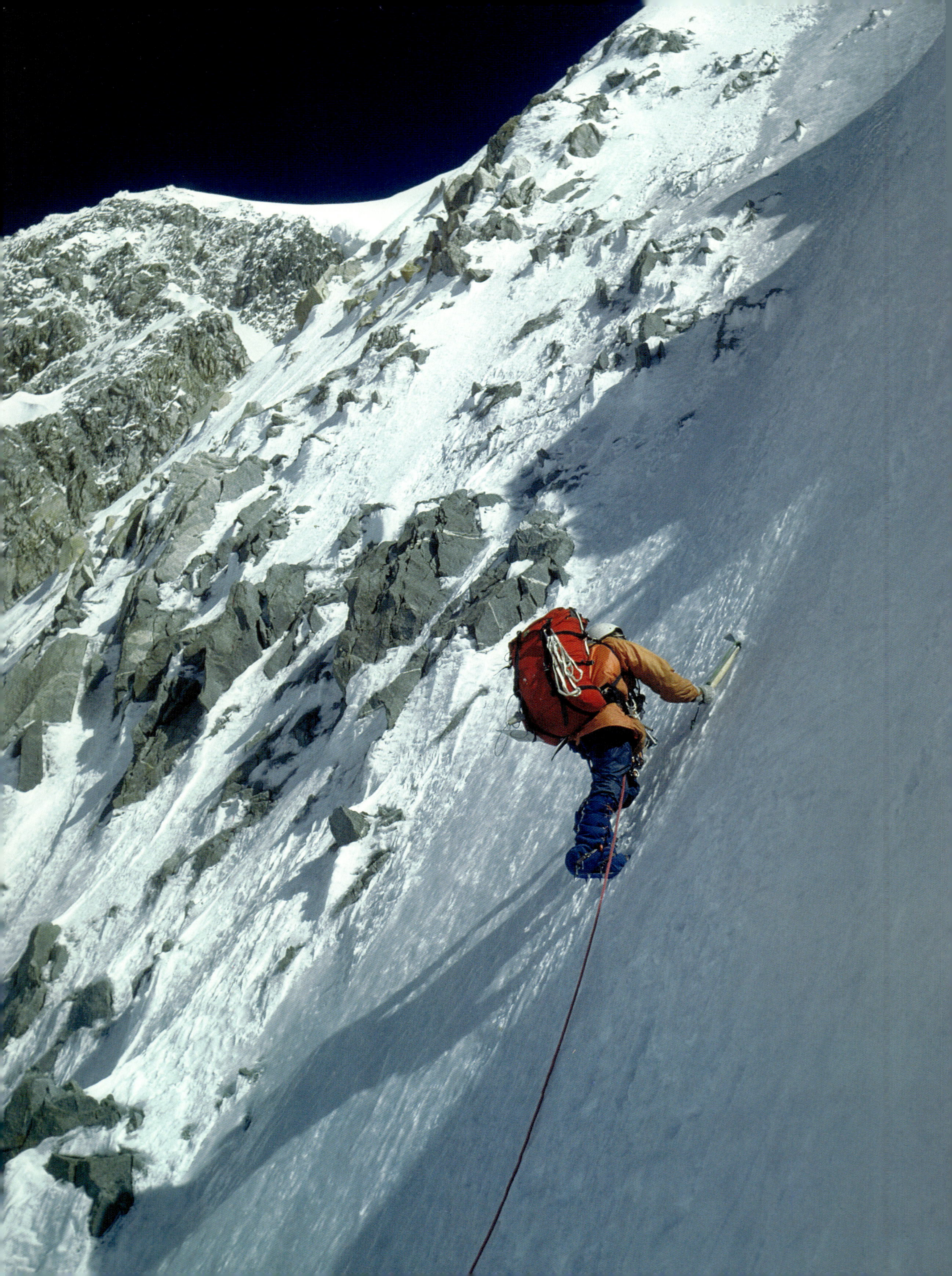

24

MICHAEL KENNEDY
THE INFINITE SPUR, MOUNT FORAKER, ALASKA RANGE, ALASKA

MICHAEL KENNEDY—TAKING THE LEAD
Since he started climbing in 1970, Michael Kennedy has proven again and again that he knows how to lead. As an alpinist, he's organized numerous big trips to the world's great ranges. As the editor and publisher of *Climbing* magazine from 1974 to 1998, his insights and vision have guided an entire generation of climbers. And as president of the Access Fund, he was a tireless advocate for a climbing community that faces a broad array of access and conservation challenges.

Kennedy enjoys all types of climbing, but is best known for high-standard alpine routes in Alaska and the Himalayas. On his first big trip to Alaska in 1977, he and George Lowe (see Climb 28) made an alpine-style ascent of Mount Foraker's Infinite Spur—the route he chose here as his favorite. In 1978, he joined Jim Donini (see Climb 14), George, and Jeff Lowe (see Climb 29) for an alpine-style attempt of the still-unclimbed North Ridge of Latok I, making it within about 600 feet (200 m) of the summit. In 1981, Kennedy made a solo ascent of the Cassin Ridge on Denali. Four years later, he and Carlos Buhler (see Climb 7) made the first ascent of the Northeast Face of Ama Dablam, in winter. And in 1994, he established the technically demanding Wall of Shadows on Alaska's Mount Hunter with Greg Child (see Climb 9). In 2000, he attempted to climb 26,545-foot (8,091-m) Annapurna, but was denied success by the weather.

When he's not climbing, Kennedy uses his writing and photography skills to share his personal experiences with others. His riveting adventure stories, insights, and philosophies are a perennial source of inspiration for climbers and outdoor enthusiasts around the world.

THE INFINITE SPUR
On June 25, 1977, Michael Kennedy and George Lowe faced an important decision: Should they attempt a new route on the 9,000-foot south face of Mount Foraker, or try something less committing? They had come to the Alaska Range with a third partner, Jeff Lowe, to attempt two new routes: the north face Mount Hunter and then the south face of Mount Foraker. Four thousand feet up Hunter's north face, Jeff rode a broken cornice 60 feet and snapped his ankle. After a tricky, 36-hour retreat to the glacier, he flew out to Anchorage for treatment. A few days later, Kennedy and George Lowe returned to Hunter, completing the north face. But now, without Jeff, the technically strongest member of their team, they had serious doubts about the south face of Foraker. Their proposed route was daunting—half again as big as the north face of the Eiger, technically just as difficult, and at much higher elevation. After considerable deliberation, Kennedy and Lowe decided to go for it.

The anxious pair started the long approach to Foraker's remote south face that evening. Skiing through the night, they reached a snow shoulder that offered the first complete view of the spur by morning. As they expected, it looked gigantic, even by Alaskan standards. Yet they were pleasantly surprised to see that their climbing route wasn't quite as steep or as blank as they thought it would be. With stable weather and no apparent rockfall, their confidence grew. They started climbing at 3:00 A.M.

They expected the first third of the route to be the most difficult. Although the rock climbing was challenging—up to 5.9 in places—it was delightful. The pristine, alpine granite was fractured enough to offer good protection and, surprisingly, most pitches could be climbed with a pack. Alternating leads, they climbed for 19 hours straight, reaching a comfortable ledge by 10:00 P.M. They were exhausted but thrilled with their progress.

The next morning they picked their way through an interesting mix of rock and ice toward the bottom of the ice rib—the central feature of the face. As they climbed, the vaporous mist that swirled above the glacier started to thicken. A few hours later, when it turned to snow, they instinctively began to assess their options, but all too soon they realized that they didn't really have any. With 3,000 feet of technical terrain below them, retreating would exhaust their entire supply of gear; going down from any higher would be out of the question. Oddly enough, Kennedy felt liberated by the sense of commitment. "Once you get to that point," he explains, "it frees your mind from all of the bullshit, because it doesn't matter anymore." Kennedy and Lowe continued up the ice

Fueled by commitment, not equipment, George Lowe uses his wood-shafted ice ax to negotiate the ice rib on the Infinite Spur in 1977.
© Michael Kennedy, portrait © Greg Child

The Infinite Spur follows the obvious ridge in the center of the face. The upper two-thirds of the 9,000-foot route climb the ice rib just left of the ridge crest. © Joe Terravecchia

rib, eventually stopping to chop out a small bivouac ledge. Another long day.

After a cold and uncomfortable night, the weary climbers forged ahead. As the weather deteriorated, they were pelted by spindrift avalanches. Eighteen hours and countless pitches later, they approached the top of the ice rib, and a surprise crux. The ice rib narrowed, forcing them into a rock band on their left. They knew that they would have to climb through it to get to the easier snow ridge above, but the rock was loose and impossibly steep. Kennedy traversed up and right until he found a slight weakness in the rock band, a wicked-looking gully that poured with snow. It looked more difficult that any mixed pitch he'd ever climbed, but it was their only option. After taking one look at it, Lowe suggested they bivouac and attack it in the morning. But Kennedy wanted to get it over with. Fueled by a second wind, he offered to lead the pitch. What happened next remains one of his most powerful climbing memories.

Intellectually, Kennedy understood that he was climbing a delicate and difficult mixed pitch. Yet emotionally, he entered a separate reality. In fact, he recalls very little about the technical details of the pitch. What he does remember is looking up and visualizing himself climbing the gully and then, sometime later, looking back down at his partner as Lowe came up. Kennedy had floated outside of his own consciousness into a surreal, hypnotic state—a feeling he has since experienced only a handful of times.

As they hoped, easier ground came after a few moderate pitches. And the weather started to improve. Before long, they had hacked out a comfortable ledge, cooked a hearty meal and drifted into a deep, restful sleep. Although the technical crux was behind them, Foraker continued to challenge them physically and mentally. The seemingly endless upper ridge shattered their hopes of making it to the summit the next day, and inspired the route's name. They enjoyed a comfortable bivouac, but their progress was stalled by a violent 40-hour storm. By Alaskan standards, it was a short delay. But the uncertainty was draining; they wondered if it might be one of those legendary 10-day blizzards that would outlast their supply of food and fuel.

On July 3 the weather improved just enough to allow them to make the long slog to Foraker's frigid summit. After a few obligatory photos, they began the tedious descent down its treacherous southeast flank. Just as they were starting to taste success, a massive cornice fracture sent Lowe plummeting down the north side of the ridge, only to be saved by Kennedy when the rope went taut. Both men dangled on opposite sides of the ridge like a human teeter-totter, miraculously unhurt. After their narrow brush with death, they belayed every pitch down the ridge, finally reaching the safety of the glacier 2 days later.

Their 11-day adventure is considered one of the crowning achievements in the history of North American mountaineering. (The route has been repeated only three times since 1977.) But, more importantly, it was one of the most intense and rewarding experiences of Kennedy's life. While reflecting on the climb in March 1999, he wrote, "Twenty-two years and many mountains later, it remains my most influential climb, an experience that opened my eyes to the possibilities in the big mountains of the world. But as much as anything, Foraker awakened in me a deep sense of spirituality and reverence for life that has helped define my life since then."

ROUTE DESCRIPTION

Area: Alaska Range
First ascent: George Lowe and Michael Kennedy, July 1977
Base elevation: Approximately 8,000 feet
Summit elevation: 17,004 feet
Difficulty: Alaska grade 6, 5.9, M5
Time required: 7–12 days on route, 1 day for approach, 2 days for descent; first-ascent party took 11 days round trip from Kahiltna Glacier, averaging 14 hours of climbing per 24-hour period
Equipment: Set of stoppers, set of cams to 3 inches, 6–8 pitons (knifeblades, Bugaboos, small angles), 6–8 ice screws, 2 snow pickets or deadmen, 8 full-length runners, plus quickdraws, biners; 2 ropes, 1 10–11 mm and 1 8–9 mm, 50-m OK; small-footprint single-wall tent, hanging stove, 2 ice tools per person, clothing suitable for major Alaskan route; skis useful for approach
Season: Mid-May–mid-July; June best, depending on snow cover
Special considerations: Retreat is difficult to impossible after second day on route; descent route is long and serious, so have some reserves on summit
References: *American Alpine Journal* (1978, 1991, 1997); *High Alaska* by Jonathan Waterman (The American Alpine Club, New York, 1989)
Maps: USGS Talkeetna D3, D2

Approach: Fly from Talkeetna to Kahiltna Glacier. Ski 6.5 miles west, over a 7,200-foot pass south and west of the bottom of the French Ridge. Drop onto the upper Lacuna Glacier, cross to its west side, travel upglacier (north), then over a 7,700-foot pass to a broad snow shoulder. Bivy here (good view of route).

Route: Drop down and move quickly across the glacier to the bottom of the route (exposed to seracfall, especially from the east/right). Cross bergschrund slightly right of the crest of the spur, then angle up and left on snow/ice to several pitches of moderate rock. Bivy on small ledges at about 9,500 feet. Continue up moderate to difficult rock (some 5.9), then moderate mixed terrain, reaching the prominent snow/ice rib that forms the central part of the route. Follow this for fifteen to twenty pitches (55 degrees) to an open bivy (at about 11,500 feet). The snow/ice rib narrows, with steep, rotten rock on the left and a steep drop toward the south face on the right. When the rib peters out, traverse left on difficult mixed ground to the crux mixed gully (85 degrees). Climb this to another open bivy at about 13,500 feet on easier snow/ice. Traverse up and left (north) for ten to twelve pitches on the west side of the horizontal ridge. Bivy (tent) in seracs at about 15,000 feet, where the ridge joins upper snow slopes. Moderate snow and ice lead to the south summit (16,812 feet), then easy walking on the broad summit ridge leads to the true summit (17,004 feet).

Descent: Descend via the Southeast Ridge or the Northeast Ridge/Sultana Variation. Be wary of cornices.

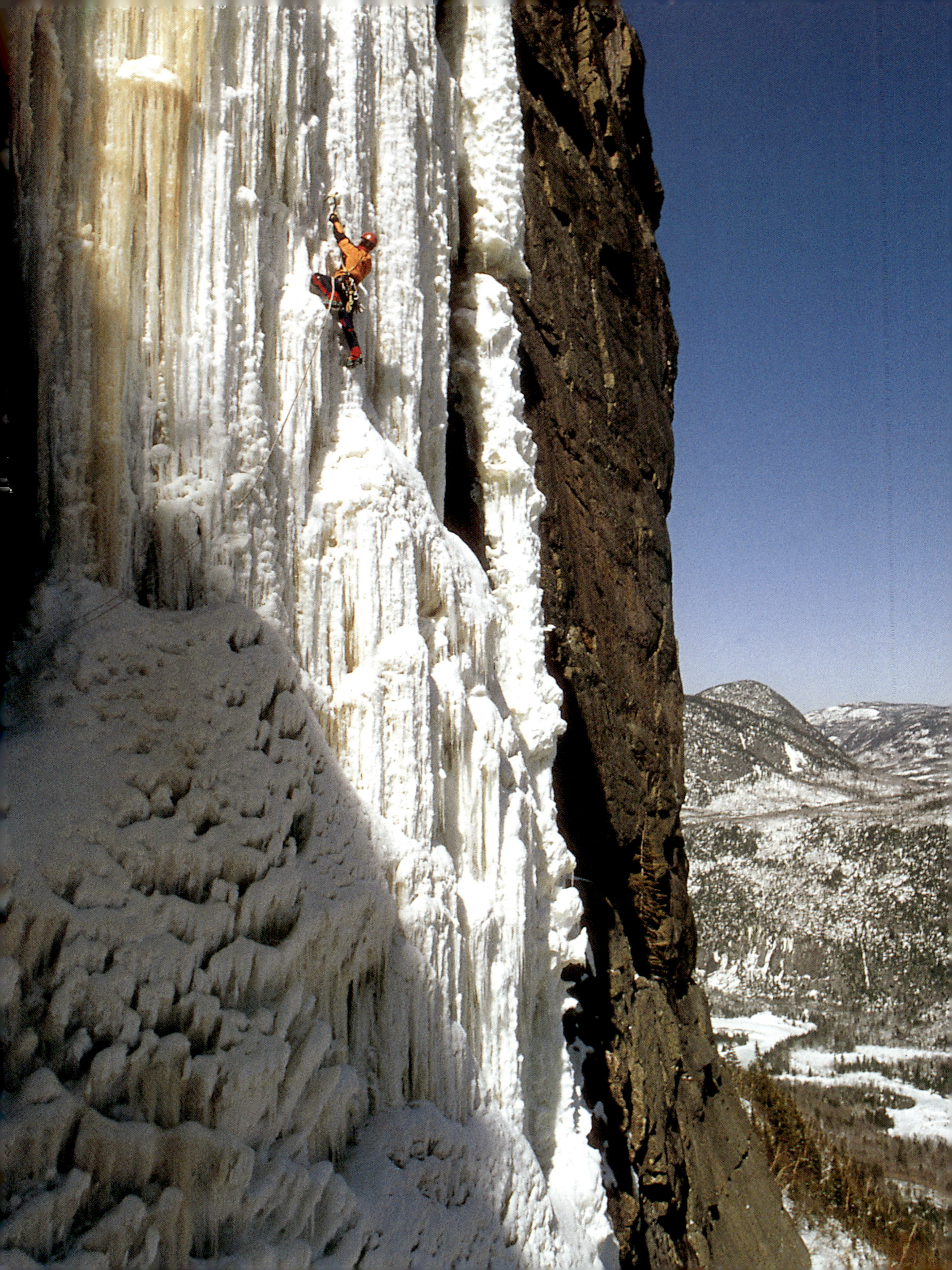

GUY LACELLE

LA POMME D'OR, HIGH GORGE OF MALBAIE RIVER REGIONAL PARK, QUEBEC

GUY LACELLE—ICE TECHNICIAN

Guy Lacelle is one of those climbers you hear about, not from. He's quiet and unassuming. He isn't flashy. And he doesn't self-promote. Yet those who have seen him climb will tell you that he is one of the best ice technicians to ever strap on a pair of crampons.

Although Lacelle has climbed countless difficult ice routes in his two-decade career, his distinction as an ice climber is about volume. He climbs full-time during the winter months—and usually solo. There is little that escapes the gentle tap of his tools. While most climbers are happy to squeeze in a dozen routes each season, he typically climbs several hundred.

Lacelle was raised in rural Hawkesbury, Ontario, just west of Montreal. The French-Canadian (whose first name is pronounced like "see") was introduced to climbing while earning a degree in physical education from the University of Ottawa. His first ice climb was the moderate 300-foot La Congelee (WI 3), an ascent that took him and his partner 7 hours. Years later, he soloed the route in less than 5 minutes.

In search of more ice, Lacelle moved to the Canadian Rockies in 1983. He spent five years climbing and guiding in Canmore, Alberta, often teaching winter courses at the Yamnuska Mountain School. In 1988 he stepped back from guiding to adopt a lifestyle that would allow him to spend more time climbing. He now spends the summer months with his wife, Marge, and their five dogs, working as a tree planter near their home in Prince George, British Columbia. After working hard all summer, he climbs virtually nonstop during the winter. Some of his favorite solo ascents include classics such as Terminator (WI 6), Sea of Vapors (WI 5), Curtain Call (WI 6), and, of course, La Pomme d'Or (WI 5+).

LA POMME D'OR

Despite its reputation as a cold and scary activity, waterfall ice climbing has surged in popularity in the last fifteen years. Dramatic improvements in equipment, better information, and man-made ice parks such as Colorado's Ouray have all contributed to the sport's growth. Part of the appeal is that, in most cases, ice climbing isn't fraught with the hassles of winter camping; most ice climbs take place within the span of a single winter's day. They often start with a hot meal, maybe even a latte, and end as the high-tech explorers lounge in front of the fireplace sampling microbrews, sharpening ice picks, and catching the latest scores on ESPN.

For better or worse, not all frozen waterfalls can be climbed in such a civilized fashion. One of the more notable exceptions is Quebec's La Pomme d'Or. When the 1,100-foot wall of ice was originally climbed in 1980, the first ascent party skied 22 miles to reach its base—unsupported by helicopters, snowmobiles, or cozy ski huts. Their remote adventure was one of the most celebrated mountaineering accomplishments of the year. The route's clever name, which translates to "the Golden Apple," describes its yellowish, mineral-stained ice while reminding locals that the first ascent was plucked by two zealous Yankees from New England—a minor blow to Quebec's provincial pride.

By 1989, when Guy Lacelle decided to have a go at La Pomme d'Or, a snowmobile track up the Malbaie River valley had reduced the full-day approach to a brisk, chainsaw-loud, 1-hour jaunt. He could have easily rented a snowmobile, but opted for the self-powered approach. With Amish-like purity, he kickglided his way up the pristine valley as two dogs of his followed with a 1-week supply of food and fuel in tow. "The valley is so magnificent, especially if you experience it on skis," stresses Lacelle. "There is so much more to La Pomme d'Or than just doing the climb."

As Lacelle skied up the valley, he imagined how La Pomme d'Or might look when it came into view. In the previous two months he'd soloed some of the longest ice routes in the world—from Alaska to the Canadian Rockies to Norway—and had grown accustomed to their visual impact. He assumed that he'd want to climb La Pomme d'Or the instant he saw it. But when the 1,100-foot wall of tawny ice fangs finally revealed itself, his confidence momentarily wilted. There he stood, alone in the dead of winter, 22 miles from the nearest road, wondering if he really wanted to solo the route. "When you first see La Pomme d'Or, it's really intimidating," explains Lacelle. "You have to remind yourself that you're not climbing the whole thing all at once. It's like eating an

La Pomme d'Or, which means the Golden Apple, is named for its tawny, mineral-stained ice. Lacelle made the first solo ascent of the 1,100-foot route in 1989. © Joe Josephson, portrait © Ace Kvale

© Joe Josephson

elephant: You do it one bite at a time."

Lacelle arrived at camp and quickly built an igloo to shelter him and his dogs from the stinging winds and subzero temperatures. Inside, where it was 30 degrees warmer, he prepared dinner and formulated a plan: He would spend the next 3 days warming up on some of the shorter ice climbs near camp, and save La Pomme d'Or for last.

Although Lacelle climbs solo—without a partner, a belay, or any margin for error—he still brings a 100-meter rope and a selection of ice screws on each outing. "It takes the stress out of soloing," he explains. "If I don't like the ice conditions, or I break a pick, I know I can always go down." Lacelle is also very conservative about the routes he will solo. "When I choose a climb to solo," he explains, "I try to pick something that I have quite a margin on, so it feels reasonable. I am actually quite a safe climber."

When someone who climbs skyscraper-size frozen waterfalls without a belay refers to himself as a safe climber, it smacks of self-delusion. But having seen Lacelle in action, it's hard to disagree. He always looks smooth and solid—as if he's climbing a rung ladder. And his motives are pure. He doesn't solo to show off. He does it because it enables him to keep moving, to delight in the kinesthetic rhythm that is inherent to ice climbing. "When I stop to place protection, it feels like I mess up the activity," adds Lacelle. "It just cuts the flow."

After a few days of warm-up climbs, Lacelle made his first attempt at La Pomme d'Or. He saw that La Pomme d'Or had yet to be climbed that season. There were no signs of human passage: no footprints, pick holes, or crampon marks. "Getting the first ascent of the season is a big plus," beams Lacelle. "Because the climb was not there that summer, it's sort of like doing a first ascent. You're on virgin ice." Unfortunately, he was forced to retreat from the lower half of the route when he broke a crampon—luckily, he had a spare pair at base camp. He couldn't wait to try again.

The following day Lacelle awoke to clear skies and frigid temperatures. Wanting to climb the route during the warmest part of the day, he didn't leave camp until 10:00 A.M. As he hiked, he thought about the adventure ahead: He would stab his crampons and picks into the wall of ice more than 1,000 times in the next 3 hours. Every single placement, he realized, had to be solid. There was no margin for error.

Lacelle got into a rhythm right away: swing, swing, kick, kick. Taking it one placement at a time, he worked his way up the lower half of the route in about an hour. By noon he was just below the upper headwall, which hung above him like dripping wax. The ice was brittle, demanding what he calls "light placements." Still, he was having the time of his life: The setting was spectacular, he felt great, and the climbing was brilliant. He paused to take it all in, then gently ticked his way up the 300 feet of chandeliered ice to the top of the route.

When Lacelle returned to the company of his dogs, he felt deeply satisfied. It wasn't because he was the first person to solo La Pomme d'Or. Or that the magazines would write all about it. It was because he climbed La Pomme d'Or in control—in a style that allowed him to enjoy the experience. "One of the reasons that this climb felt so good to me is that I was able to climb it feeling safe through the whole adventure," explains Lacelle. "If I solo a climb and there was a moment of uncertainty, to me it's a failure."

ROUTE DESCRIPTION

Area: Malbaie River valley
First ascent: Kurt Winkler and Jim Tierney, 1980
Difficulty: V, WI 5+–6
Time required: 1 long day on the ice
Equipment: Standard rack of 10 ice screws, 2 60-m ropes, selection of pitons and small nuts in case of thin conditions
Season: Late winter; early March ideal
Special considerations: Be prepared for subzero temperatures and unpredictable ice conditions in remote setting; there are more than forty established ice routes in the Malbaie River valley, and lots of potential for new lines
Reference: Le Guide des Cascades de Glace du Quebec by S. Lapierre and J. C. Maurice

Approach: From Quebec city, drive northeast on Road 138. A few miles before the town of Clermont (about 2 hours), look for signs for Saint-Aime-des-Lacs. Take that road and follow signs for Parc Regional des Hautes Gorges de la Riviere Malbaie. Ski or snowmobile 22 miles up the Malbaie River valley. La Pomme d'Or climbs the west side of the valley (east-facing).

Route: With 60-meter ropes, the route goes in seven pitches. The first 130 feet are moderate. A diagonal mixed traverse takes you left to La Rampe, 300 feet of steep ice leaning to the left that can range from WI 4 to 6. One more pitch brings you to the crux: a 260-foot pillar of vertical ice offering no rests. See photo.

Descent: Rappel the left side of the route.

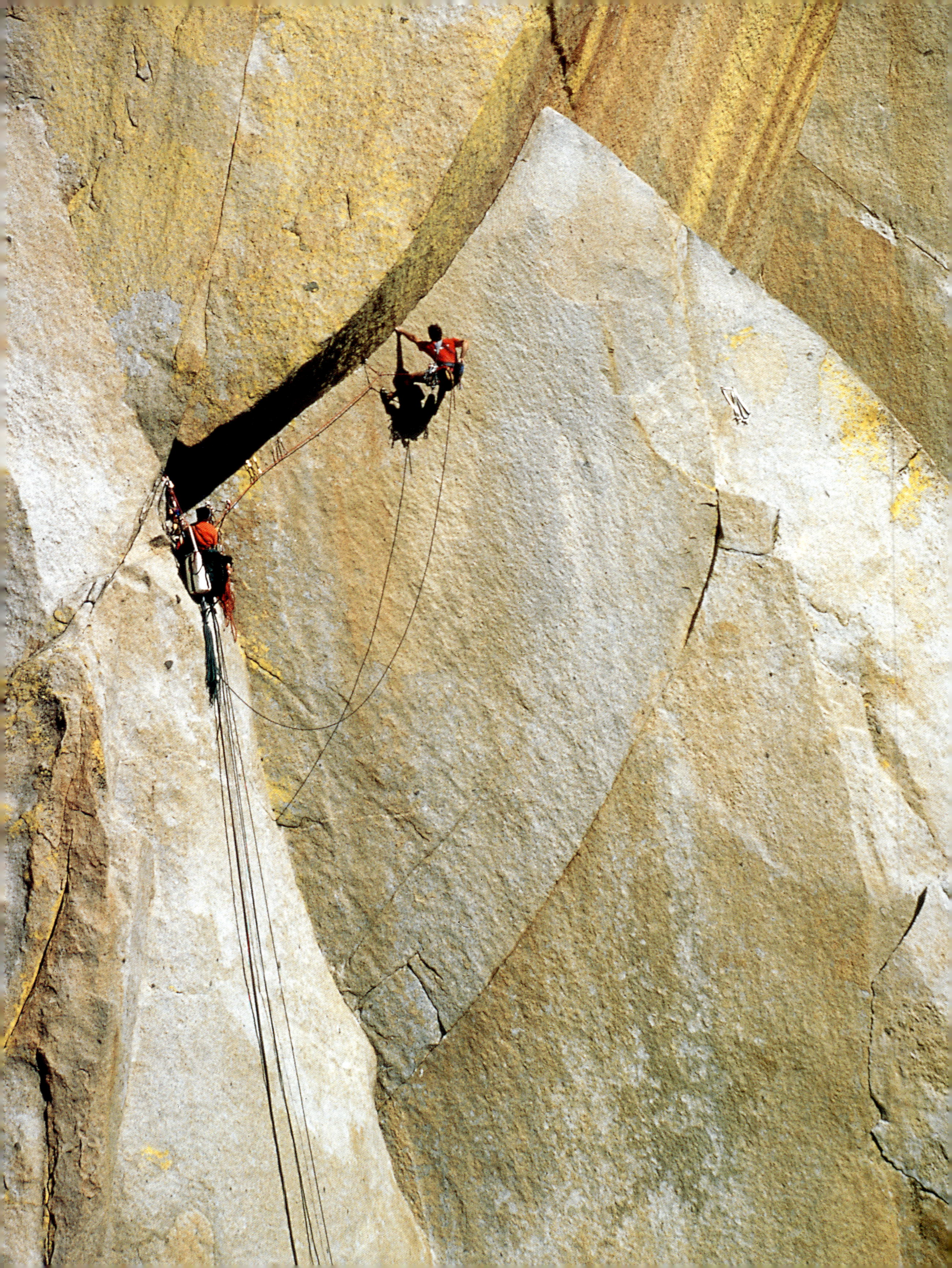

RANDY LEAVITT

ROMANTIC WARRIOR, WARLOCK NEEDLE, THE NEEDLES, CALIFORNIA

RANDY LEAVITT—MASTER OF STONE

Randy Leavitt is a rock climber who has mastered every discipline: He's climbed 5.14 sport routes. He's done A5 nail-ups on Yosemite's El Capitan. And he's established some of the finest traditional climbs in the country—from thin finger cracks to gnarly off-widths.

Leavitt's first exposure to rock climbing was in 1972, in Yosemite. The twelve-year-old was blown away when he saw tiny climbers dangling from El Capitan's sheer face. It was that image that inspired him to pursue big walls when he started climbing three years later. In his typical type-A fashion, he immersed himself in aid climbing, making early ascents of Half Dome's Tis-sa-ack, as well as the Zodiac and Tangerine Trip on El Capitan. In 1978, he joined wall ace Dale Bard for the fourth ascent of El Cap's Pacific Ocean Wall (VI, 5.10, A5; see Climb 5).

His knack for spotting aesthetic, unclimbed lines inspired Leavitt to start making first ascents in the early '80s. On El Cap, he added Lost in America and Scorched Earth, both rated A5. His enthusiasm also resulted in many new free climbs in Joshua Tree National Park and the Needles. With Tony Yaniro (see Climb 50), he also invented a technique for climbing off-width cracks called "Leavittation." In 1987, when he was no longer satisfied with being "only" a 5.12 climber, Leavitt retired from the big-wall scene to concentrate on free climbing. His focus yielded immediate results.

In 1988, Leavitt put up La Machine (5.13d) in Joshua Tree, the first of many hard sport routes to follow. He spent most of the '90s pushing his limits at the sport crags. One of his favorite haunts is Arizona's Virgin River Gorge, where he has done scores of new routes, including test pieces such as Planet Earth (5.14a). At Clarke Mountain, he also did Tusk (5.14a/b).

Although he still enjoys clipping bolts, Leavitt's current focus is back on traditional free climbing, where he still sees unlimited potential for new routes. (He insists that Yosemite is still "untapped.") When he's not climbing, he splits his time between his investment business and surfing—two more things he's mastered.

ROMANTIC WARRIOR

The stupidity of youth has its rewards. It was Thanksgiving weekend, long after the first dusting of snow in the high Sierra, when Randy Leavitt and Tony Yaniro decided that they couldn't wait until summer to make their first trip to the Needles. The high-schoolers borrowed the car from Leavitt's parents and drove through the night. When they arrived at the dirt road that leads to the Needles trailhead, it was gated shut—closed for the season. The determined climbers jimmied the lock and skidded their way up the windy road. "We almost got snowed in until spring," laughs Leavitt. "But we found a free-climber's paradise."

For Leavitt and Yaniro, discovering the Needles in 1978 was as exciting as being Royal Robbins in Yosemite during the 1950s. It was the dawn of a Golden Age. There were only a handful of existing routes—most of which were aid climbs begging to be freed—and hundreds of unclimbed lines. They were like kids in a candy store. Everywhere they looked there were soaring dihedrals, splitter cracks, knobby faces, and funky water grooves—all garnished with neon-colored lichen. Adding to the ambiance were giant sequoias, peregrine falcons, and deep blue skies.

The relatively accessible east face of Sorcerer Needle was the site of their first several climbs. On it was an aid route called the Don Juan Wall that was candidate for a free ascent, and an obvious but unclimbed crack system they named Atlantis (5.11+). "We started by doing the first ascent of Atlantis," remembers Leavitt. "We were amazed that it hadn't been climbed. It was like walking up to the Cookie Cliff and grabbing the first ascent of the Nabisco Wall" (see Climb 2).

After climbing Atlantis, Leavitt and Yaniro turned their attention to the impressive-looking Don Juan Wall. It was rated 5.8, A1, and looked like it might go free. Leavitt vividly remembers leading the crux pitch, and the confidence it gave him in Needles granite. "There were a couple of times when the crack pinched down to almost nothing and I thought I was going to get shut down. But then I would look around and find a perfect square knob to high-step on, or a little piece of texture just when I needed it. It made me realize that in the Needles there are always more features than you can see from the ground."

In the summer of 1982, after making several trips to what felt like their very own climbing area, Leavitt and Yaniro laid their

Romancing the stone. Chris Righter belays Leavitt on the fifth pitch (5.12a) of Romantic Warrior. © Jorge Visser, portrait © Jorge Visser

eyes on the secluded southwest face of Warlock Needle. It was the longest, most beautiful swath of granite they'd seen in the Needles. Following the proudest line on the lichen-covered face was an eight-pitch aid climb from 1977 named Romantic Warrior. As soon as they saw the route, the climbers knew they wanted to make an all-free attempt. "It represented the ultimate in what we were doing," says Leavitt. "It was the greatest line in an area of great lines."

Leavitt not only had confidence in the rock, but also in his partner. "Tony was a total believer," he exclaims. "When I would point out a potential new route to my other friends, they would usually say, 'No way!' But not Tony. He was always willing to go for it." Leavitt, too, was feeling pretty gung-ho. After years of concentrating on big walls, his recent focus on free climbing was starting to pay off; he was finally able to do 5.12 crack climbs on the first or second try. Both climbers were in the ideal frame of mind. "We went up on Romantic Warrior with the belief that it would go," he recalls.

As expected, the rock was immaculate. Because of its southwest exposure, the route didn't require a bit of scrubbing. "It was as clean as if had been done 100 times," remembers Leavitt. Not only was the granite clean, it was beautiful; random patches of yellow lichen stood out like coral reefs on a sea of granite.

After following the original line for three pitches, they made a slight variation that followed a more logical line, climbing left of an incipient aid seam (A4) done by the first-ascent party. From there, Yaniro led a short traverse pitch that followed an equally difficult finger crack to a large, sloping ledge.

Above them loomed the sixth pitch, an obtuse dihedral called the Book of Deception. It looked impossibly thin, even by Needles standards. Yaniro attacked the beautiful corner with a double set of RPs and tiny nuts. The climbing was difficult (5.12b) but, like most routes in the Needles, easier than it first appeared. Just when he needed it most, a small edge or nubbin would magically appear. The second pitch of the dihedral, which was almost as spectacular, eased a little (5.11d). The last, moderate pitch led to the rounded summit.

Seventeen years after doing the first ascent, Leavitt climbed Romantic Warrior for the second time in 1999. The route was every bit as good as he remembered. "I like long routes that follow beautiful lines, and I like routes that challenge me," he explains. "In that way, Romantic Warrior is the Astroman of the Needles."

ROUTE DESCRIPTION

Area: Southern Sierra Nevada
First ascent: E. C. Joe and John Peca, 1977; first free ascent: Tony Yaniro and Randy Leavitt, 1982
Base elevation: Approximately 6,400 feet
Summit elevation: Approximately 7,400 feet
Difficulty: V, 5.12b, or 5.10, A2
Time required: 1 long day for fit party
Equipment: Set of RPs; set of DMM "P" nuts (or HB offsets); 2 sets of Rocks (or DMM Wallnuts) sizes 1–6; set of Rocks or Wallnuts sizes 7–9; set of Aliens, purple through red (doubles on red); 2 sets of Friends, no. 1–2½, set of Friends, no. 3, no. 3½; no. 4 Friend and belay seat optional; 2 60-m ropes; runners and quickdraws
Season: Early May–October
Special considerations: Don't forget the camera!
Reference: *The Needles Area* by Sally Moser, Greg Vernon, and Patrick Paul

Approach: There are two ways to get to the Warlock. The first is to follow the approach to Climb 50, Scirocco (Tony Yaniro), and make a high traverse along the north (uphill) side of the Needles, then rappel into the gully between the Witch and the Warlock and descend for 1 hour. A better alternative is to approach the southwest face of the Warlock from the trail to Voodoo Dome, which involves different driving directions: From Kernville (north of California Highway 178), continue north through Johnsondale (1 hour). One mile past Johnsondale, turn right toward Lower Peppermint Campground. Continue north for 13.4 miles (passing Lower Peppermint Campground) to Needle Rock Creek (intersects road). Park just beyond at the large asphalt pullout. The trailhead is marked by stacked rocks 200 yards north of the trailhead. The trail is fairly well defined all the way to Voodoo Dome, then becomes less obvious. When in doubt, head left at branches in the trail. When you come to an eroding scree and dirt gully, continue up and left, steeply at times, and through boulders, to the southwestern corner of the Warlock.

Route: Nine pitches up an extremely clean, obtuse corner system. See topo for details.

Descent: Make five rappels down the route with one traverse. See topo.

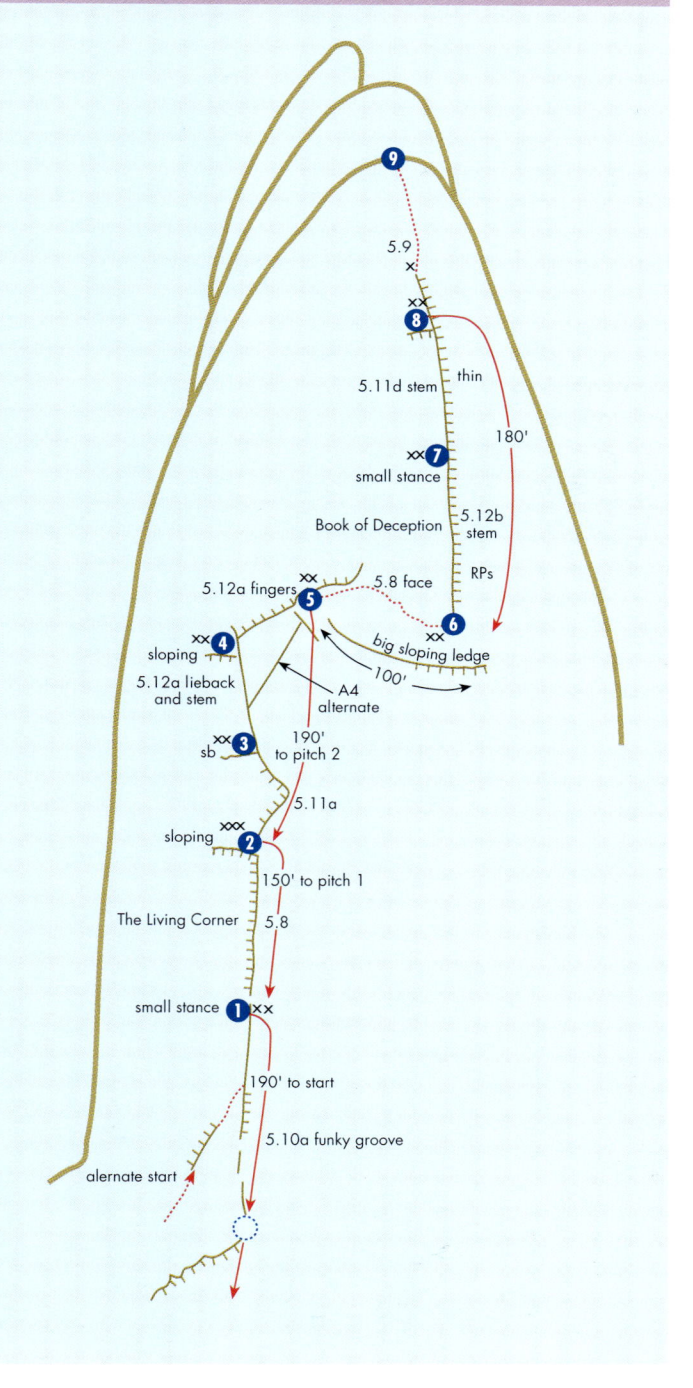

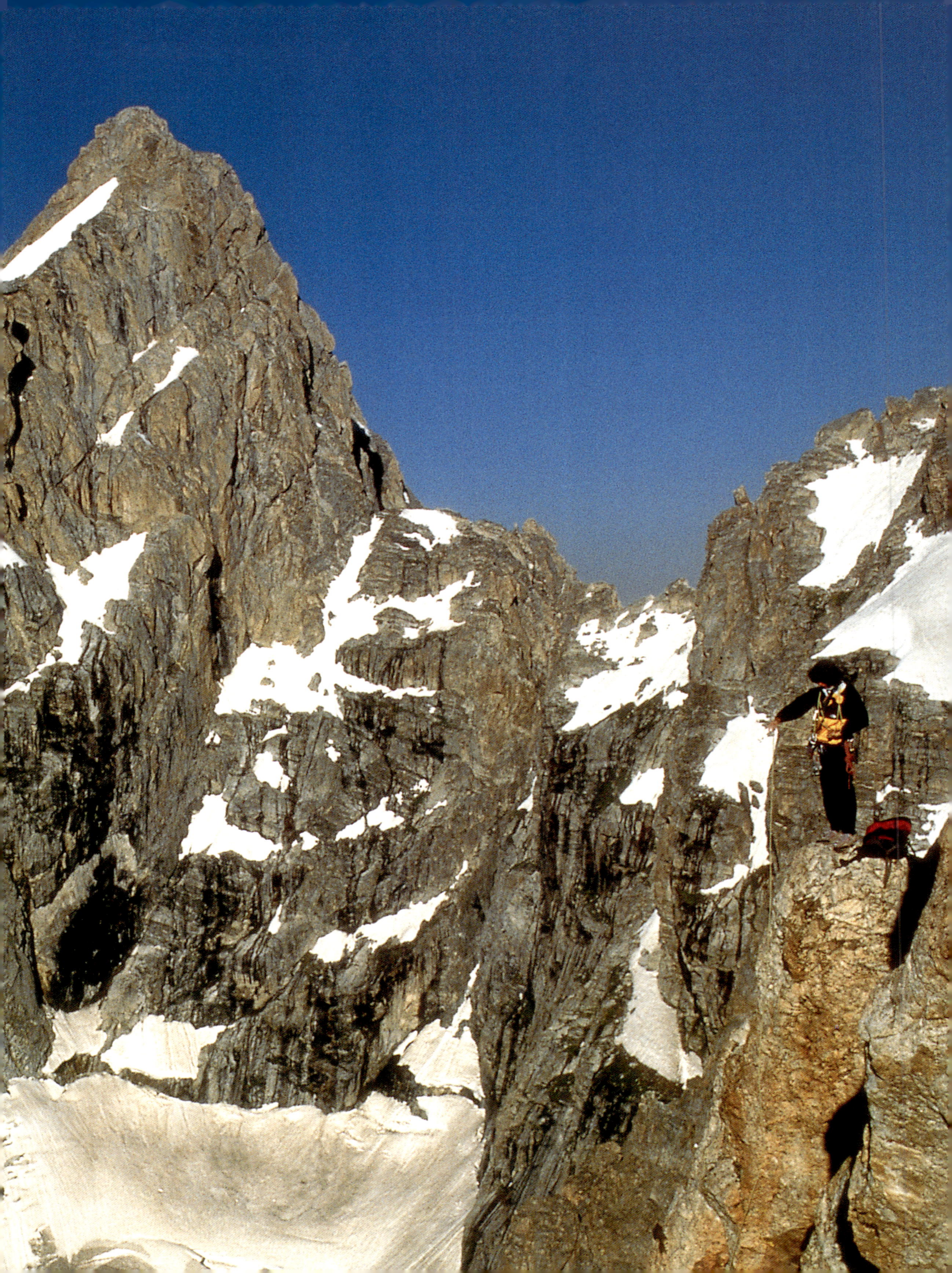

ALEX LOWE

THE GRAND TRAVERSE, GRAND TETON NATIONAL PARK, WYOMING

ALEX LOWE—1958–1999

Author's note: *I met with Alex Lowe to discuss his favorite climb in August 1999. He had just returned from his much-publicized ascent of the Great Trango Tower and was departing for Tibet in less than a month. Despite his hectic schedule, he cheerfully spent several hours telling me about the Grand Traverse. Six weeks later, on October 5, he was swept away by an avalanche on Shishapangma.*

Months later I asked his wife, Jennifer Leigh Lowe, if it was still appropriate to include Alex in this book. She agreed that any book about North America's most accomplished climbers would be incomplete without him. "If he was still with us," she said, "he would want to tell this story."

Every generation or so, an athlete emerges who is so talented, so visionary, and so driven that he or she elevates a sport to a whole new level. Michael Jordan did it for basketball. Wayne Gretzky did it for ice hockey. And Tiger Woods for golf. For climbing in the '90s, it was Alex Lowe.

Lowe, who was almost forty-one when he departed for Shishapangma, was widely regarded as America's most capable, well-rounded climber. Armed with superhuman strength and a huge repertoire of woodsy tricks, it seemed as if there wasn't anything he couldn't climb. The 6-foot 2-inch, 165-pound training maniac summitted Everest without oxygen, cranked 5.13 at the crags, set new standards for ice and mixed climbing, and pioneered new routes on Earth's biggest walls, such as the Great Trango Tower.

Everyone who climbed with Lowe has an "Alex story"—his mind-boggling fitness being the unifying theme. Stories of Lowe's physical exploits usually include phrases like "genetically superior" and "the secret weapon." Others joked that having Lowe on your team was like cheating. It's no wonder that he earned the nickname "the Mutant."

While Lowe's physical capabilities were legendary, he will be remembered most for his indomitable spirit. When the chips were down, Lowe was up. His chronic optimism inspired everyone around him. "His presence made people feel better," said Mark Twight. "You tried harder simply because you knew he was around."

Despite the blizzard of media hype that surrounded his achievements, Lowe remained unaffected—in the words of Todd Skinner, "pure Montana in an age of Hollywood." While he was often portrayed as an almighty conqueror of mountains, Lowe saw it differently; he considered himself a guest in the mountains. "I'm not conquering anything," he explained. "The key to continued success is humility, you know, really admitting that there is a lot of luck involved and that nature is very powerful."

THE GRAND TRAVERSE

Wyoming residents still remember the summer of 1988 for its abnormal weather. In Yellowstone, frequent lightning strikes conspired with howling winds to incinerate thousands of acres of parched forest. And 40 miles south, in the Tetons, the blistering sun forced the snowpack into early retirement. Despite the lingering haze from the nearby forest fires, conditions for rock climbing were never better.

It didn't take long for Lowe—then a first-year Exum guide—to figure out that 1988 was an especially good year for fast solo ascents in the Tetons. Wearing only a pair of shorts, a tank top, and running shoes, he often dashed up the Grand Teton—or one of its neighbors—in 3 or 4 hours, returning to the trailhead with daylight to spare. Tired of repeating the tedious approach hike, Lowe began climbing multiple routes in a single outing.

A logical extension of these sojourns was the Grand Traverse—a seven-summit marathon that connects all of the major peaks surrounding the 13,770-foot Grand Teton. In 1963, Allen Steck, Dick Long, and John Evans completed the traverse in less than 21 hours. Taking into account the range's geologic tilt, the trio climbed from south to north, rappelling the North Ridge of the Grand—the 5.8 technical crux. Having done all of the components of the traverse, and assuming he'd probably solo it without a rope, Lowe figured it would be easier to climb *up* the North Ridge of the Grand than to downclimb it, so if he were to attempt the traverse, he would do it in the opposite direction.

On the east ridge of Teewinot Mountain, the first of seven summits. The Grand Traverse continues up the right-hand skyline of the Grand Teton. © Beth Wald, portrait © Gordon Wiltsie

Unlike the carefully planned 1963 outing, Lowe's first Grand Traverse was somewhat spontaneous. When no guide work materialized on a blue August morning, Lowe parked his car at the Lupine Meadows trailhead and darted up Teewinot's east face, gaining 5,500 feet in less than 2 hours. Comforted by the cloudless sky and his intimate knowledge of the terrain, he decided to continue to the summit of Mount Owen. Feeling strong, and realizing he was approaching one of his favorite spots in the Tetons, Lowe kept going. "I think one of the prettiest sections of the traverse is between Owen and the Grand, through Gunsight Notch," he said. "It doesn't get done that often and has notoriously difficult routefinding, but it's just absolutely beautiful."

Less than an hour later, Lowe found himself at the base of the North Ridge of the Grand Teton. Despite the limitations of his Nike running shoes, he waltzed up the familiar eleven-pitch classic in less than an hour. "Conditions were perfect," he remembers. "The whole Teton range was nice and dry." When he reached the summit of the Grand, his elapsed time was just over 4 hours—a personal best. With three summits and the technical crux behind him, still full of energy and committing to taking it one summit at a time, he continued.

Lowe scurried down the Grand's ever-popular Owen-Spalding route and jogged across the Lower Saddle to the base of the North Ridge of the Middle Teton—a classic route in its own right. After whisking up the moderate, 1,000-foot ridge, Lowe paused for a short break on the summit. When he stood up to continue, he made a mistake that illustrates that even the best climbers have their klutzy moments. One of the countless small rocks he'd treaded on that day rolled under his foot, causing him to fall full-force on his rear. The sharp spike of rock he landed on gouged a huge chunk of flesh out of his butt. In a matter of minutes the spurting blood had soaked through his shorts. Realizing he'd need some stitches, Lowe began the painful descent down the back side of the Middle Teton. The last part of the traverse, he conceded, would have to be done another day.

By the time he reached the saddle between the Middle and South Tetons, the bleeding had stopped. With so much effort invested, Lowe decided to carry on with the traverse. There were only three summits and a few smaller towers left to be climbed. After racing to the summit of South Teton, he quickly romped up Icecream Cone, then tagged the tops of Gilkey Tower and Spalding Peak on his way up the west ridge of Cloudveil Dome. Half an hour later, Lowe completed the traverse by clambering his way to the summit of Nez Perce. A 90-minute knee-bashing sprint to the valley was all that remained.

As Lowe zigzagged down the switchbacks toward the trailhead with his shorts pasted to his leg by copious amounts of blood, he could only imagine what the swarms of hikers who watched him pass were thinking. When he got back to his car, he was dehydrated, exhausted, and pale from blood loss. Lowe's car-to-car time was 8 hours, 15 minutes—less than half the previous time.

When asked how it felt to beat the record so overwhelmingly, Lowe sidestepped the opportunity for self-aggrandizement, emphasizing that his solo time shouldn't be compared to the time for a roped party of three. "Climbing is sort of an isolated activity in which you are really competing with yourself," he explained. "To me, the best climber in the world is the one having the most fun."

On that day, it was Alex Lowe.

Author's note: *On August 26, 2000, speed-climbing ace Rolando Garibotti completed the Grand Traverse, solo, in 6 hours 49 minutes.*

ROUTE DESCRIPTION

Area: Teton Range
First ascent: Allen Steck, Dick Long, and John Evans, 1963
Base elevation: Approximately 6,700 feet
Summit elevations: From north to south: Teewinot Mountain, 12,324 feet; Mount Owen, 12,928 feet; the Grand Teton, 13,770 feet; Middle Teton, 12,804 feet; South Teton, 12,514 feet; Cloudveil Dome, 12,026 feet; Nez Perce, 11,901 feet—more than 12,000 feet of cumulative elevation gain
Difficulty: V, 5.8
Time required: 1–3 days
Equipment: Standard rack to 3 inches, 1 rope, ice ax, crampons, rock shoes recommended
Season: Late July–early September
Special considerations: Permit required for overnight camping; routefinding is biggest challenge
Reference: *A Climber's Guide to the Teton Range,* 3d ed., by Leigh H. Ortenburger and Reynold G. Jackson
Map: Grand Teton

Approach: From park headquarters on US Highway 26/89/187, drive north 8 miles to the South Jenny Lake Junction and mountaineering registration; take the short spur road southwest to the Lupine Meadows trailhead.

Route: The Grand Traverse climbs the seven contiguous summits surrounding the Grand Teton and numerous smaller towers along the way, with 14 miles of hiking, scrambling, and climbing. It is best done from north to south.

Trailhead to Teewinot Mountain: Climb Teewinot's east face route (II, class 4).

Teewinot to Mount Owen: Scramble down a west facing couloir just south of Teewinot's summit to gain the ridge between the two peaks. The big step (peak 11,840+) before the East Prong can be downclimbed (5.6) or rappelled via its west face, or avoided via its north side. Negotiate the ridge, following the line of least resistance to gain the Col at the top of the Koven couloir, from where scrambling and low-angled snow lead to Owen's summit via its east ridge (tricky). This can be avoided by climbing left (south and west) and gaining the summit via the Koven chimney.

Mount Owen to the Grand Teton: From Owen's summit, downclimb the summit chimney of the Koven route, then stay just east of the crest until forced west; scramble down until level with Gunsight Notch, then traverse easy ledges and downclimb 20 feet (5.6) into it. Climb up and then left out of the notch to gain a superb, 100-foot vertical face of flakes and knobs. Follow narrow ledges up and left to easy scrambling on the east side of the Grandstand. Climb the north ridge of the Grand (5.8).

Grand Teton to Middle Teton: Descend the Owen-Spalding route (5.4 or rappel) to the Lower Saddle. Climb the North Ridge (5.6) of the Middle Teton, then descend the southwest couloir.

Middle Teton to South Teton: Follow the crest back up the Northwest Couloir (class 4) of the South Teton.

South Teton to Cloudveil Dome: Descend the east ridge (class 4) of South Teton and climb the west face of Icecream Cone (12,400+, 5.6). Descend Icecream Cone via its east face (class 3) and climb the West Ridge of Gilkey Tower (12,320 feet, class 4) then descend its East Ridge toward Spalding Peak (12,240 feet) which is climbed via its West Ridge (class 4) and descended via its East Ridge (class 3). After a short ridge traverse scramble up the West Ridge of Cloudveil Dome. For this entire section, it is best to stay on the ridgeline.

Cloudveil Dome to Nez Perce: Descend Cloudveil's east ridge (class 4) to reach a col before Nez Perce. A long traverse on the north side of the ridge passes under several small towers.

Descent: Descend Nez Perce via the same route or the east ridge (5.4), returning to the Platforms area of Garnet Canyon. Follow the trail to the Lupine Meadows trailhead.

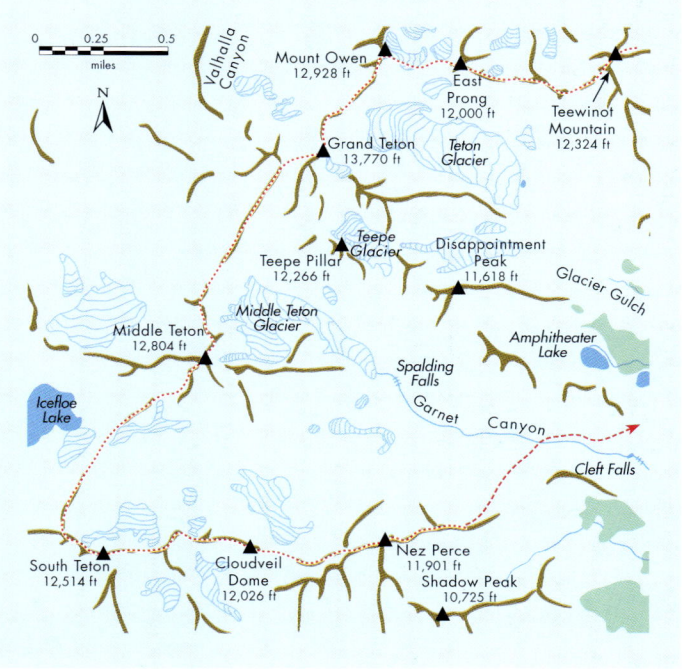

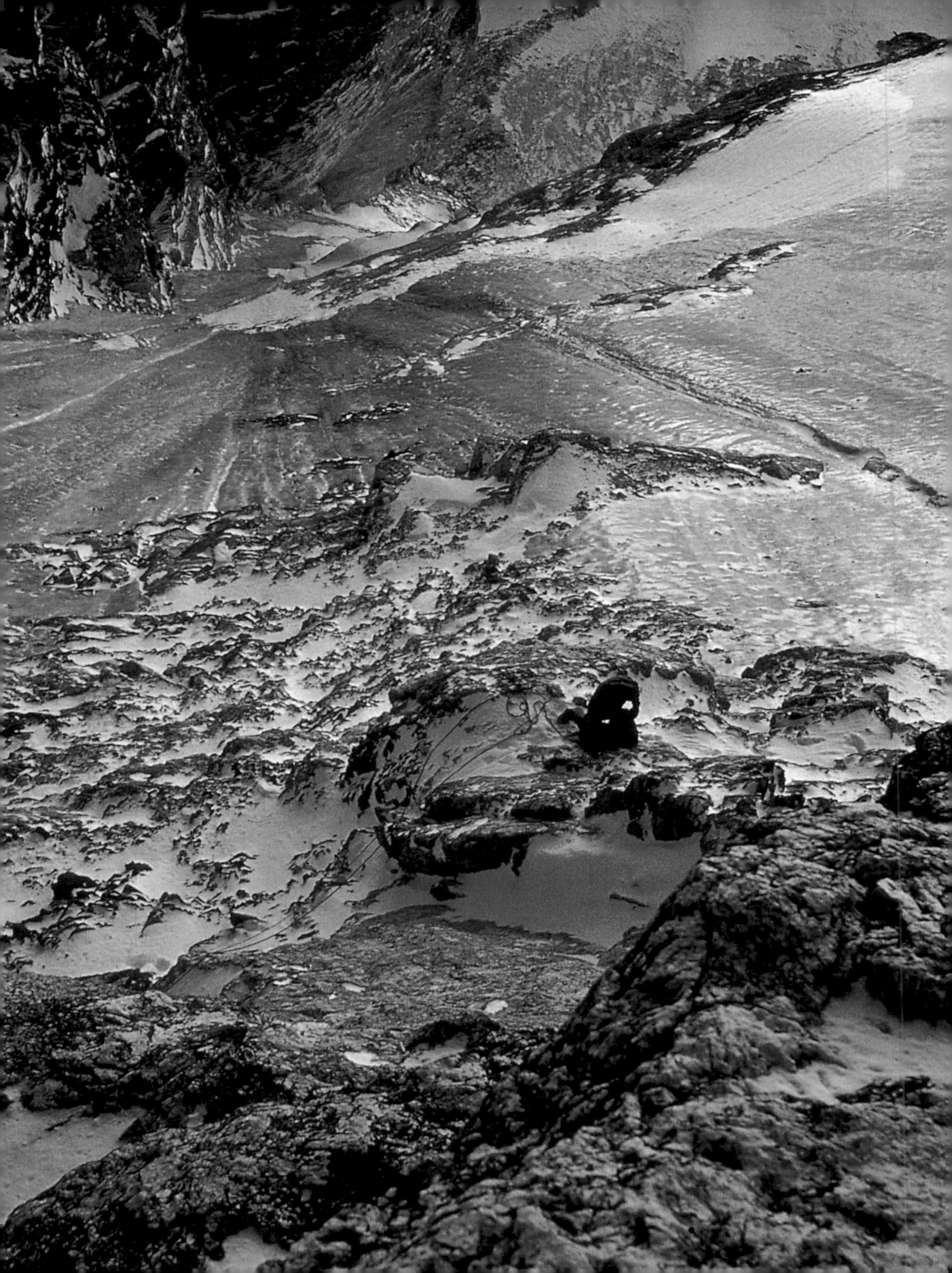

GEORGE LOWE

BLACK ICE COULOIR–WEST FACE LINKUP, THE GRAND TETON, GRAND TETON NATIONAL PARK, WYOMING

GEORGE LOWE—THE PATRIARCH

For four decades, the legendary Lowes have been the most influential family in North American climbing. The contributions of George and his three cousins—Mike, Greg, and Jeff—range from the invention of the internal frame pack to the first organized climbing competition to countless first ascents. (The late Alex Lowe, see Climb 27, was not related.)

George, the eldest of the Lowe clan, was introduced to climbing in 1956 by his uncle Ralph (Jeff's father). Seven years later, Ralph guided George and his three cousins up the Exum Ridge of the Grand Teton. Inspired, George pursued climbing with a vengeance, and was soon establishing standard-setting routes and first winter ascents in the Tetons.

In the early '70s he turned his attention to the Canadian Rockies, where many of his new routes were considered unrepeatable. His 1972 project, the North Face of Mount Alberta, wasn't climbed again until 1981 (see Climb 42). And his 1974 tour de force, the intimidating North Pillar of North Twin, remains unrepeated.

Seeking still greater challenges, the senior Lowe began exploring the Alaska Range in the mid-'70s. His drive and leadership resulted in many high-standard first ascents, including the north face of Mount Hunter and the aptly named Infinite Spur on Mount Foraker (repeated only three times since 1977; see Climb 24). In 1978, he climbed all but 600 feet of the (still unclimbed) North Ridge of Latok I with Jim Donini (see Climb 14), Michael Kennedy (see Climb 24), and Jeff Lowe (see Climb 29)—one of the all-time great alpine-style pushes in the Himalayas. Topping his list of still-unrepeated routes is the Kangshung face on Mount Everest, which he climbed in 1983.

While most of his contemporaries have mellowed, Lowe continues to climb with intensity. Like a good wine, he's improved with age. For example, he made a 1-day ascent of the Nose of El Capitan in 1991, twenty-two years after spending 5 days on El Cap's Salathé Wall. Now in his fifties, Lowe is as summit-hungry as ever. Prospective partners be warned: He still hasn't learned how to back off. Cousin Jeff cautions, "If you want to get up something, go with George."

BLACK ICE COULOIR–WEST FACE LINKUP

After being introduced to the Grand Teton—the 13,770-foot centerpiece of the Teton Range—in 1963 via the Exum Ridge, George Lowe began tackling some of its more challenging routes. He climbed numerous classics, including the North Ridge and the North Face, before turning his attention to the lesser-known West Face.

The original West Face route, which was first climbed in 1940, follows a devious sequence of ramps and snow gullies to the base of the upper headwall, where the best climbing is found. Lowe realized that the classic Black Ice Couloir—a route established in 1961—would offer a more direct and sporty approach to the upper West Face. His appetite for sustained climbs requiring a variety of mountaineering skills led him to combine the two routes in July 1967.

Lowe and his partner—cousin Mike—spent the first day approaching the West Face via the wild and seldom-traveled Valhalla Canyon. When they awoke the next morning, conditions were perfect—it was cool enough to safely climb the Black Ice Couloir, yet not too cold to rock climb without gloves. Using strap-on crampons and wood-shafted ice axes, they raced up the shady, 55-degree gully before the rising sun turned it into a bowling alley. The pitches on the upper West Face went quickly too; they reached the summit with daylight to spare and descended the familiar Owens-Spalding route.

Both Lowes felt that the Black Ice Couloir–West Face Linkup, a superb combination of two Teton classics that naturally join together to create one long alpine route, was by far the best route they'd done on the Grand. "It's a wonderful climb," says George. "It offers a variety of interesting terrain that is never easy yet never really difficult. You get a nice mix of alpine ice and excellent rock."

After making several winter ascents in the Tetons, including the first of the Grand's North Face, Lowe felt he was ready to try the West Face in winter. He made a semi-successful ascent with Dave, Jeff, and Greg Lowe in February 1971, but was forced off by a storm within 1,000 feet of the top. Not one to leave unfinished business, Lowe returned the following winter with cousin Jeff.

Jeff Lowe approaching the West Face of the Grand Teton in February 1972, with the burnished slopes of the Black Ice Couloir below
© George Lowe, portrait © Cameron Burns

© Reynold G. Jackson

When Glenn Exum, the founder of the Teton guide service that still bears his name, heard of the Lowe's intentions, he offered to let them use the Exum guide hut as a base camp. They gladly accepted. George and Jeff shared the hut with four friends who, not coincidentally, were planning to make the first winter ascent of the Exum Ridge: Jock Glidden, Hal Gribble, Dave Smith, and George's brother, Dave.

After a comfortable night in the sturdy structure, the six climbers stepped out into a world of blowing snow and swirling clouds. Undaunted by the weather, George and Jeff bid farewell to the Exum party and made the long, sometimes tricky traverse to the base of the Black Ice Couloir. There was no snow in the couloir—only hard, brittle ice that had been burnished by repeated spindrift avalanches. Solid ice-screw placements were few and far between. The storm intensified as they climbed, increasing the rate and size of the avalanches. In his account of the climb in the 1973 *American Alpine Journal,* George wrote:

> **Thoughts of the White Spider on the Eiger passed through my mind as we timed moves to avoid the avalanches . . . Jeff disappeared totally under sprays of snow several times on his lead. Following was like holding onto a water-ski rope behind a fast boat after falling."**

The weary climbers reached a large snow ledge at the base of the West Face with just enough daylight to stamp out a tent platform.

The next day dawned clear. The alpinists spent the entire day scaling the upper West Face. Rime-coated rock made for time-consuming leads and frigid belays. The ice-lined Great West Chimney forced them to climb with crampons, further slowing their progress. When they finally reached the top of the face that evening, they were exhausted—and out of good weather.

On the last day they awoke to a spindrift-filled tent and a full-on storm. The wind blew so hard it threatened to blow them off the mountain. Still, neither was willing to forego the summit. The determined climbers fought their way to the top of the mountain with almost zero visibility, then raced down the familiar Owens-Spalding route to escape the biting wind. In the *American Alpine Journal*, George described the descent:

> Backing off the standard rappel was difficult— the wind rather than the rope held us up until we reached the overhang. Jeff thought it was the worst rappel he had ever done. The rest of the descent was only miserable, graduating to pleasant when we reached our skis in the trees and skied the fresh powder in lower Garnet Canyon.

ROUTE DESCRIPTION

Area: Teton Range
First ascent: Standard West Face route, Jack Durrance and Henry Coulter, August 14, 1940; Black Ice Couloir, Raymond Jacquot and Herbert Swedlund, July 29, 1961; Black Ice Couloir–West Face Linkup, George Lowe and Mike Lowe, July 23, 1967; first winter ascent: George Lowe and Jeff Lowe, February 1972
Base elevation: 6,700 feet
Summit elevation: 13,770 feet
Difficulty: IV, 5.8, AI 3
Time required: 1 long day from Lower Saddle
Equipment: Medium rack consisting of nuts and cams to 2½ inches, ice-climbing gear, 4–6 ice screws (some short); most parties climb route in mountain boots
Season: Year-round; June–August most popular
Special considerations: Black Ice Couloir subject to natural- and climber-initiated rockfall from Owens–Spalding route, and should be climbed in early morning; keen routefinding skills required to ferret out route's many options
Reference: *A Climber's Guide to the Teton Range*, 3d ed., by Leigh H. Ortenburger and Reynold G. Jackson (pps 196–200, 206, 207; photos 47, 49, 50)
Map: Grand Teton

Approach: From park headquarters on US Highway 26/89/187, drive north 8 miles to the South Jenny Lake Junction and mountaineering registration. The original approach is via seldom-traveled Cascade Canyon into Valhalla Canyon. This is prettier, but requires gear to be carried over the top. Most parties start at the Lupine Meadows trailhead and hike the Garnet Canyon trail to the Lower Saddle (3–5 hours).

Route: From the Lower Saddle, take the Valhalla Traverse ledge to the corner of the northwest ridge of the Enclosure. Follow a faint trail down along the ledge for a short distance until a small ridge that forms the right (west) edge of a small bowl is met. Traverse on rotten rock for two rope-lengths, maintaining elevation, to the west edge of the Enclosure Ice Couloir (see photo). Continue toward two small, diagonal shelves at the base of the north buttress of the Enclosure. In two pitches (some 5.7) gain the lower shelf to the base of the main ice field of the Black Ice Couloir (approximately 11,000 feet elevation). The Black Ice Couloir consists of four distinct ice fields. The (recommended) Valhalla Traverse approach avoids the lower two, and enters the very bottom of the third (main) ice field. Assuming the West Face is climbed, the upper (fourth) ice field is also avoided. Follow the main ice field for about four pitches, trending left to the base of the West Face. Continue up the West Face on excellent rock for eight pitches (see topo), choosing between the Great Western Chimney or climbing to its left.

Descent: Descend the Owens–Spalding route to the Lower Saddle.

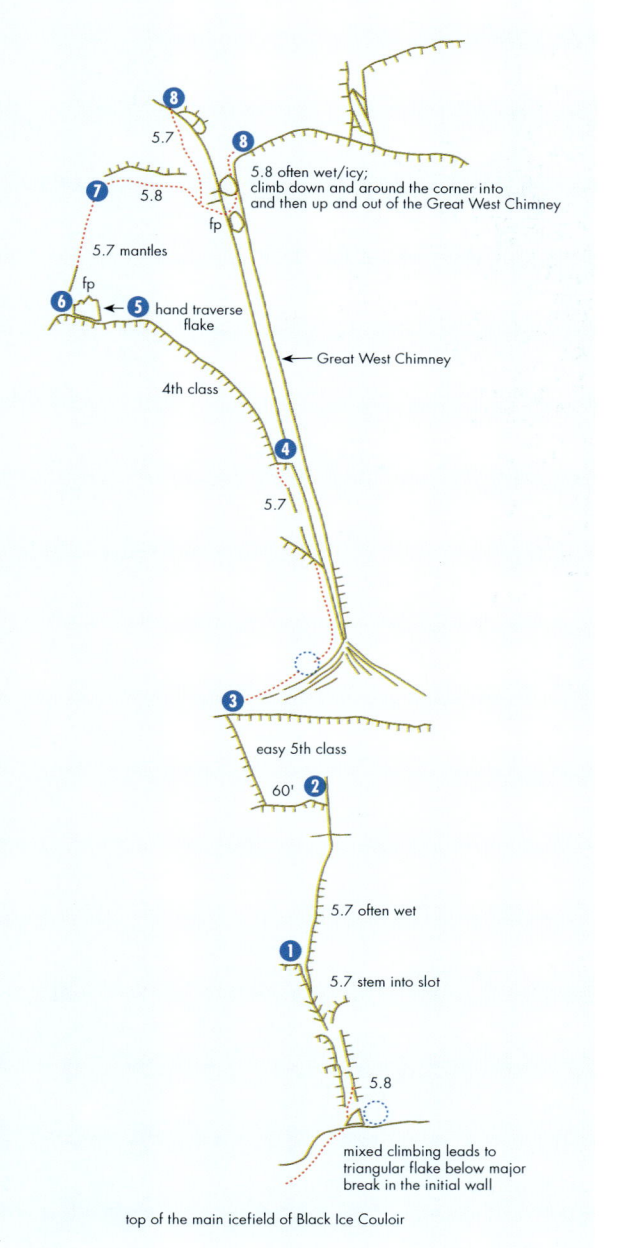

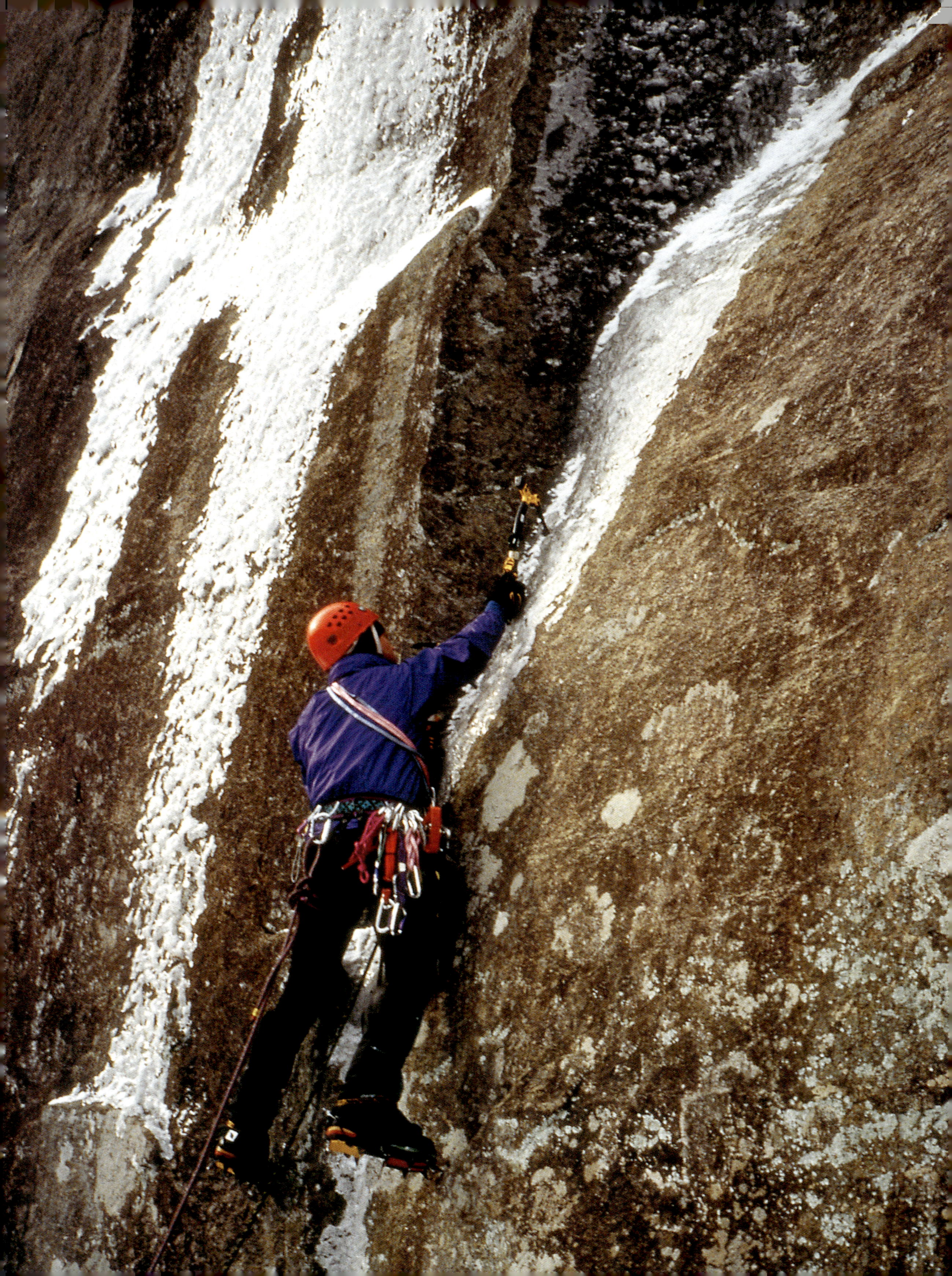

JEFF LOWE

GORILLAS IN THE MIST, POKOMOONSHINE, ADIRONDACK MOUNTAIN PARK, NEW YORK

JEFF LOWE—THE MIXED MASTER

In the fall of 1964, fourteen-year-old Jeff Lowe learned that the unclimbed North American Wall on Yosemite's El Capitan had been conquered by four of his heroes: Royal Robbins, Yvon Chouinard, Chuck Pratt, and Tom Frost. Lowe, then a mere freshman as a technical climber, was awestruck by the feat. "That seemed like going to the moon," he remembers. "It made a big impression on me." But it wasn't long before Lowe's heroes would consider him a peer. Just six years later, the talented but little-known climber made the route's fourth ascent.

Almost four decades later, with more than 500 first ascents to his name, Jeff Lowe is regarded as one of the world's premier alpinists. Yet he hardly looks the part. The clean-shaven, bespectacled Lowe stands 5 feet 10 inches, weighs about 160 pounds, and looks like he might work in a corner bookstore. His distinction as a climber is as much about style as substance. He is a purist. Eschewing large expeditions, bottled oxygen, and fixed ropes, Lowe prefers "trips with friends"—light and fast ascents of daring, technical routes in the world's most remote ranges. Mark Twight (see Climb 47), who accompanied Lowe on numerous trips during the mid-'80s, says, "For more than twenty years, Jeff Lowe led the movement toward lightweight, highly technical alpine climbing. Many of his routes were far ahead of their time."

Lowe's first ascents can be found all over North America. Over the years he has established scores of classic rock routes such as Zion National Park's Moonlight Buttress (Utah) and the East Face of Keeler Needle in the Sierra (California). But it is Lowe's bold exploits on ice—routes such as Keystone Green Steps (Alaska), Bridalveil Falls (Colorado), and the Grand Central Couloir (Mount Kitchener, Canadian Rockies)—that evoke sweaty palms among the cognoscenti.

He has also made his mark on the international scene. A small sample of his accomplishments abroad include the first solo ascent of the South Face of Ama Dablam, the North Face of Kwangde, the North Face of Tawoche, and the first solo ascent of the French Pillar of Pumori—all in Nepal. In Europe, he challenged the status quo with an almost-free ascent of the Direct Bonatti Route on Grand Capucin, and soloed a new route on the North Face of the Eiger, in winter, without bolts. The 9-day ordeal is arguably the greatest achievement ever performed by an American in the Alps.

In the early '90s, Lowe turned his attention to mixed climbing, an alpine pursuit that combines rock and ice climbing into a single discipline. Lowe's book *Ice World* is the mixed master's take on the virtually unlimited potential for mixed climbing.

GORILLAS IN THE MIST

Jeff Lowe was bored. After he had practically invented the sport of modern ice climbing, and spent two decades proving he could scale just about anything that would freeze, the sport suddenly seemed uninteresting. The standards, he felt, had not increased significantly in twenty years. And for him, the sport was no longer a challenge. "I had gotten to the point where I could be totally out of shape and still do the hardest routes," says Lowe. "Anything you can do without working at it loses its appeal."

Lowe's funk didn't last long. In the winter of 1992, while at an ice-climbers' meeting in Europe, he hooked up with a climber named Thierry Renault, one of the best ice technicians in France. Renault had spotted a new route on the nearby Tête de Gramusat, and convinced Lowe to join him for its first ascent. Thinking it would be just another shaft of frozen ice, Lowe reluctantly agreed to go.

A predawn start put them at the base of the climb just as it was getting light. When Renault set his pack down, signifying they were at the start of the first pitch, Lowe couldn't believe his eyes. The proposed route didn't look anything like an ice climb. "I'm looking up at this big, big cliff, and all I see are curtains of ice hanging from these huge overhangs," remembers Lowe. "So I say to Thierry, 'This is it, huh?' And he says, 'Yes, Jeff, we going up here.'"

Although it looked improbable, Renault's line turned out to be an outstanding, twelve-pitch mixed climb. When there was no ice for their crampons and ice picks, they hooked them on microscopic edges and torqued them into small cracks. On the fourth pitch, the pair used two points of aid to surmount an 18-foot roof. Otherwise, the route—dubbed Blind Faith—went free at M6+. Although he was disappointed that they didn't free-climb

Jeff Lowe on the crux first pitch (M6+) of Gorillas in the Mist during the route's first ascent © Mark Wilford, portrait © Greg Epperson

The ice on Gorillas in the Mist is seldom more than four inches thick, but can be remarkably solid in good conditions. © Mark Wilford

the roof, Lowe was totally energized. "The experience really sparked my imagination," he says. "After that, I just started looking for mixed free-climbing projects."

Four years and many mixed climbs later, Lowe found himself in the Pokomoonshine area of New York's Adirondack Mountains. He was teaching an ice-climbing seminar hosted by Adirondack Rock and River, a local guide service and lodge. It was his third seminar in as many years. Lowe found the teaching sessions invigorating; they enabled him to share his enthusiasm for ice climbing, make a little money, and, of course, do some climbing himself.

The students not only coveted Lowe's advice, they expected to see him perform. "Part of the fun of doing the seminars," he offers, "is that the students would want to see what I could do. So I'd always do at least one new route at each locale. I felt that it was good to show the students the reality of doing a new route on-sight, where the thing is not wired, where they see me having to take care to protect it, climbing up and down, being careful, maybe even retreating."

For the prior year's demonstration climb, Lowe picked an overhanging dihedral with a beautiful tongue of ice hanging out of it. He climbed the dicey corner while his eager students gathered below and watched his every move. As he dangled from the ice curtain with one arm and placed an ice screw with the other, a disgruntled truck driver pulled over and yelled, "Get a job, asshole." And so the route was named.

His 1996 demonstration climb was even more spectacular. Far right of the area classic Positive Thinking, Lowe spotted a tantalizingly thin, discontinuous drip of ice about 500 feet high. "From a distance," Lowe recalls, "it was nothing more than a smear of mist plastered to the wall. It looked really improbable." He walked to the base of the route for a closer look. Conditions were perfect. "The ice was very well bonded," he explained. "And the verglas was locked to the rock, which is critical."

He recruited Ed Palen, president of Adirondack Rock and River, to join him on the climb. Lowe, who led the entire route, says that the hardest part was getting to the first ribbon of ice. "For the first 15 feet, I was climbing up a seam with my picks, and then I found a little ice in the corner. I had to carefully tick my way up that corner for another 30 feet before getting my first piece of protection."

After the initial crux (M6+), the technical difficulties eased—a little. The rest of the climb, for him, was more of an intellectual exercise than a physical challenge. "Once I got up that part, and got some protection in, the climb was not that hard, but was very intricate and interesting. It didn't just go straight up, it traversed back and forth," elaborates Lowe. "It stayed thin for the first three pitches. It was never more than 4 inches thick, and often much thinner."

Five hours after they left the ground, Lowe and Palen completed the first ascent of Gorillas in the Mist. What started as a spontaneous teaching exercise had turned into an area classic, and one of Lowe's favorite climbs.

In the years since Lowe's visit, Ed Palen has witnessed a flurry of new route development. "In his short time here," says Palen, "Jeff really energized the local winter climbing scene." While there are many new lines to choose from, Palen says none of them compare to Gorillas in the Mist. "When people pick the local granddaddy of mixed routes, the purest, most eye-catching, adrenalin-pumping mixed route in the region, Jeff's visionary climb is the unanimous choice."

ROUTE DESCRIPTION

Area: Adirondack Mountains, upstate New York
First ascent: Jeff Lowe and Ed Palen, February 1996
Difficulty: IV, WI 5+, M6+
Time required: 4–8 hours
Equipment: 6 short ice screws, 3 regular-length screws, a few thin pitons and a baby angle, double 9 mm x 60-m ropes, slings
Season: Late November–March
Special considerations: Route is very condition dependent; day-use fee collected at parking area
Reference: *Climbing in the Adirondacks* by Don Mellor (Adirondack Mountain Club, date unknown)

Approach: Pokomoonshine is located in the northeast corner of Adirondack Mountain Park, near Lake Champlain, about 25 miles from Plattsburgh. Approach on State Highway 87, getting off at the Willsboro exit. Park at the state campground at the base of the cliff.

Route: A 500-foot, continuous line of smears and thinly iced corners up one of the highest walls in the area. Four pitches. See topo for details.

Descent: Walk north through the woods at the top of the cliff until it's possible to descend with little difficulty down wooded slopes back to the base.

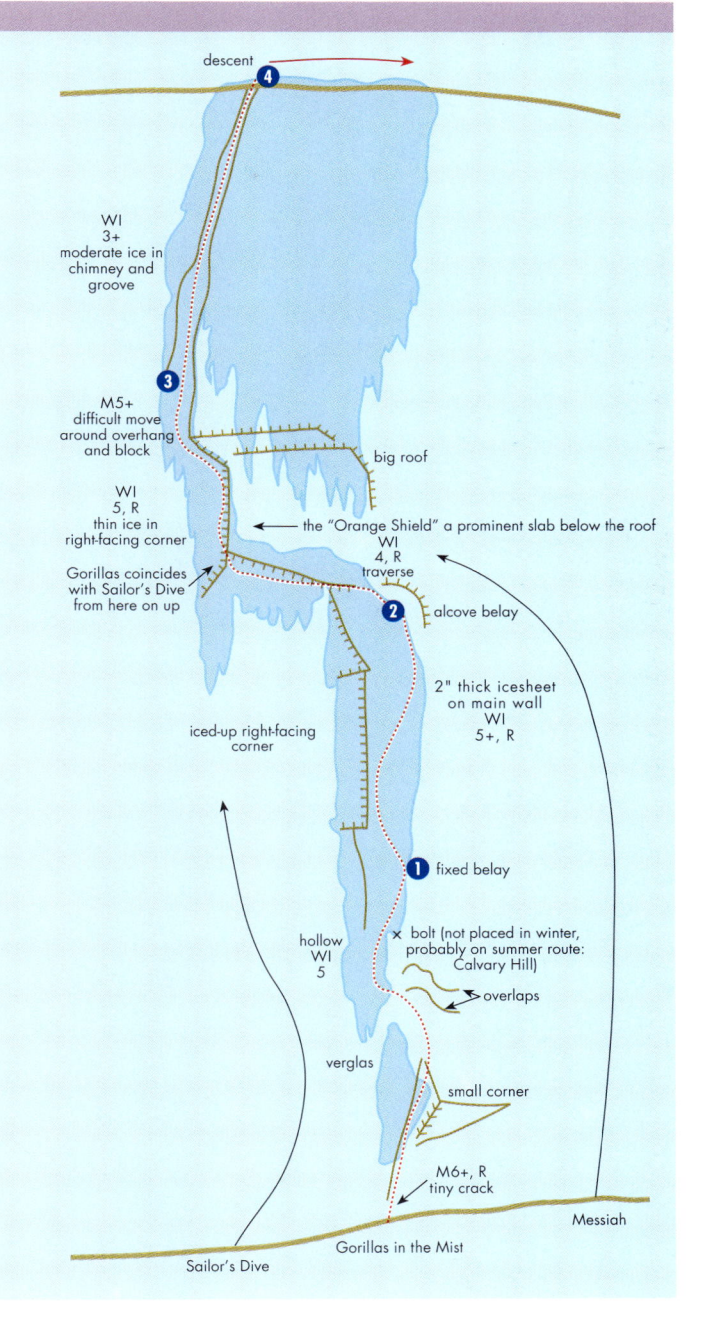

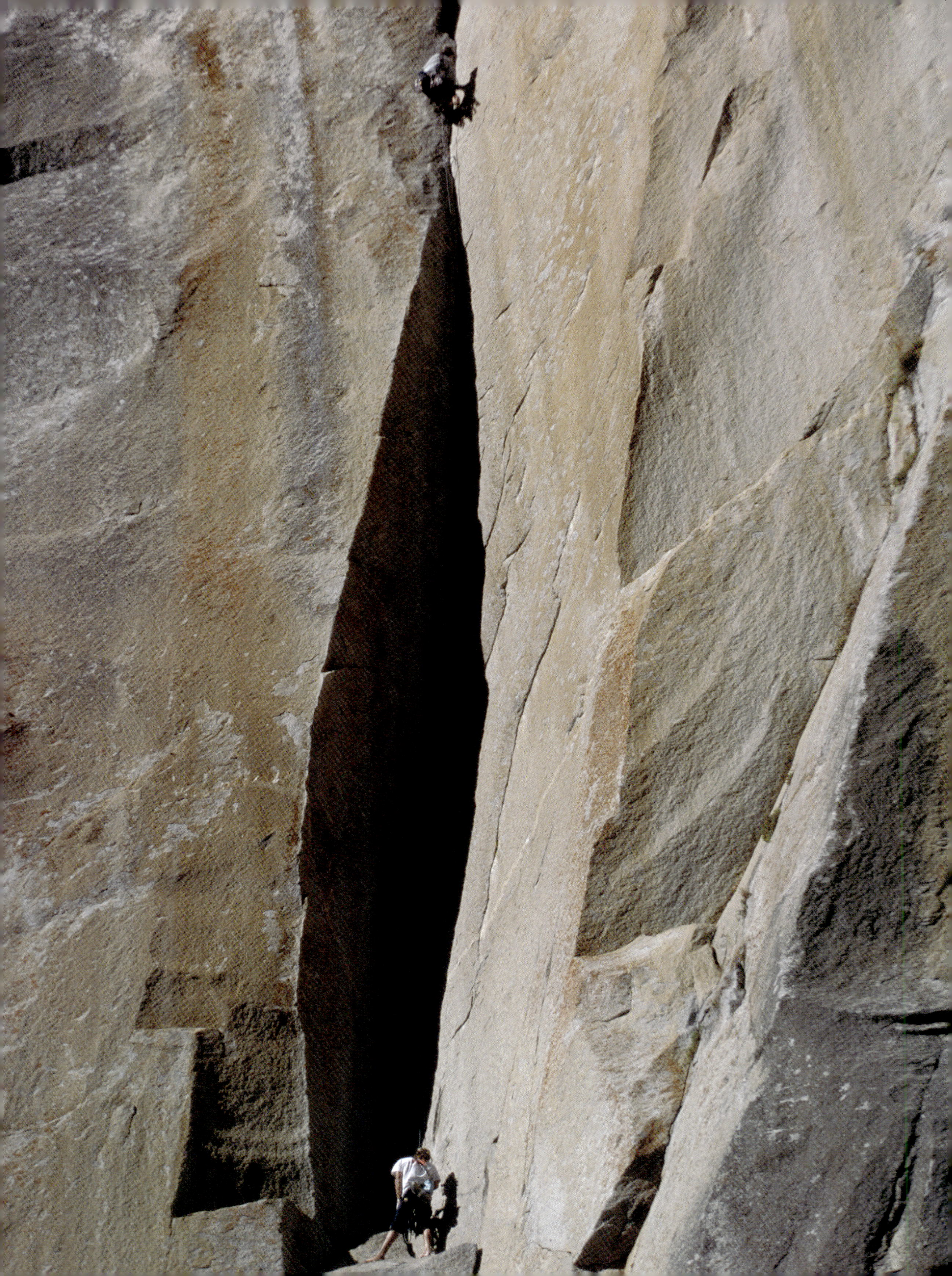

SUE MCDEVITT

ASTROMAN, WASHINGTON COLUMN, YOSEMITE NATIONAL PARK, CALIFORNIA

SUE MCDEVITT—KEEPING IT SIMPLE

Sue McDevitt's blissful life can be explained in three words: Less is more. There are many things she doesn't have, or want—such as a waterfront condo, a high-pressure job, or a convertible Saab. Yet the things she does want, she has.

She has Dan McDevitt, her husband and favorite climbing partner. She has Makayla Rose McDevitt, born on July 7, 1999. She has a home in Yosemite West, a woodsy community at the park's edge. And she has more than twenty-five ascents of El Capitan under her belt. In fact, Sue McDevitt has the one thing most people don't have: a life.

Sue Bonovich met Dan McDevitt while she was bike touring through Yosemite in 1984. "I saw him sitting at a picnic table," she reminisces, "and it was love at first sight. We've been together ever since." Prior to meeting Dan, Sue had run four marathons and biked from Europe to Africa, but had never been rock climbing. A year after meeting Dan, Sue was climbing 5.11 (that's Yosemite 5.11—off-width cracks and all). And a few years after that, she quietly emerged as one of the best all-around rock climbers in North America.

For someone who scales big walls and sends 5.12 cracks, McDevitt hardly looks the part. When you see her petite, 5-foot frame, wavy brown hair, and Wheaties-box smile, you imagine her doing triple toe-loops on ice skates, not hauling 100-pound loads up El Capitan. Yet hidden below her girl-from-Minnesota exterior is the adventurous spirit that led her to Yosemite in 1985, and has kept her there ever since, leading a life she wouldn't trade for anything. "We're kind of in our own little world here," says McDevitt. "It's a nice, simple lifestyle."

ASTROMAN

Back in 1958, when Warren Harding started aid-climbing his way up the 1,100-foot east face of Washington Column, it would have been hard to imagine that the route would eventually become one of the most classic free climbs in the world. And the notion that a girl from Minnesota would one day race up the climb to "train" for a 1-day ascent of El Capitan would have been even more inconceivable. In those days, simply getting up the wall—in a week or a month—was a huge undertaking.

Harding's first attempt to climb Washington Column was the result of a ranger-enforced climbing ban on El Capitan. That year, he had come to Yosemite with a single, overriding objective: to make the first ascent of El Cap's 3,000-foot face. In an effort that spanned many months, Harding and his cronies made it halfway up the cliff by late May. But when their highly visible assault started causing traffic jams on the valley floor, the park service ordered them to postpone their climb until after Labor Day. Determined to accomplish something during the summer months, Harding shifted his focus to Washington Column.

Although any route on the unclimbed granite pillar would have given him bragging rights, he chose the proudest line on the east face. Harding made it halfway up the orange-tinted wall in two separate pushes, but retreated when confronted by an intimidating squeeze chimney—what would later be dubbed the Harding Slot. He didn't get back to Yosemite until after Labor Day, and when he did, El Cap beckoned. He spent the rest of the season completing the historic first ascent of the Nose.

In the spring of the following year, Harding returned to Washington Column to resume his project. Like his ascent of El Capitan, it turned into a multimonth, multipartner siege. After pounding in more than 100 pitons and fixing 1,000 feet of Goldline rope, Harding, Chuck Pratt, and Glen Denny finally reached the top on July 30, 1959. It wasn't as big a deal as climbing El Cap, but was still a significant achievement.

The route didn't make headlines again until June 1975, at the height of the free-climbing revolution. That's when three of the most talented free climbers of the era—John Bachar (see Climb 2), Ron Kauk (see Climb 23), and John Long—looked at the climb with new eyes. Armed with EB rock shoes, nylon ropes, and Hexentric nuts, they free-climbed every pitch of the route, and renamed it Astroman. Stories of their achievement spread quickly, and it wasn't long before Astroman was the most sought-after free climb in the Valley. It was considerably harder than the Nabisco Wall (see Climb 2), and way more continuous.

Ten years later, when Sue Bonovich rolled into Yosemite on her touring bike, Astroman had a reputation as *the* route to do. Although

Climbers on Astroman's famous third pitch, the sustained "Enduro Corner" (5.11c) © Jared Ogden, portrait © Kennan Harvey technically harder climbs existed, few were as clean or sustained. It seemed that someone was always talking about Astroman in Camp 4. Famous pitches such as the Enduro corner and the Harding Slot were the subject of many fireside tales. It sounded like the ultimate climb to Sue. Someday, she hoped, she'd be good enough to do it.

Dan McDevitt spent the next year helping his girlfriend (and now wife) hone her climbing skills. He put her through the full Yosemite curriculum: chimneys, off-widths, flaring cracks, stemming corners, the whole bit. At first, she was terribly discouraged. "I would get 4 feet up an off-width crack and I'd have bruises all over my body," laughs McDevitt. But she quickly mastered the specialized techniques of Yosemite climbing. She also learned that her small size was often an advantage. Her petite hands fit neatly into thin cracks, and her 5-foot frame wedged securely into narrow chimneys.

By the spring of 1986, after a year of continuous climbing, Sue was a solid 5.11 climber. She climbed regularly with Dan, but also with Werner Braun, a talented and generous Yosemite "lifer." One morning, while strolling through Camp 4, Braun walked into the McDevitts' campsite to see if they wanted to go climbing. Dan had to work, but Sue eagerly agreed to go. When Braun asked her what she wanted to climb that day, she told him Astroman. She'd said this before, but always in jest. This time she was serious. Having done the route several times, and well aware of its difficulty, Braun looked at Dan, and said, "Do you think she's ready?" He nodded.

To ensure it would be a positive experience for his friend, Braun insisted on leading every pitch. As he charged up the cracks, she often wondered if she could follow. "Every time he led a pitch, I was thinking, 'I hope I can make it up this one,'" she recalls. "Looking back, I don't know how I did it. It must have been adrenalin." They completed the climb with enough time to descend the North Dome gully before dark. McDevitt was euphoric. "Up until that point," she remembers, "it was the best day of my life."

The successful outing on Astroman bolstered her confidence and inspired her to train even harder. After doing the route for the second time with Dave Shultz, one of the fastest and boldest Yosemite climbers of the '80s, she decided to team up with Mary Braun (Werner's wife) and make the first all-woman ascent of Astroman. Swinging leads, the pair completed the feat in the fall of 1990.

Since then, McDevitt has climbed Astroman at least seven times, sometimes leading every pitch. In addition to guiding the route, she's climbed it three times with Nancy Feagin (see Climb 15), another female climber who specializes in such endurance-oriented climbs. (She and Feagin have also made 1-day ascents of the Nose and Half Dome.)

What is it that keeps McDevitt returning to Astroman year in and year out? "First of all," she explains, "the rock is just so clean, every pitch is pristine." It's also her favorite way to build endurance for even longer climbs. Finally, McDevitt appreciates the beautiful setting. "It's in the prettiest part of the Valley," she explains. "You're looking at Half Dome, Quarter Dome, and Glacier Point Apron. You see golden eagles and falcons, and there are no tour buses or crowds below you. It's just nice to be over there."

© Mark Kroese

ROUTE DESCRIPTION

Area: East face of Washington Column, Yosemite Valley
First ascent: Warren Harding, Glen Denny, and Chuck Pratt, July 30, 1959;
  first free ascent: John Bachar, John Long, and Ron Kauk, 1975 (renamed Astroman)
Difficulty: IV, 5.11c
Time required: 1 long day
Equipment: Nuts and cams to 3½ inches, extra ¼-inch to 2½-inch pieces; 2 ropes recommended
Season: Spring and fall
Special considerations: Route gets morning sun; descent down North Dome gully notoriously tricky
Reference: *Yosemite Climbs, Free Climbs* by Don Reid

Approach: From the State Highway 140 entrance into the park, proceed to the Ahwahnee Hotel (recommended) or North Pines campground and park. Follow the trail to Indian Caves, then head up (north) where the bike path and the horse trail almost intersect. From here, follow the drainage that comes down from the left side of Washington Column, then head right on the climbers trail that skirts the cliff.

Route: Twelve pitches of consistently difficult, exposed, clean crack climbing. See topo for details.

Descent: From the top of Washington Column, a trail traverses east all the way to the forested gully above the so-called "death slabs." Don't be tempted down into the gully too soon. If contemplating a rappel, continue to veer left, to the far (east) side of the gully. Don't try the descent at night.

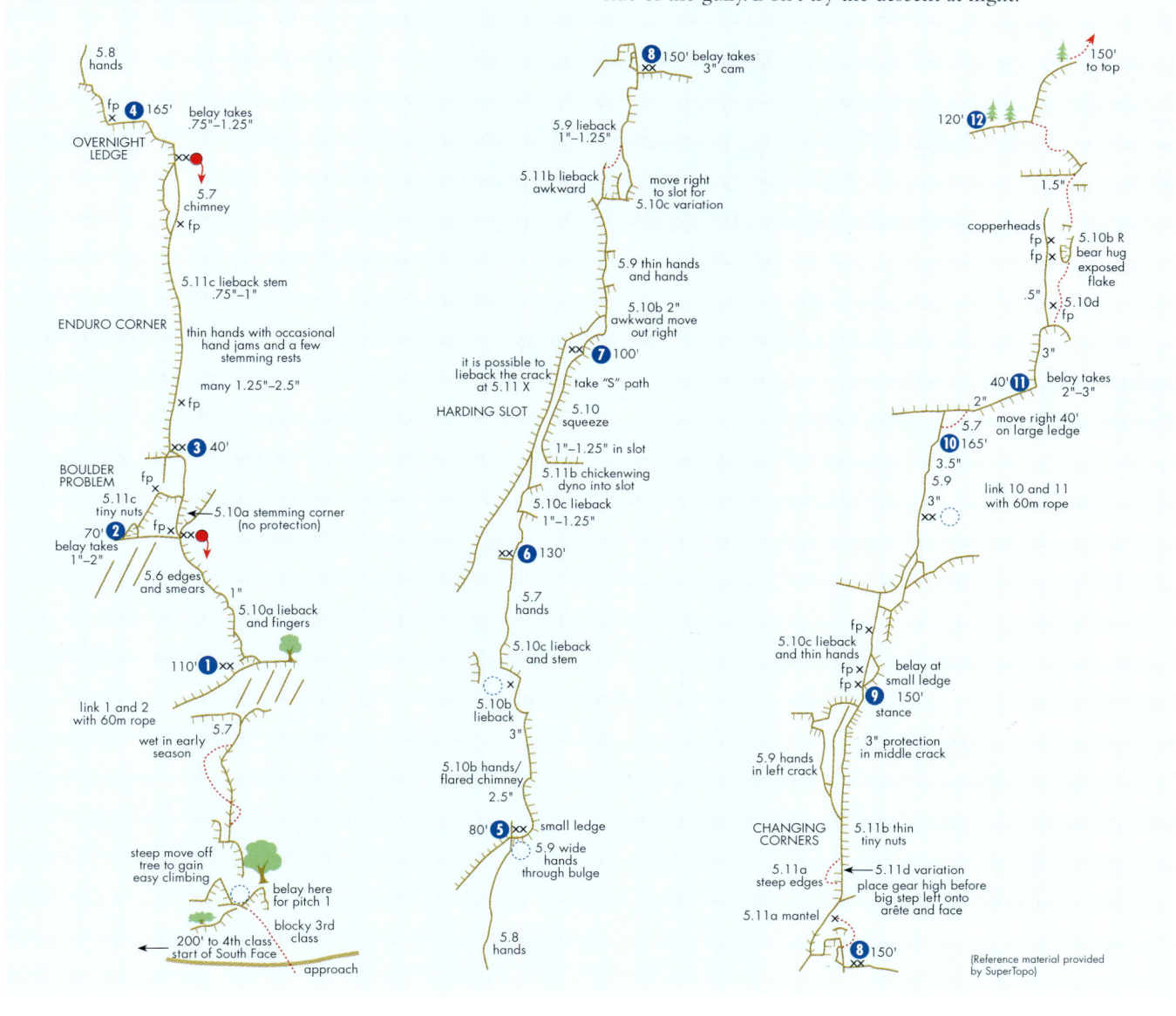

(Reference material provided by SuperTopo)

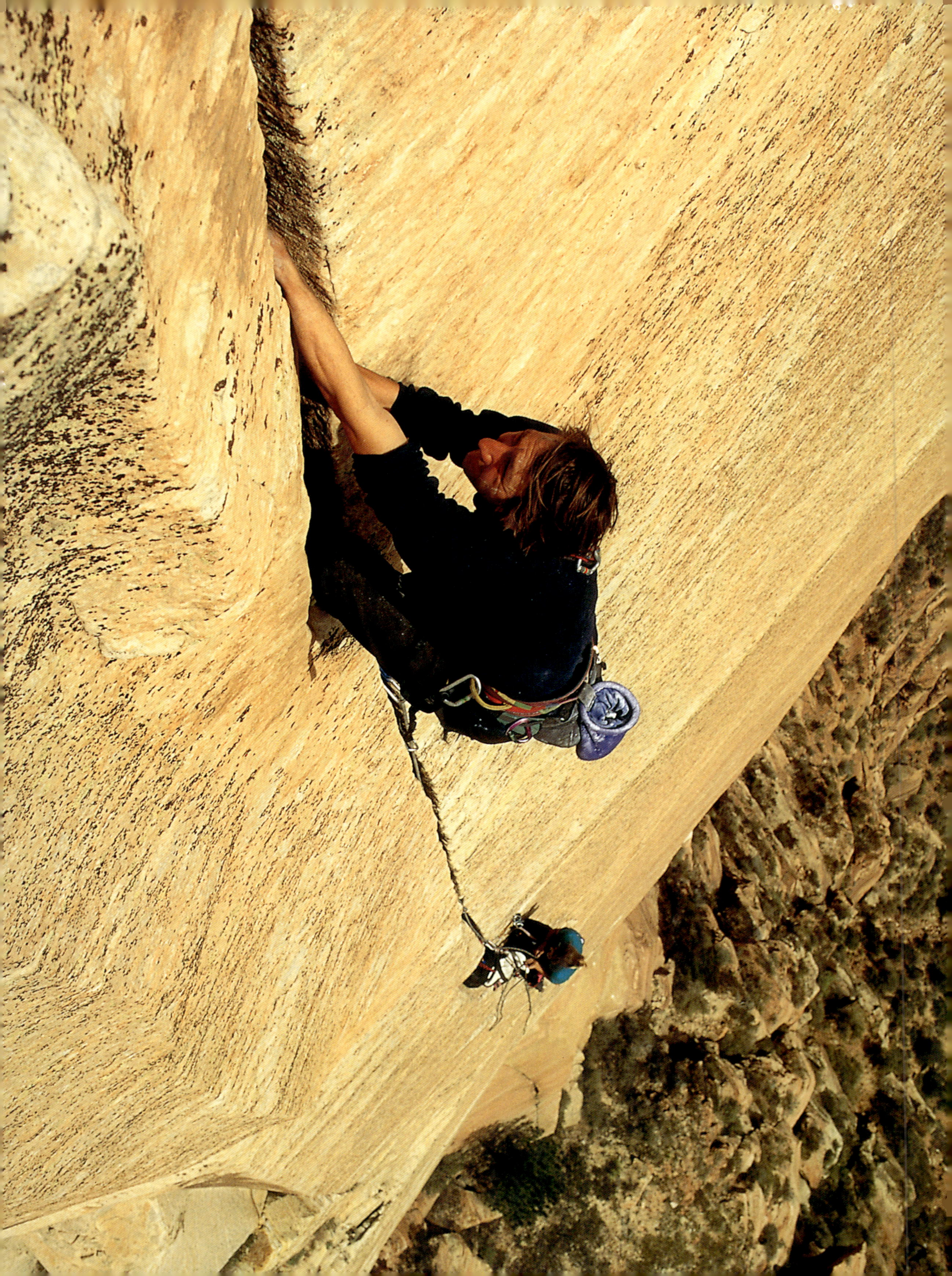

JOHN MIDDENDORF

TRICKS OF THE TRADE, ISAAC, ZION NATIONAL PARK, UTAH

JOHN MIDDENDORF—THE DEUCE

Shortly after earning his mechanical engineering degree from Stanford University in 1983, John Middendorf decided to quit climbing. He announced his retirement to his friends, sold his gear, and began looking for a job. But his resolve to lead a normal life didn't last long: Several months later, while interviewing in San Francisco, he made a weekend excursion to Yosemite—and stayed for three years.

When Middendorf showed up in the Valley in 1984, there was a lull in big-wall activity. "Most people were coming to the Valley to free-climb," he explains. "There were only about eight or ten of us doing walls." Middendorf helped reenergize the scene. Over the next three years, he did more than thirty wall routes, including the first ascent of the Atlantic Ocean Wall (VI, 5.10, A4+) on El Capitan. He also earned his nickname, which evolved from Middendorf to Dussendorf to just Deuce.

The lanky engineer's second retirement came in '87. Anxious to put his education to use, and determined to improve the quality of big-wall equipment, he founded a specialty gear company called A5. He spent the next three years building the business and designing state-of-the-art wall-climbing equipment, such as the modern portaledge.

Middendorf's advanced designs spawned a whole new generation of big-wall climbers, and inspired him to test his gear on remote, wilderness walls. After failing to stay retired for the second time, in 1992 he pioneered the Grand Voyage (VII, 5.10, A4+, WI 3) on Pakistan's Great Trango Tower, one of several ultralong routes he has established. He's been pushing big-wall standards—and himself—ever since.

Middendorf shares his extensive repertoire of wall-climbing tricks in *Big Walls*, a how-to guide he co-authored. The book tells you everything you need to know about big-wall climbing—except how to quit.

TRICKS OF THE TRADE

A thousand feet of sandstone feels like 2,000 feet of granite.

—*John Middendorf*

Not far from the road that leads to the popular Zion Lodge is a seldom-visited cirque of sandstone spires known as the Court of the Patriarchs. Presiding over the desert landscape is a proud trio of towers named after the original three biblical fathers: Abraham, Isaac, and Jacob.

The Court of the Patriarchs is a beautiful place in any season, but is especially divine after a spring rainstorm. The freshly soaked Navajo sandstone radiates with color as soon as the sun reappears. In April 1992, John Middendorf happened to be driving through Zion Canyon just as the skies were clearing from a cloudburst. From his car he caught a glimpse of the unclimbed southeast face of Abraham, bathed in a rainbow of color. It was begging to be explored.

Later that year, Middendorf persuaded his longtime friend Walt Shipley to join him for an ascent of Abraham. Albeit difficult, their new aid route (the Radiator, VI, 5.10, A4) was even better than expected, and offered a spectacular view of the tallest of the three patriarchs, Isaac. Middendorf spent numerous multihour belays staring at its unclimbed, 1,800-foot southeast face. Of particular interest was an 800-foot hand crack that split the upper headwall like a zipper. Even to a climber who had spent much of the '80s living in Yosemite, it looked too good to be true.

After a year of dreaming about what promised to be the ultimate hand crack, Middendorf returned to Zion the following spring. His first order of business was to find a partner with whom he could inspect the lower section of the route. Zion's reputation for poisonous fauna, long bushwhacks, and searing heat discourages most climbers from venturing beyond the established routes. But it wasn't long before he met Calvin Hebert, a gung-ho lad from Boulder, Colorado. Hebert had only 1 day left to climb, but was eager to try something new.

Rather than fully disclose his plans to his new friend, Middendorf simply told Hebert that there were an abundance of worthwhile single-pitch climbs at Isaac's base. The promise of Indian Creek–quality crack climbing was enough to lure Hebert through the fortress of manzanita that guarded the sandstone tower. From the base of Isaac, Middendorf spotted a crack system that led to a

John Middendorf making the first ascent of the coveted hand crack on Tricks of the Trade. The 19-pitch route has only 60 feet of aid.
© Bill Hatcher, portrait © Bill Hatcher

When he spotted a hand crack inside the shady slot, Middendorf was convinced the route would go. Satisfied with the reconnaissance, he suggested they descend. But instead of using a double line for the rappel, which would have enabled them to retrieve their ropes, Middendorf set up a single-line rappel. By leaving two fixed ropes, he reasoned, he'd have a head start when he returned to complete the route.

When Hebert, who was supposed to be back in Boulder the next day, asked Middendorf why he was fixing his lines, the wall whiz divulged his plan. Sensing that something really big was going down, Hebert wanted in. Right then and there, he told Middendorf that, if need be, he would quit his job to join him for the ascent. In Middendorf's account of the climb, he described Hebert's change of heart: "Such is the nature of Zion climbing: At first, the walls seem too intimidating to climb, but once the initial pitches are tasted, desire overwhelms rational reason and the real world suddenly becomes unimportant."

After calling his boss, Hebert was invited to spend the night in nearby Springdale with Middendorf and his friend Brad Quinn. That evening, while they drank potations and enjoyed a Dutch-oven dinner at Quinn's house, Brad decided to join the adventure as well.

As luck would have it, the spring rains started to fall as soon as they got to the base of the route. The weather was uncooperative for several days, but they managed to continue the project after a few false starts. As Middendorf hoped, the chimney system granted four pitches of reasonable, well-protected climbing, the best being the final so-called "Calvinator" pitch. From there, four meandering, mostly fourth-class leads brought them to the spacious ledge below the headwall. The solitary crack loomed above.

The next morning they were reminded, once again, that it was still spring. Sheets of rain fell, soaking them and the rock. When Navajo sandstone gets wet, says Middendorf, "It takes on the consistency of slush." They were forced to retreat.

By now a week had passed since Hebert had talked to his boss, and his resolve was starting to wane. As Middendorf put it, "The realities of his employment had gained in relative importance." Absent the promise of stable weather, he headed back to Boulder.

When the weather finally improved, Middendorf and Quinn recruited renowned photographer and climber Bill Hatcher to join the team. The threesome spent a long day regaining their high point. There were satisfied with their progress, but exhausted. Says Middendorf, "We drank whiskey, told lies, and passed out."

By 5:00 A.M. the wall was a visual inferno of golden rock and sunshine, coaxing the climbers into an early start. A difficult off-width pitch led to more enjoyable terrain and, finally, the coveted hand crack. Just as they had dreamed, it was a perfect splitter. The sweet monotony of the moves took them on an Oz-like, five-pitch ride up the wildly exposed, slightly overhanging wall. "My only complaint was that it went by too quickly," laments Middendorf. With the exception of 60 feet of aid, the crack was entirely free.

The weary climbers found a scarce bivy spot near the top of Isaac just as it was getting dark. Refreshed by cold water from remnant snow patches, they fell asleep to the tingling afterglow of a dream come true.

© Bill Hatcher

large platform below the upper headwall. After warming up on a few of the existing lines, he led the first pitch of what would soon become his favorite climb. As far as Hebert knew, they were doing just another of Isaac's so-called "base routes."

After completing the first pitch—a strenuous 5.10+ off-width—Middendorf and Hebert continued up the wall. A 5.9 squeeze chimney led them to the base of an even wider chimney system.

ROUTE DESCRIPTION

Area: Court of the Patriarchs, Zion Canyon
First ascent: John Middendorf, Brad Quinn, and Bill Hatcher, April 1993 (Calvin Hebert worked on lower pitches)
Difficulty: V, 5.10+, A2
Time required: 2–3 days
Equipment: 3 sets of camming units to no. 5 Camalot; 3 sets of TCUs; set of stoppers; small selection of thin pitons
Season: April–May, September–October
Special considerations: Lots of off-width climbing; permit required to bivouac in park
Reference: *Selected Climbs in the Desert Southwest* by Cameron M. Burns

Approach: From the T intersection of Zion Canyon Road–Mount Carmel Highway, drive 1.7 miles on Zion Canyon Road to a parking spot along the road. Hike for 1 hour into the Court of the Patriarchs and head for Isaac, the middle patriarch. From below Isaac, head for the "toe" of the most prominent central buttress on the formation. Tricks of the Trade starts in a clean, 4-inch-wide crack, 50 feet to the right of a huge chimney system on the outside of the buttress.

Route: A nineteen-pitch, 1,800-foot wall that is all free except for 60 feet of moderate aid. The route features an 800-foot, perfect hand crack on the upper headwall.

Descent: From the summit of Isaac, scramble down slabs to the northeast. Several rappels may be necessary to gain the drainage between Isaac and Jacob (the patriarch to the east of Isaac). Hike down the drainage into a hanging valley, then make several more rappels to reach the ground. Advanced routefinding and "canyoneering" skills are required.

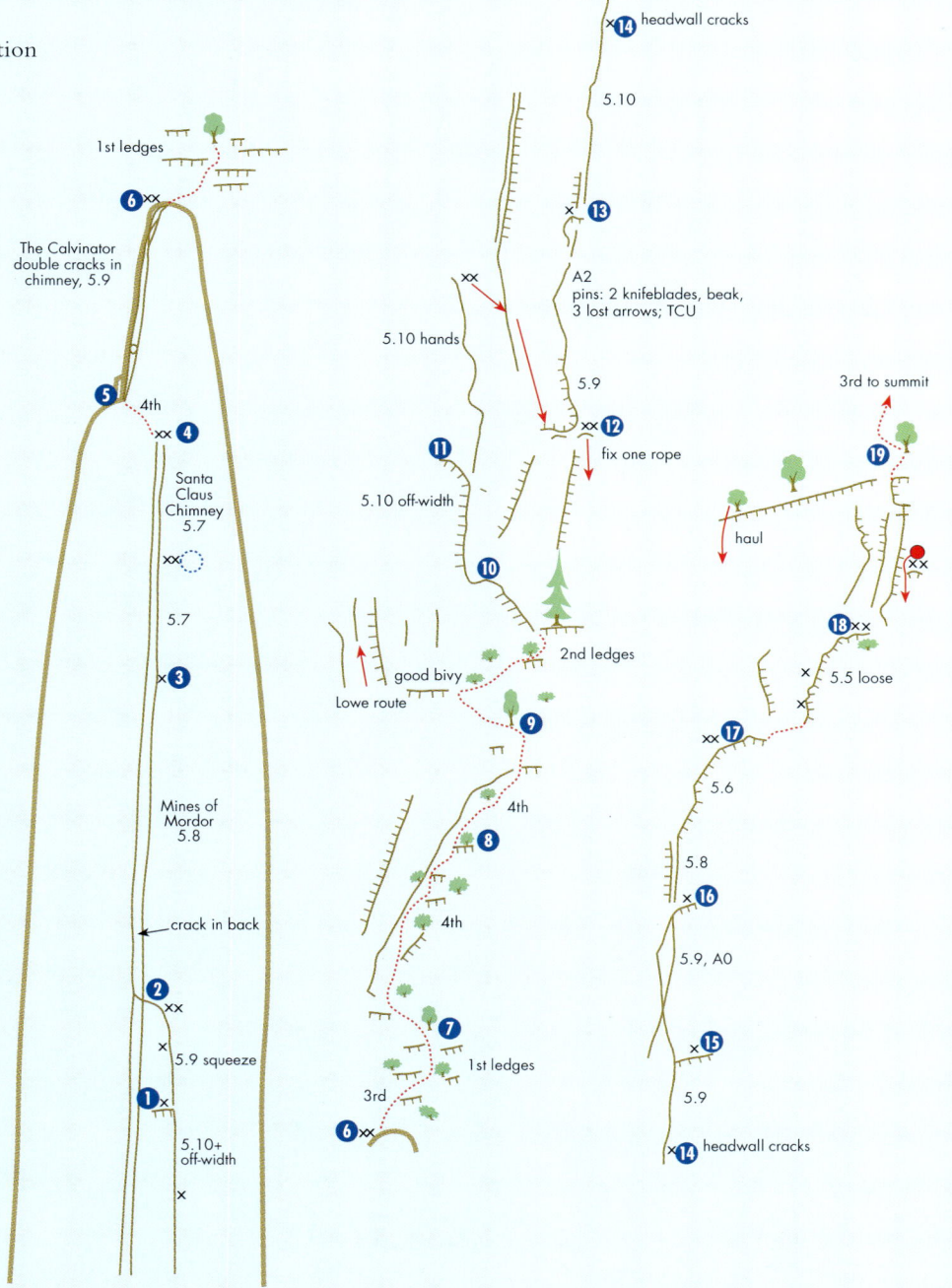

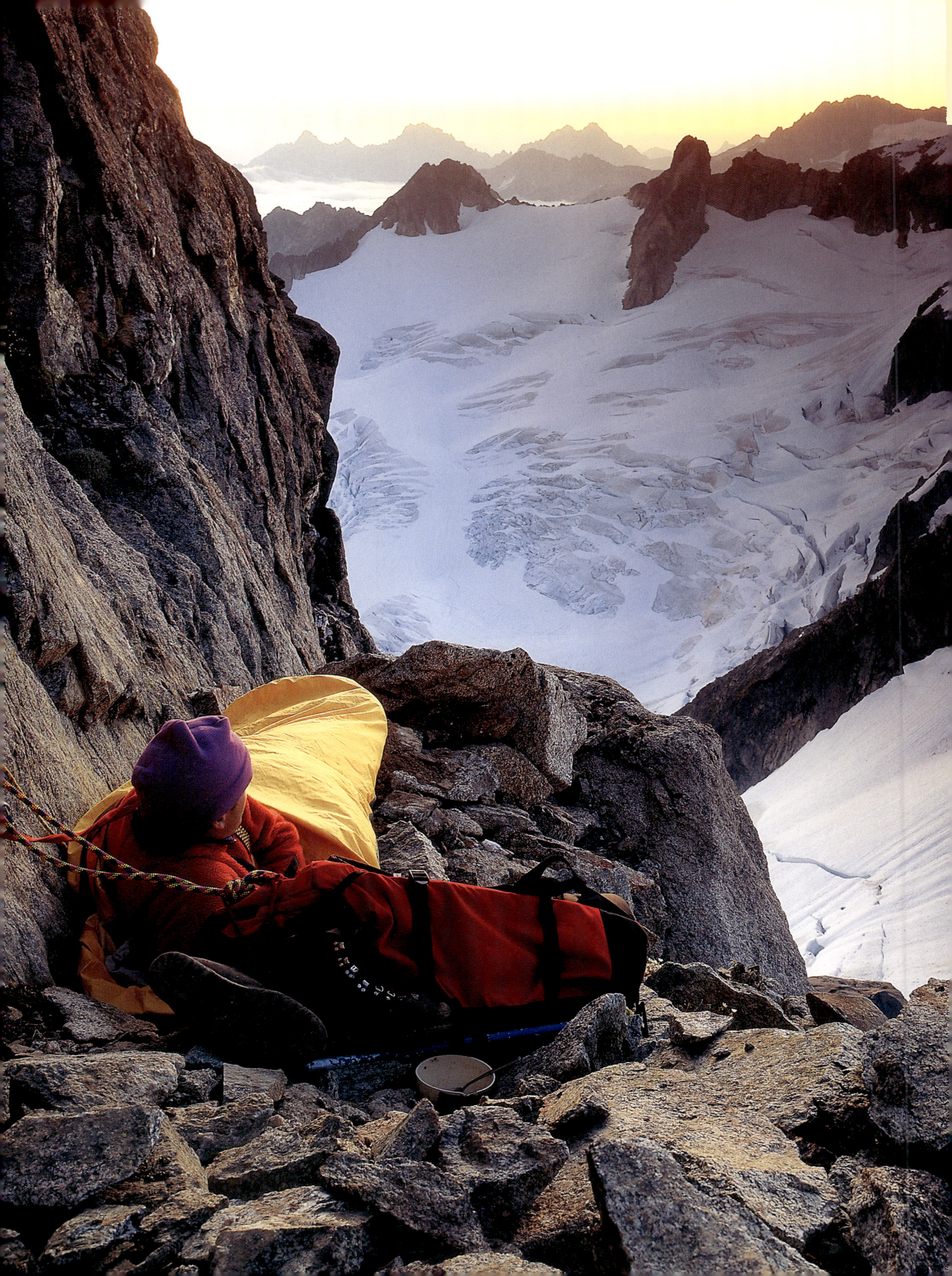

JIM NELSON

THE TORMENT-FORBIDDEN TRAVERSE, NORTH CASCADES NATIONAL PARK, WASHINGTON

JIM NELSON—CASCADES EXPLORER

If any Cascade climber can possibly follow in Fred Beckey's very big bootprints, it's Jim Nelson. For more than two decades, he has been quietly carrying the torch of Cascade exploration that Beckey lit back in the 1940s. Nelson is an accomplished alpinist, guide, author, and photographer—his contemporary knowledge of the Cascades is second to none.

Nelson first became interested in climbing in 1972, when he read Beckey's absorbing *Challenge of the North Cascades*. Like Beckey, Nelson has a penchant for doing new routes. In fact, many of his first ascents are on peaks that were originally explored by Beckey. On the north side of Mount Stuart, he and Kit Lewis added the modern classic Girth Pillar (V, 5.11, A1) next to the ever-popular North Ridge. The same pair also made the first winter ascent of Beckey's 1963 prize, the Northeast Buttress of Slesse Mountain. On the north tower of Gunsight Peak, a remote summit that Beckey first climbed in 1940, Nelson snagged the first ascent of its stupendous west face.

Beyond the Cascades, Nelson has made notable ascents in British Columbia's Coast Range and the Bugaboos, Wyoming's Wind River Range, Yosemite in California, and Alaska. In 1988, he made the second ascent of Mount Foraker's Infinite Spur (see Climb 24) with the late Mark Bebie. The 9,000-foot Alaskan route, which was first done in 1977, has only recently seen its third and fourth ascents.

Near his home in Seattle, Nelson owns and manages Pro Mountain Sports, a mountaineering shop that specializes in lightweight alpine climbing equipment. His customers rely on him for state-of-the-art gear, as well as advice on the best places to use it. His two authoritative guidebooks—*Selected Climbs in the Cascades, volumes I and II* (cowritten with Peter Potterfield)—can keep even his most enthusiastic customers busy for ten years.

THE TORMENT-FORBIDDEN TRAVERSE

Although the idea of climbing multiple contiguous summits—ridge traversing, as it's called—didn't gain popularity until the mid-'80s, it is by no means a new concept. The annals of mountaineering are peppered with accounts of multipeak marathons that, even by modern standards, boggle the mind. Above all others is the 1938 traverse of the Cascade crest by a hard-core group of climbers who called themselves the Ptarmigans.

The Seattle-based clan was famous for their forays into remote pockets of the North Cascades. They penetrated the Chilliwack range as early as 1936. They fought their way into the inaccessible Pickets in 1937. And in 1938, they completed the legendary Ptarmigan Traverse, a 13-day, thirteen-summit odyssey from Dome Peak to Cascade Pass. More than sixty years later, Jim Nelson still considers it the most impressive achievement in the history of Cascade mountaineering—it has yet to be repeated. (The traverse has become a popular high route, but no one has managed to climb the same peaks as the original 1938 Ptarmigan party.)

With a little more time and food, it's conceivable that the Ptarmigans would have continued their traverse from Cascade Pass to nearby Mount Torment, making the first traverse of the ridge between Torment and Forbidden Peak, and beating Fred Beckey to Forbidden's summit in the process. As it turns out, Beckey and party snagged the first ascent of Forbidden in 1940, via the West Ridge. But it wasn't until 1958 that Ed Cooper, another intrepid explorer, connected the sweeping ridge between Forbidden and Torment.

It's easy to see why the Ptarmigans kept returning to the North Cascades. The Alp-like range is filled with jagged summits that soar more than a vertical mile above the deep, forested valleys. Many of the peaks are draped with expansive glaciers that are nourished by eight months of almost constant snowfall. (In the La Niña winter of 1998–99, when a record-breaking 95 feet of snow fell on nearby Mount Baker, it earned the distinction as the snowiest place on Earth.) During the summer, when the skies are clear and the days are long, the North Cascades is arguably the most sublime range in the United States.

When Jim Nelson started climbing in the early '70s, it didn't take him long to discover the allure of the summits in the Cascade Pass region. In *Challenge of the North Cascades,* Beckey waxed poetic about mountains such as Johannesburg, Eldorado, Torment,

Carl Skoog enjoying a glorious Cascade sunrise on the Torment-Forbidden Traverse © Jim Nelson, portrait © Mark Kroese

Forbidden, Buckner, Logan, and Goode. After seeing the rugged peaks for the first time, Nelson realized why. He spent the next decade making numerous trips to the area.

By 1988, Nelson had climbed all of the major summits in the Cascade Pass area. He'd done numerous routes on Forbidden and Torment, but never traversed the ridge between them. Not until Ed Cooper told him that it was his favorite outing in the Cascades did Nelson decide to give it a try. Later that summer, Nelson and his partner Carl Skoog made it halfway through the traverse before realizing they should have brought crampons. "We thought we could get around the steep sections of snow on the north side by staying on rock, but we couldn't," he remembers. Rather than retreating to the soft meadows of Boston Basin, they decided to bivouac on the ridge, and enjoyed a glorious sunrise the next morning.

Nelson didn't get back to the unfinished project until the summer of 1999. He and partner Tim Bonnet started by climbing the familiar south ridge of Torment—a worthwhile climb in its own right. After tagging the summit, they found their way onto the exposed ridgeline. Stretching for more than a linear mile, it hangs like a suspension bridge between the two summits, offering spectacular views in every direction: The south side drops off sharply to the verdant splendor of Boston Basin. The north side plunges into the jumbled morass of the Forbidden Glacier. And the craggy summits of Torment and Forbidden, which emphatically demarcate the high points of the journey, sit to the east and west.

Although the ridgeline isn't technically difficult, climbing it requires good all-around mountaineering skills. "It's long and physically demanding, and has some routefinding challenges," explains Nelson. "You can't make up for that stuff by just bringing a bigger rack." The traverse is also committing. Once on the ridge, the only escape is on either end. Like a train trestle, it dares to be crossed.

By late afternoon, the climbers had reached the bivouac spot that Nelson so fondly remembered from his first attempt. They spent an equally memorable night under a star-streaked sky. They continued moving east in the morning, using their crampons to negotiate some steep snow on the north side of the ridge. As they approached the western flank of Forbidden Peak, the ridge pinched down to just a few feet in places. "The second half of the traverse is by far the best," says Nelson. "The exposure and the scenery are really great. It's way cooler than being on a steep face—you get twice the view."

Moving at a steady pace, but still allowing time to take photos, Nelson and Bonnet reached the summit of Forbidden by early afternoon. Even though Nelson had climbed Forbidden's classic West Ridge several times, it was still a treat. "The only way to improve on this traverse is to make it longer," says Nelson, who is looking forward to doing it again. "Next time I'm going to start on Eldorado and go all the way to Sahale."

ROUTE DESCRIPTION

Area: North Cascades
First traverse: Ed Cooper and Walter Sellers, via South Ridge of Torment, July 1958
Base elevation: 2,200 feet
Summit elevations: Torment, 8,120 feet; Forbidden, 8,815 feet
Difficulty: V, 5.6
Time required: 1–2 days
Equipment: Crampons, ice ax, small rack to 2½ inches
Season: July–September
Special considerations: An emergency descent from the ridge would be difficult; obtain backcountry permit at ranger station in Marblemount (360-873-4500)
Reference: *Cascade Alpine Guide, vol. 2 (Stevens Pass to Rainy Pass)* by Fred Beckey (The Mountaineers Books, 1989, pps 294–304)

Approach: From Interstate 5, take exit 232 east to State Highway 20 (North Cascades Highway) in Sedro-Woolley. Drive 47 miles to Marblemount and turn onto Cascade River Road; drive approximately 20 miles, and park near a bridge where the road crosses the Cascade River, about 1 mile beyond the Eldorado Creek parking area. From the car (approximately 2,200 feet elevation), a faint climbers trail begins 50 feet upstream of the bridge. Follow it up through steep forest, crossing talus fields, some slide alder, and grassy moraines, to the glacier below the south face of Torment. This approach takes 3 to 4 hours. It is also possible to approach via Boston Basin (park at 22 miles), and then traverse west.

Route: Start in Torment basin, climb the south ridge of Torment, then follow the connecting ridge toward Forbidden. Continue up the West Ridge of Forbidden, then descend its East Ridge. A deep notch marks the beginning of the South Ridge of Torment. Climb toward and up a mossy, left-facing corner, on the west side of the South Ridge. Climb up (several low fifth-class pitches) to a notch in the South Ridge leading to the Southeast Face, just below the summit. Dash to the summit and return to the notch, then descend 200 feet down the Southeast Face of Torment. Make a rising traverse past a gendarme and on to the first high point on the ridge proper. Bivy between the first and second high points on the ridge. Continue east on steep snow on the ridge. Follow the long, narrow, and exposed ridge to the notch that marks the start of Forbidden's West Ridge. Follow the ridge to the summit.

Descent: Descend the northeast ledges below the East Ridge. From the summit horn, make five single-rope rappels (400 feet) to a series of ledges (exposed third- and fourth-class) that are followed east. Otherwise, descend the ever-popular West Ridge.

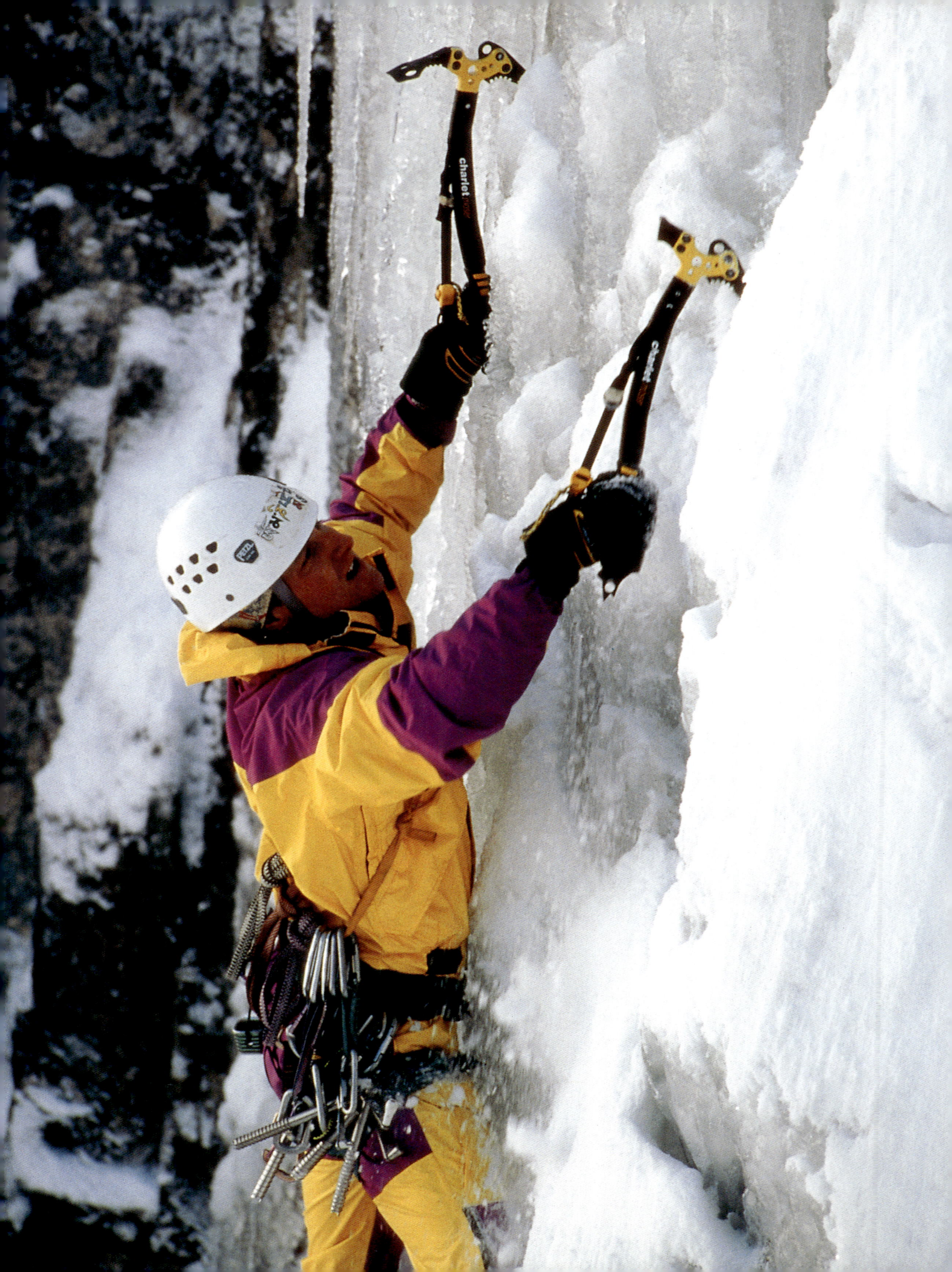
charlet

JARED OGDEN

BIRDBRAIN BOULEVARD, OURAY, COLORADO

JARED OGDEN— JUST DOING IT

Jared Ogden came out of nowhere. From the time he started climbing in 1990, it took him less than five years to emerge as one of North America's most accomplished all-around climbers. From hard free routes to steep ice to monster big walls, he does it all.

Ogden's go-for-it approach got his big-wall career off to a fast start. Although he had never used a pair of Jumars or set up a portaledge, he figured it out on El Capitan's Zodiac (VI, 5.11, A2+) in Yosemite. The 4-day experience taught him plenty, including the importance of learning to improvise, when he dropped a Jumar halfway up the route. Not one to take baby steps, his next two El Cap routes were the historic Wall of the Early Morning Light (VI, 5.9, A3) and the heady Zenyatta Mondatta (VI, 5.10, A4+). In 1995, after completing his big-wall apprenticeship with a roped-solo ascent of Zion's Moonlight Buttress (V, 5.10, C2) in Utah, Ogden headed for Pakistan.

There he and three partners attacked the sheer, 3,800-foot unclimbed North Face of Nameless Tower (20,463 feet). The team spent three frigid weeks establishing Book of Shadows (VII, 5.10, A4, WI 4). The confidence-building trip, which he describes as "a big eye-opener," whetted his appetite for more Himalayan walls. In 1997, he and Mark Synnott (see Climb 43) made the second ascent of Pakistan's Shipton Spire via the all-new Ship of Fools (VII, 5.11, A2, WI 6). The following year he joined Synnott, Alex Lowe (see Climb 27), and Greg Child (see Climb 9) for a new route on Baffin Island's Great Sail Peak. And in 1999, he returned to Pakistan with Synnott and Lowe for a highly publicized ascent of the forty-four-pitch northwest face of Great Trango Tower (VII, 5.11, A4).

Between his big-wall adventures, Ogden thrives on a steady diet of rock, ice, and mixed climbing. He has used his broad range of skills to do everything from M8+ mixed climbs to a 17-hour linkup of Half Dome and El Cap. To Ogden, it's all just part of a natural progression. "Once you start doing these things, you get a knack for it and you get hooked," he explains. "You want that thrill, that adrenalin rush of not knowing what's ahead. It makes you want to get out there and just do it."

BIRDBRAIN BOULEVARD

Jeff Lowe (see Climb 29) did Birdbrain Boulevard's first ascent with Mark Wilford (see Climb 48) and Charlie Fowler (see Climb 17) in February 1985 while on a catalog shoot for his old equipment company, Latok. Birdbrain Boulevard is located just west of Ouray, across the road that leads to the Camp Bird Mine. The route—which looks improbable compared to the nearby classic the Ribbon—got its name when Lowe and his friends joked that only a birdbrain would seriously consider climbing it. As it turns out, completing the climb demanded a *Homo sapien*–size brain, advanced ice-climbing skills, and rather large *cajones*.

When Birdbrain Boulevard was first climbed, Jared Ogden was still in junior high school, and blissfully unaware of Jeff Lowe or any of his accomplishments. Five years later, however, when he was bitten by the climbing bug, names such as Lowe, Wilford, and Fowler took on a weighty, heroic significance. "Those guys were my idols," remembers Ogden, who read every mountaineering book he could get his hands on during his early years.

Unlike most new climbers who spend years at the crags before they venture onto frozen waterfalls, Ogden's early climbs were mostly on ice. As a college student living in Durango, Colorado, he was surrounded by good ice climbing. He frequented the local routes and made regular excursions to nearby Telluride, Ouray, and Silverton. In addition to climbing pure waterfall ice, Ogden did a number of "mixed" routes—even though the discipline hadn't yet been given its official name.

Despite his rapidly developing skills, Ogden didn't consider climbing Birdbrain Boulevard for another few years. "It was notorious for being sketchy and run-out," he remembers. "I was totally scared of it." But in 1993, when some friends from Durango struggled their way up the route, its inviolable reputation softened a bit. They were the first party that he actually knew to repeat the route. "I was in awe," he remembers of his friends' feat. "They were better climbers than me, but it made me think that I might be able to do it someday."

During the next two years, while attending college, Ogden spent every spare minute climbing. His skills advanced on all fronts: bouldering, waterfall ice, mixed routes, pure rock, and big

Jared Ogden quickly moving up the relatively fat first pitch of Birdbrain Boulevard © Ace Kvale, portrait © Gordon Wiltsie

walls. Although he was more than ready for Birdbrain Boulevard by 1995, he focused on bigger projects abroad. (In 1995, Ogden did his first major new route, on Nameless Tower in Pakistan.)

Ogden finally found time in his globe-trotting schedule to climb Birdbrain Boulevard in March 1997. While training for an upcoming trip to Shipton Spire, another gargantuan granite tower in Asia, he hooked up with extreme snowboarder and alpinist Steve Koch. When they heard that conditions were perfect, they sharpened their tools and drove to the historic mining town of Ouray—also known as the "Switzerland of America."

By this point in his career, Ogden was an expert climber. He'd done a lot of advanced routes such as Telluride's Bridalveil Falls and the Ames Ice Hose, and wasn't the least bit intimidated by Birdbrain Boulevard. Blessed with a strong partner and good conditions, Ogden didn't plan to just climb the route—he intended to *attack* it. "I basically went into it with a 'take no prisoners' attitude," he laughs. "I get pretty *agro* on these routes and give it everything I've got."

To the casual observer, Birdbrain Boulevard looks more like a rock climb than an ice climb. The route follows a chimney system through an ominous-looking band of conglomerate rock. Inside the chimney, and barely visible to the untrained eye, is a ribbon of ice that varies in width from 1 to 10 feet. The route has two cruxes: The first is about halfway up. The second is 200 feet from the top, where the line appears to end under a hopeless-looking overhang. The route is typically done in seven pitches, over a period of 8–12 hours.

Ogden and Koch dashed up Birdbrain Boulevard in less than 4 hours. By climbing some of it simultaneously, they were able to reach the top in four long pitches. "It wasn't that bad," says Ogden of the climb he once considered a death wish. "I think it was because we had lots of experience, and took a very confident approach to it."

The first crux involved pulling through a bulge in the chimney. "It's a pillar about 1 foot in diameter that barely touches down," he explains. "You have to wrap your legs around it, then tiptoe your way up. It's pretty airy." From there, they followed a series of ice pillars and ramps inside the chimney to the second crux—a circuitous path around the right side of the overhang.

© Cameron Burns

Both climbers negotiated the M6 moves without incident.

The confident partners made it back to their car before noon, with energy to spare. They topped off the day by driving to Telluride and "warming down" on the area-classic Ames Ice Hose. Such endurance days are a regular part of Ogden's routine. For example, in 1999, he became part of an elite group to climb Yosemite's Nose of El Capitan and the Northwest Face of Half Dome in less than 24 hours.

Ogden spent the next day resting and reflecting on the experience. He was amazed that Birdbrain Boulevard, which once seemed far beyond his abilities, could be so much fun. Realizing that conditions were perfect—not just on the route but in his head—he went back the following day and soloed the climb. "It might have seemed crazy, but I felt really secure about my ability to do the route," says Ogden. "I went in without any mental hang-ups, knowing I would do it."

ROUTE DESCRIPTION

Area: San Juan Mountains
First ascent: Charlie Fowler, Jeff Lowe, and Mark Wilford, February 1985
Base elevation: Approximately 8,500 feet
Summit elevation: Approximately 9,500 feet
Difficulty: IV, WI 5, M6
Time required: 8–12 hours round trip from the car
Equipment: 2 ropes, 60-m ideal, 50-m OK (possible to climb and rappel the route with 1 50-m rope); 5 ice screws; set of Camalots to no. 3; a few medium stoppers; several knifeblade and angle pitons (although many are fixed)
Season: February–early May
Special considerations: Route forms late and is very condition dependent; approach is subject to significant avalanche danger, but the route is relatively safe; call the Victorian Inn (800-84-Ouray) for current conditions (and accommodations)
References: *Ice World* by Jeff Lowe; *Colorado Ice* by Jack Roberts (Polar Star Communications, Inc., 1998); *San Juan Ice Climbs* by Charlie Fowler (self-published annually)

Approach: Birdbrain Boulevard is a few miles from Ouray, Colorado (which is on US Highway 550), off the Camp Bird Mine Road. Take County Road 361 west from town (four-wheel drive recommended) for 4.5 miles to the parking spot. Drop into the main drainage; ski or snowshoe up the avalanche-prone slopes to the base of the climb, about 1 mile. Allow 20 minutes–1 hour.

Route: Follow a narrow chimney system with ice runnels for seven pitches.

Descent: Make six or seven rappels from trees down the rib to the left of the climb.

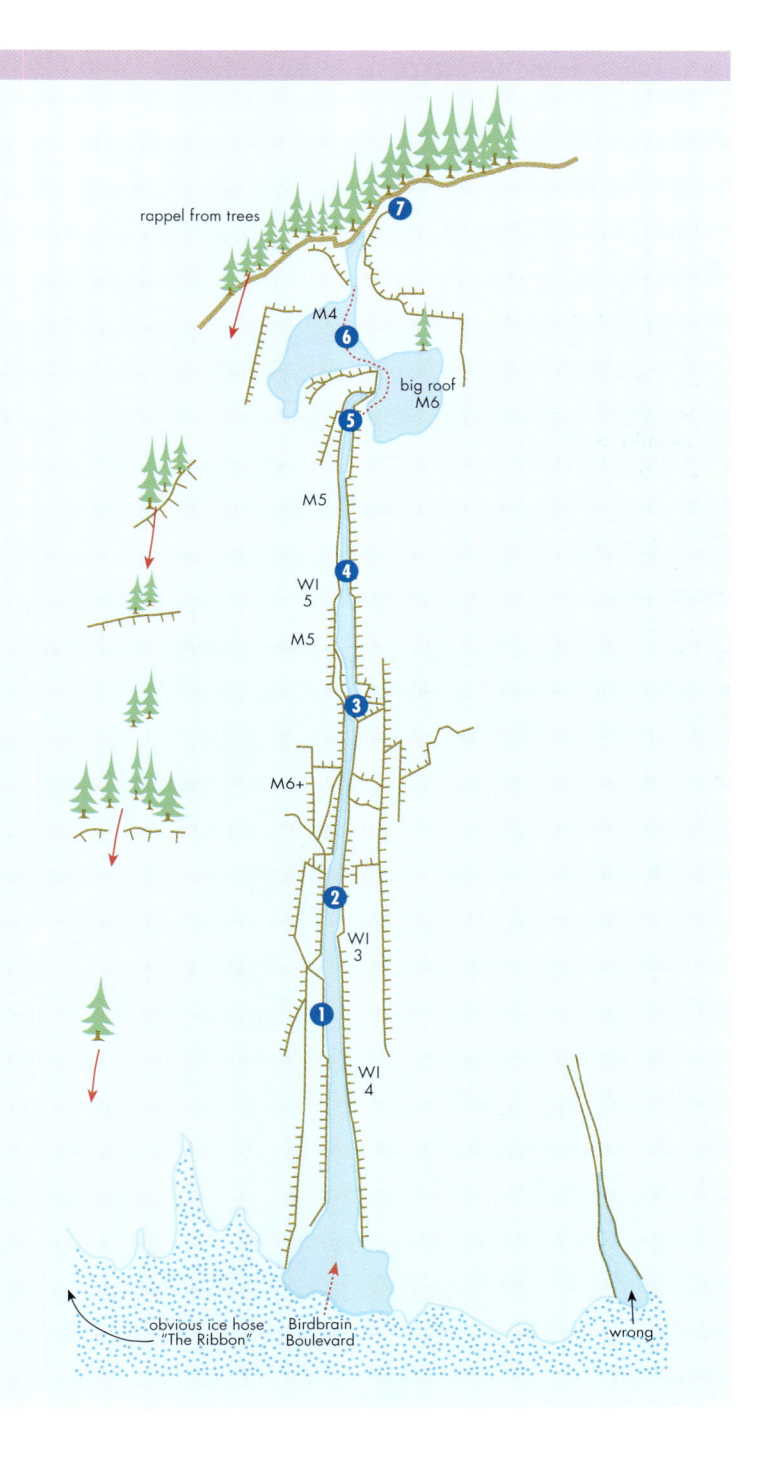

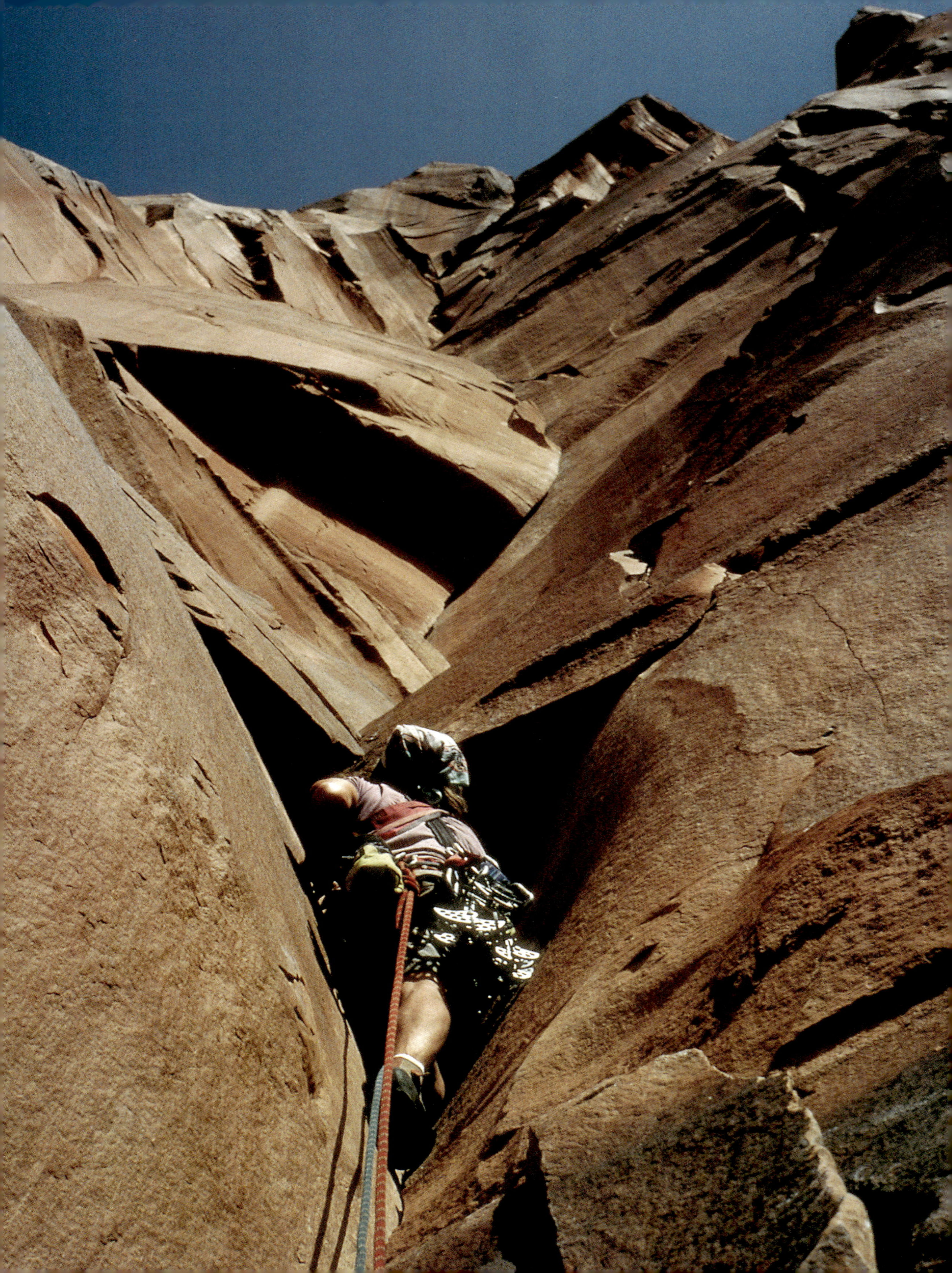

ALISON OSIUS

PRIMROSE DIHEDRALS, MOSES, CANYONLANDS NATIONAL PARK, UTAH

ALISON OSIUS—THE RIGHT BALANCE

Alison Osius's resumé challenges the conventional wisdom that you can't have it all. Since graduating with honors from Middlebury College in 1980, she has climbed all over the world, earned her master's degree from Columbia University's School of Journalism, won three national sport-climbing championships, written a book, married a fellow writer, and given birth to two beautiful children—and those are just the highlights.

Since she first discovered rock climbing in college, Osius has achieved an ideal balance between work and play. For six years after graduating from college, she avoided the toil of year-round employment, yet continued to advance her career in journalism. She climbed almost nonstop during the summer months—visiting crags from Washington to Wales—while working as a freelance writer or graduate student during the off season. And when she finally settled down in a full-time job, it was with *Climbing* magazine, the ideal place to marry her writing skills with her passion for climbing.

When she's not writing about other climbers, she's sometimes being written about herself. Osius, who bears a striking resemblance to Meryl Streep, has been profiled in dozens of magazines and appeared in numerous TV segments—often related to her success in climbing competitions. In 1988, when competitive climbing gained popularity in North America, she earned a spot on the U.S. Climbing Team. She has since competed in more than forty national or international competitions, winning three national titles and placing in the top ten in a half dozen World Cup events.

In 1997, Osius's leadership skills were tapped to serve as president of the American Alpine Club. Her unflappable, easygoing nature helped with the job's numerous challenges, including the proposed ban on the use of fixed anchors in wilderness areas. Negotiating with the Forest Service was a tricky balancing act. And who better to lead the charge?

PRIMROSE DIHEDRALS

In the fall of 1977, Alison Osius took a break from her studies at Middlebury College to watch the *Eiger Sanction*—Clint Eastwood's action thriller about international intrigue. In the movie, Eastwood takes a trip to the Utah desert to brush up on his rock-climbing skills before flying to Switzerland for an assassination assignment. His training program culminates with an ascent of the Totem Pole, a dramatic, pencil-like formation in Utah's Monument Valley.

Osius, who had just started to dabble in climbing, watched in awe as Clint Eastwood pulled onto its tiny summit. "I had this incredibly wistful feeling," she remembers. "I just kept thinking how much fun it would be to be up there." She was captivated by the idea of climbing the Totem Pole, or a godly tower such as Moses or Zeus, but dismissed it as a romantic fantasy. "To me, it was sort of like taking off in a rocket ship," she laughs. "It looked cool, but I didn't really think I'd ever do it." The following spring, her good friend Dave Gustafson climbed Moses, but she could still barely imagine it.

Two years later, Moses, the grandest of Utah's sandstone towers, was profiled in *Climbing* when desert rock pioneer Ed Webster soloed a new route on its unclimbed east side. He named his classic line the Primrose Dihedrals and described Moses as "a giant exclamation point mocking the forces of erosion." Webster's legendary ascent was anything but routine. While he was aid-climbing the fifth pitch, several loops of his rope became tangled when he pulled some slack rope through the system. Unable to free the rope, Webster proceeded to Jumar up it—a grievous error. After he ascended half the distance to the knot, the rope suddenly untangled itself, causing him to drop through space like a bungee jumper. He plummeted more than 50 feet, finally stopping with a terrifying, upward jerk. Astonished that he was still alive—and unhurt—he noticed that his top Jumar had nearly bitten through the rope. He pried it free with his hammer, then collected his scattered wits and proceeded with the climb.

After completing her graduate work in New York, Osius finally succumbed to the allure of the West in 1988. When Colorado-based *Climbing* magazine offered her a job, she bid farewell to her East Coast friends and headed for the Rockies. Despite her apprehensions, things fell into place when she arrived in Colorado:

Looking up the fourth pitch of the Primrose Dihedrals. The 5.11b off-width crux is directly above the climber, near the top. © Jeff Widen, portrait © John Heisel

She loved her new job. The climbing was fantastic. And she made some wonderful new friends. "It's sort of exhilarating when you meet people you like a lot," says Osius.

It wasn't long before Osius was invited to climb Moses with three of her new friends, Keith Gotschall, Michael Dorsey, and Michael Benge. As she prepared for the weekend trip, she found it amusing that the thought of climbing Moses—which once seemed as improbable as winning a gold medal in the Olympics—now felt like a reasonable thing to do. She was thrilled by the prospect of standing on top of the slender spire, and even more excited about spending time with her new friends. The chemistry was perfect. "I felt like I could talk and laugh with these guys for hours," remembers Osius. And she did.

That Friday night, as the raucous foursome drove to Utah, they laughed and joked constantly, pausing only to sleep at the trailhead below Moses. The joshing and repartee resumed in the morning, shortly after the first cup of coffee, and continued as they hiked to the base of the Primrose Dihedrals.

They climbed as two separate rope teams, with Osius and her partner Michael Benge leading off. Both of them were dazzled by the quality of the climbing and the dramatic setting. "The pitches were consistently wonderful," she recalls. "And they were filled with pleasant surprises." Osius remembers being impressed by Webster's ingenious routefinding on the third pitch, which starts with 40 feet of downclimbing toward the prominent corner system. And higher up, a dubious-looking wide crack turned out to be quite enjoyable when she discovered a large, hidden foothold.

The hours passed quickly as the two teams, sharing belays, worked their way up the spectacular corner system. After wrestling with the testy off-width on the fifth pitch, Osius and Benge cruised to Moses' breathtaking, flat summit, their friends not far behind.

Author's note: *Alison Osius and Michael Benge exchanged wedding vows in 1991. They live in Colorado with their two children, Roy and Teddy, and climb as much as possible.*

ROUTE DESCRIPTION

Area: Taylor Canyon, Canyonlands

First ascent: Ed Webster (solo), April 1979; first free ascent: Ed Webster and Steve Hong, October 1979

Difficulty: IV, 5.10, C1 or 5.11+

Time required: 1 full day

Equipment: Double set of cams to 3 inches; set of TCUs; set of wired stoppers

Season: Year-round; spring and fall ideal

Special considerations: Four-wheel-drive vehicle with good ground clearance required for approach; clean climbing only—Canyonlands has a strict "no piton" policy; most parties aid the Ear pitch (pitch 5)

Reference: *Selected Climbs in the Desert Southwest* by Cameron M. Burns

Approach: From Moab, drive north on US Highway 191 to State Highway 313, 9.1 miles north of State Highway 128 (River Road). Turn left (west) and follow Highway 313 for approximately 12 miles. Turn right, onto Horsethief Trail, and follow it for a dozen miles or so across the mesa. The road reaches the mesa edge, then switchbacks steeply down the canyon. At the canyon bottom, turn left and drive 4.3 miles to the boundary of Canyonlands National Park. Continue on the road, passing Charlie Horse Needle 1.2 miles south of the park boundary. Continue another 1.2 miles to a fork in the road. Take the left fork (Taylor Canyon Road) and follow it 5.4 miles to its end, where there is a small parking lot for Moses tower. Four-wheel drive is required for the last 3 miles. From the parking lot, hike east toward the southeast side of the tower. Primrose Dihedrals is the prominent crack system on the right (east) side of the south face. The route starts near the junction of Moses and Zeus (the next tower to the east).

Route: See topo for details.

Descent: Rappel the route or, if it's crowded, rappel the Diretissima route to the left.

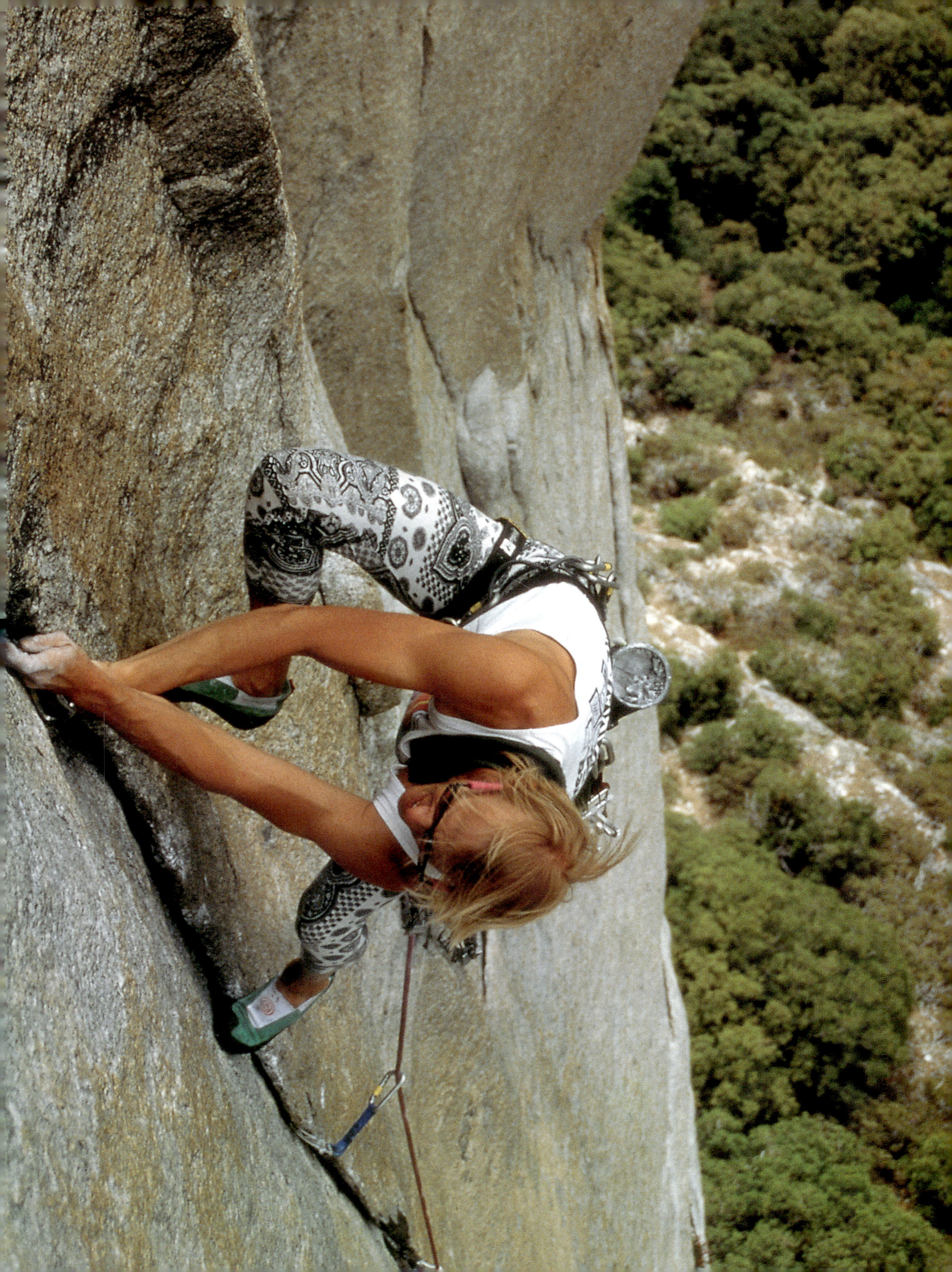

STEVE SCHNEIDER

LURKING FEAR, EL CAPITAN, YOSEMITE NATIONAL PARK, CALIFORNIA

STEVE SCHNEIDER—SHIPOOPI

In the spring of 1981, twenty-one-year-old Steve Schneider settled into Yosemite's Camp 4 for what he thought would be a one-semester break from his studies at Chico State. Obsessed with climbing, Schneider never returned to college, but graduated with honors from the Yosemite school of hard rock.

It didn't take long for him to achieve what he calls "big boy status." In 1983, Schneider did the second ascent of the notorious Bachar-Yerian, Tuolumne's knobby test piece with the potential for 80-foot falls. In 1984, he joined Yosemite's elite rescue team, a ten-year association that gave him legitimate residence and the opportunity to climb full time. Refusing to specialize, Schneider quickly mastered everything from insecure face climbs to heinous off-widths.

In 1988, Schneider nabbed the first solo 1-day ascent of the Nose in less than 22 hours. In 1992, he soloed the even harder Salathé Wall in about the same time. And in 1994, Schneider and Hans Florine (see Climb 16) climbed *three* El Cap routes in a single day—the Nose, Lurking Fear, and the West Face. They finished the seventy-three-pitch marathon in a jaw-dropping 23 hours.

Born and raised in Oakland, Schneider is pure California: blond, perennially tanned, and outrageously fashionable. He earned his nickname when he wouldn't stop talking about his new Tuolumne route, Shipoopi. Schneider's goal is to be the most well-rounded climber in California, which he defines as the first to climb 100 5.13s, 50 El Cap routes, and 3 26,000-foot (8,000-m) peaks. With the first two completed, Schneider has shifted his focus to alpine climbs. During three consecutive seasons in Patagonia, he completed seven major routes, including a new line on the 4,000-foot east face of the Central Tower of Paine. Schneider started his alpine-style ascent with a partner, but finished the upper half of the route by himself after his ropemate bailed. Emboldened by the 11-day solo, Schneider has many similar adventures planned. "My biggest problem," he allows, "is that I want to go everywhere and I want to do it all."

LURKING FEAR

El Capitan has always been a place for aid climbers. Most of the cracks on the granite monolith are too thin, too steep, and too continuous to be climbed free. But there are a few routes on the cliff—mostly on the left side—that afford outstanding free climbing for expert climbers. As Steve Schneider realized in 1985, Lurking Fear is one of them.

Back then, the southwest-facing wall route was gaining popularity, but had not yet become the moderate classic it is today. During a spell of unseasonably mild weather in January, Schneider and partner John Barbella climbed Lurking Fear at a very orderly, 3-day pace. Schneider did the route as an aid climb but was struck by its potential as a free climb. "It had some amazing free-climbing possibilities, but it was beyond me at the time," he remembers. He believed that a tenacious 5.13 climber could eliminate most of the aid from the route. Someday, he hoped, he would be good enough to try.

Seven years later, in 1992—four years after Todd Skinner and Paul Piana freed the Salathé Wall—a stronger, smarter, and vastly more experienced Steve Schneider returned to Lurking Fear, this time approaching it as a free-climbing project. He was teamed with two highly skilled crack climbers, Jeff Shoen and Alan Lester.

Lurking Fear's natural line—the crack system—starts about 300 feet from its base. To reach the crack, aid climbers follow a series of disconnected flakes and arches, with long sections of almost featureless granite in between. Typically, these blank sections are scaled via a series of straightforward bolt ladders. Schneider suspected that these lower pitches might not go free, and was surprised when they did. "I thought there would be a fair amount of aid on the first few pitches, which were blank," he recalls. "But I was able to free-climb the first pitch at a reasonable 5.12c." To do so, Schneider did not follow the original line of bolts; the free passage was a body length to its left. To accommodate the free climbing, Schneider chopped and camouflaged the old bolts and installed new ones 5 feet to the left. Even though his variation still allowed parties to aid climb, he had altered the original line. Schneider knew his variation would be controversial. "But I figured that since I was free-climbing the route, I had creative license to do a little makeover," he explained.

The second pitch turned out to be even more difficult.

Steve Schneider freeing the fourth pitch (5.12a) of Lurking Fear. He made a virtually all-free ascent of the route in 1992. © Jeff Shoen, portrait © Jeff Shoen

© Mark Kroese

Schneider's free-climbing line followed a series of dime-thin edges left of the original bolt ladder, and required six new bolts. Knowing that most parties would not follow his variation, he left the original bolt ladder intact. Schneider free-climbed the pitch at a stiff 5.13a, but broke a key handhold in the process. Unable to repeat the now more difficult move, and anxious to get to the crack climbing above, he resigned himself to using a bolt to pull through a short, blank section. The almost-free second pitch is rated 5.13a, A0.

After adding a four-bolt, 5.12d variation to the start of the third pitch, Schneider finally reached the system of laser-cut cracks that are the hallmark of Lurking Fear. Ranging from ½ to 3 inches wide, the splitter cracks are the only weakness in the vertical ocean of rock. "The fourth, fifth, and sixth pitches are the three most beautiful 5.12 continuous crack systems I've ever seen in Yosemite," declares Schneider, who has spent two decades exploring the area's most classic lines. Schneider, Lester, and Shoen were able to climb all three pitches free, at 5.12a, 5.12b, and 5.12c, respectively. "The sixth pitch is the all-star pitch," he adds. "It starts out with wide fingers, pinches to 1 inch, then down to fingers, then goes down to RP size. It's the best pitch on the climb."

The threesome quickly disposed of the next three pitches, the hardest being 5.10d. But the tenth pitch was a different story. "It gave us a really hard time," recalls Schneider, who spent 2 full days unlocking the 5.13a sequence with Lester and Shoen.

At this point the team had been on the wall for more than a week. With most of the hard climbing below them, Schneider was euphoric and fully committed to the project. Unfortunately, Shoen had injured his finger and Lester was out of time. Both men wished Schneider luck and rappelled fixed ropes to the Valley floor.

Determined to complete the route, Schneider scoured Camp 4 in search of a partner, but to no avail. As a last resort he made an advertisement for the Camp 4 bulletin board. Schneider remembers a low moment as he stood there looking for a place to hang his ad. "I'm realizing, 'This is desperate.' I'm trying to free-climb this great project and I should have all these great free climbers lining up to join me, and here I am having to advertise for a partner." The despondent Schneider shook his head in disbelief.

"What's the matter?" asked a caring voice behind him. Schneider turned around, then explained his dilemma to the young climber about half his age. His name was Calder Stratford. Despite his limited experience, Calder was keen to climb—especially on El Cap. He agreed to join Schneider without hesitation. By the next evening, Schneider and his new partner had Jumared eleven pitches up the wall and were preparing to climb at first light.

Belayed by Stratford, Schneider spent the next morning engineering a creative solution to pitch twelve, dubbed the Grand Traverse. His two-bolt variation went free at 5.12d. Next was a thin, right-facing corner on the thirteenth pitch, which Schneider sent handily after a few tries, rating it 5.12b. The following day, Schneider cruised the remaining seven pitches—mostly 5.9 and 5.10 climbing that followed the original route—and topped out before dark. Having done all but a few moves free, Schneider was ecstatic. And his partner, a fledgling wall climber, had just completed his first El Cap route.

Schneider has since climbed Lurking Fear four times—a testimony to his love for the route. He has climbed it with his wife, Heather Baer, done it as a speed climb with Hans Florine, warmed up on it as a season opener, and even guided a disabled climber up the route. "No matter how you do it," insists Schneider, "it's a classic."

ROUTE DESCRIPTION

Area: Southwest face of El Capitan, Yosemite Valley
First ascent: Dave Bircheff, Phil Bircheff, and Jim Pettigrew, May 1976
Base elevation: 4,000 feet
Summit elevation: 7,000 feet
Difficulty: VI, 5.13, A0 or 5.8, C2
Time required: 2–5 days
Equipment: 2 sets of nuts, offsets useful; 1 set of RPs; Cams: 3 each .5–1.5 inch, 2 each 2–4.5 inches; hooks: 1–2 each, cam hooks; 6 rivet hangers; 3 heads (in case fixed heads on pitches 3 and 11 are missing)
Season: Spring and fall; summer OK, but hot
Special considerations: Water, human waste disposal; all bolts replaced by the American Safe Climbing Association in 1999
Reference: *Yosemite Big Walls: SuperTopos* by Chris McNamara (SuperTopo Publishing, 2000)

Approach: Use the State Highway 140 park entrance into Yosemite Valley. Park 0.1 mile west of El Capitan bridge. Follow the trail that heads directly to the Nose, then traverse the base to the far left (west) side of the cliff.

Route: The easiest aid line on El Cap, a moderate classic. See topo for details.

Descent: Descend the East Ledges (recommended) or hike the long way down the Yosemite Falls trail.

Author's note: In June 2000, Tommy Caldwell and Beth Rodden eliminated the last points of aid on Lurking Fear, making its first all free ascent.

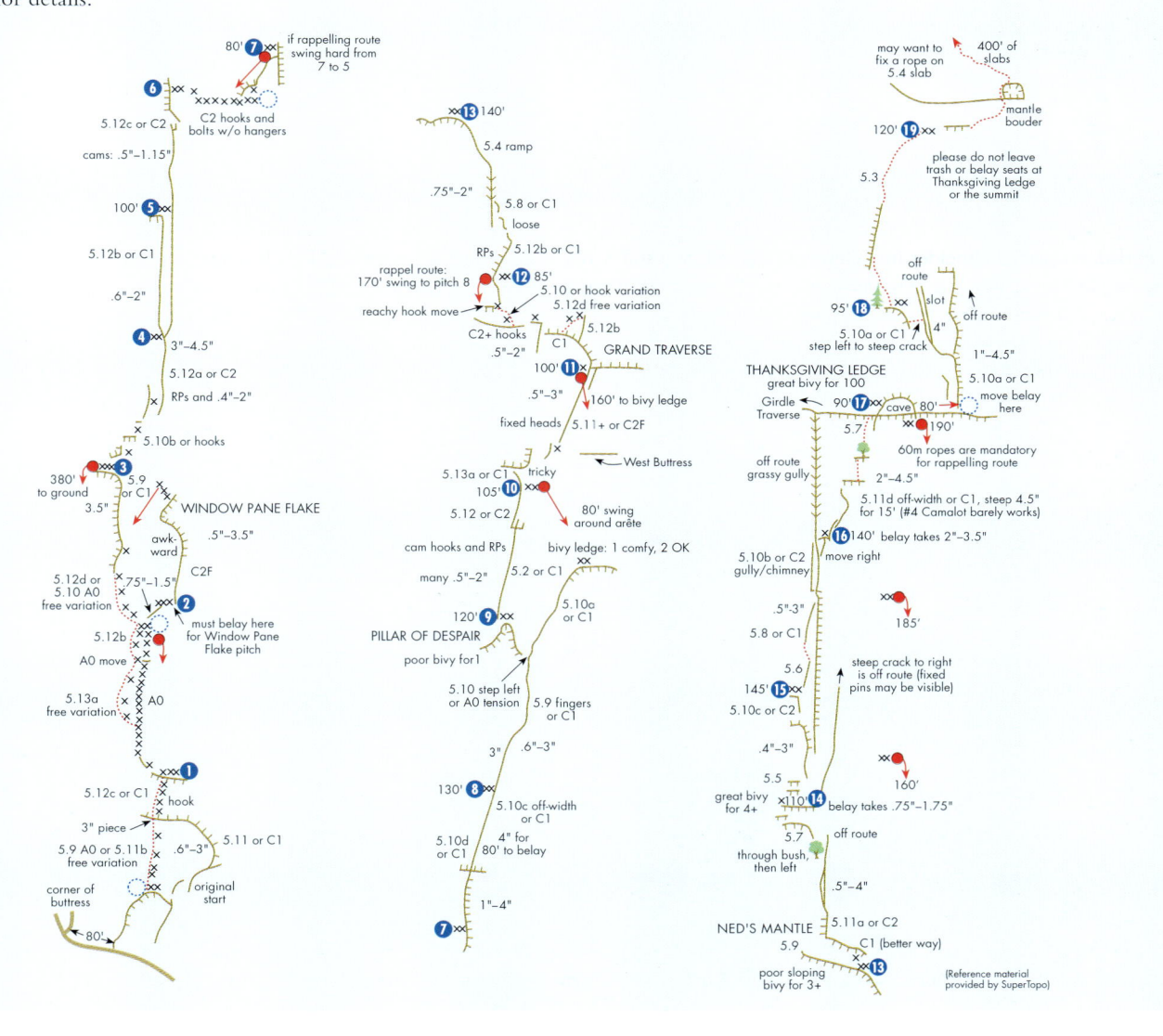

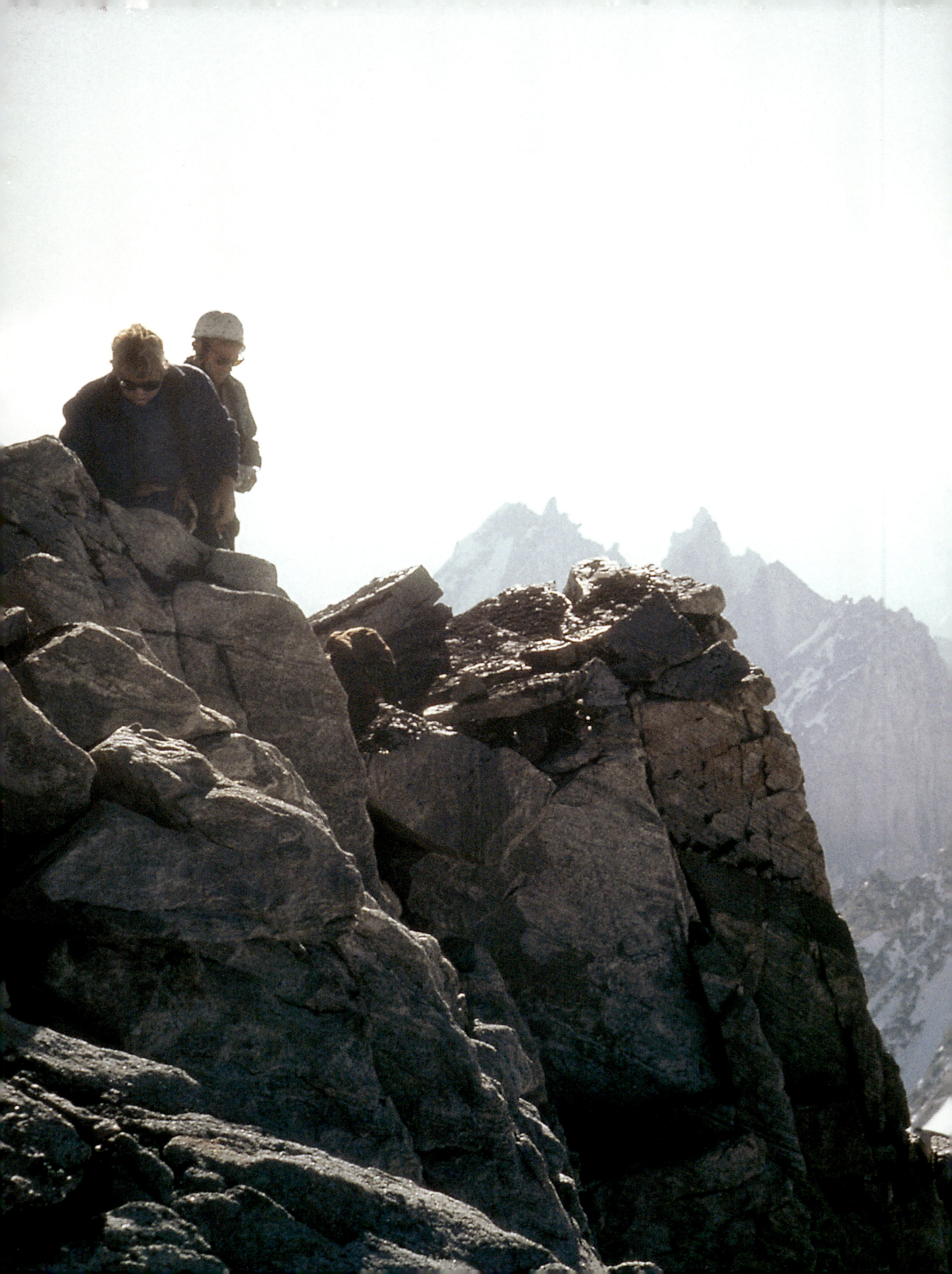

DON SERL

THE WADDINGTON TRAVERSE, COAST RANGE, BRITISH COLUMBIA

DON SERL—COAST RANGE EXPLORER

Don Serl is an unlikely alpinist. He didn't set foot in the mountains until age twenty-four. As a child growing up in Kamloops, British Columbia, he was a scrawny, bookish honor student who preferred science to Little League. And after graduating from the University of British Columbia with a degree in chemistry, he moved to mountainless Toronto, to work in a lab. Unaffected by the allure of alpinism, Serl continued with his scholarly ways until moving back to Vancouver, British Columbia, in 1972.

Shortly after Serl moved west, his co-workers invited him on a weekend hike. One hike led to another, day hikes led to backpacking trips, and before long, Serl was climbing one mountain after another. "Almost immediately, I found myself powerfully drawn to summits," says Serl. Twenty-seven years later, with more than 150 first ascents to his name, Serl jokes about his humble beginnings. "I was terrible at athletics, poorly coordinated, noncompetitive, and not very strong," he laughs, "But I was strong in ways that worked for climbing—good grip strength and a strong cardiovascular system."

Even though he got a late start, Serl has climbed all over the world—from Alaska to the Himalayas to the Peruvian Andes. Yet he loves nothing more than exploring British Columbia's Coast Range with close friends who share his passion for adventure. In more than a dozen trips to the rugged Waddington Range, Serl has established some of its most classic lines; the south face of Mount Tiedemann, the north face of Mount Hickson, and the Waddington Traverse are some of his favorites.

Despite all of his success, the lanky Canadian remains circumspect. His outlook on life was forever changed after he almost died in a rappelling accident in 1976. "Since then," he shares, "life has been a gift."

THE WADDINGTON TRAVERSE

The nine-summit Waddington Traverse was long considered the prize of BC's Coast Range, but was nothing more than beer talk until the spring of 1985. That was when Don Serl learned that fellow Canadians Peter Croft (see Climb 11) and Greg Foweraker were as interested in the project as he was. Recognizing that it wouldn't go unclimbed forever, the threesome began formalizing their plans.

Deciding where to begin the traverse was their first task. By starting from the east, with the rugged Serra peaks, they would confront the most technical and committing climbing first. However, they knew that earlier attempts from that direction had failed—the east face of Serra V looked insurmountable. The topography of the ridgeline suggests starting from the west, with Mount Waddington, but the prospect of getting to Serra IV or V after a few days and being stranded by bad weather was dreadful. After much debate, the team bet on the unusually reliable weather and decided to start from the west. Mount Waddington would be their first objective.

On the evening of July 26, the team flew by helicopter into Fury Gap. A 4-hour ascent by headlamp took them to their first bivouac at the base of Waddington's west ridge. The night was cut short when Croft—ever the early bird—got up at 3:00 A.M. to brew coffee for the long day ahead.

The trio crunched their way up the Angel Glacier as the morning sun warmed Waddington's rocky summit tower. After surmounting the final bergschrund, they unstrapped their crampons and climbed toward its 13,186-foot summit. The conditions were perfect. "The snow was superfirm and the rock was really dry," remembers Serl. "We soloed the entire rock tower in 90 minutes." On top of the Coast Range, they enjoyed a 2-hour snooze in the warm sun before retracing their route to camp.

Their next objective was Combatant Col. They followed their steps from the previous day to the lower basin of the Angel Glacier, then ran below its ice cliffs en route to the col—the most dangerous section of the traverse. As the sun climbed, the team made tracks up the western slope of Combatant, then gained the north ridge for a few pitches of easy fifth-class climbing. They reached the northwest summit by 1:00 P.M., and took another nap while waiting for firmer snow conditions. "We did a surprising amount of relaxing on this trip," notes Serl, who remembers Croft using his sleeping pad as a sun shield. The well-rested crew continued

Miles to go before they sleep: Greg Foweraker and Peter Croft on the Waddington Traverse, with the rugged Serra summits in the background
© Don Serl, portrait © Jim Elzinga

climbing through the cooler evening hours: They scrambled to Combatant's main summit, down to Chaos Col, and up the west ridge of Tiedemann. By midnight they reached their third bivy, on Tiedemann's convoluted east ridge, the halfway point of the traverse.

The trip's insouciant tone turned serious on the morning of July 29. The weather was starting to deteriorate. The sputtering stove was threatening to quit. And Greg had fallen ill. Serl remembers his anxiety as Foweraker lay curled in a fetal ball, retching. "I was thinking, 'We're fucked. We're halfway through the traverse, and it's 7,000 feet down one side and 5,000 feet down the other.'" Croft and Serl coaxed some tea into their suffering partner and watched nervously as he slept. Several hours later, Foweraker perked up just enough to pack and start moving again.

From the Asperity-Tiedemann Col, the threesome ascended Asperity's moderate west ridge, belaying only one 5.7 pitch before reaching the summit at 10:30 A.M. Racing against the heat, they climbed without a rope down Asperity's icy, 50-degree east face. Serl took the lead, and made it halfway down the slope before he heard a loud crackle. He looked up, then watched in horror as a fusillade of ice crashed toward him. It broke into smaller chunks as it fell, most of which swept by to his right, but one circular piece arced toward him like a stray hubcap. With no place to hide, he braced himself against his ice tools and waited. At the last instant, he jerked his head and body out of its path, but it smashed into his arm, threatening to spit him off the mountain. He moaned in pain, but managed to hang on until Croft and Foweraker—who were unaffected by the incident—joined him. They climbed tentatively down to the safety of the Asperity-Serra V Col. Luckily, his arm wasn't broken.

The weary threesome spent the next 2 hours pulling themselves back together. Serl remembers feeling overwhelmed. "I was really sore, Greg was still a bit sick, and we still had the Serra Peaks in front of us."

The team started up Serra V under ominous gray skies. Feeling healthy—and very committed—Croft quickly led the four rock pitches, enabling them to reach the summit by 5:00 P.M. Twenty-one years after its first ascent, they were the third, fourth, and fifth climbers to stand on the most elusive summit in the Coast Range. The note left by the first-ascent team echoed their sentiments. It ended, "Now how the hell do we get down from here?" It was a good question.

Avoiding the sheer east face of Serra V, they downclimbed until they found a suitable rappel anchor. Minutes later, Croft set out into the unknown, carefully engineering a diagonal rappel. Toward the end of the second rap, they came to a small stance that Serl describes as "a horrible affair of loose blocks and plaques of basalt, vaguely attached to the cliff." From the rotten stance, the three men gaped at the next rappel, which was slightly overhanging. With his prusik slings ready, Croft attached himself to the rope and, once again, slid into the void. After a long silence, Foweraker and Serl heard the distinctive ring of a hammer pounding in a piton. The ropes went slack a few minutes later as Croft instructed his teammates to descend. As Serl started to rappel, the rotten block Foweraker was standing on made a heart-stopping grating sound, then shifted. Serl, who was directly below it, knew the block was going to fall. Not wanting to be taken with it, he smeared his way out of the line of fire, then shouted down to Croft to tie in to both ropes and disconnect himself from the rappel anchor—in case he needed to jump out of the way. Foweraker then nudged the block into the abyss, missing Croft by about 10 feet.

The harried teammates reached the safety of the Serra IV-V Col just before dark. In his account of the traverse in the 1986 *Canadian Alpine Journal,* Serl wrote of their relief: "We jabbered, jittered, and ate convulsively, the ancient animal in each of us unquenchable in hunger for life."

The last day was anticlimactic. They quickly reached the summit of Serra IV, then did a straightforward traverse to the top of Serra III. Two rappels and some scrambling took them to the Serra II-III Col, where they ditched their packs before bagging the final two summits, Serra II and I. The successful trio reached the security of the Tellot Glacier by 8:00 P.M., all smiles as they ambled their way to the Plummer Hut (9,121 feet). The first traverse of the Waddington Range was theirs. Many first ascents later, it's still Serl's favorite climb. Says the proud Canadian, "You can't do mountaineering like this anywhere else in North America."

ROUTE DESCRIPTION

Area: Waddington Range
First ascent: Peter Croft, Greg Foweraker, and Don Serl, July 26–30, 1985
Base elevation: Fury Gap, 8,136 feet
Summit elevations: Waddington, 13,186 feet; Combatant, 13,323 feet; Tiedemann, 12,625 feet; Asperity, 12,192 feet; Serra V, 11,877 feet; Serra IV, 12,008 feet; Serra III, 11,949 feet; Serra II, 11,614 feet; Serra I, 11,286 feet; cumulative elevation gain more than 13,000 feet
Difficulty: VI, 5.9, AI 2 or 3
Time required: First-ascent party took 5 days
Equipment: 2 50-m 9 mm ropes; standard ice ax plus 45–50 cm hammer; crampons; 1 screw per person; 10–12 pitons (mostly thin) plus 4–6 cams to 2½ inches, 8–10 wired nuts (nothing tiny); glacier travel gear; good bivy gear
Season: Late July–August; September possible, but days are short
Special considerations: Make the traverse from west to east; a good weather window is needed to make it through the committing Serra peaks
References: *Canadian Alpine Journal* (1986, pps 4–6); *American Alpine Journal* (1986, pps 179–81); *The Waddington Guide* by Don Serl (Elaho Publishing, 2000)
Map: 92 N/6 Mount Waddington, 1:50,000

Approach: From Williams Lake, British Columbia, follow Highway 20 west 140 miles (225 km) to Tatla Lake, then south 12.5 miles (20 km) to Bluff Lake, located northeast of the Waddington Range. Fly from Bluff Lake to Angel Gap by helicopter with Mike King's Whitesaddle Air Service (250-476-1182). (Alternatively, Long Beach Helicopters, 250-286-8863, flies out of Campbell River on Vancouver Island. The flying route, 50 percent longer, is more expensive.) See Climb 9.

Route: The 5.9 terrain is on Serra V; ice to 50 degrees; minor mixed terrain to 75 degrees on the Serra III-IV ridge. See map overlay for route.

Descent: Descend the Tellot Glacier to the Plummer Hut.

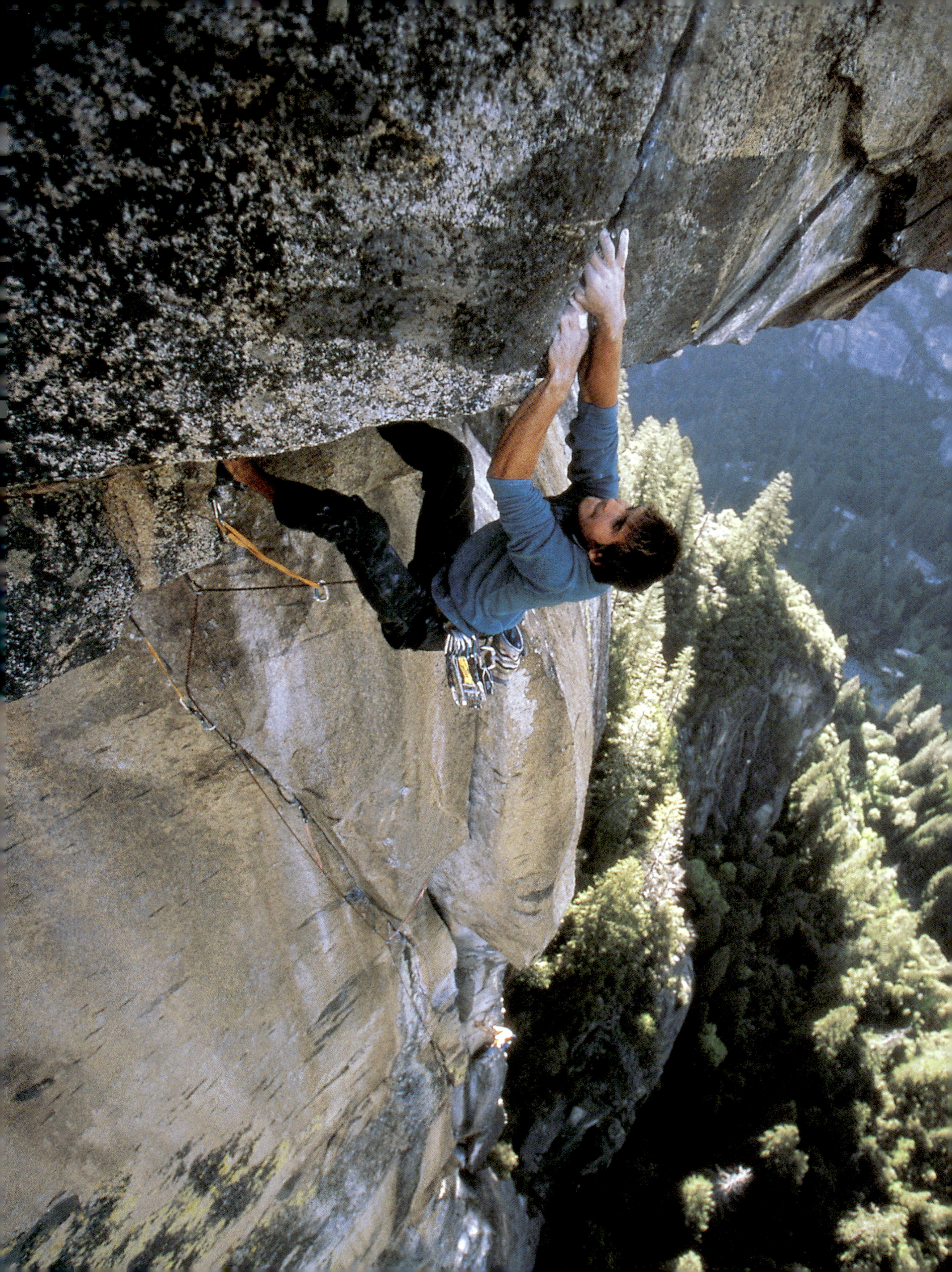

CHRIS SHARMA
NORTH FACE OF THE ROSTRUM, YOSEMITE NATIONAL PARK, CALIFORNIA

CHRIS SHARMA—THE NATURAL

Until he was twelve, Chris Sharma was a normal California kid from Santa Cruz. He rode his bike, dabbled in Little League, did a little surfing—the usual stuff. Then he paid a visit to his local climbing gym: The staff watched in awe as the child prodigy discovered his calling. The specialized techniques of the sport came to him naturally, without any coaching or instruction. "It was amazing," says Sharma, who remembers the moment vividly. "For the first time in my life, everything just clicked."

Within eight months of his first gym visit, Sharma placed second in his age group at a Junior National climbing competition. Within two years, he was competing—and winning—against adults. He won several national championships at age fourteen, then won the North American championship at age fifteen. The following year he won the Junior World Cup in France and the World Cup in Slovenia. A knee injury forced Sharma to take a break from competing, but he came back with a vengeance when he won the summer '99 X Games. Sharma made history once again on July 19, 2001, when he snagged the first redpoint ascent of *Realization* in Ceuse, France, the world's first 5.15a.

Sharma, whose life has been "pretty unstructured," says, "I'm really happy that I found climbing. It totally changed my life in many positive ways. It's given me a lot of direction." Sharma's initial focus was on sport climbing, but his repertoire now includes crack climbing and, mostly, bouldering. (In 2000, he won the Phoenix Bouldering Contest with more than twice as many points as the closest competitor.)

Despite his prodigious talents, the youthful Sharma simply wants to have fun climbing with his friends. When asked if he has some big master plan for his climbing, he just shrugs and says, "I'm still not very serious about it."

NORTH FACE OF THE ROSTRUM

When Chris Sharma tries something new, he does it in a big way. He won an indoor climbing competition within five months of touching his first plastic hold. He made the first ascent of Necessary Evil (5.14c), once considered to be the country's hardest sport climb, at age fifteen. And he sent one of the most difficult bouldering problems in the world, Fred Nicole's Scarface (V14), after just a few days of effort.

Given Sharma's tendency to jump into new activities with both feet, it's no surprise that his first multipitch crack climb—or "trad route," as he calls it—was the classic north face of the Rostrum, a lectern-shaped pillar of granite renowned for its so-called "splitter" cracks. Prior to climbing the Rostrum, Sharma had led only a couple of single-pitch 5.10 cracks. "I just threw myself into it," he laughs.

In the spring of 1999, Sharma was in Yosemite visiting ace crack climber and friend Andy Puhvel. Sharma had heard about the Rostrum, but didn't realize what a classic route it was—a lifelong goal for some—until Puhvel began waxing poetic about it. Puhvel explained that, unlike most Yosemite climbs, the Rostrum is approached from the top. Starting at the Wawona Tunnel parking area, interested parties must hike *down* and rappel to reach the start of the climb. Puhvel also explained that the close proximity of the parking area to the top of the Rostrum makes it easy to sample its final pitch—a spectacular 5.12b splitter called the Rostrum Roof—with just one rappel. Sharma couldn't resist.

As he lowered himself over the edge of the 1,000-foot face, Sharma was thrilled by the outrageous exposure. He described the experience with a refreshing, childlike zeal. "I'd never been that high off the ground before. It was awesome." As he dangled at the base of the roof, a 1,000-foot smorgasbord of crack climbing unfolded below him—finger cracks, hand cracks, and, of course, 4-inch "off-widths." He fantasized briefly about climbing the entire route, then refocused on the irascible 1-inch crack that stood between him and the top of the Rostrum.

The difficulty of a crack climb is determined by width more than by steepness. Cracks ranging from 1½ to 2½ inches, known as hand cracks, can feel as stable as a rung ladder to an experienced climber. And narrow cracks, from ½ to ¾ inch, which allow for so-called "finger locks," can feel equally secure to a seasoned practitioner. But it's cracks in between these sizes, from ¾ inch to 1½ inches, that demand a true mastery of the art. They are too narrow to afford a secure hand jam, yet too wide to offer a tight finger lock. The Rostrum Roof is just such a crack. (Most parties finish the regular north face route via a wider, 5.10a crack to the right,

Quick study: Chris Sharma perfecting his finger locks on the Rostrum's Excellent Adventure (5.13b) © Jim Thornburg, portrait © Jim Thornburg

© Mark Kroese

bypassing the 5.12b pitch altogether.)

With the security of a top rope, Sharma started up the crack, experimenting with different techniques as he went. Without the added challenge of placing gear, he was able to climb the crack without falling. "I just sort of figured it out," he recalls. The experience bolstered his confidence and whetted his appetite for more. With the crux under his belt, he was even more psyched to climb the entire route—and lead every pitch.

Sharma returned 3 days later with a friend who was happy to let him do all of the leading. As he worked his way up the route, the ratings of the various pitches seemed arbitrary. For example, he sailed through the first crux—a 5.11c finger crack that called on his phenomenal finger strength—but found the 4-inch, 5.10a off-width to be quite a challenge. "It was totally weird, kind of scary," reported Sharma. "I had never really climbed a crack that wide."

After leading six long pitches, Sharma found himself at the base of the Rostrum Roof. He wondered if he was better or worse off than he was when he last climbed the crack. On one hand, he reasoned, he knew he could do the moves. But on the other hand, he had to lead the pitch. Placing gear would require extra energy, and he was already tired from the climbing he'd just done.

Determined to lead the pitch without falling, Sharma conserved energy by placing gear sparingly. This increased his chances of success, but also the length of a potential fall. About 10 feet from the top, when he was desperately pumped, his fingers began cramping shut. Sharma knew if he stopped to place protection, he'd end up resting on it. Instead, he kept climbing, finding perverse pleasure in the prospect of a long fall. "I was so tired and gripped and scared," he remembers. "I was at my limit and had no choice but to run it out." He says he'll never forget how it felt to pull onto the top of the wall. "I remember just sitting up there thinking that this is one of the coolest things I've ever done."

Although Sharma's crash course in crack climbing was a resounding success, one small detail nagged at him. On the sixth pitch he had bypassed an optional crux, a thin, left-leaning crack that, when combined with the Rostrum Roof, is called The Excellent Adventure. Having seen it, Sharma realized it would be the ultimate "enduro pitch." When he returned the next day, he flashed the lower section of The Excellent Adventure and continued to the top via the now-familiar 5.12b crack. Sharma was tested by the 5.13b linkup, admitting that he "almost puked" when he reached the top.

Regardless of how much crack climbing he continues to do, Sharma will always remember the Rostrum as his rite of passage into the world of traditional climbing. "I used to be super intimidated by that kind of stuff," he allows. "So when I was actually able to do it, it was a major breakthrough for me."

ROUTE DESCRIPTION

Area: Lower Merced Canyon, Yosemite Valley
First ascent: Warren Harding and Glen Denny, July 1962; first free ascent to base of roof: Ron Kauk and Dale Bard, 1977; first free ascent to top: Kim Schmidtz et al., 1985
Difficulty: IV, 5.11c or 5.13b
Time required: 1 day
Equipment: Nuts and camming units to 3½ inches, with extra ¾-inch to 2½-inch pieces; can be done with 1 rope (including rappels to base), but retreat would be difficult
Season: Spring and fall; summer possible on cooler days
Special considerations: Can be done in seven pitches with 60-m ropes
Reference: *Yosemite Climbs, Free Climbs* by Don Reid

Approach: Park on State Highway 41, at the west end of the stone wall west of the Wawona Tunnel. Hike down slabs then a steep dirt gully just west of the Rostrum. Follow the gully to a drop-off. Four 70-foot rappels end at the base of the north face.

Route: An astounding column of granite with some of the best splitter cracks in Yosemite. See topo for details.

Descent: A few hundred yards of walking back *up* to your car!

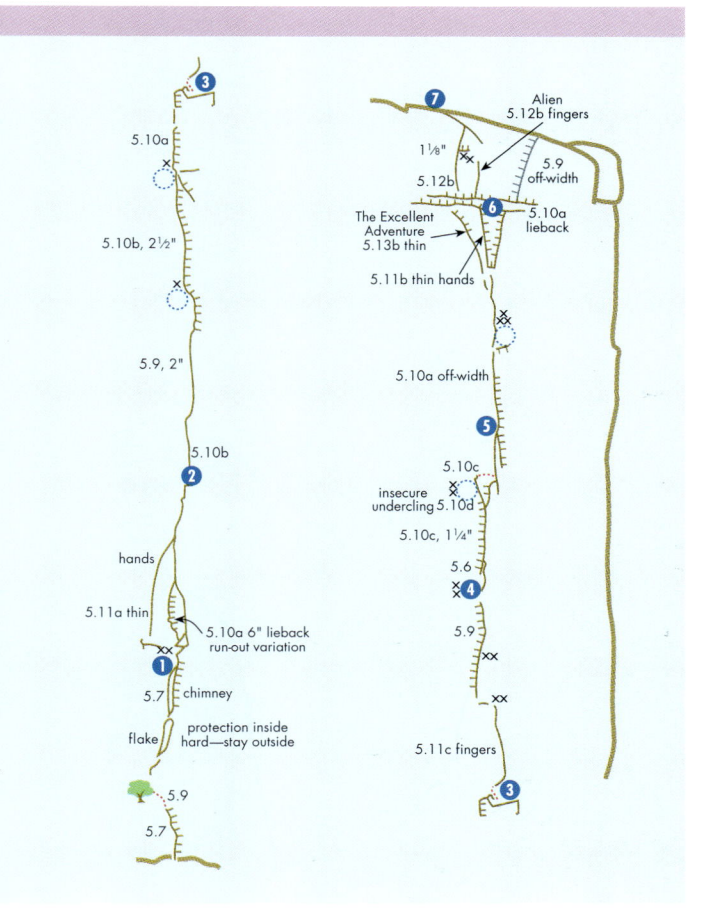

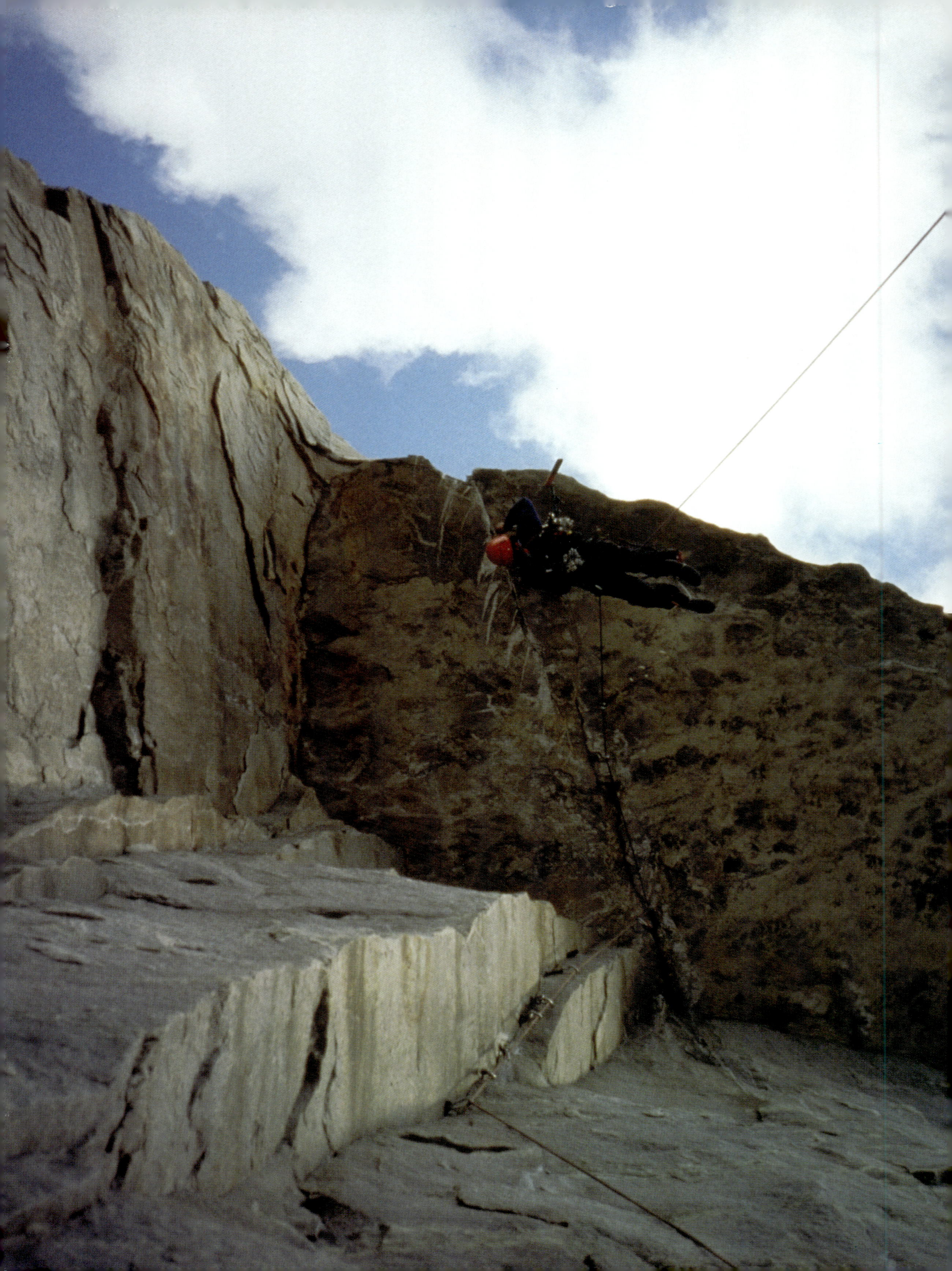

SETH SHAW

HONKY TONQUIN, NORTH FACE OF MOUNT GEIKIE, CANADIAN ROCKIES, BRITISH COLUMBIA

SETH SHAW—1961–2000

Author note: On May 25, 2000, Seth Shaw was killed by a falling serac on Alaska's Ruth Glacier. He was photographing his partner, Tim Wagner, not far from a new route they had just completed on Mount Johnston. Wagner suffered a broken leg, but was able to extract himself and limp to safety. Seth is survived by his wife, Beth Malloy, sister Suzy Shaw, and parents Ann Shaw and Tom Shaw.

Seth Shaw had his first big adventure the summer after he graduated from high school. Lured by the promise of a high-paying job in an Alaskan cannery, he steered his rickety truck up the Alaska Highway and headed for the Last Frontier. He returned three months later with everything he needed to be an alpinist: a love for the mountains, a year's supply of cash, and a tolerance for 110-hour work weeks.

The cannery experience sold Shaw on the merits of a college education. He earned a degree in meteorology from the University of Utah, and went on to become a skilled avalanche forecaster. While living in Salt Lake City, he met and climbed with the late Mugs Stump and Conrad Anker (see Climb 1). Stump's influence attracted him to the spare, hard frontiers of alpine climbing.

With Anker, Shaw did his first "big" Alaskan route in 1987. After a 100-mile approach, the pair established an impressive new technical line on Gurney Peak—a confidence-building trip that whetted his appetite for more. Shaw climbed numerous Alaskan faces during the next thirteen years, including new routes on Mount Hunter, Middle Triple Peak, the Moose's Tooth, Mount Vancouver, and Mount Johnston. He also excelled at all rock-climbing disciplines, doing everything from 5.13 sport routes to speed ascents of three Zion (Utah) walls in a single day. In 1998, he joined Steph Davis (see Climb 13) and Kennan Harvey (see Climb 19) for a virtually free ascent of Inshalla (VII, 5.12, A1) on Pakistan's 4,300-foot Shipton Spire.

In addition to being a terrific climber, Shaw was a model partner. He will be remembered for his dry sense of humor, deadpan understatement, and adventurous spirit. "Seth was an explorer," remembers Beth Malloy. "He always wanted to see new areas and climb different routes."

HONKY TONQUIN, NORTH FACE OF MOUNT GEIKIE

Each year, a few ambitious hikers venture through Maccarib Pass, a remote passage through the Canadian Rockies' rugged northern Ramparts. Those who do behold the sentinel of the Tonquin River valley, Mount Geikie (pronounced like "geeky"). Rising more than 4,500 feet from the marshy lowlands, Geikie's broad quartzite shoulders bristle with unclimbed lines.

Mount Geikie is one of Canada's best-kept secrets. Prior to 1996, there were only three routes to its summit, each yielding only a handful of ascents. The fact that one of them was established by the legendary George Lowe (see Climb 28)—whose routes often go unrepeated for decades—didn't help matters. When Seth Shaw caught a glimpse of the wildly overhanging headwall on Geikie's north face, he determined it was time for a fourth route on the mountain.

Just getting to Geikie is an experience. While preparing for the 18-mile trek to its base, Shaw and his partner Scott Simper heard a bear story so horrific it made them want to pack up and go sport climbing. "Last year at this trailhead," began the lead horse packer, "this couple was less than 100 feet from their car when a grizzly jumped out of the woods and nabbed the guy." Drawing great pleasure from their terrified faces, he continued. "So the girl runs to get help, which doesn't come for about an hour. When it finally arrives, the guy is dead, but the bear is still munching on him." Shaw and Simper exchanged troubled glances and continued loading the horses.

By evening they reached the end of the horse trail 12 miles up the Tonquin valley. From here they would shuttle loads to base camp through what Shaw called "real wilderness." As they followed game trails through the swampy meadows below Geikie's north face, there were grizzly footprints all over the muddy trail. "They were so fresh that they were still filling back up with water," Shaw explained. Wishing they had a gun, the anxious pair forced conversation until they reached camp.

The late Seth Shaw on the crux pitch (A3) of the wildly steep north face of Mount Geikie. Once over the roof, the climbing is considerably easier. © Scott Simper, portrait © Kennan Harvey

The north face of Geikie is split into three sections by two convenient ledge systems. The first third is nine pitches of mostly fourth class, with a few 5.8 or 5.9 pitches. The thirteen pitches on the middle part of the wall are mostly vertical, scattered with lots of small roofs. And the upper third is wildly steep for six pitches, overhanging like the hull of a cruise ship for 900 feet. From the top of the headwall, 700 feet of easy mixed terrain lead to the summit in seven pitches.

The previous year, Shaw and Simper had made it a third of the way up the wall, but were forced off by "cold, snotty weather." This year it was sunny and warm—perhaps too warm. As they cruised up the familiar lower third of the face, a massive rockslide released from snow-covered slopes below the summit. First they felt the rumble, then a chaos of quartzite poured over the lip of the headwall, ricocheting off the wall 100 feet to their left.

"It was super, super scary," recalled the normally understated Shaw. "We thought about retreating, but decided to sleep on it first." Their confidence was restored—slightly—after a night with no major rockfall. Lured by exceptional weather and the promise of safer climbing on the steep headwall above, they continued.

They slipped into a grueling rhythm that Shaw called "serious boot camp." Each day they were up and moving by 7:00 A.M., then spent the next 16 hours leading, fixing pitches, hauling bags, and, eventually, cooking by headlamp. They reached the upper third of the headwall late in the fifth day. After arduously hoisting themselves and their gear up the 100-degree wall, they were welcomed by a spacious, flat ledge. "It was idyllic," grinned Shaw. "Picture a Yosemite-style ledge in a wilderness big-wall setting." Adding to the ambience was a waterfall that, because of the steepness of the wall, tumbled through space 100 feet behind them.

Ironically, the climbing got easier as the wall got steeper. Despite its neck-straining tilt, the wall was dry and the climbing was what Shaw called "easy aid on great rock, fully recreational." As planned, they followed a crack system that divided the otherwise blank headwall. Although the climbing was straightforward, it didn't lack excitement. The sixth day started with a hair-raising pendulum. Cutting loose to Jumar sent the second rocketing 100 feet out from the wall—right into the waterfall. Clenching the rope like an ape on a vine, Simper suffered an unwanted shower with each outward pendulum.

On the seventh morning they awoke to cold, windy conditions. Perched on a small stance just one pitch from the top of the headwall, and downwind of the waterfall, Simper belayed patiently as his partner oozed up the climb's hardest aid pitch. Shaw nailed his way through a tricky roof while windblown droplets coated Simper in a sheet of ice. Dangling more than 3,000 feet above the glacier, Shaw was relieved when he turned the lip of the roof; he was only 40 feet from easier ground. Within an hour they were both standing atop the headwall.

Seven hundred feet of 45-degree mixed terrain stood between the weary climbers and Geikie's summit. Deep, sugary snow hampered their progress, but didn't stop them from reaching the top before dark. Standing on blessedly flat ground, they relaxed long enough to realize they'd just done the first new route on Geikie's north face in nineteen years. They were too tired to celebrate, content just to sleep on a flat surface without being tied into harnesses.

They planned to reach base camp the next day, but conceded defeat after too many rappels in the wrong direction. Shaw explained how demoralized they were as they sat in the seemingly endless gully, sharing their last PowerBar, counting the hours until first light. Then, in his inimitably deadpan way, he added, "Yeah, it could have been a lot worse. At least we didn't have to worry about bears."

ROUTE DESCRIPTION

Area: Rampart Mountains, Tonquin River valley
First ascent: Scott Simper and Seth Shaw, July 1996
Base elevation: 5,800 feet
Summit elevation: 10,700 feet
Difficulty: VI+, 5.10, A3, AI 2
Time required: 2 days for approach, 6–11 days round trip from base camp
Equipment: Double set of cams .5–4 inches, 1 5-inch; 2 sets of wired nuts from no. 2 to no. 13; pitons: 5 peckers, 5 knifeblades, 4 lost arrows; 3 angles (1 each ½–¾ inch); selection of hooks, including bat hooks; 2 ice screws; 2–6 ropes, depending on style, 60-m ideal; small, free-standing tent (portaledge optional); rubber tubing for sucking water from runnels
Season: July–August
Special considerations: Rockfall increases with warmer weather; numerous grizzly bears on approach and descent
References: *Selected Alpine Climbs in the Canadian Rockies* by Sean Dougherty; *Canadian Alpine Journal* (1997)
Map: 83 D/9 Amethyst Lakes

Approach: From Jasper, head south on Highway 16 to exit 93A. Choose either the Astoria River valley or Maccarib Pass Trail. The approach hike is 18 miles.

Route: A remote alpine wall concluding with wildly steep but straightforward aid climbing; thirty-five pitches. See topo for details.

Descent: To reach Tonquin Valley, it's fastest to traverse summit ridge to the top of the West Ridge. One rappel gains large, flat area. Some downclimbing leads to three more rappels down a rock rib to the south of a large ice gully. Rappel into the far side of the gully, then rappel back across the ice to a rock rib. One more rappel across the ice leads to talus ledges. Follow these down until stopped by a steep, 50-meter high buttress. Rappel from the northern end of the buttress to more talus ledges.

Traverse ledges along the south side of the ridge, past a bivy site, then across the north side of ridge. Rappel and traverse west to a large step in the ridge. A 50-meter rappel brings you to a large flat area in ridge. Don't scramble over the top of the couloir between Geikie and Barbican Paugak Pass—dangerous. Instead, hike down talus slopes on the north side of the ridge to the top of the large buttress. Two rappels gain easy ground and, eventually, the bottom of the face.

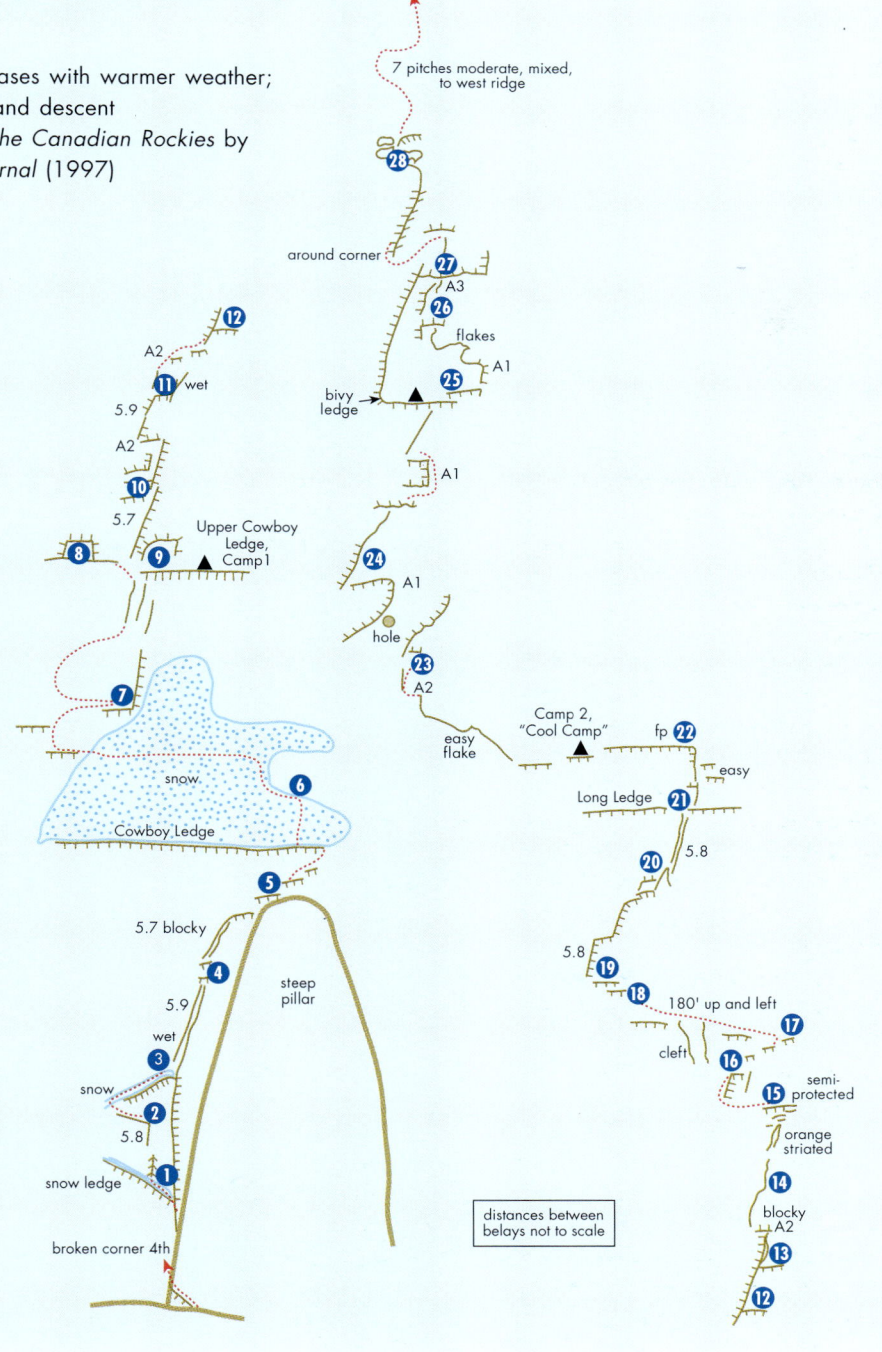

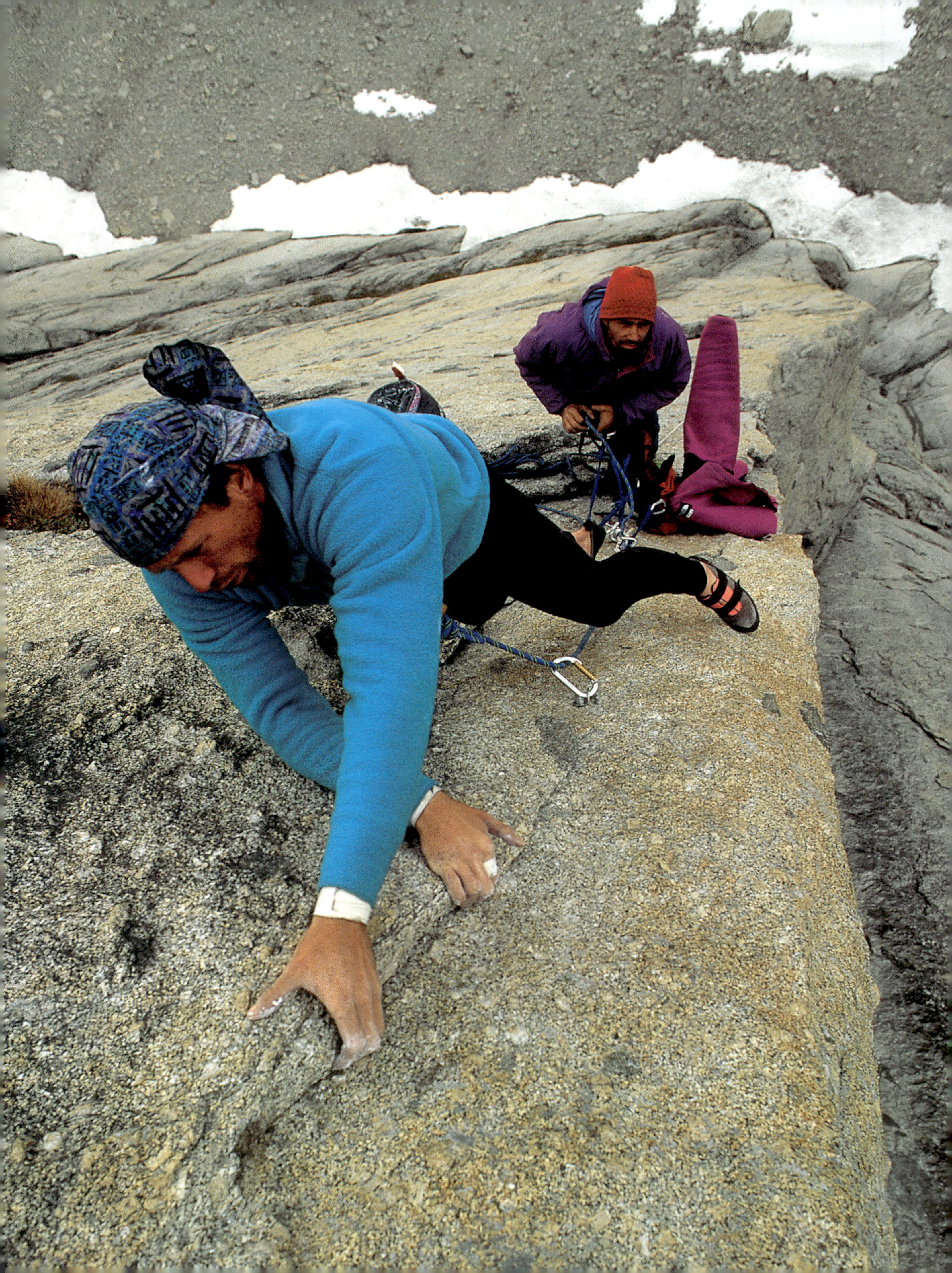

TODD SKINNER

THE GREAT CANADIAN KNIFE, MOUNT PROBOSCIS, CIRQUE OF THE UNCLIMBABLES, NORTHWEST TERRITORIES

TODD SKINNER—AS FREE AS CAN BE

Todd Skinner has been at the forefront of the North American free-climbing scene for more than twenty years. Since the mid-eighties, he has focused on all-free ascents of the biggest, most important rock walls in the world.

In 1988, Todd demonstrated his vision with the first free ascent of the Salathé Wall on El Capitan (5.13b). In 1990, he free-climbed the north face of Mount Hooker in Wyoming (5.12a). His streak continued in 1992, with a new, all-free route on the southeast face of Mount Proboscis—the Great Canadian Knife (5.13b). In 1993, he free-climbed yet another Royal Robbins route, the direct Northwest Face of Half Dome (5.13d). During the summer of 1995, Skinner took his ambitions to northern Pakistan, free-climbing the 3,000-foot east face of Trango Tower—more than 20,000 feet above sea level.

Skinner's approach, which brings sport-climbing ethics to wilderness walls, stirs heated debates among purists. While his quixotic ways may be controversial, it's impressive to see how rigidly he follows his chosen ethic. In the end, every inch of every pitch is led free, without so much as a moment of rope tension. Bolts are used only "to protect athletic passage," never for aid. The eternally upbeat Skinner is steadfast in his belief. "If we need rope ladders to ascend the peak, then we've climbed our ladders, not the mountain itself."

THE GREAT CANADIAN KNIFE

In 1963, Jim McCarthy, Layton Kor, Royal Robbins, and Dick McCracken made the first ascent of the 1,800-foot southeast face of Mount Proboscis. The trip was funded by the American Alpine Club to advance the art of technical mountaineering. According to McCarthy, their plan was for the "best American climbers to attempt the biggest wall they could find in a remote area." Using a combination of free- and aid-climbing techniques, the team proved that extremely technical rock climbs on major mountain walls were possible.

Twenty-nine years later, Todd Skinner came to Proboscis to do an all-free ascent of the same route. For the past five years, Skinner and longtime partner Paul Piana had been systematically doing all-free ascents of the biggest walls in North America—most of them Robbins routes from the 1960s. In 1991, Skinner recalls, "We were in the process of sifting out the biggest and most important walls in North America." Then Galen Rowell, an accomplished climber and world-renowned photographer, told Skinner and Piana about the southeast face of Mount Proboscis. After one look at a photo of the Half Dome–like face, the threesome planned a trip to Canada's granite paradise, the Cirque of the Unclimbables.

In July 1992, the three climbers with their gear crammed into John Witham's Jet Ranger for the final 150-mile helicopter trip to Proboscis. As the chopper dropped into the valley below Proboscis, their objective came into view: 1,800 feet of clean, vertical granite peppered with Tuolumne-like feldspar knobs. The climbing looked brilliant. The weather was good. Everything seemed perfect, until they noticed a team on the face ahead of them. For twenty-nine years, climbers ignored Proboscis's southeast face—and now there were two parties vying for the same route.

As the team hiked to the base of the wall to meet the other climbers, Skinner and Piana noticed a perfectly sculpted corner a few hundred feet to the left of the original Robbins route. The 90-degree edge soared above them like an office building. Without saying a word, they both knew what the other was thinking. When they suggested the alternative route to Rowell, who thought they were eyeing the *inside* corner of the left-facing dihedral, he was not impressed. "Look at the hideous slime in the crack," he remarked as his eyes followed a drip of water up the wall. "Not that inside corner," clarified Skinner. "I'm looking to the right, where the *outside* edge merges with the face again. It goes for more than 1,000 feet like that. It's got 'Route of the Nineties' stamped all over it!"

The knife-edged arête looked improbable—maybe impossible—from the ground, but Skinner insisted they give it a try. Rowell reluctantly agreed to their plan, but worried that if it didn't go, they wouldn't have time for the Robbins route. Unfazed by his skepticism, Skinner and Piana started the climb the next morning.

Piana led the first pitch—a slimy crack that took them to the dry but difficult arête. The twosome spent the rest of the day, and

Sweet monotony: Paul Piana belays while Todd Skinner continues up the perfectly sculpted Great Canadian Knife. © Galen Rowell, portrait © Galen Rowell

© Galen Rowell

the next three, working on the first four pitches. Because of the extreme nature of the climbing, Skinner and Piana made their ascent using modern sport-climbing techniques. Rather than trying to free each pitch on-sight, they first climbed using aid, often hanging from sky hooks to place protection and make upward progress. After establishing a secure anchor at the top of each pitch, they inspected and cleaned it on rappel. With the safety of a top rope, they rehearsed the gymnastic sequence of 5.12 and 5.13 moves before returning to lead each pitch without any support from the rope. Depending on your point of view, their controversial approach would yield either the most continually difficult alpine free climb in North America, or its longest, most remote sport climb.

Skinner and Piana made slow but steady progress, averaging one pitch per day. Meanwhile, Rowell—a perennially energetic climber in his late fifties—tracked their progress from the craggy summits of the surrounding peaks. Sooner or later, he believed, they would reach an impassable section that would force them to retreat. Skinner and Piana, however, were growing more optimistic with each new day. "We were getting euphoric," says Skinner. "Each of those pitches was, far and away, the most uniform arête I've ever been on. It was architecturally perfect. The climbing was wonderfully monotonous."

By the second week, Piana and Skinner had climbed half of the arête, leaving fixing ropes below them. After completing the seventh pitch, they rappelled to base camp to discuss their options with Galen, who, after observing their progress, was warming up to their chosen line. The threesome agreed to erect a camp at their high point and live on the wall until they completed the route.

The arête continued. And continued. Unfortunately, it outlasted their supply of bolts; they had placed just over 100 and had only a handful left. While they would have preferred to follow the arête to its top, they were forced to climb a system of cracks that drifted to the right. They would leave the upper part of the arête for a future party.

Several hundred feet from the top, they encountered the first of several off-width cracks. The insecure-looking slot was wider than their largest camming device, and neither Skinner or Piana wanted to lead. Without hesitation, Rowell, a Yosemite-schooled off-width master, grabbed the rack and started leading. "After 60 feet of 5.10+ climbing, he got in one lousy piece of gear," recalls Skinner. "Then he ran it out to the top."

Climbing by headlamp and without bivouac gear, the tired trio reached the bladelike ridge crest after midnight. To their disbelief, there wasn't a single flat spot to sit on. "The ridge was so sharp," recalls Skinner, "that you couldn't even stand on it." The weary climbers spent the rest of the night with their feet hanging over one side of the ridge and their heads over the other. "It was miserable," he laughs. "We called it the saddlebag bivouac."

When morning came, Rowell surprised Skinner and Piana with his desire to climb to Proboscis's elusive summit. While only 60 feet higher, it was six tedious 5.9 pitches to their right. Since the descent route was to their left, each rope-length would have to be climbed, and reversed, by all three climbers. To Rowell, reaching the summit mattered. But not to Skinner and Piana, who reluctantly honored Rowell's request. Skinner explains his philosophy: "We're wall climbers, not mountaineers. If you've climbed a hard wall, you've come for the journey, which ends when it's not hard anymore. When it's over, it's over."

ROUTE DESCRIPTION

Area: Logan Mountains
First ascent: Todd Skinner, Paul Piana, and Galen Rowell, August 1992
Base elevation: Approximately 6,700 feet
Summit elevation: 8,530 feet
Difficulty: VI, 5.13b
Time required: 3–6 days from lake directly below Proboscis, assuming redpoint-style climbing
Equipment: At least 2 60-m ropes (more if planning to fix pitches); 15 quick draws; standard rack of cams to 4 inches, including at least 1 5-inch piece; selection of TCUs, wired nuts, and thin pitons; assortment of hooks in case of aid moves; portaledge with rain fly
Season: Late July–early September
Special considerations: Some pitches are run-out due to first-ascent party's need to conserve bolts; black bears found in area around Glacier Lake
Reference: www.geocities.com/~gibell/cirque/ (George Bell's online guide to Cirque of the Unclimbables)
Map: Mount Sir James MacBrien 95L/4, 1:50,000

Approach: Fly directly to Proboscis, avoiding the strenuous 2-day hike from Glacier Lake. See Climb 15.

Route: Outstanding climbing on an architecturally perfect arête. A modern hardman's classic. A direct finish to the top of the arête can be added to the route by a party equipped with more bolts. See topo for details.

Descent: Rappel one of the direct routes on the face (such as the Grendel), or downclimb and rappel the South Ridge (5.7, A2) to the climber's left, then down loose, third-class shale to the lake.

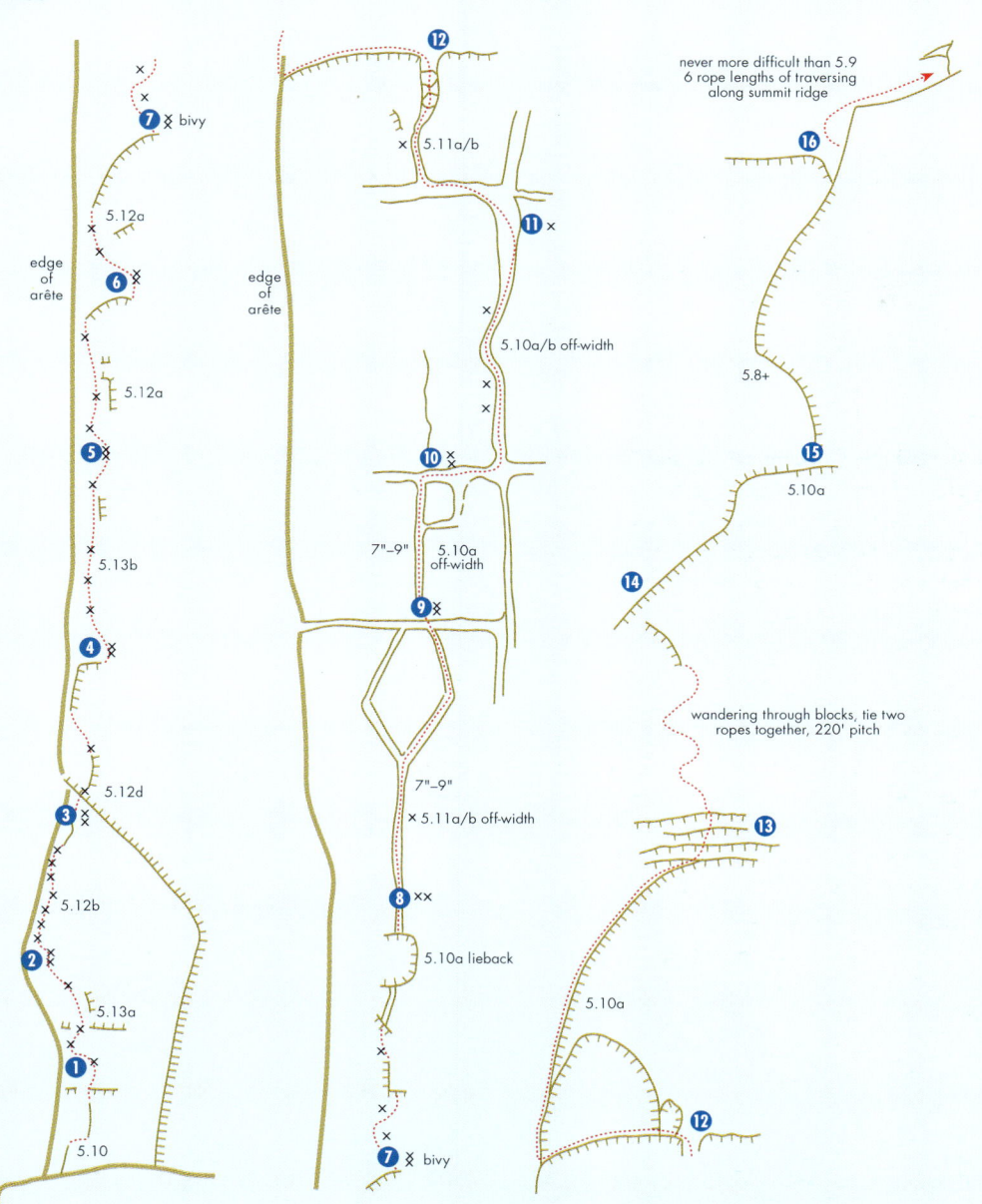

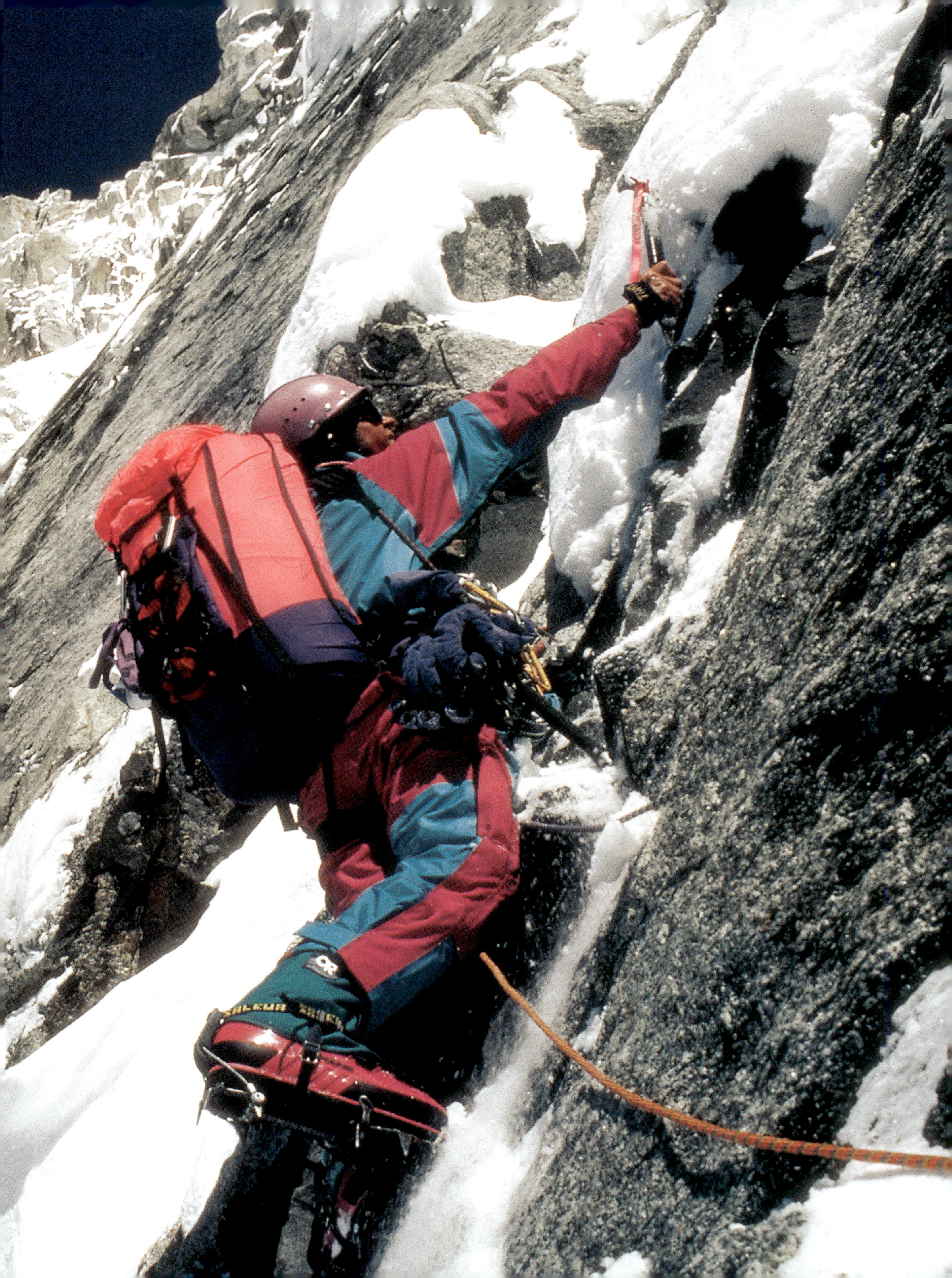

JAY SMITH

THE PHANTOM WALL, MOUNT HUNTINGTON, ALASKA RANGE, ALASKA

JAY SMITH— BEEN THERE, CLIMBED THAT

It's hard to find a place Jay Smith hasn't been, or a type of climbing he hasn't done. High-altitude mountaineering in the Himalayas? Check. First ascents of Yosemite big walls? Many. Big Alaskan routes? You bet. Exploration in Antarctica? He was one of the first. New routes in Patagonia? Seven and counting. Crack climbing in the desert? Tons. The list goes on.

The only thing that he hasn't done in the past thirty years, it seems, is stop climbing. Smith's perennial zeal comes from his refusal to specialize in a single discipline or geography. He's likely to be aid climbing on Half Dome one month, alpine climbing in Alaska the next, then heading for Australia to go sport climbing. The only common thread that runs through Smith's three-decades resume is his penchant for first ascents.

New routes have been the staple of Smith's climbing diet since 1971. As a free climber, he's done almost 200 new routes in Canyonlands National Park, Utah, 50 at Lover's Leap, California, and more than 90 at Red Rocks, Nevada. In the Himalayas, he's added technical lines on peaks such as Kangtega and Lingtreng—both above 21,000 feet. His Patagonian accomplishments include new routes on Cerro Stanhardt, Cerro Torre, and the Central Tower of Paine. In Kyrgyzstan, he plucked two new grade VI free climbs, one of them rated 5.12. And in Yosemite, he's done three new routes on El Capitan and four on Half Dome—including a highly original girdle traverse of Half Dome's entire northwest face.

If Smith isn't pioneering new routes, he's probably working as a guide. His scrupulous ways have earned him a loyal client base, including the U.S. government, which hires him to train an elite group of Navy Seals. Smith calls it the best job he's ever had. "It's pretty cool," he says. "These guys are really solid, tough climbers. We go out and do walls together, swinging leads, having a great time."

THE PHANTOM WALL

If the so-called "Seven Summits" were ranked by aesthetic beauty instead of elevation, Mount Everest would be off the list. In its place would be the architecturally perfect Ama Dablam. In South America, Aconcagua would probably cede its position to a Patagonia spire, or a summit in the Peruvian Andes. And in North America, Mount McKinley would be displaced by nearby Mount Huntington.

Since it was first photographed by Bradford Washburn in the late '50s, Mount Huntington has been considered the most beautiful peak in Alaska. At a relatively low 12,240 feet, the pyramid-shaped peak is graced by long, slender ridges and steep, ice-clad faces. The striking west ridge, also known as the Harvard Route, is included in the book *Fifty Classic Climbs of North America*.

Mount Huntington was first climbed in 1964 by a French team led by the late Lionel Terray. The following year, a young David Roberts and three Harvard schoolmates fought their way up the west ridge in a monthlong effort that inspired Roberts' first book, *The Mountain of My Fear*. Two more routes—the Colton-Leach and Nettle-Quirk—were added to the mountain's west side over the next two decades.

Jay Smith hadn't given Mount Huntington much thought until the fall of 1989, when Dave Nettle showed him a Washburn photo of its southwestern flank. As Nettle explained the intricacies of his new route, Smith's eyes locked onto a prominent line on the unclimbed southwest face. "The line was so obvious that I couldn't believe it hadn't been done," says Smith. "Paul Teare and I began making plans immediately."

Smith and Teare landed on the Tokositna Glacier below Mount Huntington the following May. They were just 8 miles from the thundering herds on Mount McKinley's west buttress, but felt like they were in the middle of nowhere. They shared the mountain, which from base camp looks like a complex maze of intersecting ridgelines and hanging glaciers, with just one other party.

The climbers came close to completing the route on their first attempt. Traveling fast and light, without sleeping bags or a multiday supply of food, they made it two-thirds of the way up the face before stopping for a quick bivy. Thanks to his partner's efforts to keep his toes, Smith didn't get much sleep. "We put on all of our clothes and laid head to toe in this little trench," he explains, "but all I heard was the sound of Paul's boots clapping together as

Paul Teare getting what he came for on Mount Huntington's Phantom Wall. He and Jay Smith completed the new route on their third attempt, in 1991. © Jay Smith, portrait © Jay Smith Collection

[Photo labels: Colton-Leach, Nettle-Quirk, Harvard Route, Phantom Wall]

© Bradford Washburn (neg. 8187)

he tried to keep his feet warm." They resumed climbing 6 hours later, but a nasty storm stopped them in their tracks. The decision to retreat was easy. "Avalanches started running down the face 10 minutes after it started snowing," remembers Smith. "We just looked at each other and said, 'We're outta here.'"

Their next attempt came about a week later, after wasting a precious day of good weather. As Paul donned his bear-trap-style crampons, he noticed that they had split the welt of his boot. "We spent a day of perfect weather watching glue dry," laments Smith. "We didn't leave camp until almost midnight." Racing against the clock, the climbers decided not to reclimb the lower part of their route, which involved traveling through a narrow, avalanche-prone valley. Instead, they stormed up the bottom part of the Harvard Route and traversed the southwest face to join their unfinished line. As luck would have it, a sudden storm denied them success once again. "We made it to the exact same spot as the first time," said Smith in disbelief. "I specifically remember the rock that marked our high point." They didn't get a third chance that trip, and left Huntington with plans to return the following year.

Their luck was better in May 1991. Even though they planned to do the route in a single push, they decided to bring sleeping bags to ensure success. The alpinists raced through the first few thousand feet of moderate terrain, what they dubbed "Death Valley." Two mixed pitches on exquisite pink granite led them to a long tongue of moderate ice, which they climbed unroped until reaching the steeper slopes above. The crux of the route was relatively short. "There are five pitches of really technical climbing," explains Smith. "but it's the best rock I've ever seen in Alaska—beautiful pink granite and deep cracks with good protection. We used only 20 feet of aid, which could be avoided if there was no ice in the crack."

After navigating through the crux pitches, Smith and Teare stopped for a quick bivy. After a short night, the determined climbers made quick work of the upper ice fields, reaching the summit under clear skies. They rappelled and downclimbed the upper two-thirds of the route, then followed the lower west ridge back to base camp. From base camp, the round trip took 32 hours, a time Smith thinks can easily be bested. "A fast party can do the route in a day. Hell, the way things are going, some young punk will probably do it in 6 hours," he laughs.

Despite the fact that it took him three tries, Smith considers the Phantom Wall the best line on a mountain filled with good lines. "I always recommend the route because it's technically reasonable and follows a striking line on the most beautiful mountain in the area," he offers. "What more could you want?"

ROUTE DESCRIPTION

Area: Tokositna Glacier, Alaska Range
First ascent: Jay Smith and Paul Teare, May 20–21, 1991
Base elevation: 6,000 feet
Summit elevation: 12,240 feet
Difficulty: Alaska grade 4, 5.10, A1, M5
Time required: First-ascent party took 32 hours; route is a great candidate for a 1-day ascent
Equipment: Ice tools and crampons, set of wired nuts, 2 sets of TCUs; 2 sets of Friends to no. 3, 5–6 pitons to ¾ inch, 4–5 ice screws, 2 pickets (optional), bivy gear (optional)
Season: April–June; mid-May ideal
Special considerations: Mount Huntington is outside of Denali National Park, thus no permit is required, but you may register with the Park Service in Talkeetna
References: *American Alpine Journal* (1992); Washburn photo 8187, Boston Museum of Science
Map: Mt. McKinley, AK (Washburn)

Approach: A 1-hour flight from Talkeetna to base camp on the Tokositna Glacier. Establish base camp under the Harvard Route beneath the west ridge. From base camp, ski west around the toe of Point 9,559 and cache skis. Contour back east, traversing along a bench (some avalanche danger) above the icefall of the Tokositna. This leads to a couloir that drops into Death Valley. Make one rappel and glissade/downclimb to its bottom. Continue upvalley to the start of the face (2 hours from base camp).

Route: Start on mixed terrain for a pitch or two, right of the hanging glacial tongue in the center of the face. Then climb several thousand feet of easy ice (first-ascent party was unroped), trending left toward the top. Then climb more difficult mixed ground (some water ice) up and left, heading for a large snowfield below a large rock headwall that bisects the face at midlevel. From the top of the snowfield, follow the highest ramp system up and right for several pitches (5.9, M5), until a discontinuous system leads up and left to the bottom of the upper snowfield in the center of the face (crux: 5.10, M5, four points of aid, A1). Continue on easy ice on the upper right-hand margin of the snowfield (possible bivy and gear stash). For the summit push, mixed climbing leads to ice flutings up and right of the bivy. Follow these straight up to the summit ice fields. Above, stay left to follow the easiest ground to the summit.

Descent: Downclimb and rappel the ascent route to the bivy site; rappel straight down when possible, using mostly rock anchors. From the bivy, traverse due west to the edge of the snowfield. Continue left across mixed ground till an obvious crack/chimney system shoots straight down the headwall. Six rappels get you to a snowfield on the west ridge. Descend the ridge. Make a few more rappels (one rock wall) until a couloir leads down off the ridge back to camp (six to eight rappels, rock and ice anchors, bergschrund at bottom). Stroll 10 minutes to camp.

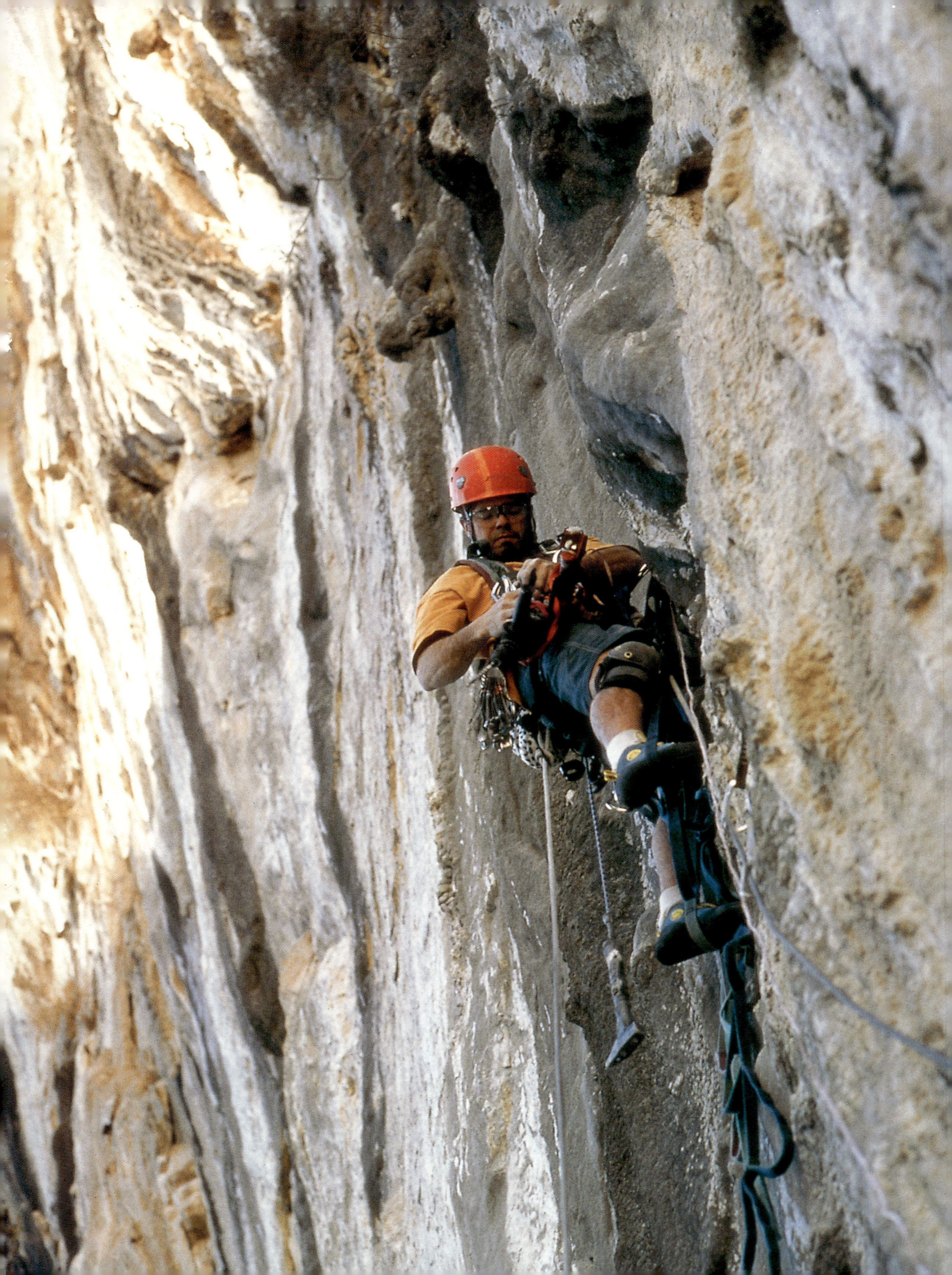

KURT SMITH

TIME FOR LIVIN', THE OUTRAGE WALL, EL POTRERO CHICO, NUEVO LEON (MEXICO)

KURT SMITH—THE GENERAL

In 1982, eighteen-year-old Kurt Smith went to Yosemite with the dream of doing a first ascent. Two decades later, that dream has been realized—about 700 times. Smith was hooked after his first new route. "The first time I drilled a bolt, it just opened up this whole new world. All of a sudden I started to look at the lines that had *not* been done yet. And I've never lost sight of that," remembers Smith. "I am a first ascensionist. It's in my heart. It's what I do."

Motivated, irreverent, and naive enough to believe he could do just about anything, Smith spent his formative years in Yosemite, challenging the status quo. Smith's tendency to take charge and rally the troops earned him his nickname—the General. A product of the MTV generation, Smith sports a mod haircut, an earring, and dresses in a way that shows he can't stomach convention. But beneath his outrageous exterior is a passionate, generous man who insists on giving back to the sport that has given so much to him. "I want to be known as someone who has given to the sport every year," says Smith.

In 1988, Smith moved to Colorado, establishing dozens of new routes at Rifle, a sport-climbing crag west of Denver. He loved Rifle's steep, pumpy routes, but missed multipitch climbing. In 1993, he found the best of both worlds—El Potrero Chico, the Mexican Yosemite. Smith remembers his awe. "All of a sudden, I'm taken to this place that has 2,000-foot walls right off the bumper. The first day I saw the Potrero, I saw about 150 lines I wanted to bolt."

He hasn't missed a season since.

TIME FOR LIVIN'

On his first trip to El Potrero Chico, Kurt Smith's well-trained eye was immediately drawn to the Outrage Wall—an improbable, overhanging sweep of streaked limestone more than 2,000 feet wide and 700 feet tall. Named by Jeff Jackson, the Texan who first climbed on the wall, the Outrage had just a few one-pitch routes at its base. Smith heard the wall crying for more. "Here was this giant canvas of untapped limestone, and *nobody* had done a route to the top of the wall. I was like, 'Man, I'm coming down for *that*.'"

By December 1996, Smith was partnered with Ned Harris, a friend from Boulder, Colorado, and prepared for the assault. The pair was armed with several hundred bolts, an assortment of sky hooks, a portaledge, and a collection of specialized gear for what Smith calls "bolted adventure climbing."

Their first job was to pick a line—a weakness in the imposing wall—that might go. Inspecting the route on rappel was out of the question; there is no easy way to the top, and it's way too steep. "If you rappel," explains Smith, "you just end up 20 feet away from the wall, dangling in space." Using binoculars, Smith found a line that might grant them passage. It started in the middle of the wall, then angled left under a series of large roofs. They had no idea whether it was possible, but there was only one way to find out. Like most first ascents in the Potrero, theirs would be done from the ground up, bolted on lead.

Smith started up the wall with his turbo drill dangling from his harness and a 100-foot extension cord in tow. Encumbered by a sizable rack of sky hooks, tiny camming devices, bolts, hangers, chain links, and wrenches, Smith used a combination of free- and aid-climbing techniques for upward progress. Stopping to drill a bolt every 10 to 15 feet proved to be strenuous—and scary. "Dicey hooks combined with soft limestone gear placements made for exciting times on the sharp end," he laughs. After 8 hours of dangling from hooks, cleaning, drilling, and turning wrenches, Smith completed the first pitch. "It's really, really demanding work. It'll break the spirit of the average sport climber—like *that*," he says, snapping his fingers for emphasis.

The hard work was rewarded with brilliant climbing that led the climbers up a snaking, diagonal passage. "It was like, 'This is where the holds are taking us, let's go there,'" recalls Smith. "The route had everything—pockets, edges, slopers, and tufas (attached stalactites) as big as beer kegs." After climbing at some of the best limestone crags in the world, Smith feels that the rock in the Potrero is as good as any he's touched. "Let's just say that the Potrero is the southern France of North America."

The first three pitches went free at 5.12a, 5.12b, and 5.12c, respectively. The higher they climbed, the steeper the wall became.

First ascensionist Kurt Smith putting up Time for Livin' (5.13a). The Outrage Wall is so tall and steep that new routes must be established from the ground up. © Kurt Smith Collection, portrait © Corey Rich

An overview of the 2,000-foot limestone walls of El Potrero Chico, the Mexican Yosemite © Kurt Smith Collection

The bolting was awkward and tedious. While placing a bolt on the fourth pitch, Harris hung all of his body weight from a hook no bigger than the tip of a screwdriver. As he teetered 15 feet above his last bolt, drill in hand, the hook placement blew without warning, spitting his outstretched body into the void. "I'll never forget the look of shock on Ned's face as he landed next to me on the ledge," says Smith. "Unscathed by the 30-footer, he charged back up there and managed to get the bolt in on his second try."

Averaging one pitch a day, and taking rest days in between, the pair reached the top of the Outrage in two weeks. But their work wasn't done. Because of the diagonal nature of the line, Smith and Harris had to install a separate rappel route, dropping straight down from the top of the sixth pitch. The wall is so steep that the first person to descend must clip the rappel rope into intermediate anchors to ensure the next rappel station can be reached. With the ends of the rope anchored to the rappel station below, the second removes the quick draws while descending, then gets pulled into the rappel station when at its level. "Now you know why I call it bolted adventure climbing," laughs Smith. "Every sport climber who comes here learns a whole new set of tricks."

With all of the bolts in place, Harris and Smith did a 1-day ascent of the route, redpointing every pitch after just a few tries. Smith says the fifth pitch, signing in at 5.13a, is the hardest. "It's 100 feet of thin crimps and shallow holds, with the crux being the surprise last moves to the belay." Smith, a big fan of the rock group the Beastie Boys, named the route Time for Livin'.

Despite all of the hair-raising moments in establishing the route, Smith insists it's safe for those who can climb at its grade. Harris and Smith used ⅜-inch bolts on the vertical sections and ½-inch bolts on the steeper terrain, with no big run-outs. "I look at it this way," says Smith: "The last thing I want is for someone to come to the Potrero and end up in a Mexican hospital."

Diablo's Path (IV, 5.11c)

Chicago residents Scott and Deanne Miller were 5.10 climbers who wanted more. They'd never done a multipitch route, never bolted a new line, and never climbed 5.11, but wanted to do all three. In the winter of 1997, they hired Kurt Smith to help them establish a new route on the Outrage. Their 5.11c route, Diablo's Path, was a three-week project that vaulted the happy couple into the world of 5.11 climbing. Smith did all of the bolting, but they did the rest, cleaning and redpointing all six pitches. Smith says it was much more than just a guiding gig. "It's the best 5.11 route I've ever done." Diablo's Path, a spectacular route that follows a diagonal line leading to a summit ledge, is located on the far right side of the Outrage Wall. The route is sustained 5.10+ and 5.11 with an awesome mixture of grips and cruxes. See topo for details.

ROUTE DESCRIPTION

Area: Hidalgo, Nuevo Leon, Mexico
First ascent: Kurt Smith and Ned Harris, December 1996;
  Diablo's Path: Scott Miller, Deanne Miller, and Kurt Smith, winter 1997
Difficulty: IV, 5.13a
Time required: 1 long day
Equipment: 2 60-m ropes, 15 quickdraws
Season: Fall–spring
Special considerations: Steepness of wall makes rappelling an adventure
Reference: www.potrerochico.com; *Mexico Rock* by Jeff Jackson (Homo-agro Press, 1999)

Approach: Hidalgo, Nuevo Leon, is about 20 miles northwest of the capital city of Monterrey, a major crossroads with an airport south of Laredo, Texas. When you drive into the Potrero canyon, park just below "the spires" on the right side of the road. From there, it's a 20-minute hike to the base of the Outrage Wall. The first pitch is located at the center of the wall and is 15 feet to the right of Palm Sunday.

Route: Time for Livin' follows a diagonal line that crosses through black and tan streaks and a small cave/roof near the top of the Outrage Wall. Pitch one is straightforward 5.12a face climbing with a mixture of crimpers and sloper pockets. Pitch two is similar to pitch one, but rated 5.12b. Pitch three is 100 feet of tufas, slopers, and crimpers. Pitch four is also 100 feet and leans left. Pitch five is the crux: 100 feet of thin crimps and shallow holds. Pitch six is a series of 5.12+ bouldering problems that throw every trick in the book at you.

Descent: Six rappels that are very overhanging; the first person rappelling must downclip the bolts to stay into the wall. The second then rappels and takes the draws off, and gets pulled back into each rappel station.

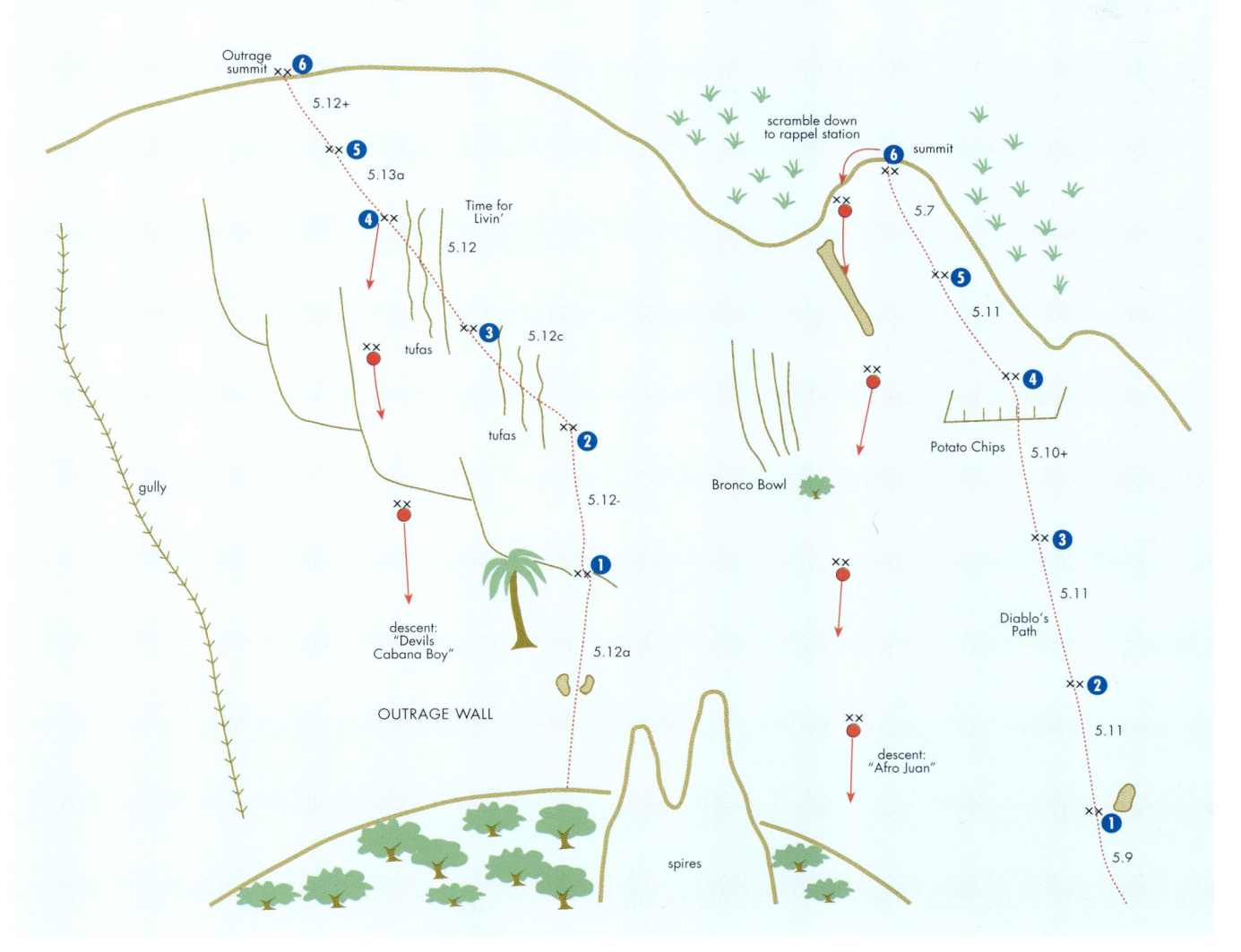

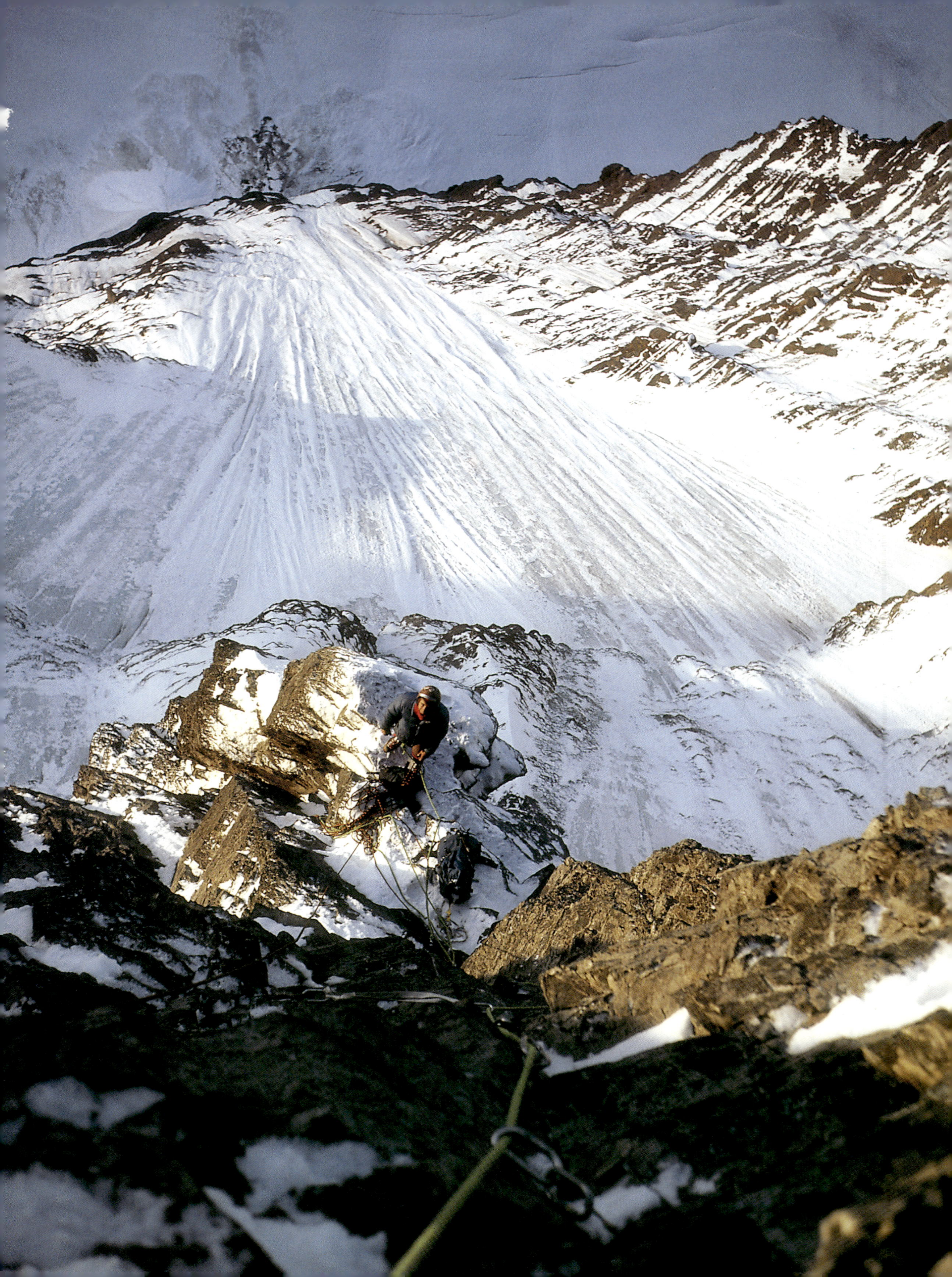

STEVE SWENSON

NORTH FACE OF MOUNT ALBERTA, JASPER NATIONAL PARK, ALBERTA

STEVE SWENSON— ACHIEVEMENT AT ALL ALTITUDES

If Steve Swenson isn't driving one of his sons to soccer practice, managing a complex civil-engineering project, or running 6-minute miles through the streets of Seattle, he's probably climbing. And climbing hard.

The gung-ho alpinist started climbing in his teens, and has been testing his limits ever since. He's climbed extensively in Yosemite, Alaska, the Canadian Rockies, the Himalayas, and, of course, his home state of Washington.

Although he specializes in high-standard alpine climbing, the well-rounded veteran is as comfortable tapping a copperhead into an incipient seam on El Capitan as he is swinging his picks into vertical ice. Swenson is an accomplished rock climber, but is best known for his unrivaled aerobic capacity. His cavernous lungs helped him make the second alpine-style ascent of Denali's Cassin Ridge, and climb the North Ridge of K2 and the North Ridge of Everest—all without oxygen. Swenson also excels on mixed terrain, having climbed the North Face of the Eiger and pioneered new routes on the north face of Kwangde Nup and the south side of Denali.

Underneath his quiet, modest exterior, Swenson is intensely driven. He maintains a rigorous training schedule, which he squeezes in between the demands of his full-time job and his family. As if Swenson were a man after his own heart, the late Alex Lowe once said, "I've always admired Steve for his ability to do it all, and do it well."

NORTH FACE OF MOUNT ALBERTA

In August 1980, Tobin Sorenson found himself clinging to a crumbling band of rock halfway up the North Face of Mount Alberta. For some reason—the details are unknown, since he was climbing solo—he fell. One can only imagine what was going through his mind as the pitons that connected him to the rotten Yellow Band began popping out like poorly sewn buttons. He'd taken plenty of spectacular lead falls in the past, but they always ended with the familiar tug of the rope, and the thankful realization that he was still alive. But not this time. One by one, the anchors he had set in the friable rock were being yanked out by the force of his fall. The gear at the belay was the last to go. And when it did, Sorenson and the tattered remains of his self-belay system cartwheeled 2,500 feet to the glacier below, abruptly ending his celebrated climbing career.

The tragedy reinforced the belief that Alberta's North Face, like many of George Lowe's routes, was unrepeatable. Lowe and his partner Jock Glidden established the bold line in 1972—back when high-tech ice tools, camming devices, and Gore-Tex were still science fiction. The route looked so intimidating that no one dared to try it for eight years. And when one of America's most talented, gung-ho climbers gave it his best shot, he was mercilessly spit off.

Steve Swenson was still in high school when Lowe and Glidden climbed Alberta's North Face. At the time, he didn't have the experience to attempt such a serious route, but hoped that someday he would. Year after year, he climbed with a vengeance, methodically building an impressive resume of hard alpine ascents. He climbed extensively in the Cascades and the Canadian Rockies, and did several big Alaskan routes.

Swenson spent the summer of 1979 climbing in France, where he and fellow Seattleite Kit Lewis polished off several difficult classics, including the North Face of Les Droites. The trip solidified their partnership and bolstered their confidence on hard alpine terrain. Despite the aura that surrounded Alberta's North Face, they were both drawn to it. Says Swenson, "The route had everything we were looking for: an elegant line on a beautiful alpine face, difficulty, remoteness, and the seriousness associated with an effort that would take several days."

In some ways, Swenson and Lewis were an unlikely pair. Swenson is soft spoken, intellectual, and trains religiously. Lewis, on the other hand, is a brash, hard-drinking wild man who relies on raw talent and a high tolerance for suffering. Yet in spite of these differences, or perhaps because of them, they had formed a strong partnership. They were both excellent alpinists. And they both wanted to climb Alberta's North Face.

In September 1981, Swenson and Lewis found themselves lying head to toe in a prototype Bibler tent at the base of Alberta's

Looking down the North Face of Mount Alberta (VI, 5.9, A3, WI 4). Kit Lewis and Steve Swenson made the route's second ascent in 1981.
© Steve Swenson, portrait © Sean Courage

© Glen Boles

northeast ridge. A recent storm had plastered the face with fresh snow, but the forecasted week of high pressure enticed them to go for it. Their adventure began early the next morning as they rappelled to the glacier below the North Face. A pitch of mixed climbing led them to the first ice field—a 2,200-foot inverted triangle of 55-degree water ice. The climbing was superb, and safe. With the security of solid ice-screw placements, they simulclimbed all the way to the base of the rock band. They arrived with daylight to spare, but couldn't pass up the deluxe ledge they found on the left side of the face. They would save the dreaded Yellow Band for the morning.

Thanks to a wet summer and the recent storm, the Yellow Band was covered with ice, allowing for a quick and safe passage to the steeper rock above. Guided by a cryptic description and keen routefinding skills, they worked their way toward a prominent, ice-filled chimney. The rock was solid and offered good protection, but their progress was hampered by the wet snow that clung to every hold. After climbing only 400 feet, they were forced to bivy on two tiny ledges just below a series of small roofs.

They awoke to clear skies and frost-covered sleeping bags. Anxious to get through the crux pitch, Lewis took the lead and started up the overhang. As he futzed with manky piton placements and dangled from wobbly sky hooks, he mocked George Lowe's technical rating for the climb. The notorious sandbagger rated it 5.7, A2; it was more like 5.9, A3. They should have known better. Several more pitches up an icy alcove and a prominent crack system led them to a spectacular pedestal near the top of the rock band. The airy perch was wildly exposed and perfectly level—the ideal bivy ledge. With the hardest climbing below them, they drifted into a deep, comfortable sleep.

Their fourth day on the face started with several pitches of enjoyable climbing on sound limestone. Unfortunately, the rock suddenly deteriorated within a rope-length of the summit ice field. To exit the rock band, Swenson had to lead a loose, nerve-wracking pitch, gingerly stepping between precariously stacked blocks aimed directly at Lewis. Miraculously, they reached the upper ice field without testing the impact strength of their helmets, and then front-pointed their way to the summit. The North Face of Mount Alberta had waited nine years for a second ascent—and it was theirs. The route had taken them a day longer than expected, but they did it safely, and in control. Swenson still remembers how it felt to repeat one of George Lowe's routes. "It was a breakthrough climb for me—a rite of passage into hard alpine climbing."

The descent down the Japanese route was almost as exhilarating as the ascent. They followed a narrow plank of limestone down Alberta's spinelike ridge that Swenson describes as "a sidewalk in the sky, dropping off thousands of feet on both sides." After a few rappels and lots of downclimbing, they reached the Sunwapta River and the seemingly endless trail back to the car.

As Lewis drove his battered Opel into Jasper, Swenson realized that their adventure was not quite over. Lewis, who had been on good behavior for far too long, was in the mood for a few beers and, much to Swenson's chagrin, some social deviance. The streets of Jasper were choked with tourists and parking was scarce. When Lewis saw a car backing out of a nearby spot, he hung a quick U-turn and snagged it, handily outmaneuvering a couple who was patiently waiting their turn. Infuriated by Lewis's callous stunt, the woman driving the other car jumped out of her vehicle and marched toward him, screaming at the top of her lungs. Without hesitation, Lewis—who hadn't shaved or showered in more than a week—pointed at her with a deranged look and yelled, "Get back in the car, bitch!" Appalled by his behavior, she looked to her husband, who was still sitting in the car, for support. "When he slid down in his seat and looked the other way," laughed Swenson, "I knew the spot was ours."

Several hours and many beers later, Swenson helped his friend back into the car, took the keys, and started the long drive home.

ROUTE DESCRIPTION

Area: Canadian Rockies
First ascent: George Lowe and Jock Glidden, August 1972
Base elevation: Approximately 8,000 feet
Summit elevation: 11,874 feet
Difficulty: VI, 5.9, A3, WI 4
Time required: 3–5 days round trip from hut
Equipment: 1–2 sets of cams to 3 inches; set of wired nuts; 12 pitons, knifeblades, Bugaboos, and baby angles; 6 ice screws; aid-climbing gear; 2 ropes, 1 10.5–11 mm, 1 8.5–9 mm; 2 ice tools each
Season: Late July–early August
Special considerations: Route is committing; retreat or escape is difficult
Reference: *Selected Alpine Climbs in the Canadian Rockies* by Sean Dougherty (Rocky Mountain Books, 1999)
Map: Sunwapta Peak 83 C/6

Approach: Mount Alberta is about 48 miles (76 km) south of Jasper via Highway 93, west of the highway. Cross the Sunwapta River, hike up Tangle Creek, then over Woolley Shoulder to the hut at the base of the northeast ridge of Mount Alberta.

Route: From the spur overlooking the North Face, walk down and onto the spur to its farthest point, and rappel from its east side using a single 50-m rope. Cross the glacier to the base of the North Face. Cross the bergschrund to the right of the obvious triangular snowfield. After some easy rock climbing, a ledge system leads left to the base of the ice field. Climb it 2,200 feet to a yellow band of friable rock (possible bivy on left). Ascend the rock band, starting directly below a prominent chimney filled with ice. Follow cracks up good rock, then bear slightly right to a short, flaring chimney. Continue straight up, through a series of small roofs (A3, hooking, nailing), then into an icy alcove at the base of a chimney. Exit the alcove and follow the prominent crack system on the right to a spectacular pedestal (bivy). Follow another good crack system straight up until it veers right. At this point, head left into a loose, shallow corner, which exits into the upper ice field. Follow it to the summit.

Descent: Descend the Japanese route.

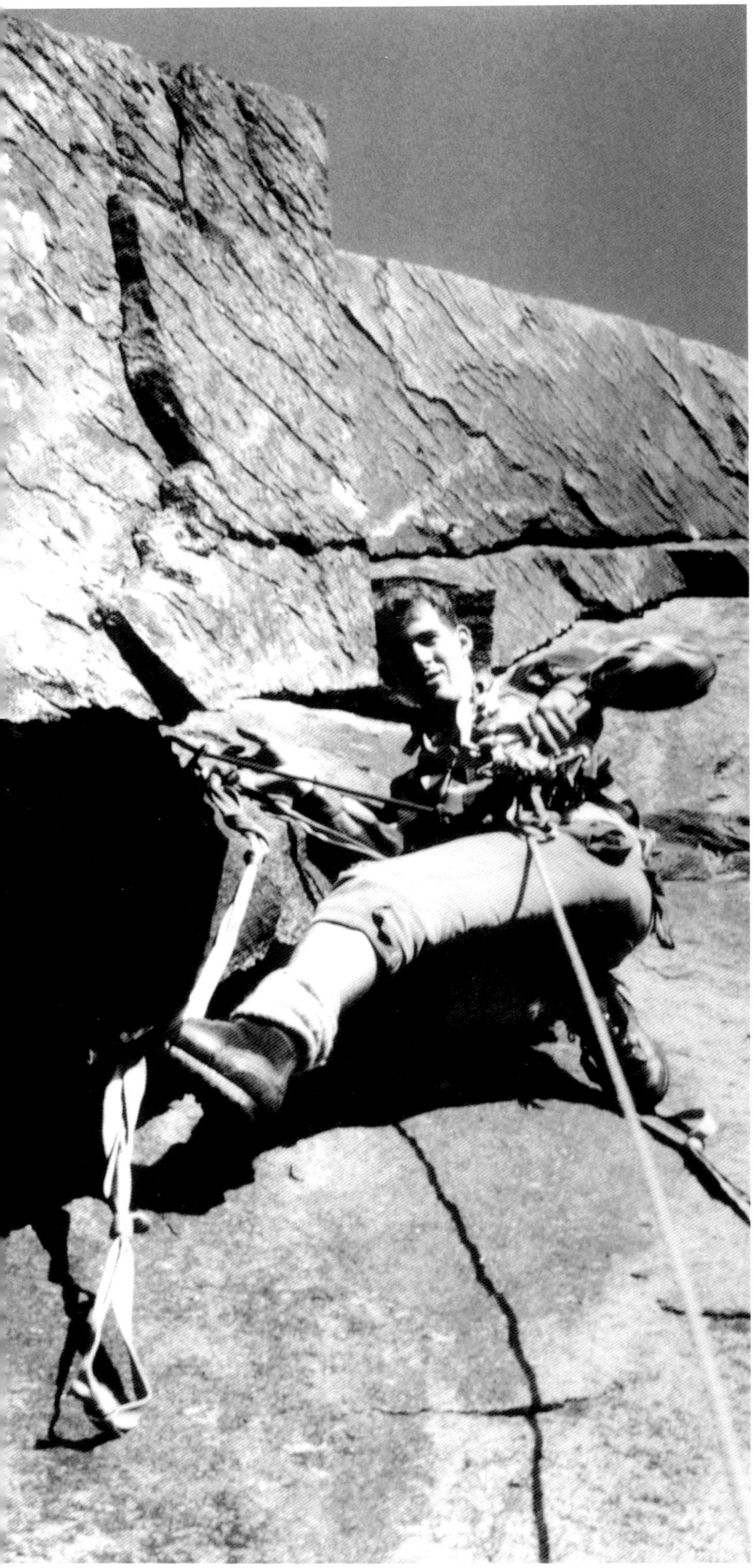

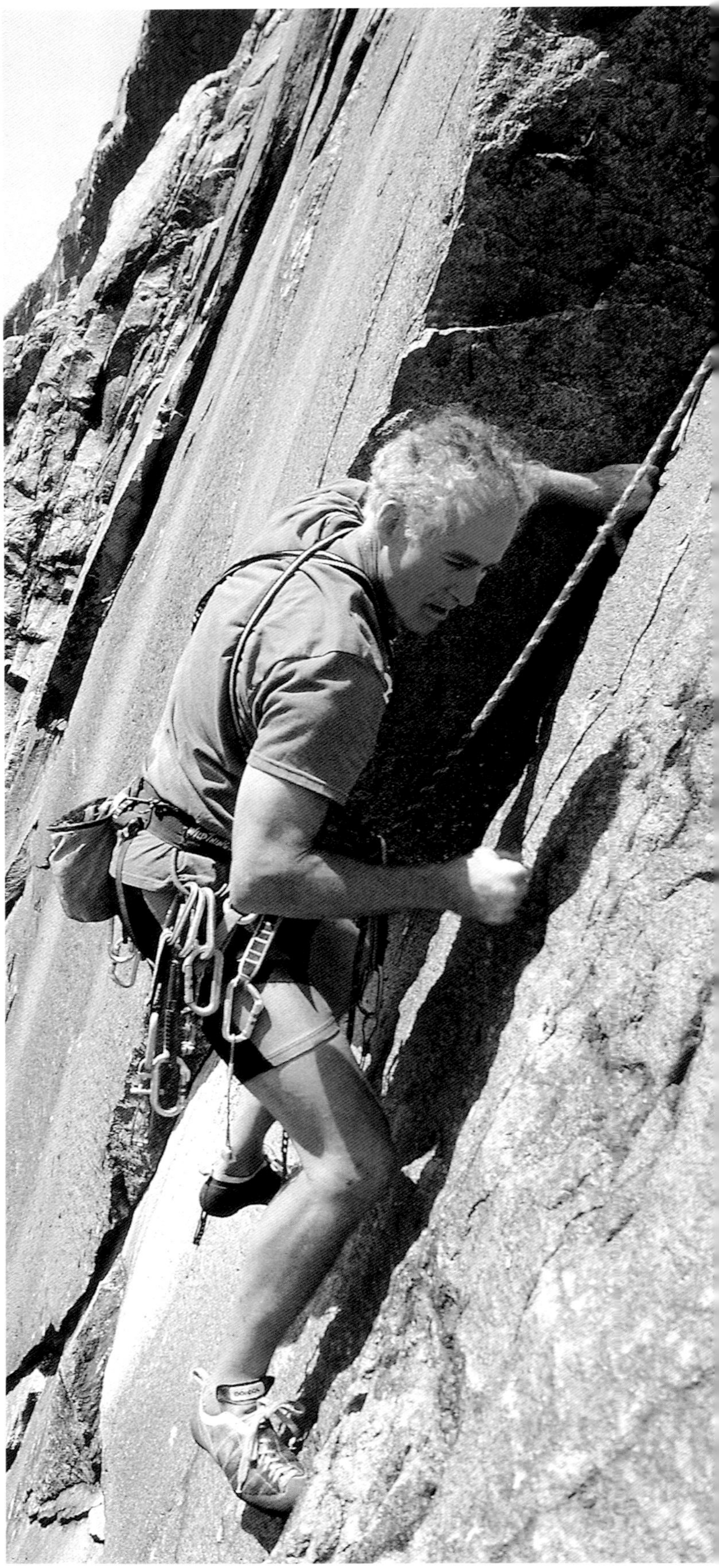

MARK SYNNOTT

VMC DIRECT DIRECT, CANNON CLIFF, WHITE MOUNTAINS, NEW HAMPSHIRE

MARK SYNNOTT—BIG-WALL MASTER

Mark Synnott is the iron man of the big-wall elite. Since the early '90s, he has been systematically climbing the tallest, steepest, and most remote rock walls on Earth. From Patagonia to Pakistan, there doesn't seem to be anything he can't climb.

Like many of his ilk, Synnott (pronounced "SIN-it") started his big-wall career on Yosemite's El Capitan. Over a period of several years, he ticked off fifteen different aid routes, including the second ascent of the Reticent Wall (VI, 5.9, A5)—El Cap's most desperate line. In 1996, on unexplored Baffin Island, he and two partners established the mother of all wall climbs, the Great and Secret Show, on the 4,700-foot north face of Polar Sun Spire. The 40-day sufferfest is a testimony to the perseverance required to scale a huge wilderness wall. His next three Baffin routes didn't take as long, requiring "only two or three weeks" each.

Synnott's first ascents in Pakistan are equally impressive. In 1997, he and Jared Ogden (see Climb 33) spent 20 days putting up the Ship of Fools (VII, 5.11, A2, WI 6) on the 4,200-foot northeast face of Shipton Spire. And in 1999, the same pair and the late Alex Lowe (see Climb 27) spent a month scaling the 6,000-foot northwest face of the Great Trango Tower (VII, 5.11, A4+). All told, Synnott has climbed more than fifty big walls on three continents—eight of them by new routes.

Looking ahead, Synnott sees himself moving from capsule-style ascents to alpine-style "single pushes" on big walls, such as his 27-hour round trip on Cerro Torre in Patagonia. Pointing at a picture of two giant Himalayan faces, the West Face of Makalu and the North Face of Jannu, he says, "Those are the ultimate."

Remote alpine walls may be the ultimate, but Synnott also enjoys doing long free climbs in his home state of New Hampshire—especially as "car-to-car" day trips. Despite his willingness to sleep in a portaledge for weeks on end, he still prefers a bed.

VMC DIRECT DIRECT

At the center of New Hampshire's state emblem is a picture of a rock buttress that shows the profile of a square-jawed mountain man—dubbed the Old Man of the Mountains. The old man's craggy visage marks the top of Cannon Cliff, New England's premier rock-climbing area and most popular tourist attraction. Cannon Cliff is the largest hunk of granite in what is officially known as the Granite State. The exfoliated dome is more than a mile wide and rises 1,000 feet above the buckled landscape surrounding Franconia Notch.

Like the rest of New Hampshire, the cliff is steeped in history. From the time it was first explored in the 1920s, the face was recognized as the biggest objective in the East. And when it was finally climbed, it was the first East Coast route to earn distinction as a Yosemite-style "big wall." The middle of Cannon Cliff, what is referred to as the Big Wall Section, was first climbed in 1965 by Dick Williams, Art Gran, and Yvon Chouinard. The trio rated their twelve-pitch route 5.7, A2 and named it VMC Direct, a reference to the Shawangunks' climbers farcical Vulgarian Mountain Club. In the 1966 *American Alpine Journal,* Chouinard described the highly celebrated ascent as the finest climb he had done in the East, and compared it to the style and quality of routes found in Yosemite.

The increasing awareness of VMC Direct spurred two of the East's finest climbers, Sam Streibert and Steve Arsenault, into making the route's second ascent. When they did, they spotted an even more aesthetic, direct start to the original line. Inspired by the potential for a major variation, they vowed to return as soon as possible. Unfortunately, their next opportunity didn't come until 1969, when Arsenault was on leave from his military tour in Vietnam. The climbers set aside the first weekend in June to attempt what they would later name the "Direct Direct."

As planned, they found themselves at the base of the cliff on Saturday morning, June 8. Although the cliff was still wet from the previous night's rain, Streibert was able to free-climb the first low-angle pitch in his wall-climbing boots. From the belay, he sized up the next two pitches while his partner followed. In his account of the climb in the 1970 issue of *Appalachia,* he described the route: "The right-facing inside corner wiggles as it rises so that there are arches, overhangs, and ramps. It looks beautiful with its top in the mist. There are two

Still climbing after all these years. Left: Steve Arsenault on the first ascent of VMC Direct Direct in 1969. © Sam Streibert
Right: Three decades later, Arsenault returns for a free ascent. © Peter Lewis, portrait © Gordon Wiltsie

leads we'll both enjoy. Above that is a question mark."

The question mark turned out to be the fourth pitch, where the sharp dihedral they had been following disappeared into a shallow, blank-looking slab. Arsenault slithered upward until there were no holds that would support his lug-soled boots. Then he pulled out the bolt kit and settled into the mindless rhythm of hit-twist, hit-twist. The iron-hard New Hampshire granite proved to be too much for his first drill bit, and his second. Both climbers breathed a sigh of relief when Arsenault completed the job with the third bit. Using the bolt to pull through the blank section, he was able to reach a crack system that eventually intersected with the original route.

The elated climbers spent the night hanging in hammocks at the top of the fourth pitch, and completed the familiar upper part of the route the next day. In his *Appalachia* article, Streibert noted that "the Direct Direct distinguishes itself not only because of the elegance of the line but also because these four pitches have an enjoyment not found in the normal start."

The next significant event on VMC Direct Direct came six years later, at the height of the so-called free-climbing revolution. In June 1975, during the same month that Astroman was free-climbed (see Climb 30), all points of aid were eliminated from VMC Direct Direct by two New England climbers, Jeff Burns and Hans Larsen. The route was rated 5.11b and became known as the hardest long free climb in the East. Only the best dared to try it.

While all of this was happening, young Mark Synnott was preparing to enter kindergarten in Wellesley, Massachusetts. But ten years later, when he developed an interest in climbing, the Direct Direct was one of the first "big routes" he learned about. As the older and wiser New England climbers briefed him on the VMC, they imbued him with a sense of reverence for the route. They told him it was serious. They helped him appreciate its history. They warned him about the "sandbag" 5.11 rating. And they advised him not to try it until he was good and ready.

Taking the advice of his elders, Synnott didn't consider trying the VMC for another ten years. "A lot of New England routes—

especially the ones on the Cannon Cliff—have big reputations," he explains. "If you grow up here and come up through the ranks as a New England climber, you hear the stories, you read about these climbs, and you respect them. You don't just think, 'Oh, I'm going to fire off the VMC.' You pay your dues first."

Synnott spent the next decade paying his dues—and then some. Visiting areas from Yosemite to Baffin Island to Pakistan, he became an accomplished free climber and big-wall master. When he returned to New Hampshire in the summer of 1998, he realized that he had yet to climb the VMC. Now there was no question that he was ready.

With partner Randy Rackliff, Synnott made an all-free ascent of VMC Direct Direct in less than 6 hours. Was the route as good as he hoped it would be? "Killer cracks and a unique history make it one of the best free climbs in the East," says Synnott proudly. Was it as difficult? "It was hard, although not as bad as I thought it would be," he allows. "But that's not what I tell the young climbers. Since I live in New Hampshire, I want to keep the myth alive."

ROUTE DESCRIPTION

Area: Franconia Notch

First ascent: Steve Arsenault and Sam Streibert, June 8, 1969; first free ascent: Jeff Burns and Hans Larsen, June 1975

Difficulty: IV, 5.9, A2, or 5.11b

Time required: 1 long day

Equipment: Large assortment of wired nuts; double set of TCUs and cams to 3 inches, with 1 4-inch piece; slings and quickdraws for fixed gear; 2 ropes, 50-m OK

Season: Late spring–fall

Special considerations: Route is often wet, needing prolonged dry, sunny weather to become free-climbable; camping not allowed below cliff, but OK to bivouac on wall

Reference: *Rock Climbs in the White Mountains of New Hampshire, East Volume*, 3d ed., by Ed Webster (Mountain Imagery, 1996)

Approach: Cannon Cliff is 2½ hours north of Boston in Franconia Notch, adjacent to the Cannon Mountain Ski Area and Interstate 93. The route starts on the right side of a small, white buttress 60 feet to the north of Triple S (Sam's Swan Song) Buttress.

Route: One of New England's premier wall climbs, but best done as a free climb. The ten-pitch route follows the obvious right-facing arch in the center of Cannon's Big Wall Section. See topo for details.

Descent: Rappel the route or bushwhack to a faint trail that drops off the north shoulder.

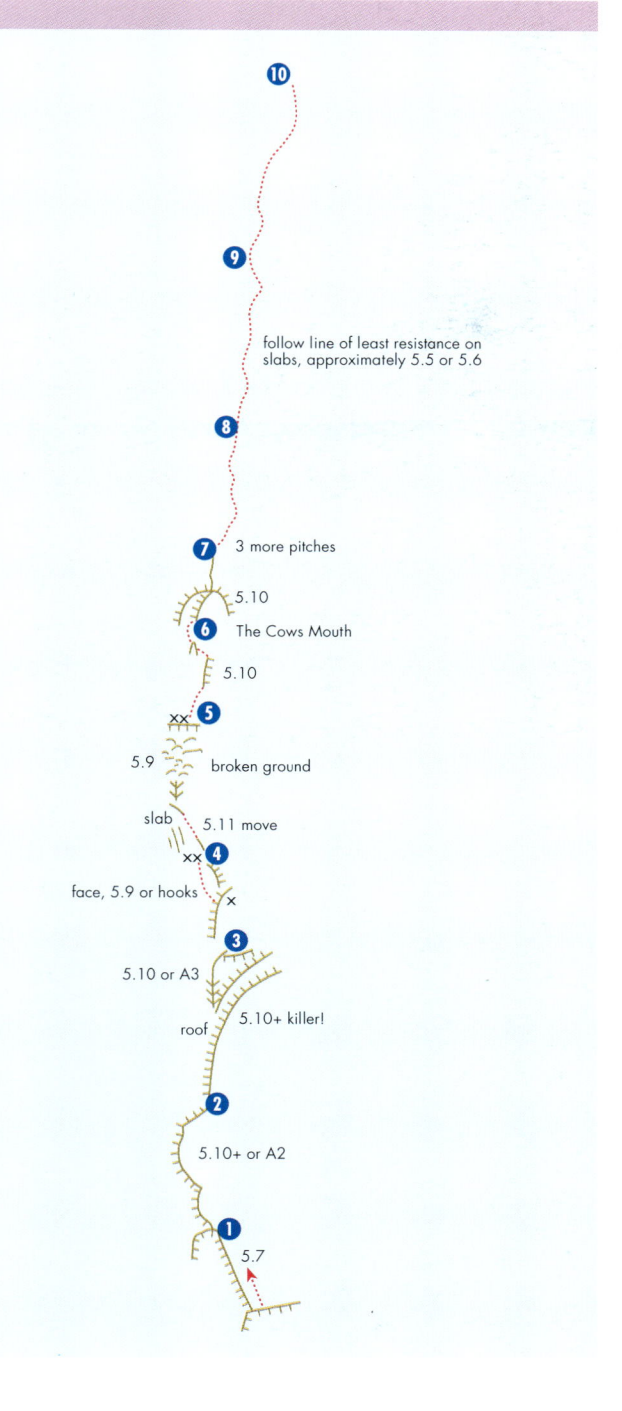

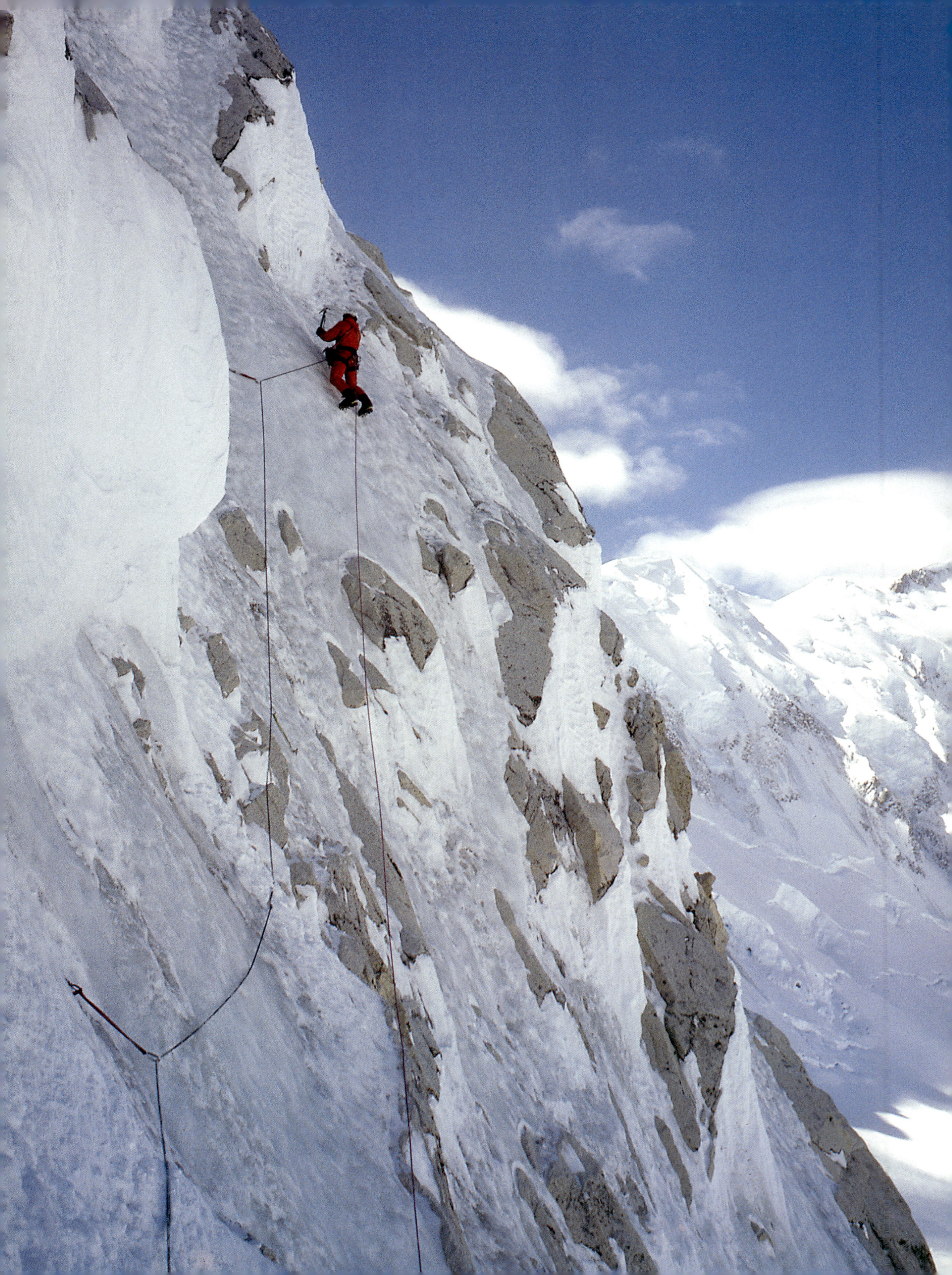

JACK TACKLE

A PAIR OF JACKS, NORTHWEST FACE OF MOUNT KENNEDY, KLUANE NATIONAL PARK, YUKON TERRITORY

JACK TACKLE— AN INEXORABLE FORCE

There ought to be a picture of Jack Tackle in the dictionary next to the word *persistence*. When this alpinist sets his mind to a climb, he doesn't give up—even if it takes numerous attempts. Consider some of his first ascents in Alaska: It took three tries over as many seasons to reach the top of the coveted Elevator Shaft on Mount Johnston. The Cobra Pillar on Mount Barrille demanded two separate efforts. Three trips to Mount Kennedy have resulted in just one new route, and he has yet to stand on its elusive summit.

Tackle's willingness to try again and again is one reason that, after more than twenty-five seasons of alpine climbing, he's still around. If conditions aren't right, he'll come back next month or next year. In addition to numerous excursions to places like Patagonia and the Himalayas, he's made more than twenty-five trips to Alaska. With so many visits to the Last Frontier, Tackle is to Alaskan climbing what Cal Ripkin Jr. is to baseball: Year in and year out, he just keeps performing.

The result is a resume that makes even the most hard-core alpinists go weak in the knees. Over the years, Tackle has made dozens of first ascents in Alaska alone, many of them still unrepeated. But don't expect him to tell you about them: His taciturn personality and refusal to promote himself mean that only his closest partners know of his accomplishments. But those who do will marvel at his dogged persistence. "Jack is an inexorable force, sort of like a glacier," says longtime partner Jim Donini (see Climb 14). "He just keeps moving forward. Nothing can stop him."

A PAIR OF JACKS

On May 10, 1996, climbers around the world were glued to their computer screens as the worst disaster in the history of high-altitude mountaineering began to unfold on Mount Everest. With each passing hour came updated reports from the world's rooftop, the highest—and most wired—mountain on Earth.

On the same day, in a remote corner of the St. Elias Range, Jack Tackle and Jack Roberts were zipped into their portaledge, halfway up the 6,000-foot Northwest Face of Mount Kennedy.

Unlike the climbers on Mount Everest, Tackle and Roberts had no radio, no fixed ropes, and no Sherpas to help with their loads. Only a handful of friends even knew of their plans. "We might as well have been on the back side of the moon," notes Tackle. "We were totally and completely on our own."

That morning, Tackle squirmed out of the portaledge into the frosty, vertical world of ice and granite and began to prepare for another day of full-on Alaskan-style climbing. As a veteran of such committing climbs, Tackle knows there are certain mistakes one can't afford to make. His first important task was to attach his crampons to his boots. With his legs dangling out of the portaledge, he affixed his left crampon with a surgeon's focus, then started on his right. After snapping the crampon's heel bail onto the back of his boot, he momentarily let go while each hand reached for an end of the ankle strap that, when cinched, would secure the whole affair. Suddenly the heel bail, which was clogged with ice, popped off the boot, allowing his crampon to fall into the gray, swirling abyss.

Tackle was furious with himself. "I started screaming and swearing so loudly that Jack (Roberts) thought I dropped the stove. When he realized it was still hanging in the tent, he asked me what the hell was going on." Tackle delivered the news. "I felt sick," remembers Roberts. "I wanted to scream and yell at Jack (Tackle), but I couldn't." The despondent climbers discussed their options. Rappelling was possible but, given their investment in the climb, an unsavory thought. Recalls Tackle, "Roberts wasn't wild about leading every pitch, but eventually it dawned on us that our feet are about the same size—so we could equip the leader with two crampons and the second could Jumar with one." Given their unappealing options, they decided to continue the climb.

Tackle first set his eyes on the Northwest Face of Mount Kennedy in 1978 while making a failed attempt on its north ridge. Only a handful of climbers knew of the classic line until 1992, when an article in the *Canadian Alpine Journal* unveiled some of the unclimbed gems in the St. Elias Range—Kennedy's Northwest Face among them. While making an unsuccessful attempt in 1995, Tackle and Roberts got an even closer look at the hefty ice

Jack Roberts, belayed by Jack Tackle, in search of thick ice on A Pair of Jacks (VI, M6, WI 5+), northwest face of Mount Kennedy
© Jack Tackle, portrait © Cameron Burns

[North Ridge]

© Bradford Washburn (neg. 5520)

runnel bisecting the face. The project appealed to Tackle and Roberts because they saw it as a way to take the discipline of mixed climbing to the next level. Mixed climbs are usually done as day trips, often at roadside crags that are comfortably close to an emergency room, a warm bed, and a hot shower. A multiday mixed climb on a remote, 6,000-foot arctic north face would be more than a test of technical competence; it would demand endurance and mental control.

When they returned in '96, after one of the region's driest winters in a decade, their intended route was barely visible. The thick swoosh of ice they had seen in '95 had been reduced to a discontinuous, translucent drip. The first half of the route involved dubious climbing on fragile smears of ice, often with marginal protection. Both climbers led their share of mentally draining pitches. "Areas of unblemished, crackless granite gave new meaning to the old saying that the leader must not fall," wrote Roberts in an account of the climb in the 1997 *Canadian Alpine Journal*. Routefinding was also a challenge. Sections that were hard to read from a distance were equally confusing upon closer inspection. But as the days wore on, their ability to improvise improved.

After 5 days of unrelenting technical climbing, they reached the upper part of the wall, which kicks back to what Tackle calls "alpine angle." But their expectations of climbing faster were only partially realized. They were chilled to the bone by the subzero temperatures. And since they were each carrying 30 pounds of gear in their packs rather than hauling, their progress was disheartening. Two days and a few sections of hard, unprotected climbing later, they reached the point where their route intersected with the North Ridge. Although they had just completed a significant new line, neither was willing to declare victory. They were still more than 1,500 feet below the summit, and were running low on food.

With their tent perched on a steep slope in an avalanche runout zone, Roberts and Tackle formulated a plan: After a good night's sleep, they would race up the ridge with light packs, tag the summit, and return to their high camp before starting the long, tedious descent. Their scheme sounded good—until they were woken by the dreaded thumping noise of snow being blown against the tent. Windblown snow was accumulating at an alarming rate. Small avalanches slid over the tent, inverting it like a dog bowl. Cold showers of spindrift sprayed through the air vent. The storm raged for 2 days.

When the weather finally cleared, about 6 feet of new snow had fallen onto the Teflon-like slopes around them. The avalanche hazard was extreme. They were almost out of food. The descent was unknown. And the missing crampon promised to hamper their progress. As much as they wanted to push on to the summit, their mountain sense told them to descend. "Let's just say it was a pretty short conversation," recalls Tackle.

After 2 days of tricky diagonal rappelling down Kennedy's north ridge, the pair of Jacks finally reached the comfort and security of base camp. For the first time in 11 days, they allowed themselves to relax and feel good about their hard-fought victory. Since they didn't reach the summit, they accepted that their accomplishment would have a footnote attached to it, but also knew that going to the top would have been a death wish. They had come in search of continually difficult mixed climbing on an unclimbed wall. They got what they came for and, more importantly, they came back. Tackle, who has lost several close friends in climbing accidents, has no regrets. "Having the discipline to make a sound judgment call is what matters in the end."

ROUTE DESCRIPTION

Area: Wrangell–St. Elias Range
First ascent: Jack Roberts and Jack Tackle, May 1996
Base elevation: Approximately 8,000 feet
Summit elevation: 13,905 feet
Difficulty: VI, M7, WI 5+
Time required: First-ascent party spent 5 days climbing, 4 days in storms, 2 days descending
Equipment: Double set of cams to 2 inches; ample assortment of pitons, including Bugaboos, knifeblades, lost arrows, and baby angles; 12 ice screws (many short if ice is thin); 3 ropes, 2 lead ropes and 1 tag-line; third ice tool, single-wall tent/portaledge combination, clothing for full-on Alaskan conditions
Season: Late April–early June
Special considerations: Obtain permit in advance from Kluane Park Service
Reference: *Canadian Alpine Journal* (1997)

Approach: From Yakutat, Alaska, fly Gulf Air, or from the town of McCarthy, Alaska, stay at the Chitina Lodge and use Paul Klaus's air service.

Route: Thirty-one 60-m pitches of modern, mixed climbing. See topo for details.

Descent: Descend the Northwest Ridge route.

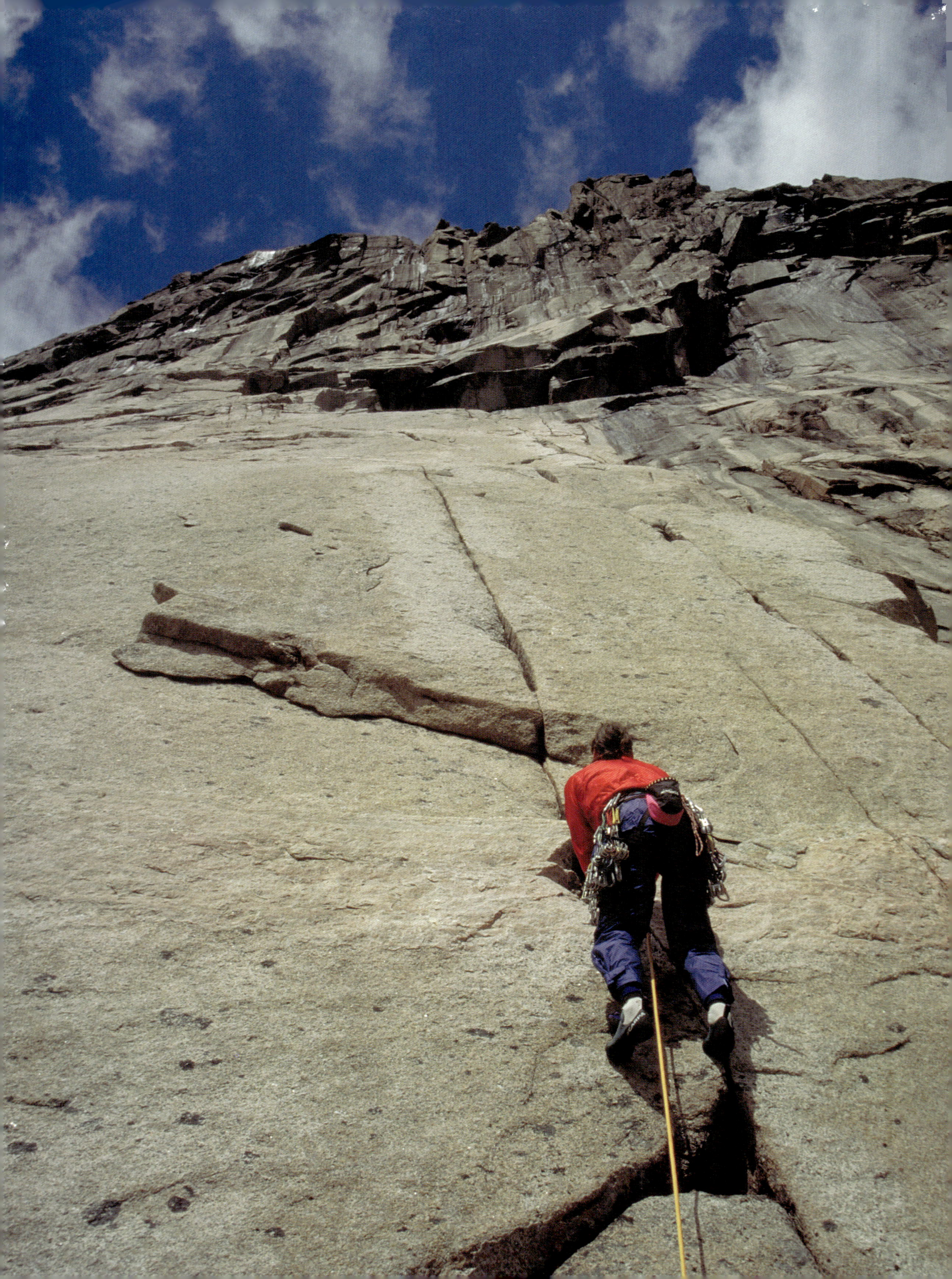

JOE TERRAVECCHIA

LEVIATHAN, BLOW-ME-DOWN CLIFF, DEVIL BAY, NEWFOUNDLAND

JOE TERRAVECCHIA—
OFF THE BEATEN PATH

Whether he's climbing on rock, ice, or both, Joe Terravecchia likes to get away from it all. Since he started climbing in 1975, the well-rounded explorer has been scouring North America for new and different adventures. When he first climbed Mount McKinley in 1986, it was via its seldom-climbed East Buttress. Throughout the '90s, he made seven trips to undiscovered Newfoundland, establishing more than 200 rock and ice pitches in the process. And in 1999, he and partner Steve Larson established a bold new line on the 9,000-foot south face of Alaska's Mount Foraker, just right of the legendary Infinite Spur. Says Terravecchia, "Given the option, I'll go someplace where there aren't any people."

When Terravecchia does visit a popular climbing destination, such as Yosemite, he doesn't mess around. In 1996, he and partner Peter Coward were the second team to climb the Nose of El Capitan and Half Dome in less than 24 hours. The fifty-six-pitch link-up was first done in a day by John Bachar (see Climb 2) and Peter Croft (see Climb 11) in 1986.

Terravecchia is as comfortable on rock as he is on ice. The modest, compact New Englander has redpointed 5.13 at the crags and led more than his share of "the-leader-must-not-fall" ice pitches. His strong technical foundation has given him the confidence to explore the spare, hard frontiers of the world's great ranges. As far as future projects are concerned, assume they'll be big—just don't be surprised if you've never heard of them.

LEVIATHAN

In July 1989, Ned Gillette, his seventy-five-year-old father, and longtime friend Earl Wiggins spent three weeks cruising the southwest coast of Newfoundland on a 42-foot Hinckley Souwester named *Janorah*. Several months later, the legendary explorer wrote an article about the trip that ran in the May 1990 issue of *Cruising World* magazine. The story included a tantalizing photo of a monstrous sea cliff and the following description: "In Devil Bay, Earl and I explored the 'Blow-Me-Down,' a 1,280-foot-high dome of clean granite whose south face was perfect for climbing."

Two years later, at Joe Terravecchia's home in Portsmouth, New Hampshire, one of his climbing buddies showed him Gillette's article. When his eyes locked onto the riveting, glossy photo of Blow-Me-Down, his first question was "Where's that?" followed by "Are there any routes on it?"

As far as he knew, the answers were: "in the middle of nowhere" and "hopefully not." Further investigation revealed that getting to Blow-Me-Down would involve a 700-mile drive to Nova Scotia, a 7-hour car ferry to Port aux Basques, Newfoundland, another 3 hours of driving to the road's end in Burgeo, and a 4-hour passenger ferry to the fishing village of François—population 180. From there, according to the owner of the François general store, a fisherman named George Durnford would gladly float them the last 15 miles to Devil Bay, unless the forecast called for "dirty weather." A subsequent conversation with George himself, a lifelong François resident, confirmed there had been no rock-climbing activity on Blow-Me-Down.

Terravecchia wasn't able to organize his first trip to Blow-Me-Down until 1994. Early that summer, he showed the picture of Blow-Me-Down to fellow rock jocks Chris Kane and Jeff Butterfield. Dazzled by what they saw, they immediately committed to going in early September. The like-minded threesome could hardly wait.

September finally came and, with it, a bleary-eyed, 2-day car and ferry trip. When the eager climbers finally arrived in Francois, it took less than 5 minutes to locate George Durnford. But thanks to high winds and big swells, it was another 5 days before they departed for Blow-Me-Down. In lieu of renting a room, the thrifty climbers spent the first night in the community fish shack, where the fishermen bait their hooks. The sturdy shack protected them from the rain, but they didn't get much sleep. "It reeked so badly that we had to sleep with our heads sticking out the door," remembers Terravecchia. "We broke down and rented a room after the first night."

When calm seas finally arrived, the climbers piled into Durnford's boat and shoved off. They cruised along the uninhabited coastline for about an hour, then headed into Devil Bay. At its

Casey Shaw on the first pitch of Leviathan. The ten-pitch line is one of a dozen routes that Terravecchia and partners have established on Blow-Me-Down. © Joe Terravecchia, portrait © Carl Tobin

In addition to Leviathan, Terravecchia and partners have established more than a dozen routes on Blow-Me-Down. From left to right: **1.** *Leviathan* **2.** *Screech (I, 5.8+)* **3.** *Central Pillar of Aestheticism (IV, 5.11d, A2)* **4.** *Weightin' for the Train (V, 5.10, A4)* **5.** *The Heart of the Matter (V, 5.10, A3+)* **6.** *Project (5.12)* **7.** *Devil's Advocate (I, 5.9)* **8.** *Straight to Hell (I, 5.10a)* **9.** *unnamed (IV, 5.10, A2)* **10.** *Savage Seas (II, 5.11a/b)* **11.** *Save the Ales (I, 5.12b)* **12.** *Dead Reckoning (III, 5.11b)* **13.** *Hydro Slave (I, 5.11)* **14.** *Lost at Sea (III, 5.10d)* **15.** *The Moratorium (III, 5.10)* © Joe Terravecchia

northern terminus was Blow-Me-Down—a nearly 1,300-foot south-facing dome of sparkling granite, just begging to be climbed. After George found a place to dock on the craggy shoreline—which was tricky—they bid farewell to him and set up camp.

The climbers had high expectations for Blow-Me-Down, and it didn't disappoint. The immaculate granite required almost no cleaning. Crack systems lined the wall like pin stripes on a suit. And there wasn't a single sign of human trespass. "Imagine the best rock in Yosemite," explains Terravecia, "but instead of the throttle of a tour bus, all you hear is rolling surf."

Although the quality of the rock was impeccable, it was rarely dry enough to climb. Brief windows of fair weather limited their progress to a few pitches at a time. When they weren't tentbound, they passed the time watching whales breach and eagles soar. If the forecast called for several days of bad weather, George or his partner Paul Lushman would motor into the bay and bring them back to Francois for a spell. "They would just kill us with kindness," remembers Terravecchia of the legendary Newfoundland hospitality.

The New Englanders grew very fond of their gracious hosts. They learned to understand their broken dialect—a quirky mishmash of Irish, Canadian, and pidgin English. They began to appreciate the economic fallout of the 1992 fishery closure. And they experienced an entirely different kind of cuisine. "When we stayed with locals throughout the province, they fed us morning, noon, and night," explains Terravecchia. "The native foods such as cod, scallops, caribou, and partridge are excellent. But in other parts of the province, canned 'mystery meat' is gaining in popularity. Let's just say we don't share their enthusiasm for the stuff. Sometimes, in order to be polite, I would heap my portion onto my partner's plate when no one was looking. After all, what are friends for?"

After two weeks of on-again, off-again weather, the ambitious threesome completed the first route on Blow-Me-Down—a ten-pitch tour de force dubbed the Central Pillar of Aestheticism (5.11d, A2). Their route followed a direct line up the middle of the face, with eight of the pitches 5.10b or easier. Not only was the climbing brilliant, it was predictable. Since they had previewed the route with binoculars, and it was just as they expected, their confidence in their ability to scope out new lines grew. Finally, they understood the cliff's potential for new routes. And it was vast.

Terravecchia returned to Blow-Me-Down the following summer with his then-girlfriend and now wife, Karin Bates, and longtime friend Casey Shaw. The team's first objective was to explore a line to the left of the Central Pillar of Aestheticism.

Since it skirted the overhanging arch that split the cliff, it looked like it would go free. Blessed by a window of good weather, Terravecchia and Bates established a ten-pitch odyssey named Leviathan. The climb was even better than the Central Pillar and, like its predecessor, easier than the rating suggested (seven of the pitches are 5.10b or easier). Leviathan was one of the most memorable climbs of Terravecchia's life. "There's something about being high above the ocean on perfect granite, with whales swimming below," he says. "You can't beat it."

Terravecchia has made several trips to Blow-Me-Down since 1995, establishing more than a dozen new routes in the process. While he admits that he's plucked the best lines on Blow-Me-Down, the potential for new routes still exists. And then there's the rest of Newfoundland's 11,000-mile coastline. "There are other bays like this one," hints Terravecchia, "and some of them have more granite than all of New England."

ROUTE DESCRIPTION

Area: South coast of Newfoundland
First ascent: Joe Terravecchia, Karin Bates, and Casey Shaw, September 1995
Base elevation: Sea level
Summit elevation: 1,280 feet
Difficulty: IV, 5.10b, A2 or 5.11b–5.12a
Time required: 1 long day
Equipment: 2 sets of Camalots to no. 2; 1 no. 3 Camalot, 6 Aliens, set of wired nuts, set of small brass nuts, 8–10 runners and quickdraws, 2 60-m ropes
Season: Early June–late September
Special considerations: Bring extra ropes to fix traverse from camp (see Approach); expect black flies in June and cooler temperatures in September
Reference: None available
Map: Cape La Hune, Newfoundland, 11P/10, 1:50,000

Approach: Drive to North Sidney, Nova Scotia, and catch the car ferry to Port aux Basques, Newfoundland. Call Marine Atlantic for a schedule and rates (800-341-7981). Then drive north on Route 1, then south on Route 480 to Burgeo (3 hours). Or fly to Deer Lake or Stephenville, Newfoundland, then from either airport, take the Stews Bus Line to Burgeo; schedule and rate information (709-886-2955). From Burgeo, take a small, passenger-only ferry to François (4 hours); reservations (709-292-4327) (sea-sickness pills recommended). In François, contact George Durnford or Paul Lushman for transport by fishing boat to Blow-Me-Down. Expect to pay about $150 Canadian, round trip. Anticipate weather delays and respect the judgment of the locals. Bivy left (west) of the cliff by a stream in open tundra. This necessitates a fourth-class approach to the base of the cliff. Bring five ropes to fix the low-angle traverse. Allow 2 hours to establish fixed ropes, 35 minutes to cross thereafter. A camp can also be made at the cliff's base, but no potable water is available.

Route: Ten outrageous, clean pitches of granite crack climbing on splitter cracks in a spectacular sea-cliff setting. See topo for details.

Descent: Walk off to the west (climber's left).

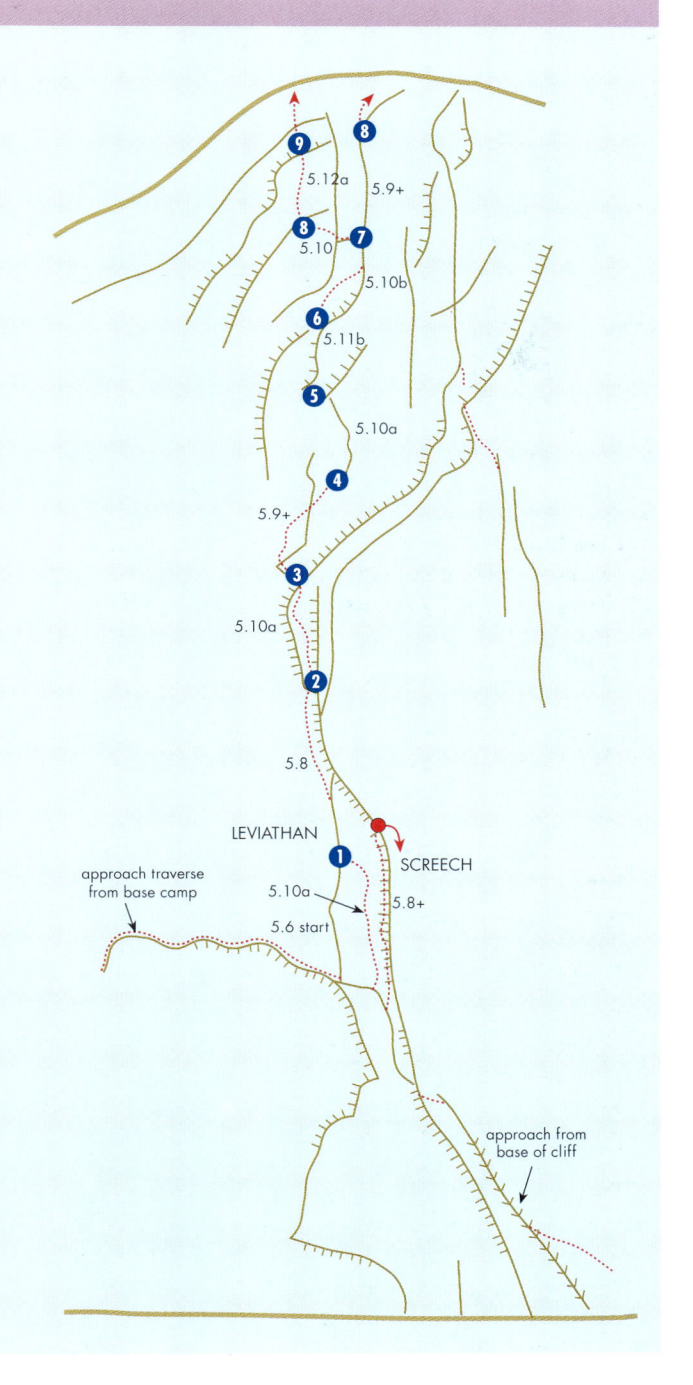

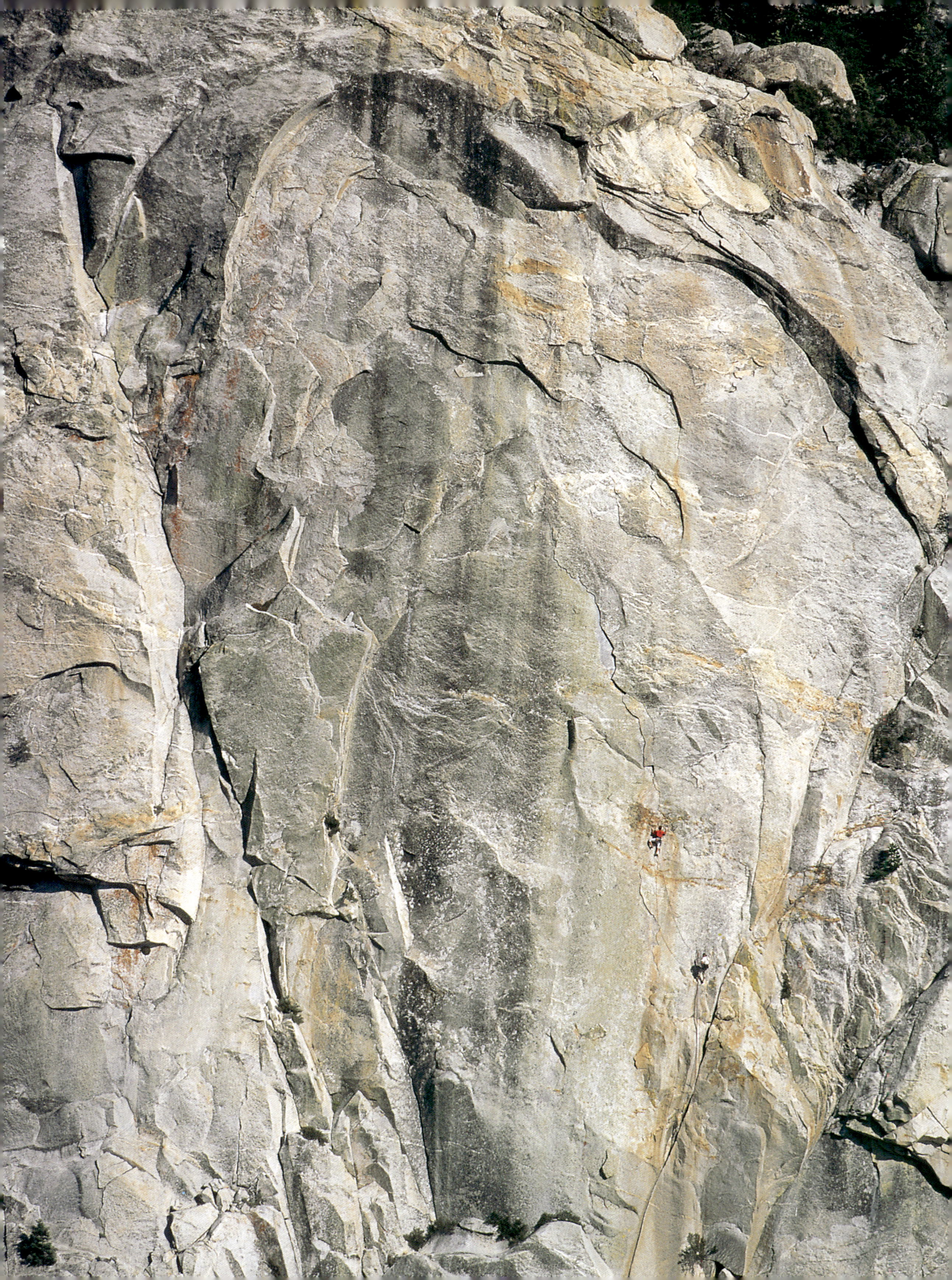

46

KEVIN THAW

THE VAMPIRE, TAHQUITZ ROCK, SAN JACINTO MOUNTAINS, CALIFORNIA

KEVIN THAW—ALL OVER THE MAP

What do Patagonia, the French Alps, Yosemite Valley, and England's gritstone crags have in common? They're all places where Kevin Thaw has made notable ascents. And what do frozen waterfalls, giant boulders, big walls, and ice-clad spires have to do with each other? They're all things that he is exceedingly good at climbing. Meet Kevin Thaw, the globe-trotting generalist.

Since learning to climb at the impressionable age of twelve, Thaw has been—literally and figuratively—all over the map. He got "silly strong" on the gritstone edges near his home in northern England, where he led seldom-climbed test pieces such as Master's Edge (5.12d, R–X), a boltless arête that imperils the leader with a potential 70-foot ground fall (the late Wolfgang Gullich broke his back attempting an on-sight ascent). He then headed for the French Alps, polishing off numerous high-standard alpine routes. After a stint of limestone sport climbing on the Mediterranean, he cruised the North Face of the Eiger—an anticlimactic ascent that taught him that "contemplation is always worse than action."

After graduating from Oldham College in the United Kingdom, Thaw found himself in Quebec, Canada. There he honed his ice-climbing skills and made an early ascent of the 1,100-foot classic La Pomme d'Or (see Climb 25). In search of warmer climes, he moved to southern California in 1990, where he has lived ever since. From his L.A. base camp, the ex-patriot makes frequent trips all over the world. One day he's ice-climbing in Canada, the next he's exploring ancient granite cliffs in Madagascar, and then he's off to Patagonia. When he's not traveling, you can probably find him racing up the granite cracks at nearby Tahquitz Rock.

Does he ever feel the temptation to slow down or specialize? "Not really," says Thaw. "To push yourself down just one avenue can be limiting." Clearly, he knows no limits.

THE VAMPIRE

For much of its rich history, Tahquitz Rock has existed in the very long shadow of its northern cousin, Yosemite Valley. When climbers rave about "perfect granite," they are usually referring to a Yosemite climb. In truth, Tahquitz granite is even better. Most climbers associate Royal Robbins with his legendary ascents on Half Dome and El Capitan, but Tahquitz is where he learned his craft. And the rating system used by North American climbers—the so-called Yosemite Decimal System—was actually developed at Tahquitz.

Tahquitz Rock is a towering hunk of white granite east of Los Angeles, near Mount San Jacinto. Unlike the ice- and water-polished slabs found in Yosemite, Tahquitz granite is textured and knobby—ideal for friction climbing. In the '50s and early '60s, when illustrious figures such as Royal Robbins, TM Herbert, and Yvon Chouinard were regulars, Tahquitz was the epicenter of the West Coast climbing scene—and the site of numerous climbing "firsts."

In 1952, just two years after he started climbing at Tahquitz, seventeen-year-old Robbins earned his place in history by climbing the hardest route in the country, the Open Book (5.9). In doing so, he saw the need to revise the existing (European) rating system, which designated all free routes that required pitons for protection as "class 5." Aware of the growing disparity between the easiest and hardest class 5 routes, Robbins and Don Wilson devised a new rating system that divided class 5 into ten subcategories, 5.0 through 5.9. Tahquitz's Open Book was the first route in the country to be given a rating using this new system. It caught on, and later gained broad acceptance in Yosemite. Hence, it erroneously became known as the Yosemite Decimal System.

Robbins's reign in southern California lasted until about 1959, when he began to focus on bigger projects in Yosemite. His last big route at Tahquitz, dubbed the Vampire, turned out to be his finest. After establishing two lines on the periphery of a prominent feature known as the Bulge, he pieced together a series of cracks and thin flakes through the steepest part of the headwall. Because of its 5.9, A4 rating, it was the most serious route at Tahquitz for many years.

In 1973—the year that Henry Barber established his standard-setting Butterballs (5.11c) on Yosemite's Cookie Cliff (see Climb 2)—the Vampire was free-climbed by four leading climbers from

Climbers on the third pitch of The Vampire (5.11a). Many consider it the best rock climb in southern California. © Kevin Powell, portrait © Corey Rich

201

Los Angeles: Rick Accomazzo, Bill Antel, Mike Graham, and John "Largo" Long. Rated 5.11a, the route became an instant classic among an elite group of climbers and earned a reputation as the finest free climb in southern California.

Kevin Thaw was unaware of the Vampire when he moved to Los Angeles in 1990, but it didn't take long for him to hear about it. While he was climbing at Joshua Tree National Park that spring, his friend Steve Edwards told him that the Vampire was billed as the best free climb in southern California. Thaw was skeptical, but figured that if Edwards's assertion was even half true, it would still make a worthwhile outing. With a third friend, John Reyher, they agreed to do the route the following week, on Thaw's twenty-third birthday.

Anticipating his birthday climb, Thaw asked other climbers about the Vampire. Every person he spoke to seemed to have *heard* about it, and many of them could give him details about each pitch, but it was difficult to find someone who'd actually done the route. Even his friend Edwards, who kindly "offered" to let him lead every pitch, had never been on it. Thaw began to wonder what he was getting into. "The Vampire had tales way beyond its grade," he remembers. "There was the endless crack pitch, the famous run-out mantle move, and mysterious flake pitch. It all sounded pretty desperate."

Knowing that the anticipation is often worse than the reality, Thaw stuck with the plan. And he was glad he did. Leading every pitch of the Vampire turned out to be a wonderful birthday present. The route was well within his abilities as a solid 5.12 climber; he enjoyed every move. Although much of the route was challenging, it had everything he was looking for—superb rock, a spectacular position, and variety.

On the first pitch, Thaw chose the direct start (5.10d), which is now the most popular way to begin the climb. "With a 60-meter rope you can make it all the way to the second belay in one long endurance pitch," notes Thaw. "You climb a 1½-inch crack up a perfect, right-facing corner. The crack is filled with sweet spots—

little constrictions to lock your hands in." On the upper part of the first pitch, climbers encounter a short, bolt-protected crux. Despite its 5.10c rating, Thaw cautions that "it may be the hardest pull on the route." By stringing the first two pitches together, the extended pitch ends with the famous mantle move, which the understated Brit describes as "not desperate, but not a good place to fall."

The second pitch starts with the first of two technical cruxes. "You paste your left foot out on this little smear," says Thaw, "then delicately stretch to this total cutter-jug." Using a 60-meter rope, he likes to continue past the original third belay, and through the second crux, belaying in a left-facing arch. From there, an easier and varied pitch leads to the top. "You can do the route in three, four, or five pitches," he explains. "It just depends on what kind of experience you're looking for."

Over the years, Thaw has done the Vampire every possible way. Although he prefers three long "endurance pitches," he insists there is no bad way to do it. And he would know: When asked how many times he's done the route, he cracks a satisfied smile and says, "So many that I've lost count."

ROUTE DESCRIPTION

Area: Southern California
First ascent: Royal Robbins and Dave Rearick, June 1959; first free ascent: Rick Accomazzo, Bill Antel, Mike Graham, and John Long, 1973
Base elevation: Approximately 7,500 feet
Summit elevation: 8,000 feet
Difficulty: 5.11a
Time required: 4–8 hours
Equipment: Double set of cams to 3 inches, ample selection of wired nuts; 1 rope (2 advised in case of need to retreat)
Season: Year-round; spring and fall are best
Special considerations: Several possible variations: the Direct Start (recommended) follows a 5.10d crack directly up to the Bat Crack; the Direct Finish on the third pitch avoids the second 5.11a crux with a 5.10c undercling and flake to the left (worthwhile, but not recommended)
References: *Guide to Tahquitz and Suicide Rocks* by Randy Vogel and Bob Gaines (Falcon Press, 2001)

Approach: From Los Angeles, follow Interstate 10 east to the town of Banning, then take Highway 243 south for 26 miles to Idyllwild. Follow North Circle Drive (Fern Valley Road) through town to the road's end at Humber Park, the trailhead. Follow the Ernie Maxwell Trail across Strawberry Creek, then another 200 yards until a faint climbers trail heads uphill (left) for 0.4 mile to Lunch Rock. The Bulge routes are directly above Lunch Rock.

Route: A three- to five-pitch classic up the central bulge of Tahquitz's west face. Many consider it the finest free climb in southern California. See topo for details.

Descent: There are several options, the most popular being the Friction Route (class 3 or 4) down the southern side of Tahquitz Rock. Those unfamiliar with this descent route should not try it at night, as there have been fatalities.

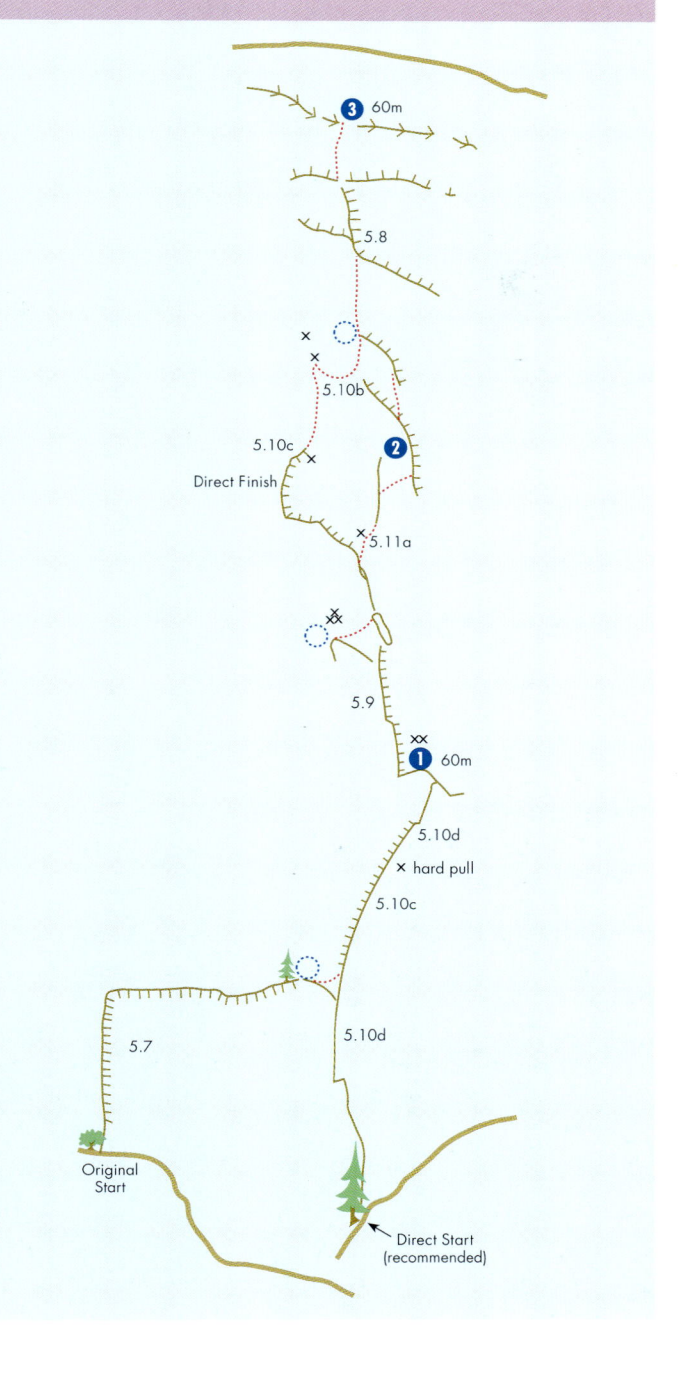

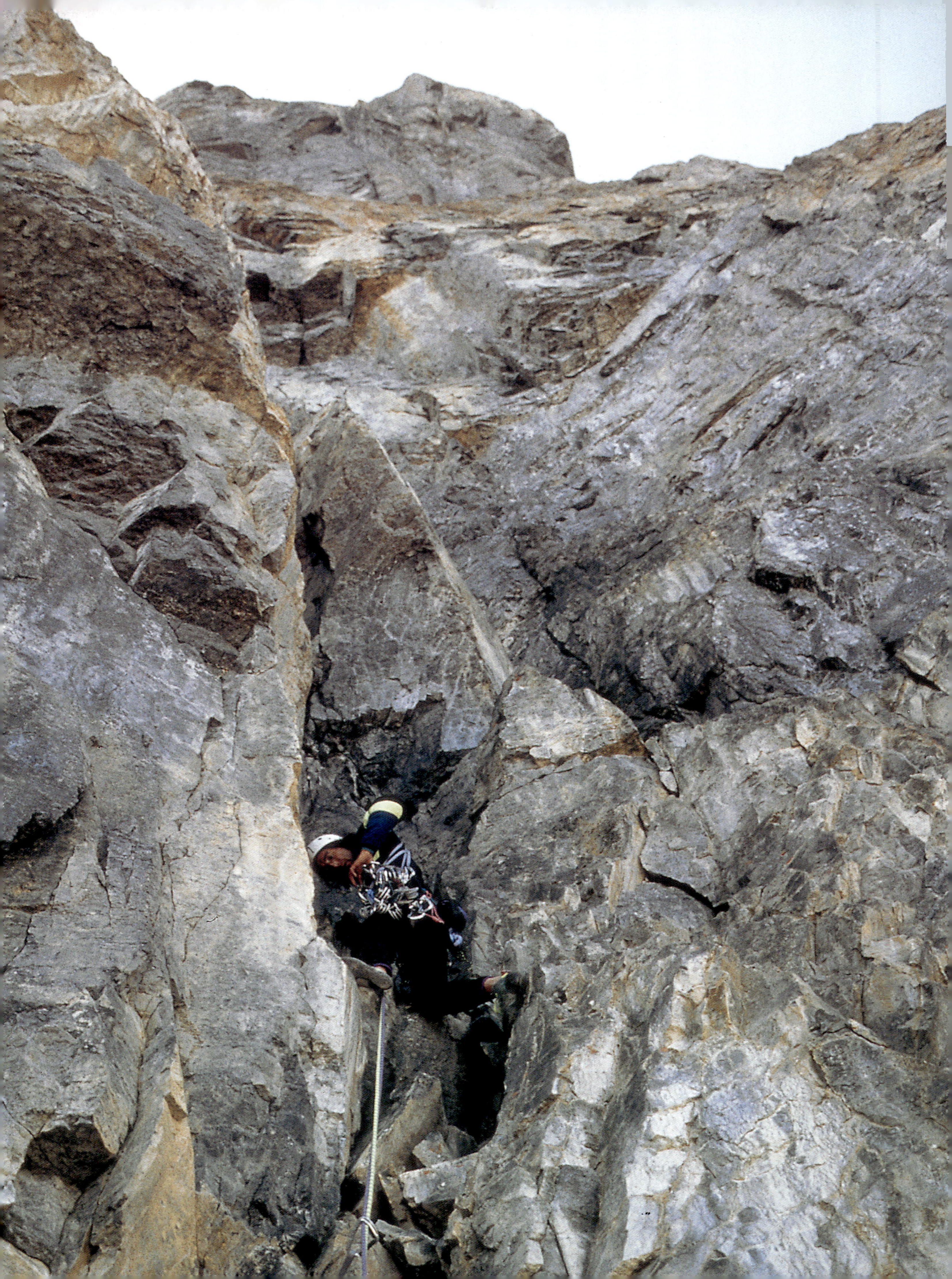

MARK TWIGHT

EAST FACE OF MOUNT BABEL, BANFF NATIONAL PARK, ALBERTA

MARK TWIGHT—ATTITUDE AT ALTITUDE

> At some point on a climb that stretches the limits, the only strength that matters is in the mind.
>
> —*Mark Twight,* Extreme Alpinism

In the early '80s, an inexperienced Mark Twight got freaked out on a difficult alpine route in Washington's North Cascades, and decided to quit climbing. He spent the next year plumbing the depths of his soul, trying to understand why. With the help of martial-arts training and the writings of nineteenth-century German philosopher Friedrich Nietzsche, Twight realized his "programming" was all wrong. He confronted his demons and began to reinvent himself.

The new and improved Mark Twight emerged a few years later. He was stronger, tougher—and enlightened. His thorough self-analysis taught him that there was more to climbing than simply tagging summits or conquering difficult terrain. Climbing was "emotional surgery," a path to the inner sanctum of his mind. "To me, it's an experience-oriented activity, not a goal-oriented activity," says Twight. "I don't care what I climb, I just care about how it affects me."

In 1988, Twight transplanted himself to the birthplace of alpinism—Chamonix, France. After testing himself on the hardest routes in the area, he began to establish bold new lines of his own. In 1992, Twight challenged the status quo by adding Beyond Good and Evil on the Aiguille des Pelerins, a north face long ago considered "climbed out." Most of his other new routes—with telling names like Money Is Not Our God, and Deprivation—also reflect Nietzsche's influence. Some are still unrepeated.

These days, Twight splits his time between his passion for alpinism and the desire to share his experience with others. Pearls of wisdom and practical advice gleaned from two decades in extreme situations can be found in his highly acclaimed book, *Extreme Alpinism: Climbing Light, Fast, and High.*

EAST FACE OF MOUNT BABEL

Ba · bel *n.* In the Old Testament, the site of a tower that was being built to reach the heavens. God halted its construction by suddenly causing everyone to speak different languages.

Not only does Mark Twight define himself as an alpinist, it's a distinction he wears on his sleeve. To go rock climbing for the sake of rock climbing, he argues, is pointless. To him, simply following a "connect-the-dots" topo is a hollow, meaningless pursuit: There is no adventure, no uncertainty, and no opportunity for "emotional surgery." He has lived in Boulder, Colorado, for several years, and is proud of the fact that he has yet to climb in nearby Eldorado Canyon. Alpine climbing, he insists, is what matters.

The pursuit of alpine climbing led him to the Canadian Rockies in the summer of 1995. Twight had made numerous forays to the Alp-like range over the years, and always came away satisfied. Easy access to big alpine faces made it the perfect place for his "light and fast" tactics. (In 1988, he climbed a 3,000-foot frozen waterfall called Slipstream in 2 hours and 4 minutes, a record that still stands.) With his freshly sharpened ice tools at the ready, Twight was prepared for glacial combat.

As it turned out, the only combat that occurred was between the crumbling seracs and whatever was in their path. It was hot. Unseasonably hot. By the time Twight showed up in Lake Louise, there wasn't an ice route in the area that could be done safely. His ice tools never left the trunk of his car.

Realizing that there is always *something* to climb, Twight and his partner Peter Arbic mulled over their options. Arbic's vast reservoir of local knowledge came in handy. He had lots of ideas, but being aware of Twight's Nietzschean need for intense experiences, suggested the East Face of Mount Babel. He told his partner that the fifteen-pitch rock face—which was first climbed in 1969—had seen only two repeat ascents. And then, as if he were baiting a hook, casually mentioned that it had never been done "car-to-car" in a day. (The second-ascent party almost made it, but was benighted on the descent.) Twight took the bait.

Peter Arbic storming up the East Face of Mount Babel. Twight and Arbic made the first one-day ascent of the route in 1995. © Mark Twight, portrait © Mark Twight Collection

Depending on where you stand, Mount Babel looks either wholly unremarkable or downright frightening. The west side of the mountain pales in comparison to neighboring Mount Fay, and may go unnoticed altogether. But the east side is dramatic, and looks like it belongs in the Italian Dolomites. The quartzite pyramid lords over the Consolation Valley with a Darth Vader–like presence.

The idea of climbing such an imposing face on a major peak appealed to Twight. Even though it was a pure rock climb, it was a mysterious puzzle. Other than the fact that the rock was reported to be exceptional, he knew very little about the route. And the requisite commitment made the proposition even more appealing. It promised to be an exhilarating experience and a spiritual journey—just what he was looking for.

Twight and Arbic awoke at 5:00 A.M. and made most of the 6-mile approach in the dark. They arrived at Consolation Lakes just as the morning sun was sweeping down Babel's East Face. The low-angle light revealed hidden features on the wall. It looked less intimidating than Twight remembered, but it was still enormous.

Because of the meandering nature of quartzite, they chose to climb with two 9 mm ropes instead of a lead rope and a haul line. The technique not only reduced rope drag, it saved weight. And, since the route had few established belay stations, they climbed a full 200 feet (60 m) on most pitches. Swapping leads, they made good time up the moderate lower slabs.

By early afternoon, they reached the halfway point of the climb: a large, horizontal ledge that slices across the face with such geologic precision that, from a distance, it looks like it was cut with a chainsaw. The rock above them was considerably steeper, and uncharacteristically solid. Says Twight, "There were times when I felt like I was climbing in the Verdon Gorge" (one of the best crags in France).

Looming above them was the route's first major obstacle. "There is this massive roof on the upper headwall," he explains. "It's a honker. It must stick out 50 feet. You just look up and think, 'Oh my God, how are we going to get through that thing?'" Following the path of least resistance, Arbic and Twight snuck around the left side of the ominous roof, then traversed back right to a wildly exposed stance directly above it. They could no longer see the lower part of the route. The only thing between them and the valley below was 1,500 feet of air.

Two more pitches of well-protected 5.10 climbing led them to a 4-inch off-width—the crux. When Twight first saw the crack, he envisioned an elbow-scraping, Yosemite-style grovel. But when he reached inside it, he was relieved to find a series of small edges that he could pull on, lieback-style. Better yet, there were smaller cracks within the main crack that could be used for protection. Thankful for every fingertip pull-up he'd ever done, he cranked on the tiny holds while his feet smeared against the highly textured quartzite.

Even more classic than the crux was the climb's dramatic finish. The final pitch continued steeply toward the top of the wall, then abruptly ended at a spacious, flat ledge. "It was crazy, sort of like pulling onto a dance floor," laughs Twight. From there, a short scramble would have taken them to the true summit—but they didn't bother.

As they made the tedious, 4-hour descent down Babel's north ridge, Twight was filled with a sense of satisfaction that, until that moment, he'd only experienced on hard alpine routes. "It changed the way I think about rock climbing," he allows. "Something happened inside of me. I got what I came for."

ROUTE DESCRIPTION

Area: Valley of the Ten Peaks, Canadian Rockies
First ascent: Brian Greenwood and J. Moss, August 1969
Base elevation: Approximately 8,000 feet
Summit elevation: 10,174 feet
Difficulty: IV, 5.10, A2 or 5.11d
Time required: 1 long day from base of route
Equipment: Double set of TCUs or Aliens; double set of Camalots to no. 3, 1 no. 4 Camalot; assortment of wired nuts; optional no. 0.5 and no. 1 Tri-Cam; 2 ropes, 50-m OK, 60-m ideal
Season: Late June–September
Special considerations: Hauling difficult on lower part of climb; wide assortment of camming devices essential for parallel-sided cracks; double ropes useful for wandering pitches; be wary of afternoon thunderstorms
Reference: *Selected Alpine Climbs in the Canadian Rockies* by Sean Dougherty (Rocky Mountain Books, 1999)
Map: Lake Louise 82 N/8

Approach: From Trans-Canada Highway 1, take the Lake Louise exit and follow Moraine Lake Road (south) to Moraine Lake. From the Moraine Lake parking lot, follow the Consolation Lakes trail (east, then south) to Consolation Lakes. From the north end of the southern lake, climb talus slopes toward two gullies at the base of the East Face of Mount Babel. Pass the first gully and climb the next one, moving out to the left on broken rock near the base of the face.

Route: A classic Canadian Rockies quartzite route on an impressive face and surprisingly solid rock. The majority of the fifteen pitches are moderate, with four pitches of harder climbing up high. See topo for details.

Descent: Downclimb and rappel the north ridge to Moraine Lake. The easiest line is somewhat left (west) of the ridge. Resist the temptation to peel off to the east too soon.

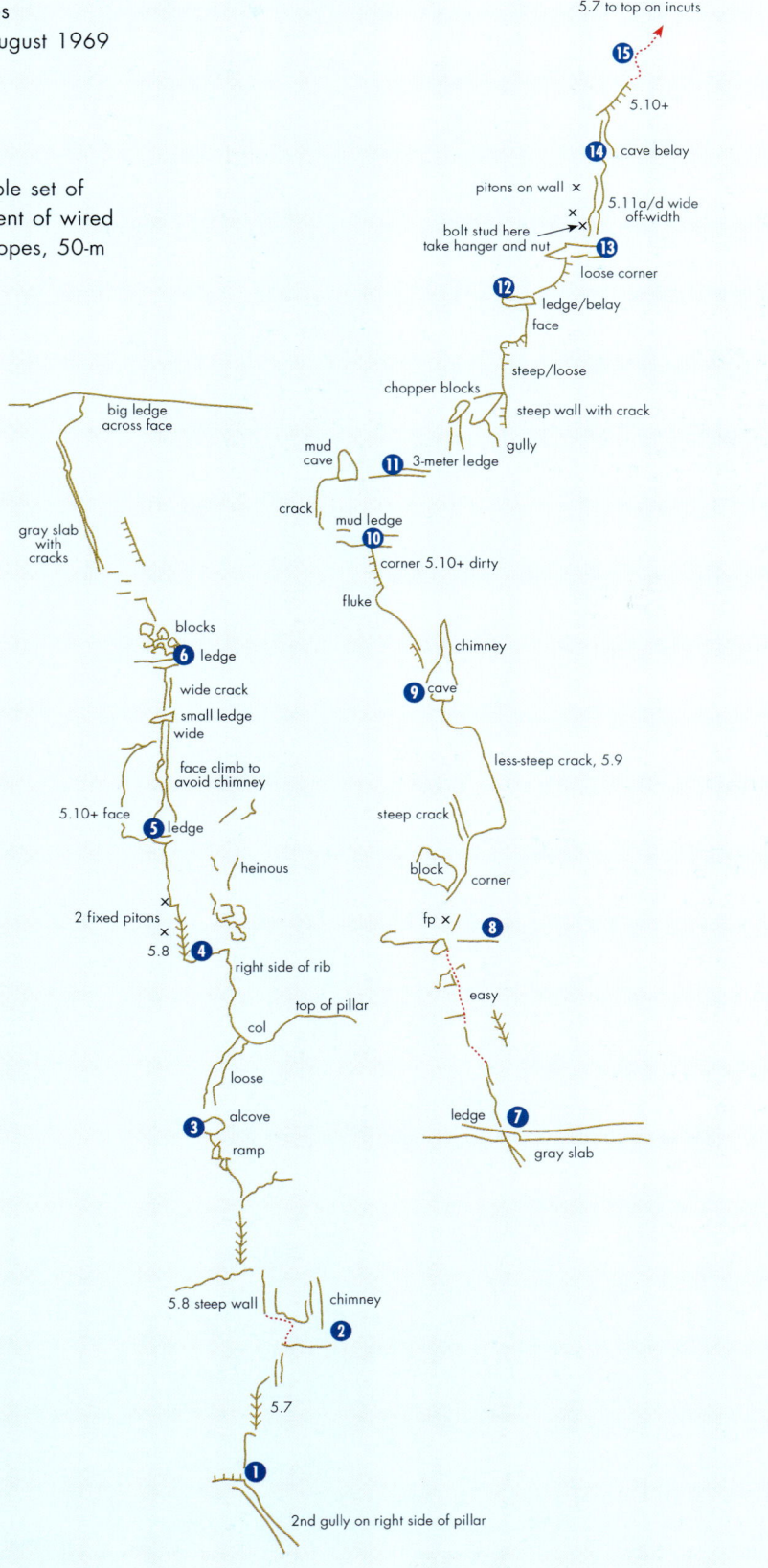

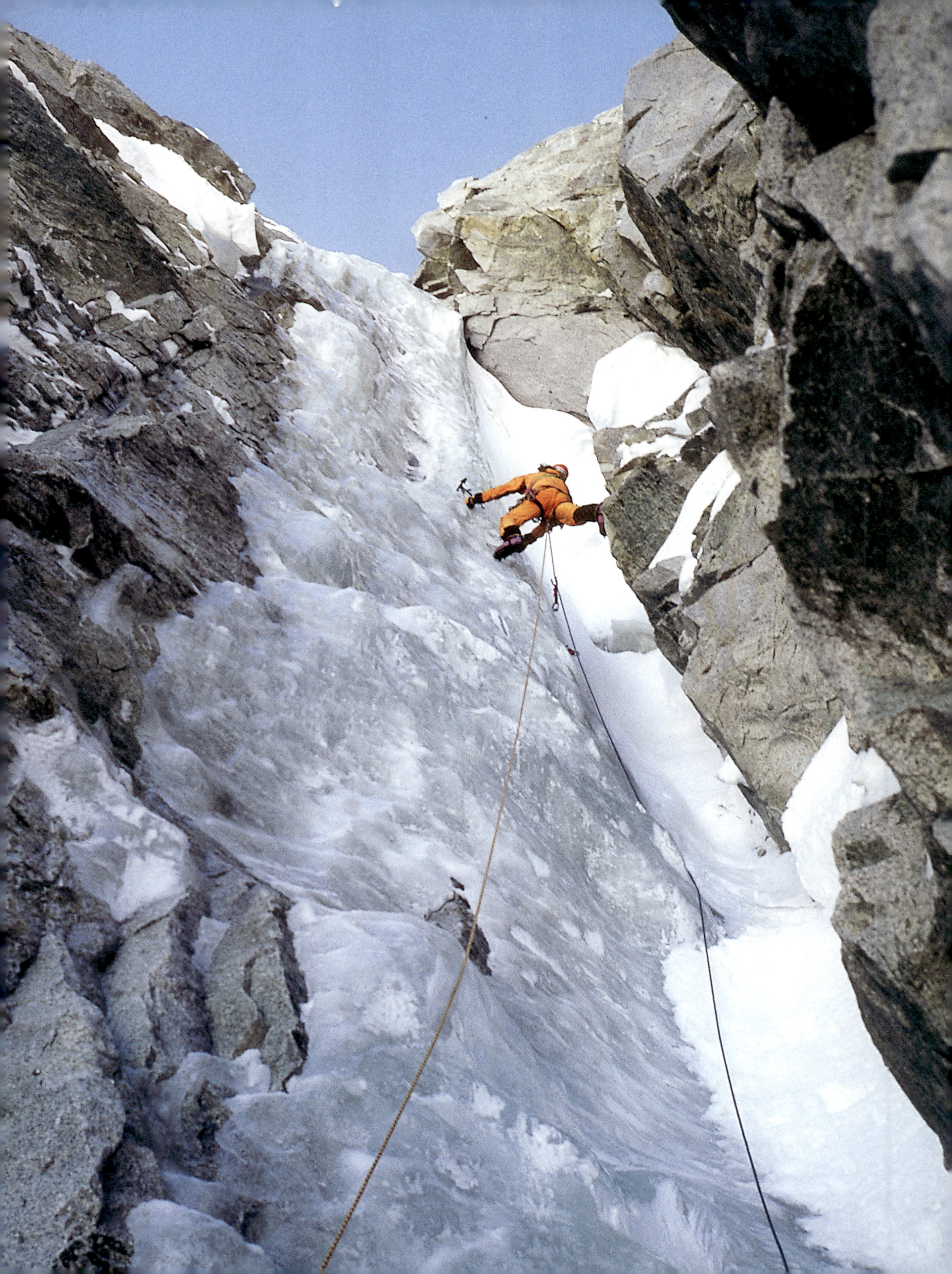

MARK WILFORD

THE PUGILIST AT REST AND WILFORD COULOIR, "POINT BLANCHARD," KLUANE NATIONAL PARK, YUKON TERRITORY

MARK WILFORD—TRADITIONAL ETHICS, MODERN STANDARDS

Mark Wilford is one of North America's great all-rounders. His climbing resume spans three decades, and is as audacious as it is diverse. Highlights from the past fifteen years vary from climbing floating icebergs in Antarctica to establishing the seldom-repeated Colorado climb Spinal Tap (5.13, R/X), pioneering a new line on Pakistan's 20,000-foot Great Trango Tower, soloing the North Face of the Eiger in a blistering 9½ hours, and taking second place in the Phoenix Bouldering Contest.

In a climbing world increasingly driven by big numbers, risk-free ascents, and media hype, Wilford stands out as an adventure-seeking traditionalist who thrives on difficult, high-stakes climbing. Inspired by the no-compromise ethics of legends such as Reinhold Messner and John Bachar (see Climb 2), Wilford is a vocal proponent of the preservation of traditional climbing areas. "You can open all the sport crags you want, but don't rap-bolt in traditional areas or put bolts next to cracks," pleads Wilford, whose climbing has always revolved around ethical, from-the-ground-up, in-control ascents.

Wilford's traditional bent hasn't been without peril. His reluctance to place bolts has resulted in some harrowing, gear-popping lead falls. He has tweaked his knees and ankles countless times after bailing from risky bouldering problems. And he's had several close calls in the mountains—with and without a rope. Still, Wilford contends that climbing is safer than some of his other pastimes, like fast driving. He has survived six roll-over accidents and numerous spin-outs—suggesting that his most important piece of equipment might be his Volvo.

THE PUGILIST AT REST AND WILFORD COULOIR

Six years after the 1992 *Canadian Alpine Journal* was published, Barry Blanchard (see Climb 4) was flipping through his dog-eared copy of it, shopping for a cause. On page 11 was a Bradford Washburn photo flaunting the sweeping west flank of Mount Alverstone—6,000 feet tall, and unclimbed. He faxed the picture to Mark Wilford in Fort Collins, Colorado. A short phone call is all it took. Tickets to Yakutat, Alaska, were booked for May 7.

On May 8, Blanchard and Wilford loaded as much food, fuel, and technical gear into a single-engine Cessna as their pilot Kurt would allow. As they flew over Mount Alverstone, they noticed a pair of golden granite pillars to its northwest. It looked like a chunk of the French Alps rising from the northern terminus of the Alverstone Glacier. It was the steepest, cleanest feature around. Blanchard described it as "the stuff dreams are made of." They stared at it until the last second, craning their necks as the pilot swooped toward the glacier.

Ten minutes later, they were skidding to a stop at the head of the Alverstone Glacier, their home for the next three weeks. The tent was set up just in time for a 2-day storm. Three feet of snow fell. They exercised by shoveling it away from the tent. Inside, they made pancakes, talked, drank whiskey, and slept. On the third day it cleared up. Clouds clung to Alverstone's ample granite hips, but the unnamed pillars glistened in the sun. Wilford admired them with his binoculars. "There's a dihedral splitting the base of the right-hand pillar," yelled Wilford, trying to entice Blanchard outside. "Oh man, we have to check it out." After Alverstone, they agreed, they'd take a closer look.

The west face of Mount Alverstone is structured like a high-angle bowling alley: gully, ridge, gully, ridge. The right-hand ridges were threatened by giant seracs that calved as they watched, roaring down the face with reckless abandon. But the leftmost ridge enticed them with a safe passage. They left base camp early the next morning with a 4-day supply of food. The ridge turned out to be considerably easier than expected. They completed half of the face on the first day, then cached everything except a light rack and dashed to the summit ridge. From there they followed the Northwest Ridge route to within 600 vertical feet of the summit before being forced to retreat by a storm. The completion of a new route offset the disappointment of not reaching the summit, but they were still far from satisfied. "We weren't super psyched about the route on Alverstone," says Wilford, "and we couldn't stop thinking about those granite pillars."

At 1:00 A.M. on May 17, after a 2-day rest, Blanchard and

Barry Blanchard enjoying perfect conditions on the 3,000-foot Wilford Couloir (V, 5.9, M4, WI 5), one of two adjacent routes he and Wilford climbed in 1998. © Mark Wilford, portrait © Mark Wilford

Wilford began skiing toward the unnamed pillars. (They later named the formation "Point Blanchard.") The closer they got, the better it looked. "I'd never seen an unclimbed piece of rock like that anywhere in my life," marveled Wilford. The open book at its base screamed *start here*.

Blanchard led the first pitch, camming the pick of his ice tool into the crack while his crampons stabbed for purchase. The granite was superb. Three more rope-lengths brought them to the top of the 5.9 corner, where some precariously balanced blocks encouraged them to exit left. In search of another crack system, Wilford made a 50-foot pendulum to a scrappy crack near the arête. He leapfrogged up the flaring seam, back-cleaning his aid placements to avoid rope drag. When he was level with his pendulum point, the piton he was standing on shifted, threatening to swing him into the corner like a wrecking ball. Adrenalin surged while he gingerly placed another anchor, then sighed with relief.

Several more mixed pitches took them to a 5.10 traverse—the route's hardest free pitch. Wilford led, shuffling his front points across a horizontal fault, until a continuous crack system pointed him upward. It was a flawless lead. Inspired by his partner's performance, Blanchard forged ahead on mixed terrain to a small snow patch, the site of their first bivy.

Above it was a roof—the route's technical crux. In the 1999 *Canadian Alpine Journal,* Blanchard described it as "a mixed pitch that would grow bolts and sprout photographers if it were next to a golf course in Colorado." Wilford's lead again. After muscling his way to the lip of the roof, he eyed an ice vein about the width of his thigh. To reach it, he drilled a stubby screw through a 2-inch-thick shovel-blade of ice hanging from the roof. Using it as an aid placement, which Wilford remembers as "super scary," he was able to stand high enough to stick his tool into the ice. Not just bold—brilliant.

After another half-dozen moderate mixed pitches (M4), their weather window started to close. The wind howled, and communication became impossible. Blanchard scared himself trying to pull through a loose overhang, then reversed his moves in a lonely panic before escaping left into an ice gully. The Pacific wind pestered from all directions as they neared the top. Chunks of rime-ice the size of golf balls swirled around, inspiring them to name the penultimate pitch "the popcorn machine." The final pitch was a gift; an ice tube allowed them to bore through the cornice instead of climb over it.

On the summit the now-raging storm chased them off the mountain. A combination of downclimbing, rappelling, and navigation skills led them back to the glacier for another bivy and, the following day, base camp. The next day, they decided to name their route after a collection of short stories by Thom Jones which they'd read during the last storm. They were inspired by Jones's macho writing about boxing, warfare, and Friedrich Nietzsche.

Five feet of snow fell over the next 7 days. Tentbound, Wilford and Blanchard talked about many things, including the tantalizing couloir 200 feet left of the Pugilist at Rest. It looked brilliant, and a bit easier: mostly water ice, some rock. Rested and restless, on May 25 they left camp with light packs and no bivy gear, and blasted up the Wilford Couloir. (After naming the entire formation Point Blanchard, it was only fair.) From the summit, they radioed their pilot to get them in the morning.

ROUTE DESCRIPTION

Area: Wrangell–St. Elias Range, Yukon Territory
First ascent: Both routes: Mark Wilford and Barry Blanchard, May 1998
Base elevation: Approximately 7,000 feet
Summit elevation: Approximately 10,000 feet
Difficulty: The Pugilist at Rest: VI, 5.10, A3, M5; Wilford Couloir: V, 5.9, M4, WI 5
Time required: (First-ascent party) The Pugilist at Rest: 2 days; Wilford Couloir: 24 hours
Equipment: The Pugilist at Rest: 2 9 mm ropes; 3–4 ice screws; 10–12 pitons, mostly knifeblades; full set of cams, double 1½–2½ inches; set of wired nuts; many runners; 2 ice tools each; rigid crampons; full Gore-Tex; light bivy gear; Wilford Couloir: 6–8 ice screws, small selection of nuts and cams, 6–8 pitons
Season: Late spring–early summer
Special considerations: Be prepared for full Alaskan conditions, subzero temperatures; skis needed to travel to and from routes; bring many wands for glacier travel, and comfortable base-camp tent for long spells of bad weather
References: *American Alpine Journal* (1999, pps 265–67); *Canadian Alpine Journal* (1999); Bradford Washburn Photographic Collection, accession no. 5661

Approach: Fly to Yakutat, Alaska, then take a bush plane (Gulf Air) to the head of Alverstone Glacier. Ski north-northwest to a hanging cirque below the west flank of Mount Alverstone, using rope on the glacier/icefall, and wands for the entire approach. Once in the cirque, "Point Blanchard" is obvious.

Route: The Pugilist at Rest: Climb the longest, most prominent arête on "Point Blanchard" (approximately 3,000 feet), starting in the large dihedral system. Wilford Couloir (approximately 2,700 feet): Start about 200 feet left. See topo for details on both.

Descent: For both routes, traverse to climber's left (west) along the corniced ridge (crevasse danger) for approximately 1 mile, then downclimb a 500-foot ice face. Rappel bergschrund, then traverse back under the face to your skis.

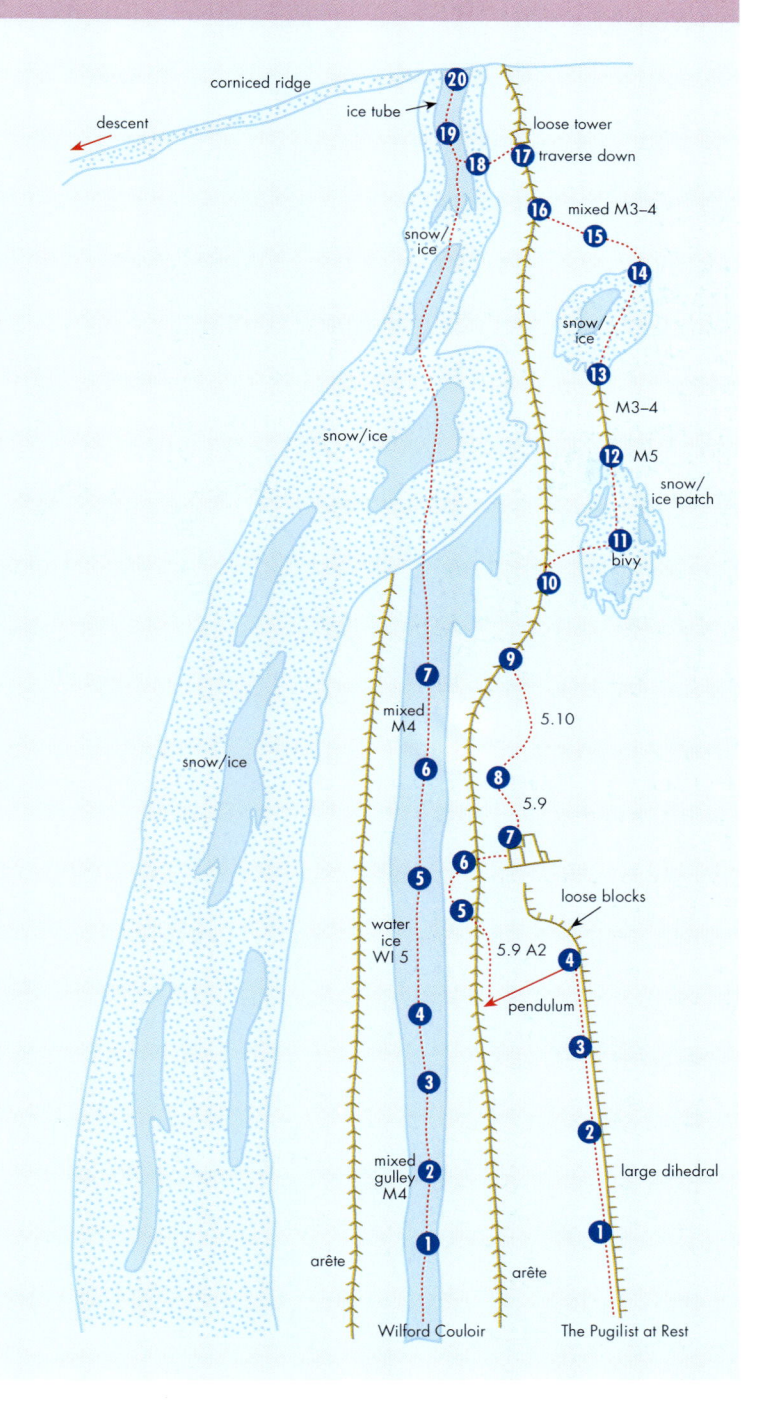

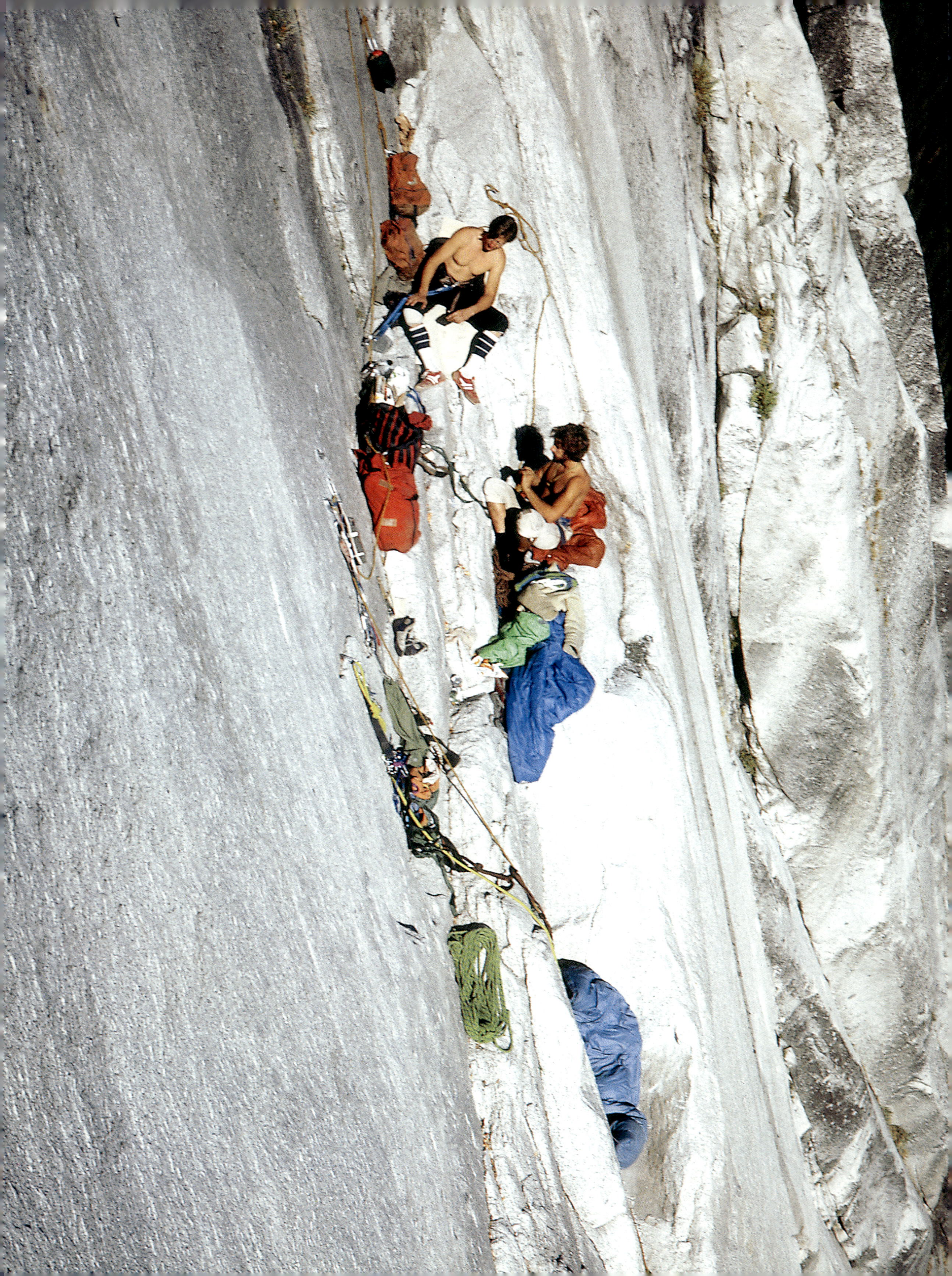

JONNY WOODWARD

HALL OF MIRRORS, GLACIER POINT APRON, YOSEMITE NATIONAL PARK, CALIFORNIA

JONNY WOODWARD—TRUE BRIT

Jonny Woodward started bouldering on the short gritstone edges near his home in Macclesfield, England, at the youthful age of ten, and was instantly hooked. The rest of his childhood, he says, was "pretty monomaniacal." He spent every free moment at the crags—and still couldn't get enough.

The pivotal moment in his climbing career came during his freshman year at Macclesfield University. While suffering through a lecture about special relativity, time dilation, and length contraction, he decided that higher education wasn't his cup of tea. Says Woodward, "I thought, 'Screw this, I'm going climbing.'"

And climb he did. Woodward soon became one of England's leading free climbers, repeating many of the Peak District's desperate classics such as Old Friends, Strapadictomy, and the London Wall. He also established some testy climbs of his own, including Beau Geste, once the hardest route on gritstone.

Lured by Yosemite's sweeping granite walls, Woodward headed for California in 1982, and has been exploring the West ever since. The expatriate enjoys both traditional and sport climbing, and is particularly known for his ability to climb hard routes on the first try. "The thing that gives me the biggest reward is to walk up to something that is at my limit and climb it without falling," muses Woodward. "Sight-reading the moves is what demonstrates the absolute mastery of climbing."

HALL OF MIRRORS

As eighteen-year-old Jonny Woodward contemplated his escape from Britain's Margaret Thatcher–era economy, he picked up a copy of *Mountain* magazine to read about the latest developments in the world of rock climbing. He was immediately drawn to an article about a new, all-free route to the top of Yosemite's Glacier Point Apron named Hall of Mirrors. The route was billed as a landmark achievement for two reasons: It was the first entirely free grade VI climb in the Valley, and only the second route to be given a rating of 5.13.

Back in 1980, Woodward spent most of his time climbing on the small gritstone crags scattered throughout Britain's Peak District. Like many Brits, he dreamt about doing long, multipitch routes on Yosemite's grand, monolithic formations. He was particularly awed by the scale and sweep of the Valley's slabs. As Woodward put it, "Climbing them represented the conquest of the featureless." Since Glacier Point Apron was known to be the ultimate slab, Hall of Mirrors, he concluded, was the ultimate slab climb.

Woodward made his first visit to Yosemite in 1982. Although he never consider climbing Hall of Mirrors on that trip, he tried to learn as much as possible about the route. Because of its status as the sole grade VI free climb in Yosemite, the sixteen-pitch slab was the subject of many conversations in Camp 4. Wherever he went, someone was talking about it. Yet after numerous discussions with Valley locals and visiting foreigners, he couldn't find a single person who had actually climbed more than the first few pitches. He began to wonder if Hall of Mirrors had seen a second ascent. Intrigued, he vowed to become a master slab climber and do the route himself.

Hall of Mirrors is the collective creation of six visionary climbers. The first two nerve-wracking pitches were established as an independent climb in 1975 by Mark Wilford (see Climb 48) and named Misty Beethoven. Three years later, Chris Cantwell, Dave Austin, and Bruce Morris added six pitches to Wilford's original line before reaching an impasse on the ninth pitch. Despite their best efforts, the soap-smooth granite was too slick for the EB rubber of the day. They dubbed the featureless slab the Unfinished Ninth. Then, late in the fall of 1979, sporting a pair of prototype Galibier Contacts, Cantwell and Scott Cole managed to smear through the crux and pushed the route to the base of the thirteenth pitch before winter set in. Finally, in the fall of 1980, Cantwell and Scott Burke added the last four pitches.

After moving to California in 1984, Woodward began making frequent excursions to Yosemite. By May 1992, after dozens of trips to the granite Mecca and years of establishing bolted routes of his own, he had the confidence to tackle Hall of Mirrors. On the heels of making the first free ascent of Zion's Moonlight Buttress (5.12c) with Peter Croft (see Climb 11), Woodward drove

Dave Austin and Bruce Morris hanging out at The Hang bivouac, seven pitches up Hall of Mirrors, in 1978 © Chris Cantwell, portrait © Greg Epperson

from Utah to Yosemite, where he met his partner Darrell Hensel. Armed with an extensive selection of rock shoes—hoping one of them would stick to the hard Apron glass—he and Hensel started up the route the next morning.

Getting up Misty Beethoven proved to be more difficult than they expected. "Those first few pitches are notoriously hard," remembers Woodward, who contends that the sparely protected 5.11a slab is more like 5.11d. The stout introduction revived their rusty slab-climbing skills, enabling them to reach the top of the eighth pitch—known as the Glass Menagerie—before a spring thunderstorm halted their progress. Knowing they'd be back, they fixed ropes on the hardest pitches as they rappelled to the Valley floor.

After 3 days of rain, they returned to Hall of Mirrors only to find the fourth and fifth pitches acting as a granite gutter system for the spring runoff. Not wanting to wait until fall to continue the route, they spent the day establishing a dry, two-pitch variation to the left of the original line.

With only 1 day left to climb, they realized that a clean ascent of Hall of Mirrors was not going to happen. Instead, they decided to climb as high as possible—standing on bolts or aid-climbing if necessary—to reconnoiter the upper part of the route for an attempt in the fall. Their fixed ropes enabled them to quickly reach the crux pitch, the Unfinished Ninth. When Woodward wrote about the experience in *Climbing* magazine, he described it as "the blankest section of climbed rock I had ever seen, desperate and unattainable." After several slides down the crux, he tried everything he could think of to avoid climbing it.

Much to his chagrin, he found no way to get across the featureless slab without actually doing the moves. He tried standing on bolts and running between them, but they were too few and far between. He tried making an "upward pendulum" on the low-angle slab, but to no avail. Finally, he resigned himself to doing it the hard way. After countless rubber-shredding attempts at what he described as "a series of weight transitions so tenuous that they had to be executed in a single, flowing motion," he eventually made it to the belay ledge.

The momentum continued until the twelfth pitch, which proved to be almost as hard as the Unfinished Ninth. When they reached the base of the thirteenth pitch—which Cantwell christened as the 5.13a crux—their hearts sank when they saw a line of hangerless bolt studs and tattered cord leading up the wall. Lacking the hardware to continue, and nonplused by Cantwell's decision to install hangerless bolts, they were forced to retreat.

With Hensel trapped in a new job, Woodward returned to Hall of Mirrors the following October with slab-climbing ace John Bercaw. They gave themselves 3 days to climb the route: The first would be spent regaining their high point, the second re-equipping the upper pitches, and the third making a clean, 1-day ascent. It was a straightforward but ambitious plan.

The first day went as planned. The second day was arduous; Woodward described it as "a day of toil, best forgotten." But the third day made it all worthwhile: In one fell swoop, Woodward and Bercaw re-led the heady lower pitches, squeaked through the hideous ninth, and dispatched the upper section of the route with relative ease.

The thirteenth pitch, which they expected to be troublesome, wasn't 5.13 after all—it was more like 5.12b—and the pitches above it were considerably easier. Still, the infamous thirteenth was the finest, most sustained edging pitch he'd ever done. In fact, every pitch was memorable. In Woodward's account of the route's second ascent in *Climbing* magazine, he summarized the experience: "If you are not one of those for whom slab climbing has become the hip thing to despise, you're in for a treat. The quality of the pitches, the difficulty of the climbing, and the historical notoriety ensure its status as America's archetypal slab."

ROUTE DESCRIPTION

Area: Yosemite Valley

First ascent: Chris Cantwell, Bruce Morris, Scott Burke, Dave Austin, and others, 1978–80; dry variation: Jonny Woodward and Derrell Hensel, May 1992

Base elevation: Approximately 4,000 feet

Summit elevation: Approximately 7,000 feet

Difficulty: VI, 5.12c

Time required: 1–3 days

Equipment: Assortment of wired nuts and set of camming devices to no. 1 Camalot; quickdraws

Season: Spring and fall

Special considerations: Glacier Point Apron has been the site of several catastrophic rock slides, most recently in 1999, which result in occasional closure of the Apron; consult Park Service prior to attempting this and other routes on the Apron; the Hang is a natural water drainage for upper Apron, hence a bad place to be when it rains

References: *Yosemite Climbs, Free Climbs* by Don Reid; "Smoke and Mirrors," *Climbing* magazine, by Jonny Woodward

Approach: From the east end of Yosemite Valley, follow the horse trail immediately west of Happy Isles. Head up the hill where a concrete slab with a pipe abuts the trail. The route starts above Misty Beethoven on the Glacier Point Apron.

Route: Sixteen pitches of flawless granite slab climbing on one of Yosemite's most historic landmarks. See topo for details.

Descent: Rappel from the top of the fifteenth pitch, or continue one more pitch to the top of Glacier Point.

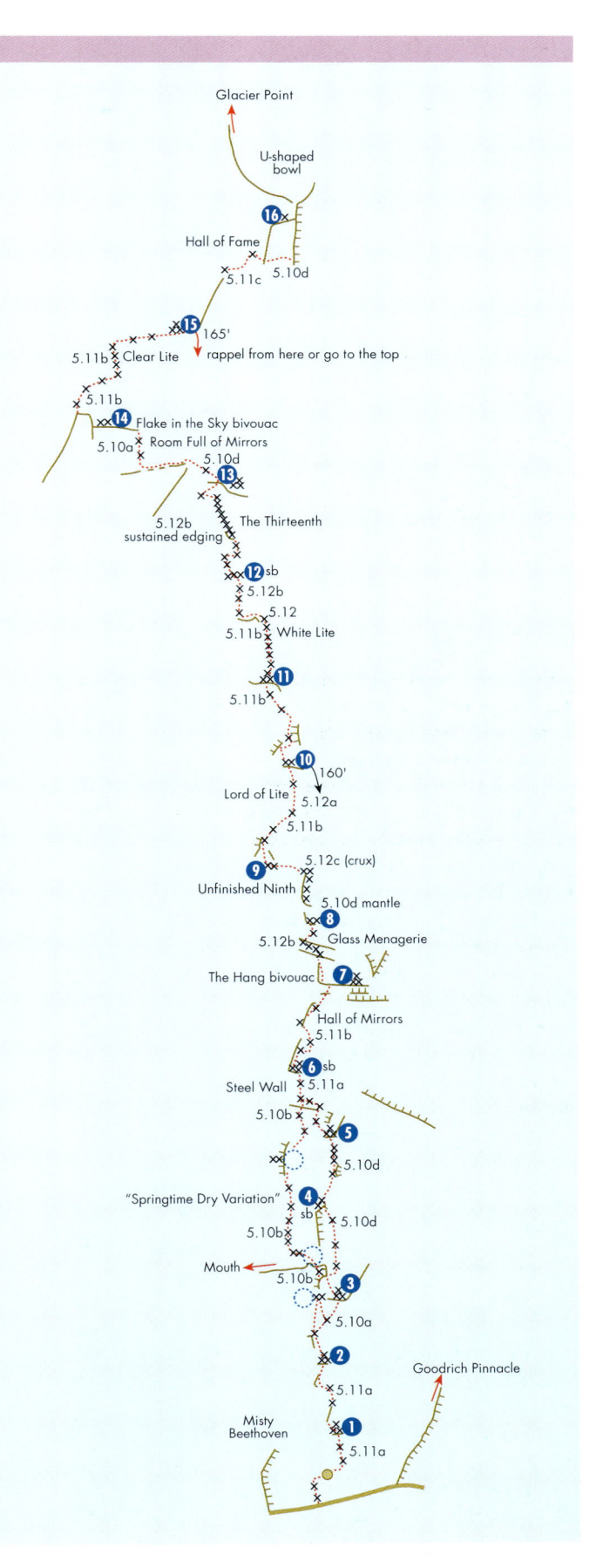

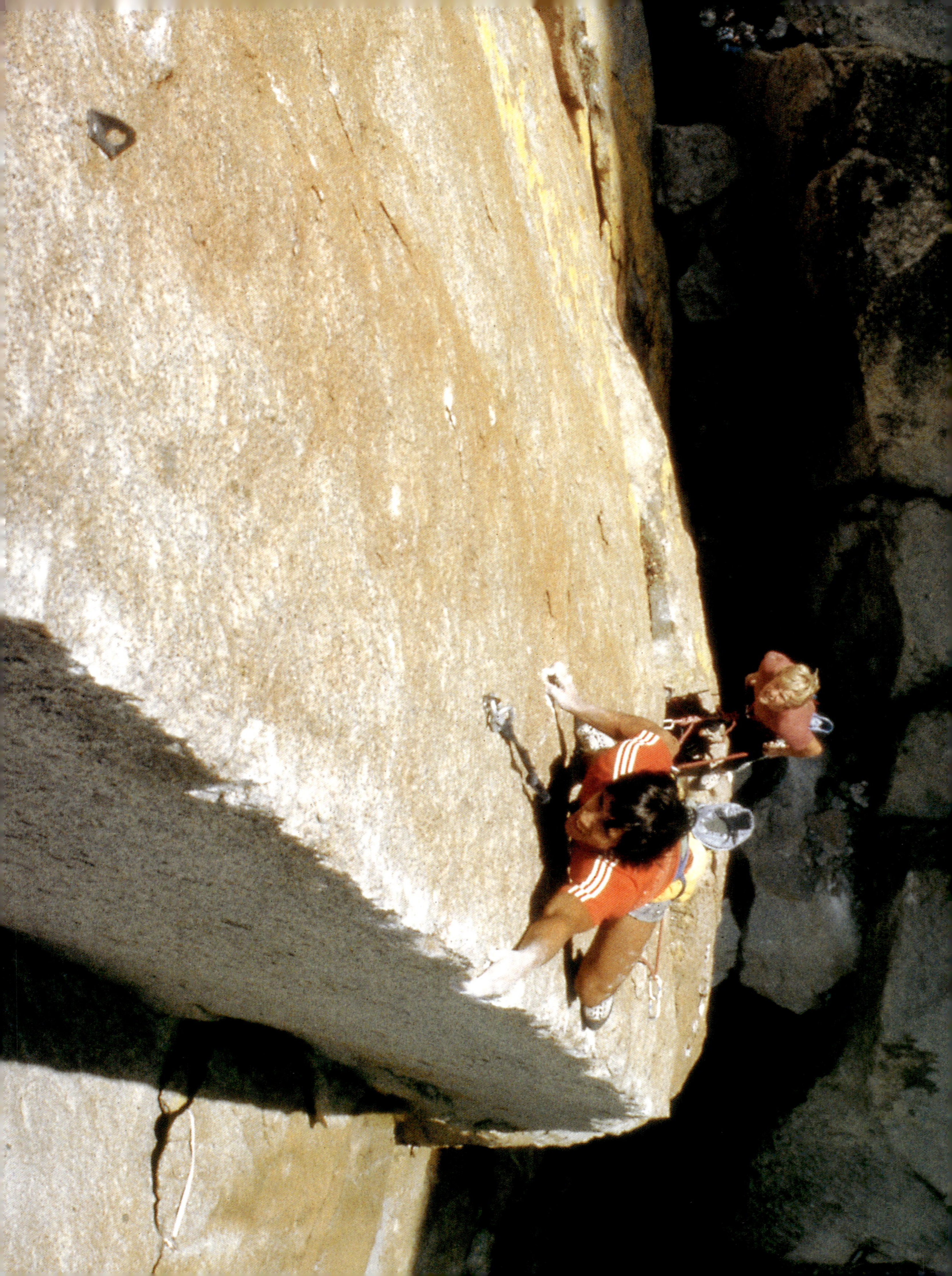

TONY YANIRO

SCIROCCO, EAST FACE OF THE SORCERER, THE NEEDLES, CALIFORNIA

TONY YANIRO—AHEAD OF HIS TIME

Tony Yaniro started rock-climbing in the early '70s, back in the days of rugby shirts, swami belts, and unyielding traditional ethics. Back in the days when bolts were placed on lead, if at all. And back when it was taboo to rehearse routes—the hardest of which were rated 5.11.

Although he initially abided by the purist tactics of the era, Yaniro saw limitations with them. He believed that advancing the standard of free climbing would demand new training techniques and a controversial change in ethics. The compact Californian was one of the first to develop training programs for specific routes—a practice that is commonplace today but drew criticism in the '70s. As a teenager, he did fingertip pull-ups on his door jams until he was strong enough to climb the Drainpipe (5.11a) at Suicide Rock, near Idyllwild in southern California. When he saw the benefit of being able to do one-arm pull-ups, he trained until he could do nine with his right arm and seven with his left. And in 1979, when he was working on his Sugarloaf, California, masterpiece, the Grand Illusion (5.13b/c), his homemade "crack machine" gave him the strength to do the route.

Yaniro's willingness to challenge the "ground-up" first-ascent ethics in traditional areas also drew criticism. In the early '80s, when he realized that placing protection—not physical ability—was the limiting factor for many potential new routes, he used aid-climbing techniques to place bolts on lead. It was a small but symbolic transgression that eventually led to the modern practice of drilling bolts on rappel.

In 1988, Yaniro's ways were vindicated when the French brought what we now know as sport climbing to the United States. The country's first organized competition at Snowbird, Utah, was the turning point in the great debate. "When the French kicked our butts in the competition," remembers Yaniro, "everyone was suddenly interested in sport climbing and training on artificial walls."

As sport climbing grew in popularity in the early '90s, Yaniro focused on developing hard routes on limestone crags such as Mount Charleston in Nevada. He has numerous 5.14 routes to his credit. When he's not climbing, he spends his time doing a variety of aerobic sports, coaching and course-setting for indoor climbing competitions, and practicing naturopathic medicine. Although traditionalists once considered Yaniro a radical, history has proven him to be more of a visionary. "Looking at Tony in the early '80s," says longtime partner Randy Leavitt (see Climb 26), "was like looking at the future."

SCIROCCO

Tony Yaniro spent his first several climbing seasons visiting popular areas such as Joshua Tree, Tahquitz Rock, and Yosemite Valley—places blessed with perfect weather, solid granite, and an abundance of brilliant routes. It was hard for Yaniro to imagine anything better, until he discovered the Needles of the southern Sierra.

Yaniro was awestruck when he made his first trip to the Needles in 1980. He marveled at the missilelike granite towers brushed with yellow lichen. He drooled at the abundance of unclimbed cracks. And he didn't see any other climbers. The place had a mystical, almost supernatural feeling that explained why the rock formations had names like the Sorcerer, the Witch, and the Warlock.

Yaniro began making frequent trips to the granite paradise with fellow Needles enthusiasts Dick Leversee, Randy Leavitt, and Brett Maurer. "We just went hog-wild," he remembers. "We would do these burnout weekends where we would wake up at 5:00 A.M., hike in with giant packs, and spend all day scrubbing and cleaning routes. Then we'd stumble down the trail in the dark, eat a bowl of cereal, and fall asleep. We'd go nonstop for 3 or 4 days in a row, sometimes doing eight new pitches a day."

The first phase of their route rampage resulted in numerous classic lines such as Atlantis, Love at Sea, and the Don Juan Wall. While establishing these routes, they diligently adhered to the area's traditional ethics. Although some of the pitches had to be cleaned on rappel, they were all led from the ground up. And if bolts needed to be placed, which was rare since the routes followed crack systems, they were drilled while the leader stood balanced on a stance. It's the way things had been done since Fred Beckey first started exploring the area in the early '70s.

Tony Yaniro on the first ascent of Scirocco (5.12a) in 1983. Back then, the route was controversial because Yaniro used aid-climbing techniques to bolt the route on lead. © Randy Leavitt, portrait © Jim Thornburg

Unlike the polished, featureless granite found in Yosemite, Needles granite is highly textured, speckled with small edges and nubbins; it's possible to climb not only the cracks, but the faces between the cracks. "There are little features and patina edges all over the place," explains Yaniro, who spotted potential new routes wherever he looked. The problem, of course, was protection: Most of the faces were too steep to be bolted on lead, and drilling bolts on rappel was taboo. Barring a change in ethics, only the natural crack systems could be climbed.

In 1983, Yaniro and Brett Maurer were planning to repeat the ultraclassic Don Juan Wall—a route he free-climbed the previous year with Randy Leavitt. As they prepared for the ascent, they admired a perfectly sculpted arête just to their left. The slightly overhanging corner was dotted with small, incut edges, but offered no cracks for protection. Still, it was begging to be climbed. "We just knew it had to be done," remembers Yaniro. "We weren't sure how we were going to do it, but decided to just start climbing."

About 15 feet up the arête, Yaniro found a tiny seam in which he placed two stoppers about the size of his little fingernail. Suspecting that they wouldn't hold a fall, he decided to place a bolt. If he were aid-climbing, say, on El Capitan, it would have been OK to support his body weight from a sky hook while drilling the bolt. But free-climbing ethics dictated that he had to support his own weight while pounding the drill bit into the rock. While this is easily done on a 70-degree slab, it's impossible on an overhanging arête, where the climber needs at least one hand to hang onto the rock. Fully aware that he was stretching an ethical boundary, Yaniro placed a hook on a small edge and hung from it while he drilled. Short of placing the bolt on rappel, which was even more unthinkable in those days, he knew it was the only way to do the climb. Says Yaniro, "I knew it would be controversial, but I just decided to take the crap."

To a nonclimber or someone who started climbing after sport climbing gained acceptance in 1988, such an ethical subtlety seems arcane, if not frivolous. But to climbers of the late '70s and early '80s, it was an issue of religious importance.

Tony Yaniro on the first pitch of Scirocco in 2000, seventeen years after making the first ascent
© Jim Thornburg

Yaniro spent the entire day hooking, drilling, and climbing his way up the two-pitch arête. The moves were athletic and sporty: Sometimes he would have to climb 20 feet above his last bolt before finding the next hook placement. And not all of them were good. The hooks would occasionally pop off, causing an unexpected plummet. One time a hook blew when the drill bit was buried in the rock, snapping it when he fell. When he regained his high point, he simply tied off the broken stub and hung from it to drill the next bolt.

After laboriously placing fifteen bolts—some ¼ inch and some ⅜ inch—Yaniro finally reached the top of the arête. He, Maurer, and Leavitt returned the next week to lead the route in one continuous push, without any tension from the rope—a style of ascent now known as a redpoint. As Yaniro enjoyed the fruits of his labor, he became more and more convinced that he'd done the right thing. The route was every bit as good as he dreamed it would be, and he felt his actions were justified in the spirit of advancing the standard of free climbing.

As predicted, the ascent was highly controversial. "We got a lot of flak," he laughs. "Everyone accused us of overbolting the route, even though some of them are 20 feet apart." He gave his critics permission to chop every bolt that they were willing to skip when they climbed the route.

Twenty years later, all the bolts are still there.

ROUTE DESCRIPTION

Area: Southern Sierra Nevada
First ascent: Tony Yaniro, Brett Maurer, and Randy Leavitt, 1983
Base elevation: Approximately 7,000 feet
Summit elevation: Approximately 7,400 feet
Difficulty: III, 5.12a
Time required: Half day
Equipment: 10–15 quickdraws; set of cams to 3 inches, set of TCUs, full set of stoppers
Season: May–October
Special considerations: High elevation can mean drastic temperature swings
Reference: *Southern Sierra Rock Climbing, Book 2, The Needles Area* by Sally Moser, Greg Vernon, and Patrick Paul

Approach: The Needles are about 42 miles east of California's Central Valley. From Porterville (about 70 miles south-southeast of Fresno via State Highway 99), follow State Highway 190 east for 20 miles to Springville, then continue another 24 miles to road 21S05 and follow it to its end. Hike 3 miles from the end of the road. Sorcerer Needle is about a 10-minute walk from the Lookout, and due south of the Charlatan. Scirocco is located on the left side of the east face.

Route: A striking, three-pitch granite arête on the east face of the Sorcerer. Can continue to the top via Wailing Banshees (5.11b). See topo for details.

Descent: Rappel with two ropes down the north side of the Sorcerer.

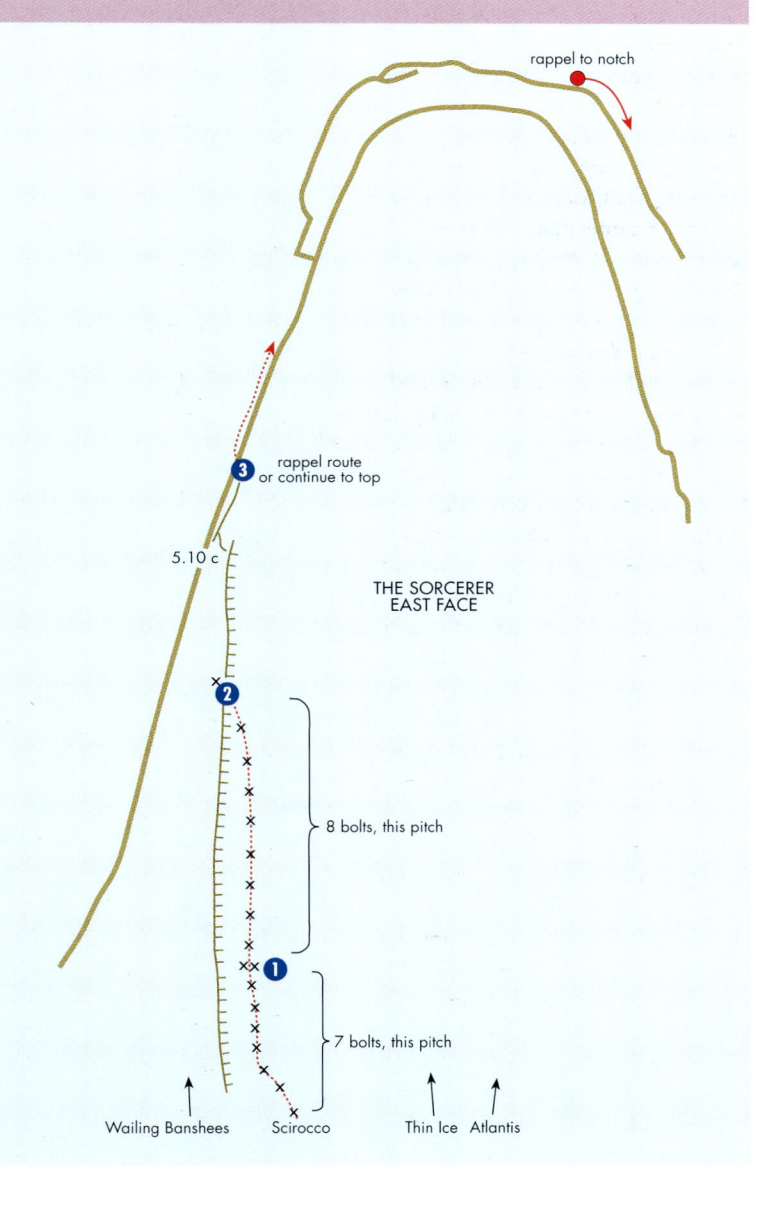

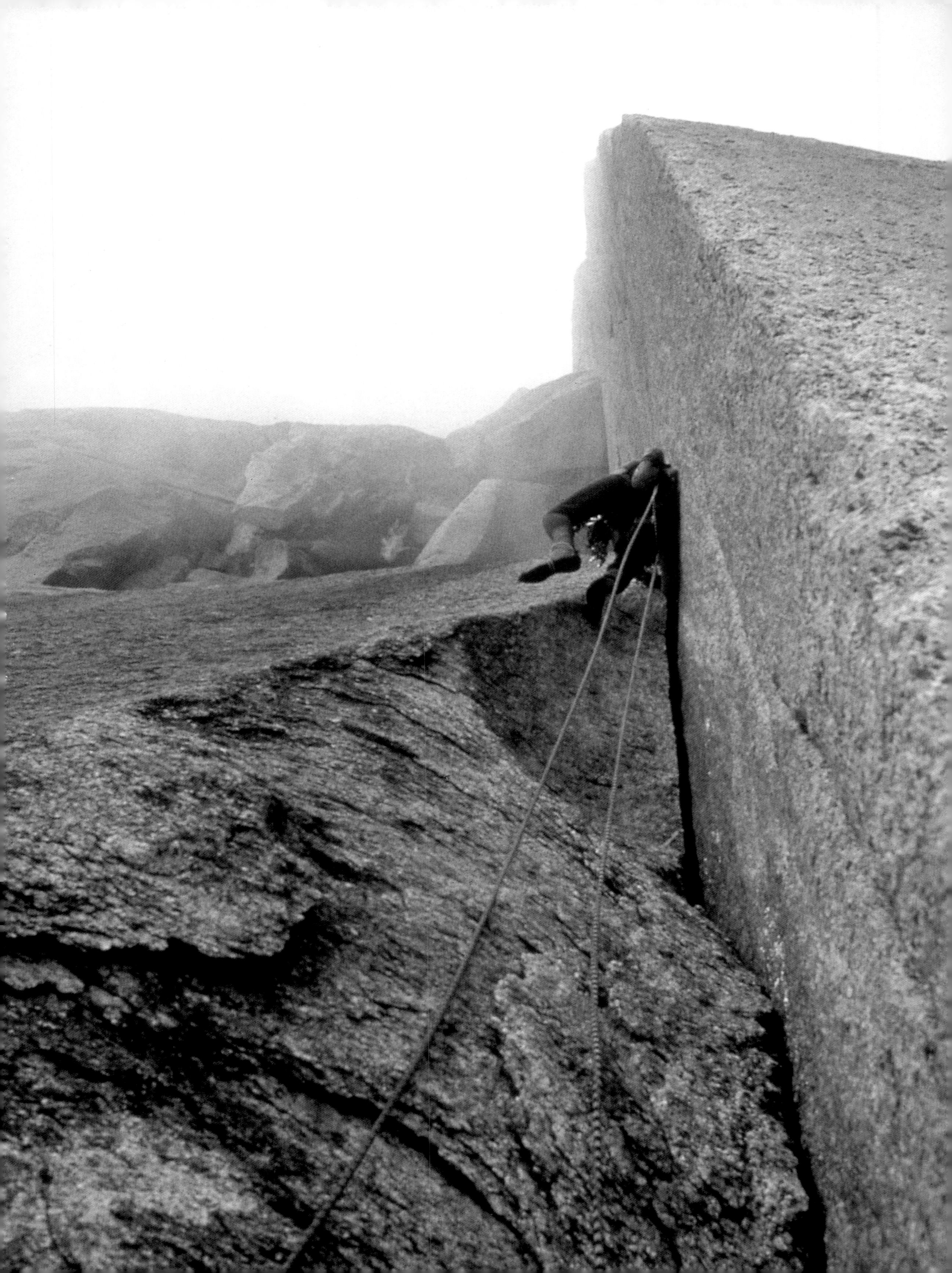

GLOSSARY

The ever-swelling lexicon of climber-speak continues to confuse climbers and nonclimbers alike. There are about thirty key terms and concepts used repeatedly throughout this book. Understanding them will help readers—from armchair mountaineers to hardcore climbers—get more out of this book.

Aid, aid climbing. Aid is the term for protection devices (pitons, spring-loaded cams, bolts, etc.) used to support a climber's weight and assist in upward progress. Aid climbing, the direct use of fixed or climber-placed aid, is very different from free climbing; it is a mechanical process, not a gymnastic performance. Solid protection makes for easy aid climbs with ratings such as A0 and A1, and "bodyweight" protection makes for difficult aid climbs, with ratings like A4 and A5. The most difficult and risky aid climbs are rated A5.

Alpine style. An ultra-lightweight method of mountain climbing in which equipment and food rations (i.e., comfort and security) are trimmed to the bare minimum in order to facilitate a swift ascent. Alpine-style climbing involves more commitment and risk than expedition-style climbing, which relies on load-carrying Sherpas and fixed ropes. *See also* fixed rope.

Belay. A safety technique in which a stationary climber provides protection, by means of ropes, anchors, and braking devices, to an ascending partner. It is possible, but uncommon, to self-belay and make a roped solo ascent.

Beta. Information and advice to use while climbing a route.

Big-wall climb. A long and sustained technical rock climb that usually requires more than 1 day to ascend.

Bivouac. A temporary camp that provides little or no shelter from the elements; bivy for short.

Cams. A generic term for mechanical, spring-loaded devices of varying sizes and manufacture (such as Friends, Camalots, and TCUs) that can be inserted in cracks for protection.

Class 3. Straightforward but exposed scrambling that requires the use of hands for upward progress. Most climbers don't use a rope on "third-class" terrain.

Class 4. Harder than class 3, but steep and exposed enough that most climbers will want a rope.

Class 5. Rock that is sufficiently steep or difficult to require the use of a rope or technical gear for protection. Class 5 climbs are broken down into subcategories, from 5.0 to 5.14 (5.0 being relatively easy and 5.14 being impossible for all but elite climbers). Climbs from 5.10 to 5.14 are further classified by letter ratings: a, b, c, and d. For example, 5.10c is harder than 5.10b, and 5.11a is harder than 5.10d. This rating system is also known as the Yosemite Decimal System (see Climb 46).

Clean. To remove protection placed by the climbing leader while ascending. Usually accomplished by the following climber, or "second."

Clean climbing. A style of ascent; free or aid climbing without the use of a hammer to place pitons, and usually without pitons altogether. Most "clean climbs" rely on nuts and cams—which don't scar the rock—for protection.

Crux. The most difficult section of a pitch, or the most difficult pitch on a route.

Dihedral. A crack or corner system formed when two walls meet in a right-angled inside corner, like an open book.

Flash. A style of ascent in which the climber successfully leads a climb never previously attempted with no falls or rope-assisted rests, but with prior knowledge of the intricacies of the route. *See also* on-sight.

Fixed rope. A rope anchored to a route by the lead climber and left in place for those who follow. Fixed ropes are used to ascend and descend the lower pitches when the climbers want to sleep on the ground. Also known as "fixed lines."

Free climbing. A style of ascent in which the climber uses natural features to make upward progress, using ropes and protection only in case of a fall. The opposite of aid climbing. Many old "aid routes" have been "freed" as free-climbing standards have increased.

Free solo. To climb with no protection whatsoever, relying solely on strength, agility, and a cool head. Typically, climbers free-solo routes well below their physical limits. Free soloing is often referred to as just "soloing," and should not be confused with self-belayed, roped soloing.

Jumar. The first popular brand of mechanical rope ascender, now used as a generic term referring to all brands of ascenders. Several companies manufacture mechanical ascenders, but climbers still refer to them all as Jumars. Also, the act of using an ascender to climb a fixed rope is known as Jumaring. A slang term for Jumars is "jugs," which can also be used as a verb, as in, "They let us jug their fixed ropes."

When in doubt, run it out. Jim Donini high on the Cobra Pillar. © Jim Donini Collection

Manky. Bad, dubious, or insecure protection such as an old fixed piton or bolt, or any protection that is generally worthless.

Mixed climbing. Ascending a route by a combination of methods, (i.e., free and aid climbing), usually on terrain wherein both rock and ice, and sometimes snow, are encountered.

Nut. A metal wedge with a wire loop that is inserted in cracks for protection. Also called stoppers. RPs and HB offsets are specific types (and brands) of nuts.

On-sight. The most impressive style of ascent; leading a climb with no falls and no rope-assisted rests on the first attempt without any prior knowledge (beta) of its features or difficulties.

Pitch. A section of rock between two belay points, no more than the length of one climbing rope (165–200 feet, or 50–60 meters).

Piton. A metal spike or peg that can be hammered into the rock as an anchor. With a few exceptions, pitons have been superceded by clean protection such as cams and nuts.

Portaledge. A lightweight yet very strong cot for big-wall climbing. A portaledge can be hung from a vertical rock face to provide a place to rest or sleep.

Protection. Any anchor (such as a nut, chock, camming device, piton, or stopper) used to protect the leader in case of a fall. Also known as "pro."

Rack. The collection of gear on a shoulder sling, usually carried by the leader while climbing. The rack typically consists of an assortment of protection and spare carabiners.

Rappel. To make a controlled descent of a rope using a mechanical braking device. Also known as "rapping."

Redpoint. A style of ascent; to lead a route (usually a sport climb) from bottom to top without falling or hanging on the rope. Only the first bolt may be pre-clipped. *See also* Yo-yoing.

Run-out. An uncomfortably long, scary, and sometimes dangerous distance between two points of protection that can result in a long fall.

Sandbag. To intentionally downplay the difficulties of a climb in order to convince a dubious partner to try it; for example, "He is a total sandbagger!" or, "That route is a sandbag."

Simul-climbing. The act of two or three people simultaneously climbing on the same rope, secured by protection, but not belaying in the traditional sense. Sometimes called a "running belay." This technique helps a party climb faster, but increases the length of a potential fall.

Sport climbing. Free climbing that focuses on extreme gymnastic difficulty rather than adventure and risk. Such climbs are protected with preplaced bolts.

Top rope. A climbing rope that is secured from above. Climbing a pitch with a top rope involves virtually no risk.

Yosemite Decimal System. See Class 5 and Climb 46.

Yo-yoing. A style of ascent popular in the '70s and '80s in which the leader lowers to the start of the pitch after each fall, rather than rehearsing it with the aid of rope tension. Today, most climbers practice the redpoint style of climbing on harder routes.

SELECTED REFERENCES

BOOKS

Burns, Cameron M. *Selected Climbs in the Desert Southwest*. Seattle: The Mountaineers Books, 1999.

Dougherty, Sean. *Selected Climbs in the Canadian Rockies*. Calgary, Alb.: Rocky Mountain Books, 1991.

Green, Randall, and Joe Bensen. *Bugaboo Rock, A Climber's Guide*. Seattle: The Mountaineers Books, 1999.

Jones, Chris. *Climbing in North America*. Seattle: The Mountaineers Books, 1997.

Josephson, Joe. *Waterfall Ice Climbs in the Canadian Rockies*. Calgary, Alb.: Rocky Mountain Books, 1994.

Long, John, and John Middendorf. *Big Walls*. Evergreen, Colo.: Chockstone Press, 1994.

Lowe, Jeff. *Ice World*. Seattle: The Mountaineers Books, 1996.

McLane, Kevin. *Rock Climber's Guide to Squamish*. Vancouver, B.C.: Elaho Publishing, 1999.

Moser, Sally, Greg Vernon, and Patrick Paul. *Southern Sierra Rock Climbing, Book 2, The Needles Area*. Evergreen, Colo.: Chockstone Press, 1992.

Ortenburger, Leigh H., and Reynold G. Jackson. *A Climbers' Guide to the Teton Range*. 3d ed. Seattle: The Mountaineers Books, 1996.

Reid, Don. *Yosemite Climbs, Big Walls*. Evergreen, Colo.: Chockstone Press, 1996.

———. *Yosemite Climbs, Free Climbs*. Evergreen, Colo.: Chockstone Press, 1994.

Roper, Steve. *Camp 4, Recollections of a Yosemite Rockclimber*. Seattle: The Mountaineers Books, 1994.

Roper, Steve, and Allen Steck. *Fifty Classic Climbs of North America*. San Francisco: Sierra Club Books, 1979.

Swain, Todd. *Rock Climbing, Red Rocks*. Helena, Mont.: Falcon Press, 2000.

Twight, Mark, and James Martin. *Extreme Alpinism*. Seattle: The Mountaineers Books, 1999.

Vogel, Randy, and Bob Gaines. *Guide to Tahquitz and Suicide Rocks*. Evergreen, Colo.: Chockstone Press, 1993.

JOURNALS

Buhler, Carlos. "University Peak." *American Alpine Journal* (1998): 78–87.

Davis, Steph. "Shipton Spire." *American Alpine Journal* (1999): 80–89.

Ogden, Jared. "Ship of Fools." *American Alpine Journal* (1998): 21–33.

Rowell, Galen. "The Great Canadian Knife—Logan Mountains." *American Alpine Journal* (1993): 66–78.

Turk, Jonathan. "Sam Ford Fjord—Baffin Island." *American Alpine Journal* (1993): 58–65.

Wadman, Clay. "Count Zero on Huntington." *American Alpine Journal* (1993): 79–84.

MAGAZINES

Achey, Jeff. "Long's Strange Trip." *Climbing* no. 145: 62–71.

———. "Ten Stars of American Climbing." *Climbing* no. 192: 88–95.

Anker, Conrad. "Now Going." *Climbing* no. 191: 58–65.

Benge, Michael. "Forty Days and Forty Nights." *Climbing* no. 164: 21–22.

———. "Travels with Charlie." *Climbing* no. 139: 72–81.

Child, Greg. "Mortals on Combatant." *Climbing* no. 162: 100–108.

Horgan, Candice. "Life on the Run." *Climbing* no. 191: 66–70.

Jackson, Jeff. "The Shining Path." *Climbing* no. 146: 104–110.

Josephson, Joe. "The Outsider." *Climbing* no. 173: 88–95.

Luebben, Craig. "Country Boy." *Rock & Ice* no. 82: 62–69.

MacDonald, Dougald. "The Professional." *Rock & Ice* no. 70: 48–55.

O'Connell, Nick. "Peter Croft." *Rock & Ice* no. 56: 52–57.

Papciak, Mike. "Blonde Ambition." *Climbing* no. 168: 80–87.

Perlman, Eric. "The Natural." *Rock & Ice* no. 78: 56–61.

Piana, Paul. "The Great Canadian Knife." *Rock & Ice* no. 57: 28–35.

Schneider, Steve. "Seize the Day." *Climbing* no. 153: 90–99.

Thesenga, Jonathan. "The A Team." *Climbing* no. 192: 104–112.

Waterman, Jonathan. "The Natural." *Climbing* no. 138: 70–78.

Woodward, Jonny. "Smoke and Mirrors." *Climbing* no. 141, p. 98.

Young, Wills. "Sharma's Dharma." *Climbing* no. 195: 112–19.

MARK KROESE

CLIMBER, WRITER, PHOTOGRAPHER, COMPUTER CONSULTANT, HOPELESS GENERALIST

Mark Kroese started climbing in 1976 at the impressionable age of fifteen (back in the days of swami belts and rugby shirts) and he's been exploring the high and wild ever since. His mountaineering and rock climbing adventures have taken him all over world. In addition to climbing extensively in the western United States, he has climbed in South America, Australia, New Zealand, Newfoundland, the Northwest Territories, British Columbia, and Alberta.

The majority of Mark's career has been spent in the business world. He graduated from the University of Washington in 1983 with a degree in Business Administration and spent fifteen years working as a marketing professional, including three years as an account manager for Chiat Day Advertising and twelve years as a marketing executive for Microsoft Corporation. In 1998 he decided to merge his passion for writing and outdoor photography and his passion for climbing into a successful career as a freelance writer and photographer. His work has appeared in publications such as *Climbing, Outside,* and *People,* and on numerous web sites including *mountainzone.com*.

During the last two years, Mark's son Daniel, now 13 years old, has emerged as one of his regular rock climbing partners. Daniel is frequently overheard saying, "C'mon Dad, you can do it—it's only 5.11d."

During his free time, Mark volunteers as a member of the Board of Directors for the Access Fund, a national, non-profit organization dedicated to preserving access to climbing areas and conserving the climbing environment. (Twenty-five percent of the author's proceeds from this book are being donated to the Access Fund).

Mark lives in Bellevue, Washington with his wife Lisa, and their two children, Daniel and Nicole.

THE ACCESS FUND: PRESERVING AMERICA'S DIVERSE CLIMBING RESOURCES

The Access Fun, a national, nonprofit climbers organization, works to keep climbing areas open and to conserve the climbing environment. If you need help with closures, land acquisition, legal or land management issues, funding for trails and other projects, or if you are interested in starting a local climbers' group, call us at 303-546-6772 or visit us at *www.accessfund.org*.

Climbers can help preserve access by being committed to leaving the environment in its natural state.